VIETNAM 101
A CLASS LIKE NO OTHER

Jerry C. Davis

VIETNAM 101
A CLASS LIKE NO OTHER

Veterans, serving as *instructors*, share a unique
Patriotic Education experience with
COLLEGE *of the* OZARKS® students.

Jerry C. Davis

Scripture quotations are from the King James Version.

This work was written primarily from unpublished primary sources provided by the Vietnam veterans and students thoroughly identified within. Some names and places have changed; where possible, the author utilized the names and places commonly used at the time of the War.

Due to the volume of references consulted, the entire manuscript was subjected to *iThenticate*, a leading tool for research and professional writers, for assurance proper credits were given.

Printed in the United States of America by the students and staff at the Hyer Press, College of the Ozarks.

First Printing, 2021

For additional copies of this book, or for information about College of the Ozarks, contact:

Office of the President
College of the Ozarks
P. O. Box 17
Point Lookout, Missouri 65726
417-690-2470

www.cofo.edu
www.vietnam101.org

**Dedicated to
my two brothers
who served in
Vietnam**

James "Jim" A. Davis, III
U.S. Navy
U.S.S. Ranger
Attack Squadron VA 95

Dan S. Davis
U.S. Army
HHC 2nd Battalion, 28th Infantry Regiment
First Infantry Division (Big Red One)

**and
all those who served on
the side of freedom**

"Freedom Eagle"

All proceeds from this book will go toward
Patriotic Education
at College of the Ozarks.
The College annually hosts patriotic programs and
events, produces publications, and is home to
several memorials, which serve as a
reminder that freedom is not free.

The "Freedom Eagle" photograph was gifted to College of the Ozarks by
combat veteran, professional photographer, author, ambassador, and motivational speaker,
Darren McBurnett (SEAL) Ret.

TABLE OF CONTENTS: SYLLABUS

FOREWORD

Those of us who fought in the Vietnam War are the sons and daughters of what Tom Brokaw called *The Greatest Generation*. My mom and dad are among them. They weathered the Great Depression, met at a USO dance in 1941, married in 1942, and I was born at Fort Sam Houston, Texas, in 1943, as my dad prepared to land at Normandy. For his courage under fire, he was awarded a Silver Star. He was the first American Hero I ever knew. When World War II ended in September 1945, he and his comrades in arms were welcomed home and celebrated by a grateful nation with victory parades all across America.

Unlike the nearly 17 million men and women who donned uniforms during World War II, there were no victory parades for my own U.S. Army brother's heroic service in Vietnam. Not one of the approximately 2.7 million American men and women with whom we served during the Vietnam War received so much as a "Thanks for fighting for us" note. The Vietnam War is the first armed conflict in the history of our nation in which our countrymen failed to welcome home its combat veterans as heroes. In fact, the massive anti-war movement, stimulated by ubiquitous negative war coverage—particularly on television—meant many of us were subjected to outright hostility.

From 1968 onward, American Soldiers, Sailors, Airmen, Guardsmen and Marines here in the U.S. were urged—sometimes ordered—not to wear our uniforms off base. Failure to heed these warnings often resulted in being spit upon, spattered with blood or red paint, and having our car windows smashed or otherwise defaced and damaged by anti-war protesters.

College campuses became hotbeds of violent dissent—opposed not just to U.S. government policy, but also to our troops in combat. Congressional foes of the War held a nearly non-stop series of hearings during which American military personnel were routinely described as "war criminals" and worse. American prisoners of war, estimated to be more than 1,200 in 1972—with only 591 having come home—endured torture by their captors and were denounced in televised propaganda visits by Hollywood celebrities. All of this demoralizing news was gleefully broadcast into American homes and printed in routine newspaper headlines.

Vietnam 101: A Class Like No Other is a long-awaited, healing balm for those of us who were blessed to serve with the best and bravest of a generation who never received the recognition or affirmation they deserved. This book is a salve, particularly relevant to every still-living veteran of the Vietnam War and the families and loved ones who lost a father, mother, son or daughter in what was, until 9-11-01, America's longest war.

The extraordinary research in *Vietnam 101* proffers an honest, no-holds-barred, straightforward, perspective on the War. It's based on a college course at a truly unique institution of higher learning: College of the Ozarks, located near Branson, Missouri. Frequently referred to by its nickname, *HARD WORK U.*, it is unabashedly patriotic—as is its president, Jerry C. Davis, Ph.D., the author of this spectacular work.

Dr. Davis is a dear friend, an extraordinary educator, and one of the longest-serving college presidents in America. He is renowned for having made College of the Ozarks one of our nation's best. His commitment to patriotic education is evident the moment a visitor arrives on campus.

Patriots Park, with its beautiful statues and memorials, is a reminder of heroic sacrifice made in war. The Missouri Vietnam Veterans Memorial, etched with 1,410 names of Missouri's bravest who lost their lives in Vietnam, was built by the College's staff and students.

Vietnam 101: A Class Like No Other is about another of Dr. Davis' creative and inspiring innovations. For example, the College's Patriotic Education Program includes a Patriotic Education Travel Program, wherein student "hosts" accompany veteran "teachers" to major battlefields. Together the students and veterans have visited battlefields around the world, where the veterans have had experiences—including Vietnam. I know of nothing like it in the curriculum of any other American college or university.

Herein, Dr. Davis details how the veterans/teachers of the first trip to Vietnam were selected from the U.S. Army, Air Force, Navy and Marine combat veterans of the Vietnam War. Their numbers include a Medal of Honor recipient and a U.S. Army Nurse. They were all engaged in battles—from the early fights of the 1960s through being released as POWs in 1973, to the ignominious fall of Saigon in May 1975. These "teachers" had friends and comrades in arms killed and grievously wounded.

Best of all, are Jerry Davis' exceptional descriptions of how these American Heroes interacted with their student hosts. The following are reasons why I revere him and these inspiring patriotic programs at College of the Ozarks:

- First, I believe the classical definition of "Hero" isn't someone wearing a spandex suit and a cape. Rather, a Hero is a person who willingly puts him or herself at risk for the benefit of others. That certainly defines the teachers in this course.
- Second, the best teachers I've ever had are eyewitness participants in their subject matter—whether it's physics or patriotism.
- Third [and most importantly], our Lord and Savior instructs us to be humble servant leaders who show others what that means by actions, not just words.

This program and this book boldly achieve these objectives. Read what follows, and you will know why I so much admire Jerry Davis and why he inspires me to close all my correspondence as follows:

Semper Fidelis, Oliver North, LtCol USMC (Ret.)

**"Semper Fidelis" is more than a slogan for U.S. Marines.
"Always Faithful" is a way of life.**

Lt.Col. North and Dr. Davis at the Missouri Vietnam Veterans Memorial, Point Lookout, Missouri.

ACKNOWLEDGEMENTS

The Patriotic Education Travel Program (PETP) has been in existence now for a decade. Its roots began with the effort and creativity of Dr. M. Fred Mullinax who served as executive vice president of College of the Ozarks until retirement. Dr. Mullinax implemented a program of sending students (as hosts) and veterans back to the battlefields where veterans fought. In turn, veterans of WWII, Korea, the Cold War and Vietnam have served as *instructors* for trips to different parts of the world. The work of Dr. Mullinax has paid off, with the dividends reflected in the lives of students and veterans alike. It is one of the most influential educational programs I have witnessed in my 44-year presidency, and all those involved share my appreciation to Fred for his leadership role.

We are grateful for the generosity of many supporters who joined our efforts to provide a truly unique educational opportunity. We all took comfort in knowing our physical health and well-being were monitored and cared for by Mrs. Lori Vanderpool, RN and former administrator of the Armstrong McDonald Clinic. Dr. David Dalton, professor of history, has been a wealth of knowledge and developed the required Vietnam coursework. Many students will be better citizens and appreciate the service of those in uniform because of it. For this trip, the College was privileged to have Mr. John Luck accompany the group to capture photos. Luck is a professional photographer and writer based in Washington, D.C. Luck's father was an infantryman in the Pacific during World War II and later served in Vietnam, adding to his interest of participating in a unique trip such as this.

Since I have gotten to know most of these Vietnam veterans, I am humbled and honored to have written about their stories and am still amazed at the valor and sacrifice made by all these patriots. Although the focus of this book is on the inaugural 2014 (Class One) trip of Vietnam veterans and students, the stories of those who went on subsequent trips (Classes Two, Three, and Four) are no less compelling.

My only regret is that I could not write about all 43 veterans and 56 students who have participated in these early trips. The following will show the breadth of experiences shared on four Vietnam trips with our students:

Class One (2014)

Veterans—Donald "Doc" Ballard, Navy Corpsman with 4th Marines, Medal of Honor recipient (Student Host, Sara Cochran); James "Bill" Bailey, Navy pilot, POW (Student Host, Haly Johnson); John Clark, Air Force pilot, POW (Student Host, Molly Matney); Bill Duncan, 1st Marines, Commander (Student Host, Taylor Johnson); Thomas Egleston, Army helicopter pilot (Student Host, Jacob Mullet); Lou Eisenbrandt, Army nurse (Student Host, Chase Davis); Paul Frampton, Army, 1st Division Radio Telephone Operator (Student Host, Johnathan Minner); James Greer, Army helicopter pilot, 1st Cavalry (Student Host, Jessica Turner); Steve Hansen, Army, combat soldier (Student Host, Blane Bias); John Ligato, Marine platoon leader at Hué (Student Host, Devan Spady); Tony Nadal, Army 1st Cavalry at LZ X-Ray (Student Host, Cody Pentecost); John Sorensen, Army helicopter pilot (Student Host, Caleb McElvain).

These 12 veterans were very helpful in making presentations, granting personal interviews, and graciously sharing and answering numerous questions pertaining to their Vietnam experiences. Equally impressive has been the servant attitude of the student hosts, who deserve special thanks. They were helpful, dependable, and very attentive. Their timely class reports, both on campus and on the trip, were informative and well done. As noted (and cited) throughout, much of their work was edited and used as the basis for what has been written. Their observations and comments were inspiring to the group and give hope for the future. We are grateful for their kindness.

Class Two (2016)

Veterans—Tom Center, Navy, Army, Mobile Riverine Force (Student Host, Brittany Allee); Charlie Engram, Navy, Cua Viet River (Student Host, Janna Engram-Goodwin); John Fer, Air Force pilot, POW (Student Host, Loyal Carpenter); David Garrett, Army Huey helicopter door gunner (Student Host, Michaela Schaal); Don Ivie, Navy, river patrol (Student Host, Adam Pipenhagen); Edward Lohmann, Army, howitzer crew chief (Student Host, Lauren Scott); Norman McDaniel, Air Force pilot, POW (Student Host, Kaitlin Kroese); Leonard Rutledge, Army, assault helicopter pilot (Student Host, Loran Wiley); Edward Neas, Marine, Quang Tri (Student Host, Grant Talburt); William Thompson, Army, Chinook helicopter pilot (Student Host, Katherine Yung); Joel Trautmann, Army, infantry platoon leader (Student Host, Dalton Lane); William Webb, Marine, tunnel rat (Student Host, Christian Lingner).

Class Three (2017)

Veterans—Frank Swygert, Army, physiological warfare officer (Student Host, Chelsea Johnson); Michael Bruce, Army, medevac (dustoff) pilot (Student Host, Sarah Pogue); Larry Ernsting, Air Force, security combat police (Student Host, Shaundra Sprinkle); John Flock, Army, medical officer (Student Host, Michael Galioto); Dan Glenn, Naval aviator, POW (Student Host, Hannah Gray); George Haley, Navy, attack pilot—150 missions (Student Host, Billy Rhea); Stephen Henton, Army Ranger, LRRP (Student Host, Grayson Ketron); Richard Hokenson, Army sniper (Student Host, Caden Peterson); Fred Pfohl, Navy, village assistance team (Student Host, Courtney Bressler); James "Jim" Rougeau, Army special forces trainer (Student Host, Canyon Smith); Joseph Tiscia, 1st Marines at Hué (Student Host, Sam Scaggs); William Werther, Army special forces recon (Student Host, Crenna Firestine).

Class Four (2018)

Veterans—Tom Moe, Air Force, pilot of F-4, 85 combat missions (Student Hosts, Lily Woolsey, Sara Pitts, Rebekah Eklund); John Clark, Air Force pilot of RF-4C, POW (Student Hosts, Kaylee Thieme, Courtney Hendrix, Kyle Stevens); Gary Littrell, Army Ranger, Medal of Honor recipient (Student Hosts, Michael McGinnis, Miles Mrowiec, Emma Bachali); Gary Wood, Army 101st Airborne Division, field combat medic (Student Hosts, Alex Weathermon, Annie Boyd, Allison Steuck); Robert Smith, Army helicopter, Huey and Cobra gunship (Student Hosts, Jedidiah Friedman, Braden Farris); Don Browning, 7th Marines, machine gunner at Hué (Student Hosts, Cody Neal, Christina Malzner, Jason Good).

Many students assigned to the President's Office helped with the transcription of interviews. The many notes and handwritten portions of the book were no doubt difficult. Those who helped were Lacey Bricker, Amanda Cheah, Grace Donaldson, Madison Donze, Heaven

Falconburg, Bethany Holder, Maddie Inselmann, Haley Jones, Kinley Jurgielski, Dalton Lane, Molly Matney, Shelby Moore, Madison Peters, Rachel Sanders, and Katherine Yung.

The original organization of the book was done by Molly Matney. Her creative ideas were helpful in getting the project started.

Helpful assistance was provided by Mrs. Beth Blevins and Mrs. Tamara Schneider. They are due much credit for breaking away from their duties in the President's Office and taking on atypical requests.

Ms. Gwen Simmons, associate professor of library science and media specialist at the Lyons Memorial Library was very helpful, especially in tracking down publications and pictures, and advising the use of public domain information.

Countless veterans have contributed letters, pictures, clippings and other helpful information, for which appreciation is in order. I am grateful to the late Dr. Bruce Herschensohn, a veteran and respected author, for providing useful, firsthand information from his experience in the Nixon administration. Mr. John Hamilton, Colonel Duncan's radio telephone operator (RTO), kindly reviewed and confirmed details of Con Thien. Mr. Thomas Pilsch, a decorated Vietnam veteran, offered help and graciously provided access to his website—a wealth of Vietnam resources. In addition, many thanks to former Army Ranger and my "resident military consultant" Mr. Bryan Cizek, dean of work education and director of patriotic activities.

Those who took the time to edit the manuscript are due appreciation: Shirley D. Davis, Sara June Osborne, Dr. Hayden Head, and Patricia Felton Franks.

The Vietnam Center and Sam Johnson Vietnam Archive at Texas Tech University were helpful in answering questions.

Finally, the project would likely not have reached fruition without the hard work of Mrs. Sara Franks, a multi-talented assistant. Whether it was editorial formatting, picture selection, follow-up contacts with veterans, contacting other librarians and veterans' organizations, or computer skills, Sara was extraordinary. To care for a busy family (husband and three youngsters) while working on such a project was no small task.

The Hyer Press students and staff worked tirelessly to produce this book. Led by Craig Cogdill, the team included Sammie Blackwell, Don Codillo, Karen Terry, JaMarie Thompson, Gena Farmer, Adam Evans, John Forker, Stephen Bliss, Eli Aguiar, Lindsay Hemann, and Ben Scheets. In the hallway of the Hyer Press, there is a sign: "Work is love made visible"; this talented design and print team lives out this mantra.

To all the Vietnam veterans and their families, I hope this book contributes as a reflection of their honor, courage, and loyalty to America and the freedoms we enjoy. We thank God for our country and those who have sacrificed for freedom.

INTRODUCTION

Much has been written and reported about the Vietnam War. Unfortunately, this War has been cast in a narrative irresponsibly created by the media, both in print and on television. Therefore, the American public has been left to assume that America was the source of the problem, instead of Communist North Vietnam which was aggressively trying to take over neighboring South Vietnam. North Vietnam ultimately took them over, with the help of the media, U.S. Congress, and many others.

It could be said that *fake news* originated with the reporting of the Tet Offensive, for this media narrative was neither true nor accurate. The idea that the United States lost the War is absurd. What was lost were over 58,000 Americans who tried to perform as directed (under very difficult rules of engagement), all the while winning every major battle, only to watch Congress betray our commitment and essentially retreat. The way many Vietnam veterans were treated upon returning home was a national disgrace.

So why another book, especially by a civilian?

Because the College of the Ozarks, a small Work College nestled in the Ozark Mountains, has a patriotic goal and is taking a leadership role of filling in the gaps of American history by equipping future generations with the truth. Hopefully, this book will bridge the generation that fought the Vietnam War to the current generation, which has been taught little or nothing about the War and its meaning. As you will read, when students are taught the truth, they are willing to listen.

It was, in fact, the year the War supposedly ended (1973) that trustees of the College added a patriotic goal to the four (Christian, academic, cultural, and vocational) established goals of College of the Ozarks. The trustees were very concerned about the decline of patriotism among college students, and youth in general, throughout the United States. No doubt they were influenced by a changing culture and rioting on many campuses across the country.

1

Citizenship continues as a national concern. Many of the current issues in America sound eerily familiar, as if they were right out of the '60s. Recent polling details in the *Investor's Business Daily* indicate that "younger generations…are less likely to love and respect the country… and they're less informed about American history and way more likely to embrace socialism." Critics also say that "mis-education" at all levels is to blame. It has been said about the education system that "they're producing generations of Americans who know little about their own country, other than they hate it."[1] Clearly, the public should be concerned.

Nearly fifty years since adding a patriotic goal, the College of the Ozarks trustees remain laser-focused on patriotic education as a key to fulfilling its vision of *developing students of Christ-like character who are well educated, hardworking, and patriotic.* The Patriotic Goal of the College of the Ozarks is, ***to encourage an understanding of American heritage, civic responsibility, love of country and willingness to defend it.***

To publicly prioritize patriotic education, the College of the Ozarks recently established The William S. Knight Center for Patriotic Education. The Knight Center (Figure 1) serves as a hub for initiatives related to the Patriotic Goal, which is pervasive throughout the institution.

For students, patriotic education is formally explained in the classroom with a freshman-level course (Patriotic Education 103) which is required of all students and includes military science (which may lead to commissioning); civics (including American exceptionalism, U.S.

Figure 1: William S. Knight Center for Patriotic Education rendering.

flag code, capitalism versus socialism, events in American history); government (national, state, and local); and current events. Senior-year students are required to take Patriotic Education 401—composed of an intensive CitizenTrip® to Washington D.C.

Major convocations are held annually, where the College hosts speakers such as Lady Margaret Thatcher, Prime Minister Benjamin Netanyahu, President George W. Bush, General Peter Pace, former Speaker of the House Newt Gingrich, former U.S. Olympian and WWII hero Louis Zamperini, Secretary of Human Services Dr. Ben Carson, Colonel Oliver North, and many others.

Figure 2: Aerial view of Patriots Park, the Flag Plaza, the memorials, and Veterans Grove.

Many symbols of patriotism are on display at the College. **Patriots Park** (Figure 2), near the College of the Ozarks entrance, is home to the **Flag Plaza** where each service branch flag flies next to the prominent American flag, as well as the **Veterans Grove**, which contains over 150 Legacy maples, each named for veterans who have accompanied students on Patriotic Education trips.

Also, **Patriots Park** showcases the *WWII Memorial*; the *Korean War Memorial*; the *Missouri Vietnam Veterans Memorial*; *the Global War on Terrorism Memorial*; and the *Missouri Gold Star Families Memorial*. **Patriots Park** was built and is maintained by College staff and students and serves as the locale for various activities honoring veterans throughout the year.

In addition, **Patriots Plaza,** located at the entrance to School of the Ozarks (a K-12 lab school), recognizes four prominent alumni who were general officers. Central on campus and south of Williams Memorial Chapel is a monument for the *1976 Bicentennial,* and nearby is the *Alumni Veterans Memorial,* which contains the names of alumni who fought in the armed services and paid the ultimate sacrifice. The September 11 *"Lest We Forget" Memorial* is on display close to the College's Firehouse.

In addition to these patriotic initiatives, a very unusual program of the Knight Center is briefly described here:

THE PATRIOTIC EDUCATION TRAVEL PROGRAM

One of the more creative and certainly life-changing programs is the Patriotic Education Travel Program. This program turns battlefields all over the world into classrooms and laboratories wherein the College sends veterans of those battles back to where they fought. Each veteran travels with a student host. Student participants are selected from a competitive application process, and they study the subject country/countries or events before traveling. Veteran participants submit the Veteran Biography Form and are selected based on interviews, background, battles, events and/or branch of service.

Thus far the College has sent nearly 400 students and 200 veterans on such endeavors. This program honors veterans and helps them connect with younger generations by instilling in students an appreciation for the sacrifices of American soldiers and the causes for which they fought.

International Patriotic Education trips began in 2009 and have included a visit to Pearl Harbor with Pearl Harbor survivors; two trips to England and France, with WWII veterans; a tour to Europe with Cold War veterans; a trip with WWII veterans to the Mariana Islands and Japan; two trips to Normandy for the 70th and 75th Anniversaries of D-Day ceremonies with WWII veterans; a tour of battle sites with veterans of the Korean War; a trip to England and one to Guadalcanal, each with WWII veterans; a China tour; a Holocaust Memorial tour; a trip to the Philippines; and a trip to Pearl Harbor for the 75th Anniversary. Most recently, the College has made four trips to Vietnam, again with veterans of that War. The inaugural trip to Vietnam was in the fall semester of 2014, which is the primary subject of this book.

Very little or nothing has been done to connect the generation of the American military who fought the Vietnam War with the generations who have followed them. The general public knows little about the War or its aftermath. Addressing this discrepancy has been a primary goal of this book. Other goals of *Vietnam 101* have been to:

 Provide a unique educational experience for students and veterans alike in which veterans themselves serve as instructors.

 Present students with a more truthful, close-up view of what the Vietnam War (or any war) was really like.

 Give students the opportunity to bond with Vietnam veterans and express appreciation for their service and that of their friends—long overdue.

 Reveal the actions of our elected political leaders, how the Vietnam War was politicized and micromanaged, as well as mismanaged from Washington D.C.

 Give a better understanding of how dishonorably the media, celebrities, and politicians handled their duty while 99% of Soldiers, Sailors, Airmen, and Marines served admirably.

In the case of the Vietnam War, there is no better way for today's generation of college students to understand this conflict than to travel to former battlefields with veterans who fought in these battles during their youth. The country of Vietnam (Figure 3) and the battle sites become a "classroom," and seeing these with veterans provides a "laboratory" for observations like no other. It is a *generational bridge*, connecting youth of today with Vietnam veterans.

ORGANIZATION OF THE BOOK

As mentioned previously, students who participated in the first Vietnam trip were chosen through a competitive application process. Once selected, students took a 16-week face-to-face course studying the Vietnam War with Dr. David Dalton, professor of history. An assignment for that course was for each student to contact and write a biography about his/her assigned veteran. Additionally, each student wrote a personal biography and shared it with the assigned veteran. While on the trip, students posted blogs about their experiences with the veterans. Upon returning from the trip, each student submitted a trip journal. All these pieces became part of the student experience.

The Vietnam veterans submitted the Veteran Biography Form, and their military experiences were considered for participation in the program (for example: serving as a pilot, nurse, machine gunner or mortarman, rifleman, etc.). Once selected, they spoke to classes on campus and then served as *instructors* on the tour bus and/or at various locations (Figure 3) in Vietnam aligned with their personal experiences. Veterans were paired with a student host which fostered one-on-one conversations about battlefield events.

In this text, sections providing overviews, backgrounds, and summaries are broad and intended to provide enough information to frame the needed context. Interviews were conducted once or twice after the Vietnam 2014 trip for all veterans featured in this book. In addition, supplemental sources about the War were reviewed to examine various stakeholders. Dozens of books, magazines, periodicals, and movies were studied. Some of these resources featured our trip veterans.

In no way is this an exhaustive history, as there are plenty of such materials (see pages 375-384) available. As much as possible, student submissions and responses supplied the content for this text. Each Class Topic (chapter) of the book has the following sections: Instructor, Student Host, Background, Instructor Reflections, Student Response, and Topic Summary. The primary sources for each Class Topic came from the student's trip application, Veteran's Biography Form, student-written essay about his/her veteran, student biography, transcripts of the bus tour presentations by veterans, student blog post about his/her veteran's experiences, student-submitted post-trip journal, and my (author's) personal interviews with each veteran.

It was, of course, neither possible nor necessary to visit every battle site in Vietnam before writing this book. But it was possible to visit a sampling of locations (Figure 3) that reflect various stages of the War. With veterans functioning as *instructors,* students learned without the screen through which the media framed and presented the conflict.

Stories from the veterans cover a broad spectrum, from combat to imprisonment to medical treatment. The details are intensely personal, and many are riveting. The POW experiences and combat experiences are especially dramatic. All reflect the willingness of these veterans to serve and do their best at what they were called upon to do—drafted or not!

Additionally, you will notice the style in this book is somewhat different. I have used italics for both quotes within quotes and emphasis. This is done to guide you through the text, conveying the veterans' stories most clearly.

❝ Stories from the veterans cover a broad spectrum, from combat to imprisonment to medical treatment. The details are intensely personal, and many are riveting. **❞**

Future generations need to study this most divisive American war. It should become obvious how practically every battle was won and the people of South Vietnam could look forward to a better future—until the actions of the media and leftist radicals in the streets, on campuses, and in Congress forced the South Vietnamese (along with the Cambodians and Laotians) to surrender to communist invaders who wrought untold misery and death to tens of thousands. It was the American military that served with honor and sacrifice, and this must not be forgotten.

Figure 3: Map of southeast Asia including Vietnam 2014 trip odyssey. Map adapted from public domain.

College of the Ozarks Tour to Vietnam Itinerary
September 25 – October 9, 2014
(The numbers in parentheses are odyssey stops.)

Thursday, 25 September – Friday, 26 September
Travel days and depart San Francisco (SFO), CA.

Saturday, 27 September
Arrive Taipei and travel to Saigon (1). Drive to Can Tho (2) via Vinh Long. Welcome dinner and Overnight, Victoria Hotel, Can Tho.

Sunday, 28 September
Floating Market tour early, then drive from Can Tho to Saigon. War Remnants Museum in the afternoon. Overnight, Rex Hotel, Saigon.

Monday, 29 September
Visit Chu Chi Tunnels in the morning and drive to Iron Triangle (3) in the afternoon. Overnight, Rex Hotel, Saigon.

Tuesday, 30 September
Visit Reunification Palace in the morning. Visit the Saigon Central Post Office/Notre Dame Cathedral of Saigon in the early afternoon. Fly to Pleiku (4) in the late afternoon/evening. Overnight, at Hoang Anh Gia Lai Hotel, Pleiku.

Wednesday, 1 October
Morning visit to Ia Drang (5) battle site. Drive to Qui Nhon (6) in the afternoon. Overnight, Saigon Quynhon Hotel, Qui Nhon.

-1-

	**1st Aviation Brigade, U.S. Army** SORENSEN, EGLESTON		**1st Marine Division** DUNCAN, LIGATO
	**1st Division, U.S. Army** FRAMPTON		**3rd Battalion, 4th Marines** BALLARD
	**1st Cavalry, U.S. Army** GREER, HANSEN, NADAL		**VF-143, US Navy** BAILEY
	**Army Nurse Corps** EISENBRANDT		**432nd Tactical Rec. Wing, U.S. Air Force** CLARK

Figure 4: Military insignia of the Vietnam 2014 trip veterans.

College of the Ozarks Tour to Vietnam Itinerary, cont.

Thursday, 2 October
Drive to Bong Son (7). Then to Chu Lai (8). Continue to Hoi An (9). Overnight, Ancient House Village Resort, Hoi An.

Friday, 3 October
Drive through Da Nang, Hai Van Pass and Hué to Dong Ha (10). Stop at China Beach, Marble Mountain, the Bridge, Vinh Moc Tunnels. Overnight, Dong Ha Hotel, Quang Tri.

Saturday, 4 October
Drive to Con Thien (11), Rockpile, Khe Sanh (12), Lang Vei, returning to Dong Ha. Walk to site of "Bridge at Dong Ha." Overnight, Dong Ha Hotel, Quang Tri.

Sunday, 5 October
Drive to Hué (13), cruise on the Perfume River and visit Khai Dinh Royal Tomb in the afternoon. Overnight, Hué La Residence, Hué.

Monday, 6 October
Visit the Citadel in the morning and cycle tour of Battle of Hué site. Overnight, La Residence.

Tuesday, 7 October
Fly from Hué to Hanoi (14). Visit Hỏa Lò Prison [as named by the prisoners "Hanoi Hilton"] and Water Puppet Show in the late afternoon. Farewell dinner at Seasons of Hanoi. Overnight, Hong Ngoc Hotel, Hanoi.

Wednesday, 8 October
Check out of hotel and transfer to airport. Depart Hanoi, arrive Taipei, then non-stop flight into Los Angeles, CA. Connect to domestic flights to U.S. interior cities.

-2-

Student trip participant Molly Matney remarked, "This experience truly opened my eyes to the sacrifices that our veterans have made for us, the younger generation. It is a realization that I intend to share, and be impacted by, for the rest of my life."[2]

ORIENTATION

In order to understand *why* and *how* the United States got involved in the Vietnam War, we should first consider the prior decade (1954-64) before actual combat commenced. After World War II, the French wanted their former colony, Vietnam, returned to them. The U.S., however, preferred the country granted its independence, but couldn't support Ho Chi Minh since he was a communist. The Vietnamese people were divided among themselves. Some were nationalists, some Viet Minh communists (led by Ho Chi Minh), and many were neutral. After a few years of fighting, Ho Chi Minh's forces withdrew, entering Laos. French pursuit led to the establishment of the main French base at Dien Bien Phu. (Figure 5)

Dien Bien Phu (Figure 6) was a poor choice. Located 220 miles west of Hanoi, it was composed of a long valley and surrounding hills. Such an isolated location could not be supplied except by air, and that was often hindered by fog and rain. The French did not believe the Viet Minh had any anti-aircraft ability. This turned out to be a false assumption. The Viet Minh somehow managed to bring heavy artillery and anti-aircraft weapons

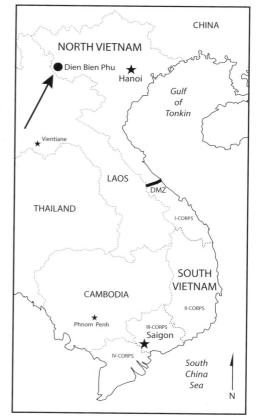

Figure 5: Map of Vietnam showing the location of Dien Bien Phu. Adapted from public domain.

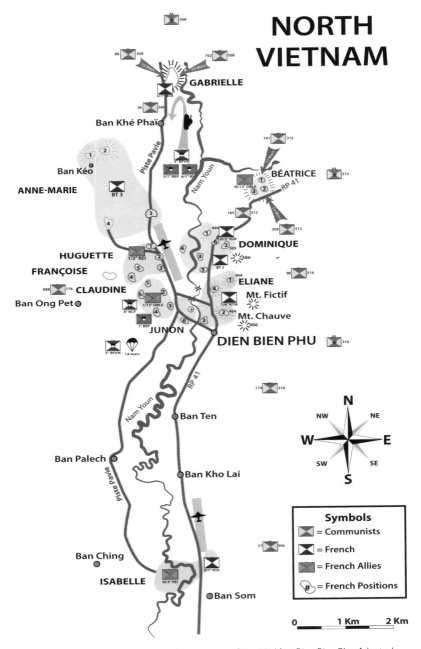

Figure 6: Troop locations for French and Communists (Viet Minh) at Dien Bien Phu. Adapted from public domain.

to battle. This feat was accomplished by the hard labor of soldiers and workers, old and young.

A two-month siege ensued, starting with a heavy artillery bombardment which the French could not answer. The Viet Minh had dug trenches from which they surfaced and launched human wave attacks. Worst of all, the French runway at Dien Bien Phu (Figure 6) was repeatedly hit and rendered inoperable for bringing in supplies. It was a self-made disaster for the French even though they had substantially more soldiers than the communists (16,000 to 3,000).[1] The French were overrun, losing 1,600 killed-in-action (KIA), 4,800 wounded and an additional 1,600 missing-in-action (MIA), compared to losses of 7,900 KIA and 15,000 MIA for the Viet Minh. As well as losing the battle, the French lost 8,000 POWs, half of whom didn't survive while being forced to march to a POW camp 500 miles away.[2]

Perhaps the French might have been spared had American airpower been available. It was not that President Eisenhower and Secretary of State John Foster Dulles were totally against involving Americans. They appealed to British Prime Minister Churchill who refused to get involved. Eisenhower and Dulles wanted other nations to form a coalition, but this did not materialize. President Eisenhower was concerned that if the French lost, the communists would have a free hand in southeast Asia – and especially Vietnam. Noted author Charles Neu quoted Senator John F. Kennedy: "Vietnam represents the cornerstone of the Free World in Southeast Asia, the keystone to the arch, the finger in the dike. Burma, Thailand, India, Japan, the Philippines and obviously Laos and Cambodia are among those whose security would be threatened if the red tide of Communism overflowed into Vietnam….If we are not the parents of little Vietnam, then surely we are the godparents. …This is our offspring—we cannot abandon it, we cannot ignore its needs."[3]

The French loss at Dien Bien Phu signaled the end of French rule in Vietnam. Subsequently, at a Geneva Conference, Vietnam was divided into North and South at the 17th parallel, and a "free election" was to be held within two years. The Vietnam emperor Bao Dai abdicated, and Ngo Dinh Diem became the Prime Minister of the State of Vietnam and Ho Chi Minh the President of North Vietnam.

The intentions of Ho Chi Minh were known quickly. He was a socialist first, who became a communist as a means to an end—independence through nationalism. Many fled south as President Minh forced a peasants' revolt wherein thousands were killed. Once Diem became Prime Minister, he quickly consolidated his power after a fraudulent election and rejected any further elections to unify the country. United States President Dwight D. Eisenhower had no other choice but to support Diem as a bulwark against the spread of communism. All the while, Ho's long-held goal was to invade the South. America's objectives were preventing a totalitarian state from being imposed on an ally and slowing the spread of communism in southeast Asia.

Over the next few years (early '60s) South Vietnam was in constant turmoil as Prime Minister Diem struggled to stay in power and fight communist infiltration from the north. The National Liberation Front (NLF), began as a group of South Vietnamese who were opposed to the corruption and tyranny of the Diem regime; they will commonly be referred to as the Viet Cong to differentiate them from the Viet Minh. The Viet Cong (VC) resorted to violence or anything else to undermine the South Vietnamese government. Across the ocean, the young, idealistic John F. Kennedy had become President of the United States. He was tested early in his presidency and the results were not encouraging. The Bay of Pigs invasion of Cuba was a fiasco. And, after talking tough about communists in Laos, he signed a treaty but didn't back it up. Also, the American response to the Berlin Wall was tepid. Kennedy appeared to be "in over his head." Vietnam required more and more American attention. Prime Minister Diem was no choir boy, but he was a strong leader, despite corruption. Kennedy increased the number of American advisors and equipment because of NLF and Viet Minh activity, but within a year the Cuban missile crisis erupted and distracted Washington from focusing on Vietnam.

American advisors were disappointed with the ARVN's (Army of the Republic of Vietnam) first battle with the Viet Minh at Ap Bac in January 1963. With incompetent South Vietnamese officers in charge, the South Vietnamese government had much work to do in improving its armed forces. The corruption and tyranny of Prime Minister Diem provoked a controversy with Buddhists that resulted in a monk setting himself on fire. This shocked the world and further undermined Diem.

The Kennedy administration lost confidence in Diem and was complicit in the assassination of the Prime Minister. Tragically, President Kennedy was assassinated the same month. Unfortunately, those who followed Diem were worse and, with so much turnover in the government and military, it became a game of musical chairs. Nguyen Cao Ky followed Diem. Eventually, Nguyen Van Thieu was elected president. Given the endless coups that erupted, most regard the American complicity leading to Diem's death to have been a serious mistake.

President Lyndon Johnson inherited a deteriorating situation. Infiltration from North Vietnam continued unabated. U.S. advisors, CIA, and South Vietnamese military used various techniques to encourage the infiltrators to "switch sides."

Captain Frank Swygert (a veteran on the College's third trip to Vietnam) explained, "A United States-based counterinsurgency program was implemented to try and win over the people, keeping the communists from taking over, and providing some stability, because the South Vietnamese government sure couldn't do it. One of the players in this effort was a MAAG (Military Assistance Advisory Group) sent out into the provinces to influence the provincial chiefs and their people. Also trying to help was another group called the United States Overseas

Figure 7: CIA "Money man" with briefcase. Interpreter (far right), U.S. Army Cpt. Frank Swygert (second from left). Photo courtesy of Frank Swygert, PETP 2017.

Mission (now known as USAID – United States Agency for International Development). And finally, there was the CIA. The CIA was known as the *money boys* (Figure 7) because they came in with briefcases of cash!"[4] The American counter-insurgency operators were called psy-warriors. Swygert relates how extensive the effort was to influence a province chief and his districts: "We were able to bring in money, the overseas mission programs, defense training, air support, medical services, and various armaments."[5] All of this was supported by a psy-warrior effort to attract converts. Helicopters equipped with loudspeakers flew low in order to talk to the communists (or get shot at). There was also a Chieu Hoi Program of dropping leaflets (Figure 8) that invited them to turn themselves in, and some, in fact, did. These counter insurgency efforts were not always successful. "One step forward, two steps back,"[6] Captain Swygert recalled.

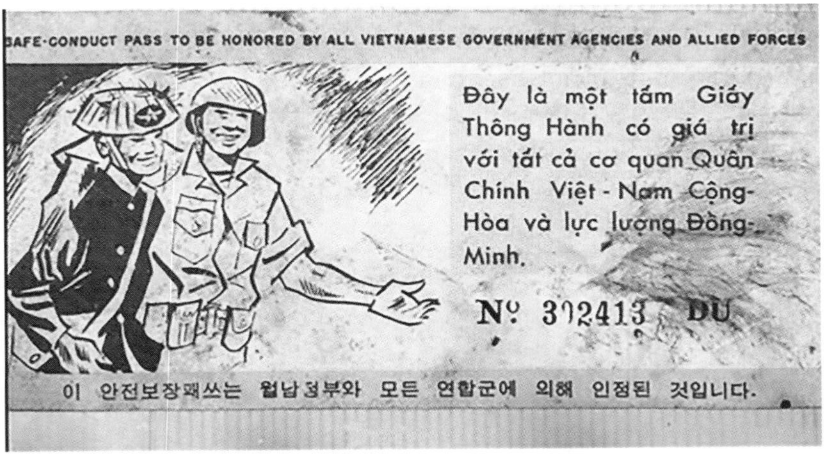

SAFE-CONDUCT PASS TO BE HONORED BY ALL VIETNAMESE GOVERNMENT AGENCIES AND ALLIED FORCES

Đây là một tấm Giấy Thông Hành có giá trị với tất cả cơ quan Quân Chính Việt - Nam Cộng-Hòa và lực lượng Đồng-Minh.

Nº 312413 DU

이 안전보장패쓰는 월남정부와 모든 연합군에 의해 인정된 것입니다.

Figure 8: Example of Chieu Hoi "Safe Conduct Pass." Image courtesy of Frank Swygert, PETP 2017.

After Diem's death, the instability in South Vietnam further encouraged the North Vietnamese to increase their infiltration into the South, via the Ho Chi Minh Trail (Figure 9), fueling the insurgency of Viet Cong and their hope that the Americans would leave. No doubt open warfare would have ensued, but an incident in the Tonkin Gulf provided President Johnson (LBJ) the opportunity to ensure he could respond to any provocation as he saw fit. It also gave him the chance to add a cloak of armor to his "peace candidate" image, because his fall opponent, Senator

Barry Goldwater, was going around the country accusing the President of being weak on the Vietnam problem and national security in general.

The factors contributing to the Tonkin Gulf Incident are worth noting. The year, 1964, was LBJ's first year in office. He inherited a bad situation from President Kennedy due to the murder of Diem and the subsequent falling apart of the South Vietnamese government. The coup against President Diem was especially problematic. As H.R. McMaster wrote in the book *Dereliction of Duty*, "Johnson's preoccupation with his domestic legislative program led him to obscure from the public and the Congress the extent of the difficulties in Vietnam. McNamara assisted his

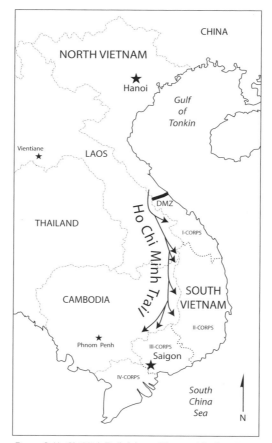

Figure 9: Ho Chi Minh Trail. Adapted from public domain.

dissembling."[7] Even with reprisal air strikes and 16,000 "advisors," the War was not improving. The South Vietnamese were also patrolling the coast of North Vietnam, risking provocation. Covert activities were "conceived and overseen by the Department of Defense with the support of the Central Intelligence Agency and carried out by the South Vietnamese Navy…the United States was playing a dangerous game."[8]

On August 2, 1964, the American destroyer, *U.S.S. Maddox*, was attacked by three North Vietnamese torpedo boats. The attack was probably a reaction to South Vietnamese covert operations. The attack was certainly unsuccessful, "with two of the three attacking boats damaged and one left dead in the water."[9] The President downplayed the incident, but on August 4, Secretary McNamara received a message that a second attack was likely. Such a possibility presented the President with a "political master stroke against his chief political adversary."[10] Shortly thereafter, McNamara received a report that a second attack had indeed occurred. Johnson wanted a reprisal, and Secretary Robert McNamara came up with a plan which disregarded the advice of the Joint Chiefs of Staff (JCS). While the JCS were preparing the ordered limited strike, a message came indicating that the second attack may not have happened. Bad weather, poor visibility, rough seas, obstructed views, radar and solar malfunction, and inexperienced personnel were likely involved. Therefore, the subsequent raid was carried out under a cloud of confusion. But it wasn't confusing to Commander James Stockdale, who flew his F-8 Crusader at dangerously low altitudes to observe what might be occurring that night. Upon his return to the carrier and in a debrief, he said, "I had the best seat in the house from which to detect torpedo boats."[11] Stockdale's confident response to the question about sighting boats, "Not a one. No boats…", was a telling conclusion and gave confirmation that there was no second incident.[12]

Some forty years later, classified documents, phone transcripts, oral history interviews, and other materials indicated that Vice Admiral Stockdale was correct. The second incident likely never happened. But Johnson wasted no time in pushing through Congress the Gulf of Tonkin Resolution, giving the President essentially a blank check to conduct war. And, he wasted no time in capitalizing on the support he received for the reprisal against North Vietnam and the passage of the

Gulf of Tonkin Resolution. Further, the President asked his advisors to develop a policy on Vietnam. They struggled to do this as the disarray in the South Vietnamese government persisted. There was concern that the government would collapse. Subsequently, a bombing campaign was authorized and, in spring of 1965, some 3,000 Marines disembarked at Da Nang to defend the base and make a statement of U.S. intent. It wasn't long before the Marines were allowed to go on the offensive, and other troops were brought in behind them. Clearly, the Americanization of the War had commenced. Soon enough, President Johnson declared, "We will not be defeated. We will not grow tired. We will not withdraw, either openly or under the cloak of meaningless agreement."[13] Big talk; but as you will learn in this text, there was big trouble ahead.

Within a short period of time, the Marines cornered a North Vietnamese Army (NVA) regiment on the coast south of Da Nang. *Operation Starlite* saw the enemy lose but slip away, something the enemy did exceptionally well. Though the Marines had prevailed, it was a taste of Vietnam-style war and not an easy fight, an additional sign of what was to come.

One of the earliest and major battles of the War was fought in the Ia Drang Valley in the fall of 1965. Those who fought there were the *instructors* for College of the Ozarks students on the first Patriotic Education trip to Vietnam. The story of the battle is told primarily by a company commander who was present. The battles at Landing Zone X-Ray and Landing Zone Albany reflect much about the War and what America and her allies faced.

PART I
EARLY YEARS (1965-67)

OVERVIEW

Section Two of the Gulf of Tonkin Resolution authorized the President *to take all necessary steps* against the North Vietnamese. The passage of such a resolution at the time paralleled strong public support. Although American advisors had been assisting the South Vietnamese Military (ARVN) for a long period of time, the years 1965-67 saw the insertion of combat troops for the first time and the escalation of fighting in multiple regions of the country. It quickly became obvious what "all necessary steps" entailed.[1]

Lyndon B. Johnson was in his first full year of office as President. As the War escalated, he seemed to rely heavily on his Secretary of Defense, Robert S. McNamara, for establishing the trajectory of how the War was to be fought. McNamara's style was not well received by the military. H.R. McMaster wrote in his book, *Dereliction of Duty,* "The officers resented the lack of respect for military experience among these whiz kids, whom they nicknamed derisively McNamara's *happy little hotdogs.*"[2] Unfortunately, most of McNamara's advisors were civilian bureaucrats with Ivy League degrees and no combat experience. Later in the War, some of these advisors were a part of the so-called "wise men" that advised President Johnson.

Subsequently, it became clear that President Johnson and his Secretary of Defense, Robert S. McNamara, had misjudged the tenacity of the communist commitment from the very start. This, along with trying to fight a war on the cheap to preserve the President's Great Society Program, placed severe limitations on military readiness. Worst of all was the conflict between the Joint Chiefs of Staff (JCS) and Secretary

McNamara. From its inception, the Joint Chiefs were troubled about the direction of the War and the way it was being managed and fought. The Joint Chiefs of Staff were granted an audience with the President, their Commander in Chief. This situation and a subsequent meeting are mentioned in *Cheers and Tears* written by Lieutenant General Charles G. Cooper, USMC (Ret.). Excerpts are telling:

> The Vietnam War was in its first year, and its uncertain direction troubled Admiral McDonald and the other service chiefs. They'd had a number of disagreements with Secretary of Defense Robert S. McNamara about strategy, and had finally requested a private meeting with the Commander in Chief—a perfectly legitimate procedure. Now, after many delays, the Joint Chiefs were finally to have that meeting. They hoped it would determine whether the US military would continue its seemingly directionless buildup to fight a protracted ground war, or take bold measures that would bring the war to an early and victorious end. The bold measures they would propose were to apply massive air power to the head of the enemy, Hanoi, and to close North Vietnam's harbors by mining.

> The Joint Chiefs intended that the prime topics of the meeting with the President would be naval matters. … For that reason, the Navy was to furnish a briefing map, and that became my responsibility.

> The Military Office at the White House agreed to set up an easel in the Oval Office to hold the map. Holding the map board as the chiefs entered, I peered between them, trying to find the easel. There was none. The President looked at me, grasped the situation at once, and invited me in, adding, "You can stand right over here." I had become an easel—one with eyes and ears. My memory of Lyndon Johnson on that day remains crystal clear.

> President Johnson turned his back on them (the Joint Chiefs) for a minute or so, then suddenly discarding the calm, patient demeanor he had maintained throughout the meeting, whirled to face them and exploded. I almost dropped the map. He screamed obscenities, he cursed them personally, he ridiculed them for coming to his office with their "military advice." … he called them filthy names. … He then accused them of trying to pass the buck for World War III to him. It was unnerving, degrading. Using soft-spoken profanities, he said something to the effect that they all knew now that he did not care about their military advice. After disparaging their abilities, he added that he did expect their help. …

> The Joint Chiefs of Staff had done their duty. They knew … despite the rebuffs.

The US involvement in Vietnam lasted another ten years. The irony is that it began to end only when President Richard Nixon, after some backstage maneuvering on the international scene, did precisely what the Joint Chiefs of Staff had recommended to President Johnson in 1965. But had General Wheeler and the others received a fair hearing, and had their recommendations received serious study, the United States may well have saved the lives of most of its more than 55,000 sons who died in a war that its major architect, Robert Strange McNamara, now considers to have been a tragic mistake.[3]

Agency historians have found no evidence of this meeting. Given the civilian-military conflict of this era, it would be understandable if one party wanted no records kept. This meeting was described by a U.S. Marine, not a politician.

As American involvement increased, the Joint Chiefs were eventually pushed aside and much of their responsibility was assumed by arrogant civilian analysts. H. R. McMaster believed President Johnson could not command the JCS respect, as he deceived the public and Congress about the War. The administration's lies to the American public had grown in magnitude as the American military effort in Vietnam escalated.[4]

It should be of little surprise that a policy of gradualism or incrementalism led to mission drift, confusion, and dwindling public support.

A policy of *gradualism* was pursued over the advice of the generals of the Joint Chiefs of Staff who had experienced war up close and personal—World War II and Korea.

It should be of little surprise that a policy of gradualism or incrementalism led to mission drift, confusion, and dwindling public support. This, along with rising causalities, was a major problem from the earliest years of the War. Add to this an activation of the draft, and turbulence both at home and abroad was understandable.

Despite such a characterization of the War, the American military answered its nation's call. Though the Marines landed near Da Nang, they didn't stay on the coast very long. Army regulars followed, including the newly untested air mobile division. Navy and Air Force planes were already actively helping ARVN (Army of the Republic of Vietnam) troops. American actions met with early success; this was not so for ARVN troops. It was clear that the American military would have to carry the load.

This they did despite rules of engagement (ROE) that were often viewed as unduly restrictive. As noted author Guenter Lewy observed, "The American command from the very beginning realized the potentially damaging effect of the great firepower of American combat forces and it therefore issued ROE governing ground and air operations which were designed to minimize the destruction and loss of life among noncombatants. In addition, General Westmoreland repeatedly reminded his commanders that *the utmost in discretion and judgement must be used in the application of fire power.*" He continues, "People, more than terrain, are the objective in this war, and we will not and cannot be callous about those people."[5]

A consistent application of ROE was difficult. After all, the lives of American troops were on the line, too. The rules of engagement were especially troublesome for aviators, as Naval Commander George Haley (Figure 10) explained to students and veterans alike:

- Don't do anything to trigger massive Russian or Chinese troop intervention.

- Don't hurt civilians and don't damage civilian property.

- Prohibit and restrict areas around Hanoi and Haiphong and along Chinese border.

- Don't hurt military leadership at the highest levels…no regime change…

- Don't mine or quarantine Haiphong harbor, sink supply ships, or damage piers.

- Don't bomb military airfields that may contain civilian planes.[6]

Commander Haley flew an A-4 on 159 combat missions into North Vietnam, South Vietnam, and Laos off the *U.S.S. Bon Homme Richard* and *U.S.S. Ticonderoga*.

He explained the futility of the situations that pilots confronted, given the ROE requirements. Though aviators were charged to, "Stop movement, materials, and equipment moving into South Vietnam,"[7] the

Viet Cong (VC) communists had no rules.

American pilots spent a lot of time shooting at trains, trucks, elephants, and barges that the VC used as transport. Meanwhile, the pilots dodged SAMs (surface-to-air missiles) which were Russian made and among the most sophisticated in the world. American usage of smart bombs was seldom, because of their expense.

American forces often paid the price for restraint as ROE

Figure 10: Navy A-4 pilot, Cdr. George Haley. Photo courtesy of George Haley, PETP 2017.

existed not only for control of tactical air power, but also the use of tanks, naval gunfire, artillery, mortar fire, and territorial borders they could or could not cross to pursue the enemy.

Another difficulty that American forces had to deal with was that targets were often selected from the White House. President Johnson said, "They can't hit an outhouse without my permission."[8] Such a foolish comment was not viewed as inspirational by soldiers 10,000 miles away, trying both to stay alive and accomplish their mission. Operating in a very hostile environment, much of it in the jungles with guerrilla warfare, made it even more remarkable that more Americans weren't casualties during the early years of the War.

Battles in the Early Years are spread throughout the various military regions or Corps Tactical Zones I-IV of South Vietnam (Figure 11). Therefore, Landing Zone X-Ray and Landing Zone Albany were located in II Corps, Bong Son was also in II Corps, the Iron Triangle was in III Corps, and Con Thien was in I Corps below the Demilitarized Zone (DMZ). During College of the Ozarks' patriotic trip to Vietnam, combat veterans shared their experiences with the entire group, as well as each student host individually. Veteran recollections reflect the honor and valor with which they and the great majority of Americans served. Unfortunately, the same cannot be said of many in Washington, D. C., who were making decisions regarding the War, or those in the streets and at many colleges and universities across our nation. The initiation of combat signaled that much sacrifice was going to be required.

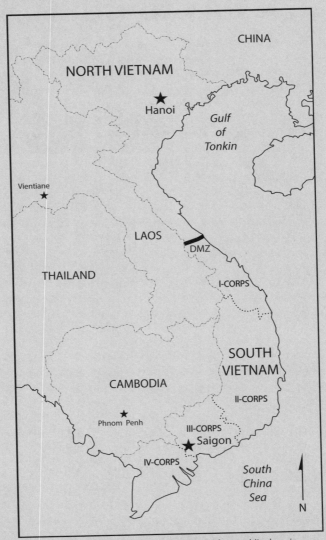

Figure 11: Corps Tactical Zones (I-IV). Adapted from public domain.

CLASS TOPIC 1: IA DRANG VALLEY, LZ X-RAY (II-CORPS)

I need fire, and I need it now...

INSTRUCTOR: COL RAMON A. (TONY) NADAL, USA (RET.)[1]

Colonel Tony Nadal served 22 years in the U.S. Army. Nadal's father was one of the first Puerto Ricans to graduate from West Point. Consequently, Nadal followed in his father's footsteps, graduating from West Point in 1958.

Tony Nadal's first tour of duty in Vietnam (1963-64) was in an area just south of the A Shau Valley (Figure 12), upper I-Corps. From this isolated outpost, he commanded Special Forces Detachment A726 in Nam Dong, from which he conducted counter-insurgency operations, ambushes, raids, and reconnaissance. Nam Dong, which is in the Central Highlands (Figure 12), was the site of repeated Viet Cong attacks. The first Medal of Honor recipient of the Vietnam War, Captain Roger Donlon, served in this same Special Forces camp.

Nadal served a second tour in Vietnam (1965-67) where he commanded A Company, 1st Battalion, 7th Cavalry at Landing Zone X-Ray, south of Pleiku (Figure 12) and at the Bong Son Plains. He also served as the operations officer (S-3) of the 2nd Battalion, 7th Cavalry.

In 1968, Colonel Nadal returned for a third time to conduct a study of allied operations in II, III, and IV-Corps tactical zones. Since the War, Nadal has served as a psychology/leadership professor at West Point and on staff of the Chief of Staff of the U.S. Army, where he was responsible for designing and implementing the largest organizational development

(OD) programs in the world. Additionally, he served as president of United Way, vice chairman of a hospital board, and vice president of Human Resources at Carlisle Syntec Systems and C&M Corporation.

As a highly decorated soldier, Colonel Nadal's recognitions include the Silver Star, two Legions of Merit, a Soldier's Medal (highest award for heroism in peace time), two Bronze Stars, three Meritorious Service Medals, Purple Heart, three Air Medals, Combat Infantry Badge, a Vietnam Cross of Gallantry, and a Presidential Unit Citation (PUC).

Figure 12: Central Highlands map.

He is also Special Forces, Ranger, Pathfinder, and Airborne qualified.

Colonel Nadal has been the topic of several books, including *Valor in Vietnam* and *We Were Soldiers Once...and Young*, the latter having been made into a movie. A sequel, *We Are Soldiers Still*, was published in 2008. In 1992, he was featured in an ABC show entitled, *We Were Soldiers Once and Brave*. After Tony's wife, Billie, of 45 years died, Tony married Gabrielle Brown, widow of one of Tony's West Point classmates. Tony has two children and one grandchild. He currently lives in Williamsburg, Virginia.

Figure 13: Student host Cody Pentecost and veteran Tony Nadal. Photo by John Luck.

 ## STUDENT HOST: CODY PENTECOST

At the time of the Vietnam trip, Cody Pentecost (Figure 13) was a senior health and wellness major from Lebanon, Missouri. He was married on May 17, 2014, to Nickie, who also graduated from College of the Ozarks. Cody worked in the Admissions Office where he met prospective students and helped them with the application process at College of the Ozarks (C of O). Cody also conducted tours for individuals or groups interested in the College.

When not in class or at work, one could typically find Cody on the baseball field, playing as an outfielder. Both of his parents were high school coaches, so he spent a lot of time on a field or court of some kind. Since his faith is very important to him, he used athletics to open doors of opportunity to share what God had done in his life.

Cody's excitement for this Patriotic Education trip was based on two things: the opportunity to travel overseas for the first time and the chance to experience Vietnam through the eyes of the veterans who were returning to their battlefields, many for the first time.

Cody's grandpa and great uncle were both enlisted in the Army during the Vietnam War. His grandpa, David Ray, was stationed at Fort Campbell, Kentucky, preparing to fight overseas, but the war ended before he was called to active (combat) duty. Even though he never fought in a battle in Vietnam, he still experienced great scrutiny for being in the military. Cody's great uncle served at Cam Rahn Bay in Vietnam, so Cody was interested in seeing the things his uncle experienced.

Cody had this to say: "The Bible [Philippians 2:3] teaches that we as Christians should be humble and selfless. There isn't a better example of selflessness than a soldier setting his/her own life and desires aside and fighting to keep this great nation free. I cannot even imagine what it would be like to fight in a war, wondering if I would ever make it home to see my family again. Being in a situation like that would be the most difficult and terrifying experience a human can face, especially if you were not appreciated by your own country."

LANDING ZONE X-RAY BACKGROUND

The Ia Drang Valley was the first major battle site of the Vietnam War. Several landing zones (Figure 14) were located in the area a few miles west of Plei Me, near the foot of Chu Pong Mountain. This large mountain lies adjacent to the Cambodian border. Landing Zone (LZ) X-Ray was a small, flat area near the base of the mountain and was judged to be of a size that would land eight helicopters at a time. After the NVA attacked a Special Forces camp at Plei Me, they were pushed out, and combat erupted in several nearby areas. NVA troops suffered heavy losses before retreating toward the Cambodian border, albeit near Chu Pong Mountain. This was a typical pattern of North Vietnamese units—ambush or attack and return to Cambodia because allied (primarily U.S.) troops were not allowed to follow in pursuit; this was a different way to fight a war and one of the major causes of the American failure. Wars are won by pursuing the enemy to his destruction without allowing him respite.

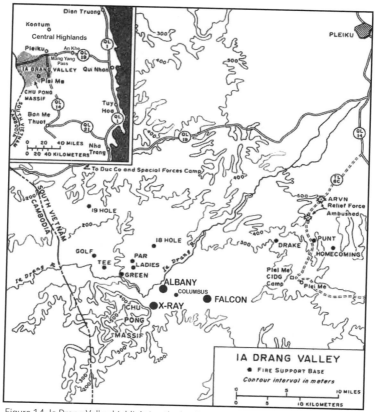

Figure 14: Ia Drang Valley highlighting the landing zones in the valley between Chu Pong Massif (mountain) and Plei Me. Adapted from public domain.

The Central Highlands (Figure 12, 15), an important region of Vietnam, was traversed by Highway 19 (originating near coastal Qui Nhon) and passed through An Khe, Mang Yang Pass, and Pleiku before reaching the Cambodian border. The NVA attacks in Pleiku and surrounding areas foretold an effort to cut the country in half. This was not successful thanks to the arrival of American combat forces along with their air power and artillery units.

Not surprisingly, after the February 1965 Plei Me attack, MACV (Military Assistance Command Vietnam) Commanding General William Westmoreland directed the 1st Cavalry Division (airmobile) to *search and destroy* enemy troops believed to be in the Chu Pong Mountain area (later determined to be the 32nd, 33rd, and 66th NVA

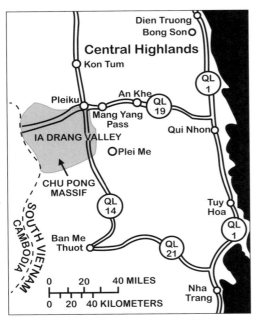

Figure 15: Central Highlands traversed by Highway 19 which passes through An Khe, Mang Yang Pass, and Pleiku. Adapted from public domain.

Regiments). Also, not surprisingly, the North Vietnamese were looking for Americans to kill to study American tactics. The battle was the first major battle to test the air mobility of the U.S. military. A captain at the time, Tony Nadal commanded A Company 1/7 Cavalry under the direction of Lieutenant Colonel Hal Moore. Lt. Col. Moore's battalion was under-strength, to say the least. He said, "The enlisted ranks had been whittled down by expiring enlistments, malaria cases, and requirements for base camp guards back at An Khe. Alpha Company had 115 men, 49 fewer than authorized. Bravo Company, at 114 men, was 50 short. Charlie Company had 106 men, down by 58. And the weapons company, Delta, had only 76 men, 42 fewer than authorized."[2] Such a situation as this undoubtedly put American troops at further risk.

 ## INSTRUCTOR REFLECTIONS

Before the group departed the hotel in Pleiku to visit the battlefields, Colonel Nadal oriented the students as to what the day would entail: "I asked for a chance to talk to you about where we are going to visit. So, the purpose of this is to give you some background as to why this event, this particular battlefield that you're going to see, is important in the history of the Vietnam War and the significance that it created for lots of things that happened during the War thereafter."

Displaying a map (Figure 16) he had made, Colonel Nadal pointed out the Cambodian-Laotian border and Pleiku. He continued to explain the area the group would be visiting: "Over here is the Special Forces Camp, called Plei Me (Figure 15), that is significant in the movement towards this battle. Chu Pong Mountain is like a big rock that rises out of a plain which is fairly flat, not a jungle. The jungle starts in Kon Tum (Figure 15), the high mountains. Now covered by tea and coffee plantations, the terrain was desolate, then with relatively small trees giving some visibility. You could see at a distance, but the grass grew about knee-high in this area. And this grass played a significant role in this event; when the soldiers went to the ground, when they hit the dirt, they couldn't see. You couldn't see them, and they couldn't see you. That created a psychological effect on a soldier of feeling isolated. He's used to having panoply of power when he's training, with all his trucks and tanks and whatever around him. But when the battle started and he hit the dirt and couldn't see the squad leader or the lieutenant, that obviously created anxiety."

Figure 16: Col. Nadal, LZ X-Ray map explanation. Photo by John Luck.

"On the other side of the border (Figure 17), was the Ho Chi Minh Trail. There were various inputs into the Ho Chi Minh Trail. One of

Figure 17: Map showing Ho Chi Minh Trail. Adapted from public domain.

the main routes came up near Kon Tum, and another one came out in this valley of the Ia Drang River. At the foot of Chu Pong Mountain there is a place called Landing Zone X-Ray which became, has become for Steve Hansen and me, a central memory of our lives."

Nadal gave some additional historical background to the battle: "In 1964, the U.S. began a major increase in the number of forces sent to Vietnam. The message had been communicated to the North Vietnamese that we were not going to negotiate. In 1963 and '64, just about everyone in the world—the Germans, the French, British, Canadians, etc.—were trying to get the U.S. to negotiate with North Vietnam. The negotiations would be around the issue of the future status of South Vietnam. The Johnson Administration viewed negotiation as basically surrendering South Vietnam to the North, because any negotiation would create a neutral country and eventually lead to the North Vietnamese taking over South Vietnam."

Colonel Nadal had beneficial insight: "They [U.S.] didn't negotiate and because the situation in South Vietnam was not very good, it was decided by the Johnson Administration to increase forces. Well, that message was heard loud and clear in Hanoi. And the North Vietnamese decided to move quickly to increase forces in South Vietnam before U.S. military arrived in large numbers.

Nadal continued "In 1964, in Hanoi, they decided to send two regular Army North Vietnamese divisions south, the 33rd and the 66th divisions. They came down the Ho Chi Minh Trail (Figure 17) starting in early '65. It took them several months to walk from Hanoi to the

Pleiku area. They didn't stay in one spot, but spread out throughout this central part of Vietnam as they arrived. The intent was to cut South Vietnam in two, right along Highway 19. Highway 19 (Figure 18) runs from Pleiku east to the coastal town called Qui Nhon. They were going to go across the narrow waist of Vietnam and separate it into two parts."

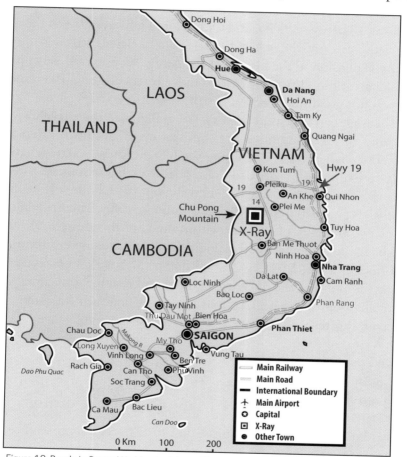

Figure 18: Roads in Central Highlands. Adapted from public domain.

Colonel Nadal elaborated on the history lesson: "The next step for the North Vietnamese was what is the classic strategy of a guerilla army. It is a tactic which the Viet Minh (North Vietnamese communists) had used time and again against the French, attacking an outpost with intent of annihilating the relief column that people inevitably sent. So, you attack an outpost, and you squeeze it, but you don't overrun it. You create a circumstance in which the other side is compelled to try and relieve the outpost."

Nadal shared his vivid memory of the battles in the area: "About the time offensive action started, August of '65, the 1st Cavalry Division arrived in Qui Nhon and moved to a town called An Khe, which is on Highway 19 between Pleiku and Quin Non. Halfway between the coast and Pleiku was An Khe, where the 1st Cav was based. This was the first airmobile division in the history of the Army. We had 400 helicopters. We had great mobility to be able to move forces around. The result of that was not good news for the North Vietnamese."

"There's a road that went from Pleiku to Plei Me. There the NVA put the camp of Plei Me under siege and set up an ambush. The South Vietnamese relief forces (including the USAF) knew exactly what was going to happen on that road. What the North Vietnamese did not know was that we had the ability of using our big Chinook helicopters (Figure 21, page 48) to move artillery around rapidly. The Army moved one or two batteries of artillery within range of this camp, but out of sight of anyone who was on this road. A South Vietnamese column and personnel carriers (M-113s) started down the road. When the NVA sprung the ambush, the Air Force fighter bombers overhead, along with the artillery on the ground, started firing. The ambush was destroyed; the camp was relieved!"

> **❝ The 1st Brigade found a hospital that was full of wounded North Vietnamese, which we moved to our hospitals to take care of them. ❞**

Colonel Nadal's perspective was helpful to the group: "The North Vietnamese pulled back and moved toward the border. At that time and for the next two weeks, the 1st Brigade—a division has three brigades equivalent in size to a Marine regiment—had a mission of going out to find and destroy them. They didn't really locate any enemy troops, but they did have small contacts. The 1st Brigade found a hospital that was full of wounded North Vietnamese, which we moved to our hospitals to take care of them. We still didn't make contact with the main force enemy. After two weeks, the 1st Brigade went home, and the 3rd Brigade was brought down (from An Khe). I commanded A Company, 1st Battalion, 7th Cavalry, in the 3rd Brigade. Steve Hansen was a mortar forward observer supporting my company, so he and I were together during all this fighting."

Colonel Nadal's recollection was fascinating:

> Our brigade started looking for enemy forces but were not finding them. We were due to fly back to our base at An Khe, I think on 15 August. Well, on the afternoon or the evening of 13 August, my boss, the guy that Mel Gibson plays in the movie, *We Were Soldiers,* got a call from brigade headquarters that said, *We have a new area we want you to look at. We don't know what's there, but we have some intelligence from radio signals and so forth that there may be a force nearby.* On that day, Lt. Col. Hal Moore and the company commanders got in a helicopter and flew over this area looking for a place to land. The only place that we found was the little clearing (Figures 18, 19) we called Landing Zone X-Ray (LZ X-Ray), located next to a big mountain, which straddles the Cambodian border. The following day we started moving the battalion with a total of 12 helicopters. A helicopter, in those days at that altitude and temperature, allowed for six soldiers and the crew. It takes a long time to move over 400 soldiers. We were scattered all over this area because we had been patrolling in small units, looking for these guys. The helicopters had to go out and pick them up in various locations and move them to LZ X-Ray. The first company to get picked up was B Company; I was with A Company. B Company arrived at LZ X-Ray and didn't find anything. It was quiet, except they captured a prisoner. A poor lone North Vietnamese soldier, who had gotten lost, was meandering across that landing zone, and he got quite a surprise when a bunch of helicopters landed around him! We had a Vietnamese interpreter with us, so we questioned the soldier, *What are you doing here?* And he said, *We're here to kill Americans.* We asked, *What unit are you with?* He responded, *We're from the 66th NVA Division.* We knew that was a big outfit. *Where are you?* And he replied, *Right here, on that mountain. Right here,* was maybe 300 yards away! We were obviously surprised; we didn't expect that size of an outfit to be up there. And they were surprised, because sitting up on the side of the mountain, they (NVA) could see what was happening. They could see our helicopters flying in, and they thought, *The enemy has been delivered into our hands.*

As soon as our commander, Hal Moore, realized the situation, he immediately changed plans. The initial plan was to land with every company going off in a different direction, searching for the enemy. Hal realized immediately that Landing Zone X-Ray was our survival. If we lost that landing zone we were done, because through that landing zone would come our ammunition, our people to control air support, evacuations for our wounded, whatever. And the rest of the battalion still had to land; there were only two companies (A and B) on the ground at that time.

"We had a Vietnamese interpreter with us, so we questioned the soldier, *What are you doing here?* And he said, *We're here to kill Americans.*"**

First person experience is a priceless teacher. Colonel Nadal's recount of LZ X-Ray no doubt relayed the significance of the engagement: "This battle was very significant. It was the first major engagement between a regular North Vietnamese Army unit and an American infantry unit. But it was not any old American infantry unit; it happened to be an airmobile division. The capabilities of the division to move forces around quickly was something the North Vietnamese had never experienced. The success of our three-day fight there—we survived; they killed a lot of us; we killed more of them—was based on the ability to move forces quickly. Before we went in there, an artillery battery was moved to a place called Landing Zone Falcon (Figure 14, page 31). When we started landing helicopters, we already had artillery to support our landing. When we came in with our helicopters, another set of gunship helicopters came alongside and strafed the edge of the landing zones as we were coming in. That's called prepping the landing zone. Consequently, the landing zone was prepared before we came in."

"The battle lasted for about three days and was very violent. There were a lot of other hard-fought battles in the country, but this will rank up near the top. I commanded a rifle company of about 90 soldiers that went to that landing zone (X-Ray). In those three days we had 16 killed and 27 wounded. So, you figure out the percentage of that. The battalion I was in had 76 soldiers killed."

"At the end of the fight, we were pulled out by helicopter. We had been reinforced during the fight, and it had been decided to call in B-52 strikes. The B-52 is a huge airplane that carries a 'gillion' bombs, and when they drop those bombs, you had to be 10 kilometers away from wherever those bombs were going to land in order to be safe. It was not the most accurate weapon system in the world. They took us (Company A) out by chopper back to Camp Holloway in Pleiku. One battalion that had reinforced us walked back to LZ Falcon and was pulled out of there. Another battalion (the 2nd BN of the 7th Cav) was given the mission to walk to LZ Albany. There were two episodes in the battle of the Ia Drang Valley. The first episode in the Ia Drang was at X-Ray and the second was the battle at LZ Albany."

> **❝ I commanded a rifle company of about 90 soldiers that went to that landing zone (X-Ray). In those three days we had 16 killed and 27 wounded. ❞**

"Landing Zone Albany was a disaster for the U.S. Army—in my mind—caused by an inept battalion commander who allowed his company (his battalion) to walk single file through the jungle. The North Vietnamese reacted quickly, proficiently, and got in position to ambush that battalion. They cut it up into sections, and then went around the line killing soldiers, even our wounded."

In 1992, Colonel Nadal went back to Vietnam and spent ten days with the colonel who commanded the North Vietnamese regiments who spent three days attacking the left flank of Nadal's rifle company: "I grew to have a great deal of respect for the man. I was impressed by his dedication and his professionalism. He was there for eight years. He joined the North Vietnamese Army as a private in Hanoi, fought as a sergeant in the Battle of Dien Bien Phu (1954), stayed in the North Vietnamese Army and became a captain in the spring or summer of '64. He was told, *take your company and march south to Pleiku*, where he had never been. He walked through the jungle, got malaria, as many of them did, but stuck with it, coming down south. Eight years; he never went home! He got an occasional letter from his wife who lived in Hanoi, but she never heard from him. He was wounded six times; once he was left on the battlefield for dead.

His soldiers carried him out. For a Vietnamese, he was tall and hefty. He was concerned the soldiers couldn't carry him, but they came back and got him and moved him to a hospital area. He told me that when you're a Viet Minh soldier (North Vietnamese soldier) and you are wounded and taken to a hospital, it was a triage as to who was going to get one of the five shots of penicillin they had. Of course, he was a very good commander and valuable asset, so they tried to take care of him."

> **The military doesn't go to war on its own; it goes as directed by civilian leaders.**

"I learned, in my view, that Americans and the American power structure at the very top had a vision of an expanding communism, and the War was fought as a way of holding the line against communist expansion. The only thing any of those Vietnamese soldiers cared about, however, wasn't communism or socialism or any "ism." It was uniting a country that had been divided for a thousand years. This country has only been united for two hundred of the last thousand years."

Colonel Nadal zeroed in on a message for students. "So the lesson is, make sure you know that what you're thinking is correct. In my view, we really misunderstood (Vietnamese motives). I have spent a lot of time reading and studying this country. My personal view is that it was a mistake for us (U.S.) to get involved as deeply as we were. Anyway, I hope that gives you a feel for why the battle was fought, what occurred, and what drove it."

Nadal gave instructions for a visit to the battlefield: "I want to do what the military would call a terrain walk. I plan to take you around and show you what happened and where. I'm going to try and help you feel or understand what it's like to be a private first class in a terrible fire fight. There are many anxieties and fears it creates, along with the confusion that exists with all these things going off around you. I hope, by the time this morning is over, you will know the importance of being here."

"All of you are citizens of our country. The military doesn't go to war on its own; it goes directed by civilian leaders. And we're now being sent to fight ISIS. We were sent to Vietnam; we were sent to Korea. And when we're sent, we try and do the best we can. And we get constraints put on us by the government agency, the Congress, when they say, *You can only have so much money*, and the White House says, *You can't cross this border or you can't bomb this target.*"

Col. Nadal discussed the lessons learned on both sides: "We learned that these guys were tenacious, they were professional, and they were good fighters. They learned we have a lot of fire power; we have a lot of ways to hurt them. They believed the best way to fight us was to get really close so there's not much space between their front lines and our front lines. Then we couldn't bring the Air Force in for fear of killing our own soldiers. The North Vietnamese used the phrase, *Grab them by the belt buckle and hang on*. The other thing I figured they learned was that we created sanctuaries. After this first battle, the 66th NVA Regiment pulled into Cambodia. They had base camps over there, and we knew exactly where the base camps were because we flew airplanes that had heat-seeking devices. We could see where their cooking fires were. We also had something called side-looking airborne radar, so we knew where the camps were."

"Our division commander, a wonderful general named Henry W. Kinnard, asked *twice* for permission to go after them and was denied. So now they had a place to hide and rest. They would come in, there would be a big fight, they would pull off to the side, and rest and recuperate. The 1st Cav fought the 66th division three times. Once here (Ia Drang), once at a place called Bong Son, and once up around the Kon Tum area. In between, they would go back to Cambodia and have a little R&R, to recuperate. We could have wiped them out."

In an effort to study the battle at LZ X-Ray, Nadal further explained the details: "I want to tell you more detail about the battle at LZ X-Ray. I have the perspective of a company commander, which is not the same perspective as people at other levels. So, I'm going to tell you how the thing went, the way it was. I landed with my company (Company A, the 1st Platoon). Lt. Col. Moore said to B Company, *Go out forward and let's do a little exploring. You, Tony, take over responsibility for the landing zone.* It was evident that the threat was from the west, so the 1st Platoon was sent over to the west. We found there was a creek bed that ran across the western end of the landing zone. (Figure 19) The landing zone wasn't very big. It could handle four helicopters at one time on the ground."

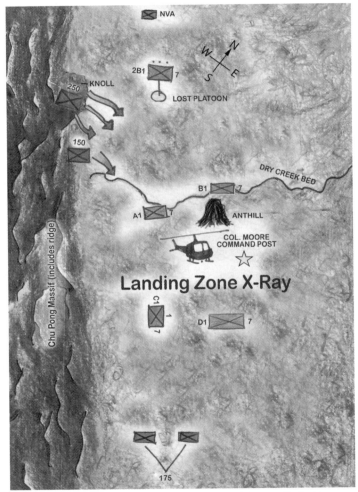

Figure 19: Troop locations at LZ X-Ray. Drawing by student artist Shelby Moore.

"A Company advanced west toward the creek bed. Moving forward, probably farther than I intended them to go, they ran into a buzz saw of North Vietnamese coming down the mountain. I was still at the landing zone because I had to wait for the rest of the company to arrive. The second platoon landed, and I sent them to their location."

"A Company was on the landing zone side of the creek bed. (Figure 19) After all my platoons had landed, and aware of the heavy firing coming from my company sector, I rushed to the 3rd Platoon area. I ran into the platoon sergeant and Captain Herren, the B Company commander, and asked the platoon sergeant, *Where is Lieutenant Taft, the platoon leader?* The platoon sergeant said, *Lt. Taft is dead.* I asked, *He's dead? Where is he?* He responded, *Well, sir, he's in the creek bed.* One of the things I had long believed and General Moore told us repeatedly, *We don't leave anyone behind* (same as the USMC). This was my first battle leading this particular company, and I was determined that nobody was going to say that I didn't do my job. So when they said, *Lt. Taft is dead and in the creek bed,* I turned to my communication NCO, Sergeant Jack Gell, an outstanding soldier, and said, *Let's go get Taft and bring him back.* We were under enemy fire as we ran to the creek bed. We got to the creek bed and found Taft. While I was in the creek bed, the enemy was throwing hand grenades at us. The hand grenades went off with little puffs of black smoke. They didn't have much power."

"I brought Taft back. While in the creek bed, we found another soldier who had been left behind. He was still alive. *Well, I've got another soldier back there, and he's alive, so I've got to go back and do it a second time.* I put my rifle down this time, because I had to carry him. My radio operator, Sergeant Jack Gell, was probably the best friend I had in the company at the time. He went with me, and we brought back the soldier. I think his name was Waluski, but I don't know that for a fact. But I do know he survived the battle; he was shot in the stomach. He made it and he wouldn't have if we had left him there!"

"Shortly, the other two platoons arrived. For about an hour there was a significant, thunderous sort of fire fight as the enemy came down the mountain. It appeared the enemy was focusing on the creek bed. My guys were either in the creek bed or just short of the creek bed. The NVA were running right in front of our guns. It's like someone had said, *Go from point A to point B.* But we were between point A and point B, and they were determined to get to point B and weren't paying a lot of attention to us in between. We created a lot of casualties in the enemy force as they streamed in front of our guns."

"Then C Company arrived. So now we had three rifle companies—B,

A, and C—on the ground. C Company served as the flank (the side). Last to arrive was D Company (mortar and reconnaissance), which served as the weapons company. One of the things that the NVA never discovered was that the back end of our landing zone was open, because we didn't have enough soldiers to cover the entire perimeter. If they had discovered that, it probably would have been all over for all of us, because there were a lot more of them. There were about 2,000 people in that NVA regiment, and we had less than 700 on the ground."

Nadal continues, "I mentioned earlier that before we landed, we had artillery in range and prepped the landing zone, so we had artillery coming in on the North Vietnamese soldiers. That resulted in casualties for them. Then there was a lull in the battle. At the beginning of the battle, not known by me at the time, a young platoon leader with B Company saw a couple of North Vietnamese soldiers in uniform running away from his platoon and said, *Let's go get them.* He wanted to capture these two soldiers, which you would initially think was not a bad idea, except by doing that he allowed his platoon to get split from his company. And because the enemy was coming down from the mountain, a gap had developed, allowing the enemy to get between his platoon and the rest of B Company. He (B Company platoon leader) was stuck, and he couldn't get back."

"At around four or five o'clock that afternoon, I got a radio call from Lt. Col. Moore saying, *You and B Company go out there and bring that platoon back.* We'd only had an hour or an hour and a half with some degree of calm. There was still sniping going on, but we weren't in assault mode. I had a particular problem: my artillery forward observer couldn't contact the artillery battalion firing in support of my company, because B Company's forward observer was on the same frequency."

Col. Nadal referred to his earlier teaching about the terrain: "Remember when I spoke about the high grass—knee-high or thigh-high grass in the area—and a lot of little trees? At the base of those trees were big termite hills (Figure 20) that could be as tall as 12 or 14 feet high, and those termite hills are harder than...whatever! The base of them could be 10 feet wide, so it was a conical, A-shaped thing which had trees growing out of it. Those termite hills made good places for the enemy to hide. The tall grass was a good place in which the enemy could crawl around. So in the time that we had been waiting (which we thought was a period of calm), the enemy had been crawling forward in the grass. I got the call at five o'clock to go out and get the platoon back, and I gathered my soldiers near the creek bed and I told them, *Ok, guys, we're going to go on assault, and we're going to bring that platoon back.* The response was *Let's go!* I reminded the guys, *These are your buddies, your brothers; we've got to get them back.* With that, I got up on top of the creek bed and said, *Follow me,* and I, personally, led the assault."

Figure 20: Termite Hill. Photo by John Luck.

"I had with me two radio operators, an artillery forward observer, and a reconnaissance sergeant, so there were five of us, and we had gone about 50 or 60 yards when all hell broke loose. We stumbled right into the enemy crawling toward us! It became up-close and personal. I had a sergeant who killed either one or two people with his bayonet. I had a machine gunner who shot guys with a .45 pistol because his machine gun ran out of ammo. In my case, I was standing, talking to the artillery forward observer; he was wearing a harness with an M2 compass, an artillery sophisticated compass. As I was talking to him, I saw that compass explode. *Boom!* His reconnaissance sergeant, who was on his right, dropped dead. The forward observer dropped dead, and my best friend on my left, Sergeant Jack Gell, was hit through the chest. I got him back to the battalion aide station, but he died there. It's hard to talk about this."

"I had to roll Sergeant Gell over and take the radio off of him, because I had a job to do. My job was to find that B Company platoon. I reached up and grabbed another soldier and said, *Here, put this radio on.* I was finally able to communicate with the artillery by using the battalion command frequencies, because I couldn't get through the regular channels. The stupid artillery man wouldn't accept the order to fire because I was not on their list of approved people. I called the battalion S3 and I said, *I need fire, and I need it now, and I want white phosphorus!* I asked for permission to withdraw back to the creek bed. The B Company commander had run into much of the same but not quite as bad. By this time, I had lost several of my soldiers; a couple of my best squad leaders had been killed, and one lieutenant had been killed."

To explain more fully serving honorably at war, Nadal shared this story: "One lieutenant received a Medal of Honor, Lieutenant Joe Marm, for actions in the middle of that fight. His story is remarkable. There was a clearing, but he was in the grass. He saw on the other side of that clearing an anthill (an anthill looks similar to a termite hill, without a tree jutting out of the apex), from where a machine gun was firing at his platoon and causing casualties. Joe grabbed what's called a LAW (light anti-tank weapon) and fired it into that anthill. Then, he picked up his rifle and grenades, charged the anthill, while crossing the clearing which was under enemy fire, threw his grenades over the anthill and wiped out the machine gunner's nest, while getting shot in the mouth. It was an action that resulted in his being awarded the Medal of Honor, which was well-deserved. I have known Joe for 50 years, and there's not a nicer, more humble guy in the world than Joe Marm. He acted without any preconceived notions other than, *I've got to do this to save my soldiers!*"

Nadal continued to tell about his actions in battle: "I called artillery fire, and said, *I want smoke.* A smoke round is an artillery round that comes out and lands and goes *POOF!* White smoke starts billowing up and provides concealment so that you can withdraw your forces without the enemy shooting at you as you're moving away. Unfortunately, there was a miscommunication. When I said I want fire mission and I want smoke, I was requesting a non-casualty producing round that would just go *POOF* and send up the puff of smoke. To my surprise, the artillery battery called back and said to the S3, *We don't have smoke; we have white phosphorus.* The battalion commander, not knowing where I called that location said, *Fire it; that makes good smoke.* The only time in that fight where I felt a sense of panic was when those rounds exploded and I thought, *I've killed my company!* It was white phosphorus, an agent that burns. If you got it on you, it would burn all the way through you until that particle was used up. There are times when one says, *Thank you, Lord,* and that was one of them for me, because none of my soldiers, as far as I know today, were hit by the WP (Willie Peter)."

"While I was leading the assault, an enemy machine gunner killed the people around me, two guys on one side and a guy on the other side. I was spared, along with my RTO standing behind me, who is today one of my very best friends. There are still mysteries in life that I can't explain. At this point, I realized that the enemy was too strong and well-concealed for us to continue the attack. I called Lt. Col. Moore and asked permission to withdraw. He approved and I ordered the company to withdraw to the creek bed. My RTO and I remained on the battlefield to provide covering fire for the company and then returned to organize the defense. We made it back to the creek bed. We got part way back, and I thought, *That smoke was so successful, let's do it again!* I called another mission; they fired the same white phosphorus, but I wanted it in the same area. We had pulled the company back and it was a lot safer the second time."

"After a day of fighting, we were absolutely out of water, having consumed every drop we had in our canteens. We were so thirsty and exhausted. The emotional intensity of battle had taken its toll. Any time you do anything that depletes your adrenaline, you crash. We were in effect crashing, and it was the role of the commander to know that was going to happen. Military doctrine is, *You attack the enemy when you're attacked, and if the enemy withdraws, you counter-attack.* You counter-attack because you want to take advantage of exhaustion that exists in his ranks. So, I was afraid we were going to get hit. My role was twofold: keep my guys alert and get them resupplied. We managed to get ammunition, but we didn't get water until later that night. A great big Chinook helicopter (Figure 21) flew in with a 500-gallon bladder of water underneath it, and we were able to send people back to retrieve it."

"The night was relatively quiet on our front, although we had a soldier that kept firing. We were telling our soldiers, *Don't fire. Don't fire your weapons unless you have something to shoot at. We don't want to give our position away.* But somewhere in my company there was a soldier who was determined to keep the enemy at bay on his own, and he had an M79 grenade launcher. Once in a while I would hear this, *POP. BOOM!* He thought he was defending his position; he was nervous and he didn't want anyone coming near him. So regardless of what orders were out, he was going to shoot that M79 and land it on someone's head. Every time he did that, I got a call from battalion. *Who's shooting in your area? Cut it out!* I'd say, *Yes, sir.* And then we'd hear a *BOOM!*"

Figure 21: Chinook Helicopter. Photo by John Luck.

"The following morning, around 4:00 a.m., Charlie Company got hit very hard by a battalion-sized attack, which resulted in the enemy getting into foxholes with C Company. C Company lost 47 soldiers killed in that morning attack, but they held on. Company Commander, Bob Edwards, was shot through the chest and called back and said, *I need to be evacuated. I've been shot in the chest.* The battalion commander said, *I can't get anyone to you.* A platoon reconnaissance leader was sent to relieve him, and he was shot trying to cross the landing zone. So, they messaged to Bob Edwards, *Hang on! We'll get to you, but it's not going to happen right now.* Bob Edwards hung on and kept fighting with his company with a bullet hole somewhere in his upper chest."

Colonel Nadal responded to the question he frequently gets: "People always ask, *Why do soldiers fight?* And the answer typically is, *Well, the American soldier does not fight for an ideological reason. The American soldier fights for his fellow soldiers. The unit develops a sense of cohesion and trust and respect for one other. They fight for each other.* The soldiers of 1/7 Cavalry had been together for two years before being deployed to Vietnam and had a terrific battalion commander, Lt. Col. Harold G. Moore, and strong unit cohesion. Though that's a good answer, in my view, it's not the total answer. There's another factor which is very important. And it's *you fight for your self-respect.* Human beings do not like to be viewed as weak, useless, unnecessary, despised, etc. If you're a good guy and you're doing your job, you're going to get a lot of positive feedback from the members of your platoon. If you're not a good guy and not doing a good job, you're going to get a lot of negative feedback from the members of your platoon. Nobody likes that and nobody wants to be viewed as a loser or a weirdo. The issue of how you perceive yourself or how you want to be perceived is important, and so you behave a certain way that earns you the respect of your peers."

Another question Colonel Nadal is asked concerns the available medical assets and evacuation: "We had the standard platoon medics assigned to each platoon, and then we had a company medic assigned to my headquarters. We had a battalion surgeon and he was a member of the medical platoon. He was a captain, doctor—M.D.—and never expected that he would be up near the frontlines. But when the fight started getting hot and we started getting a lot of wounded, either he volunteered to go up there or the battalion commander said, *We need you up here.* So we ended up with a battalion surgeon on the landing zone. He was doing tracheotomies. Afterwards I talked to him and he said, *That was rough and futile because I really didn't have anything to work with, just what was in my hands and in the first aid kit.*"

"Evacuation was another issue. When the 1st Cavalry went to Vietnam, we were assigned a medical helicopter evacuation platoon or company. They managed to earn the hostility of some of the infantry units because they were overly cautious. You got in a fight and you needed someone evacuated, and you'd call for medevac. Medevac would ask, *Do you have a clear landing zone?* And I'd say, *Hell no, I don't have a clear landing zone, but it's where we're taking casualties!* They would further explain, *We can't land unless you have a green landing zone.* So then I would call Bruce Crandall, a friend who was the company commander of a helicopter lift company, and/or his sidekick, Ed Freeman. They would dodge the bullets and whatever, land the helicopter, and keep it on the ground until we got it loaded. Bruce and Ed are credited with saving perhaps as many as 70 lives at LZ X-Ray by flying in after the landing zone had been declared officially closed. One chopper had gone down at the end of the landing zone, and some aviation guy said, *It's too hazardous to go in there!* But Bruce and Ed kept flying in and taking out six or seven soldiers at a time. Some of his crewmen were wounded, but they flew into the LZ well into the night. Both Major Crandall and Captain Freeman were later awarded the Medal of Honor for their bravery in saving so many soldier's lives while under fire. All the while, back at Pleiku we had a surgical team that could deal with the injuries."

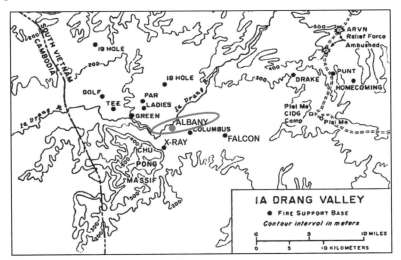

Figure 22: LZ Albany. Adapted from public domain.

Nadal returned to the battle: "Someone asked about the remainder of the battle, and what happened after the first day. The following day, early morning, as I explained, C Company was attacked. The enemy was in the foxholes with them, but C Company survived with a lot of casualties. We started getting reinforcements; two battalions landed somewhere away from us. They were air-mobiled in and walked into the landing zone. One of those battalions got the mission of going out and bringing the lost platoon back. B Company got the task of leading out, because our battalion commander wanted to make sure we brought our own guys back. B Company went out, supported by the whole infantry battalion, with only minor enemy contact."

"There is an interesting story about the lost platoon. The lieutenant was killed, so the command evolved to a platoon sergeant. The platoon sergeant was killed, and the command evolved down to a sergeant—an E5—named Ernie Savage. When Ernie Savage took over command, he surrounded himself with artillery concentrations. All night long, every time he heard movement, he'd call in artillery fire."

"One of the medics, a soldier named Doc Loss, was recommended for a Medal of Honor, but he didn't receive it. He should have, because all night long he kept moving around the perimeter treating soldiers. When he had run out of bandages, he would take bandages from dead soldiers and put them on live soldiers. He was sheltering wounded soldiers with his own body to keep them alive. There came a time when the direct fire of the enemy was reduced, and Doc kept everyone else in the platoon alive after that."

> **Some guys feigned death. I was told by soldiers that were there, that they could hear the NVA going down the line killing all the wounded.**

"The Ia Drang battle continued with the evacuation of Landing Zone X-Ray. We were picked up by helicopters and taken back to Camp Holloway, which is where the current airfield is in Pleiku (Figure 14, page 31). The 2nd Battalion, 5th Cavalry marched out to where the artillery was, and got picked up. And then the 2nd Battalion, 7th Cavalry was told to march out to Landing Zone Albany (Figure 22) and get picked up there. Well, they started out and the terrain got thick. They got into an area which I call *true jungle*. They were all strung out, and some NVA scout had seen what was happening and appropriately called his chain of command. The NVA organized rapidly and set up an ambush and these guys walked into it. Unfortunately, the battalion commander of the 2nd and 7th was at the head of the column and had just gotten to the landing zone. He wanted to organize the landing zone for their defense that night. So he called all the company commanders to come forward and with them came the radio operators, two radio operators per commander. When the enemy attacked, the rifle companies didn't have a commander with them. But worse, they didn't have any radios to communicate with their artillery or to communicate with the other units. The battalion got hammered and split into groups. Some of them fought ferociously and survived. Others were overrun. Some guys feigned death. I was told by soldiers that were there, that they could hear the NVA going down the line killing all the wounded."

"One company commander, Captain George Forrest, a good friend of mine, was a football player in college—a big, strong black guy. His company was at the tail end of that column. When the firing started, he ran the whole length of that column, while the ambush was going on. He had two radio operators with him, both of them were killed! They were trying to keep up with him. But he made it back to his company and organized that company for defense. That company probably had fewer casualties than any of the elements in that column. LZ Albany was a disaster with 151 Americans killed, but the number of NVA killed was over 300."

Colonel Nadal concluded his remarks about the battle at Landing Zone X-Ray: "My company went back to Camp Holloway. There was an officer's club there for the pilots. Lt. Col. Moore and the rest of us walked in; we smelled bad, we looked bad, and we were dirty. The guy behind the bar said, *Sir, we can't serve you. You're not meeting our dress standards here.* Lt. Col. Moore put his M16 on the bar and said, *You're going to serve me something and you're gonna do it right now!* We all had a few sodas and went back to our units. The following day General Westmoreland came and, as was his habit, got up on a Jeep and gave us an inspirational sort of talk. He was going to promote Sergeant Savage to second lieutenant, right on the spot—instant promotion—and Savage turned him down. Sergeant Savage said, *I don't want to be a lieutenant.* Eventually, Savage became a captain, and he won a Distinguished Service Cross for his actions with that lost platoon."

STUDENT RESPONSE

"After knowing Tony Nadal for only a few hours, I already had the utmost respect for the U.S. Special Forces Commander," wrote Cody Pentecost. Cody responded candidly about the opportunity he had to travel as Nadal's student host and hear firsthand about battles in the Ia Drang. Steve Hansen, another veteran at LZ X-Ray and Tony Nadal's mortar forward observer, was also helpful. Between Steve Hansen and Tony Nadal, Cody received insights that no other class in America could provide. What follows are some of Cody's deeply-held feelings, as recorded in his student journals, about what he, as a student, was experiencing.

"Today, we were able to visit Plei Me, which is close to LZ X-Ray. Although we were not able to see Landing Zone X-Ray, we were easily within a short walk over the red dirt and scrub brush. It was amazing to hear both Tony and Steve's stories—so different, but at the same time, alike."

Figure 23: Col. Nadal explained the battle at LZ X-Ray to students, veterans, and sponsors. Photo by John Luck.

"Before we even left the hotel (Figure 23) in Pleiku, we were given a little history lesson by Tony Nadal. He shared some basic information we needed to know about the terrain, lay of the land, and the battle itself. He drew a map from memory showing us where the landing zone was. He was very adept with helping us understand what his soldiers had to deal with during the battle. When our class session ended, we boarded the bus and headed to the area as close to the LZ X-Ray battle

53

site (Figure 24) as we could get. On the bus ride, Nadal and Hansen were able to enlighten the group and take questions. At one point, Tony got up and shared a step-by-step account of what he experienced on the battlefield. This was very emotional, and everyone was on the edge of their seats. It was so quiet that you could have heard a pin drop. This was one of my most meaningful days on the trip. It was a pleasure spending time with a man who has not only been impacted by the War, but also one who made a contribution to this battle."

Figure 24 (left to right): Cody Pentecost, Col. Nadal, Lt. Col. Steve Hansen, and student Blane Bias near LZ X-Ray. Photo by John Luck.

"In my opinion, the soldiers that served in Vietnam might be the toughest soldiers to have fought for our country. The contempt the Vietnam veterans experienced upon returning to the U.S.A. might be expected in another country, but nobody could have been prepared for this to happen in our own country. My heart goes out to all the soldiers who came back from war to see their fellow Americans despise and reject them for serving the United States."

"My experiences in Vietnam with Colonel Tony Nadal and all the other veterans will be a time I will never forget."

TOPIC SUMMARY

"Okay, that concludes today's class. There will be an exam tomorrow," Nadal declared with a smile, following his detailed recount of the battle at LZ X-Ray. It is easy to see how Colonel Nadal was such an excellent instructor at West Point. His combat experience placed him in a unique position. Every student, veteran, and sponsor on the Patriotic Education Trip to Vietnam benefitted from his presence.

The battle at Landing Zone X-Ray had implications for the entire War: Practically all units were understrength. According to Lt. Col. Hal Moore, "The four line companies had 20 of their authorized 23 officers, but the enlisted ranks had been whittled down by expiring enlistments, malaria cases, and requirements for base camp guards and workers back in An Khe. Headquarters Company was also understrength, and I had been forced to draw it down further by sending men out to fill crucial medical and communications vacancies in the line companies."[3] Medics were in short supply and were critically needed.

> **"** The price had been high—79 U.S. killed and 834 NVA dead at LZ X-Ray and 151 Americans KIA at LZ Albany.[6] The battle had been brutal. **"**

So, American soldiers were ten thousand miles from home, short-handed and worried about family and friends back in "the world." Officialdom in D.C. was occupied with Great Society program approvals, the first "teach-ins" had started at the University of Michigan, and President Johnson and Secretary of Defense Robert McNamara were micromanaging the War effort and trying to keep the Joint Chiefs of Staff in line.

Indeed, this early year (1965) was anything but calm. South Vietnam was not stable, the U.S. military barracks at Qui Nhon were bombed, the Marines killed two hundred in *Operation Starlite* near Chu Lai, and Commanding General Westmoreland was asking for more troops.[4]

It's hard to believe it had only been a few months since President Johnson had said, "We are not about to send American boys nine to ten thousand miles from home to do what Asian boys ought to be doing for themselves."[5] Despite all of the talk and double-talk, the U.S. troops had good morale and wanted to win the War and return home with honor.

Those who fought at Plei Me, LZ X-Ray, and LZ Albany will tell you that leadership matters. Lt. Col. Hal Moore and (then Captain) Tony Nadal are examples that students and veterans, alike, recognized. Above all else, they sensed that uncommon valor was everywhere to be found. The price had been high—79 U.S. killed and 834 NVA dead at LZ X-Ray and 151 Americans KIA at LZ Albany.[6] The battle had been brutal. Hearing of NVA soldiers shooting wounded Americans in the head and laughing about it was more than anyone expected, even in guerrilla warfare.

Colonel Nadal, as Cody Pentecost remembers, "emphasized the importance of brotherhood during war. Nadal said, *Even through the negative nature of war, sometimes flowers bloom.* Colonel Nadal cares for his men just like they are family," Cody recalled. "He told me the entire battalion from LZ X-Ray gets together every year for an anniversary." One of these reunions (Figure 25) was hosted at College of the Ozarks in 2018. Nadal expressed to Cody the effect of brotherhood: "It is important in war, so they know who they are fighting for and who they are fighting with. The respect that the men develop for their leadership and comrades could potentially determine the outcome of their battles and even the war."

"I have truly been blessed with the opportunity to get to know Colonel Nadal," Cody concludes. "I will never forget."

Figure 25: 7th Cavalry Reunion 2018 at College of the Ozarks. Infantry Line Company at LZ X-Ray (left to right) Bob Edwards, C Company; Tony Nadal, A Company; John Herren, B Company. Photo by Shann Swift.

CLASS TOPIC 2: BONG SON (II-CORPS)

Why make a friend just to see him die?

INSTRUCTOR: LT COL STEVEN R. (STEVE) HANSEN, USA (RET.)[1]

Like Colonel Tony Nadal, Lieutenant Colonel Steven R. Hansen had a long tenure with the Army, serving in Germany and Vietnam. His service began by enlisting in the U.S. Army in 1960 at the age of 17. He completed basic training and advanced individual training at Fort Ord, near Monterey, California. Upon graduation, he was sent to Bamberg, Germany, to join D Company, 2nd Battle Group, 4th Infantry Regiment, 3rd Infantry Division. Hansen served three years in Germany as an ammunition bearer, forward observer, squad leader, and eventually sergeant. Upon denial of an extension request in Berlin, he was sent to Fort Benning in late March 1963 to develop and test air assault tactics and techniques.[2]

Hansen served two tours in Vietnam. He was first deployed to Vietnam in 1965 as a part of D Company, 1st Battalion, 7th Cavalry Regiment, 1st Cavalry Division. During this tour from 1965-66, Hansen was involved in major conflicts such as LZ X-Ray in the Ia Drang Valley and the Bong Son campaigns.

A second Vietnam tour, from 1969-70, placed Hansen as the commanding officer of C Company, 1st Battalion, 20th Infantry and, later, the commanding officer of A Company, 23rd Supply and Transportation Battalion. In 1973, he left the Army and entered into the Army Reserve. Having graduated from the University of Tampa with a B.S. in Business Administration, Hansen began working as a civilian personnel management intern for the Department of the Air Force, specifically as a position classification specialist. Later, Hansen was appointed civilian personnel officer at Blytheville Air Force Base, Arkansas; Homestead Air Force Base, Florida; and Clark Air Base, Republic of the Philippines.

Lt. Col. Hansen received many decorations and recognitions during his military career. These include the Silver Star, Bronze Star with valor and two oak leaf clusters, Combat Infantryman's Badge, Air Medal, Purple Heart with one oak leaf cluster, Meritorious Service Medal, Army Commendation Medal, Army Achievement Medal, Presidential Unit Citation, Army Good Conduct Medal, and Vietnamese Gallantry Cross with Gold Star.

Hansen considers it an honor to have served under some of the Army's most highly regarded leaders at noteworthy locales: with the Berlin Brigade in Germany, in combat at Landing Zone X-Ray, in the Ia Drang Valley with Lieutenant Colonel Hal Moore, and with Colonel Tony Nadal at LZ X-Ray and the Bong Son Campaign.

Lt. Col. Hansen and his wife, Belinda, currently reside in Jonesboro, Arkansas.

Figure 26: Veteran Steve Hansen and student host Blane Bias. Photo by John Luck.

 ## STUDENT HOST: BLANE BIAS

Blane Bias (Figure 26) was the student host for Lt. Col. Hansen. Blane came to College of the Ozarks (C of O) from the small town of Centralia, Missouri. While at the College, his major was criminal justice, with an interest in becoming a Missouri State Highway Patrolman. His workstations on campus were the power plant, the maintenance department at The Keeter Center, and the fire department. He could also be found working off campus at a go-kart track to earn spending money. When asked how he spent his spare time, Blane said, "Hunting, fishing, spending time with family, training with the campus fire department, and fighting fires!"

Going on a Patriotic Education Trip to Vietnam was very personal to Blane. He relates, "My interest in participating in the patriotic trip to Vietnam stems from my grandfather, Gary B. Whitehead, who served as a combat medic with the 25th Infantry Division during the Tet Offensive in 1968. On August 4, 1968, he was wounded when he (Whitehead) and his men stepped on a booby trap. In the moments after landing (back on the ground), he crawled to the other wounded men and bandaged them all. By the time the medevac helicopter arrived, my grandpa's wounds were the only ones that had not been treated. For these exemplary deeds, he received the Purple Heart and Bronze Star."

" During our childhood, my grandpa instilled, in both my brother and me, a deep respect for the soldiers who fought for the United States, especially those who fought in Vietnam. **"**

"During our childhood, my grandpa instilled, in both my brother and me, a deep respect for the soldiers who fought for the United States, especially those who fought in Vietnam. Grandpa Whitehead also taught me to have a strong sense of patriotism, duty, and pride for America. I remember Grandpa sadly recounting how the soldiers were treated when they arrived back home from Vietnam. With glistening eyes, he'd explain, *that people spit on them and called them baby killers*. It made me really sad to hear that people did not understand that Americans went there (Vietnam) and were willing to die for their country."

In addition, Blane wanted "to see some of the places that my grandpa may have gone and experience some of the places he told about in his stories. I hope to gain a deeper understanding of the things that soldiers went through in Vietnam. Also, I want to honor the service of the Vietnam veterans who will be accompanying us and learn about some of the struggles that they have been through. I would be grateful for the privilege of honoring them by listening to their stories and sharing this time with them."

Blane considered the timing of being chosen: "On June 12, 2012, my grandpa died after a seven-year battle with Lewy body dementia, a disease in which patients slowly lose both their cognitive skills and mental thought processes, along with their ability to walk and communicate. Ironically, he died two hours after someone from College of the Ozarks called [with trip-acceptance news]. By God's grace, in 2010 my grandpa had gone with the Central Missouri Honor Flight out of Columbia, Missouri, to Washington, D.C., to visit the World War II, Vietnam, and Korean War Memorials. Grandpa went because he wanted to honor the men who died in Vietnam and to also say he was sorry to the ones that he could not save. As I recount all of this, I am reminded of how much respect I have for my grandpa and for those who have fought for this country. I want to go on this trip so that I can honor my grandpa's memory."

It's easy to see why Blane was selected to participate in the College's first Patriotic Education Trip to Vietnam with veterans.

BONG SON CAMPAIGN BACKGROUND

Bong Son is unusual in its location (Figure 12, page 28), geography, and importance during the Vietnam War. First of all, it is in the coastal part of the II-Corps Tactical Zone. Lt. Col. Hansen referred to it as a plain. To the west the mountains can be easily seen on the horizon. In fact, without looking closely, the topography (Figure 27) would be hard to distinguish from locales within the United States. The importance attributed to the Bong Son area stems from its agricultural usefulness. Some called it the "bread basket" of Vietnam, and both the Army of the Republic of Vietnam (ARVN) and the North Vietnamese Army (NVA) claimed it as their own.

The battle at Bong Son was the second major engagement between the 1st Cavalry Division and North Vietnam Regulars. Many who fought in the Ia Drang wound up warring with some of the same NVA

Figure 27: Bong Son plain. Photo by John Luck.

Regiments in the Bong Son Campaign. Such was the case for Colonel Nadal and Steve Hansen.

Hansen explained his transition from the Ia Drang to Bong Son by way of Hong Kong: "I went for rest and relaxation to Hong Kong. While most men wanted Bangkok, I preferred Hong Kong because I wanted an escape from Vietnam and anything like it! While Hong Kong was Asian, it was also British and a very nice place to visit. I enjoyed myself immensely."[3]

Upon returning to the battlefield, Hansen noted some changes to his team: "Shortly after my return, I was sitting in the NCO (non-comissioned officers) Club with some friends, and as I looked around, almost all the faces were new. Those of us who had trained together stayed together, but we were more reserved about the replacements. *Why make a friend just to see him die?*"[4]

When he returned from R&R, Hansen was also faced with a new assignment. He was now the D Company (Delta) field logistics sergeant. This position was much different from being a forward observer. Delta did not have a maneuver element; its three platoons were reconnaissance (recon), heavy mortar, and anti-tank. Supplying these platoons was a difficult task because they were scattered throughout the Battalion's area of operations. Bong Son was Hansen's first operation as a member of the company field headquarters. Though he had operated in areas around Qui Nhon (Figure 18, page 35), no major contact with the enemy had been made. The locals seemed friendly around Qui Nhon, but this wasn't the case at Bong Son, where many were hostile. Heavy fighting was ahead.

 ## INSTRUCTOR REFLECTIONS

Before Lt. Col. Hansen served at Bong Son, he had survived the Ia Drang battle at Chu Pong Mountain, near Landing Zone X-Ray. His experience at X-Ray was surreal and helped prepare him for the extended battles at Bong Son. He relayed to students and fellow veterans some experiences at X-Ray that almost fifty years later still stand out in his mind: "LZ X-Ray was not *hot* when I arrived; it was quiet. I came in with a different lift from the first. I came in with the second half of the second lift and was assigned to A Company under Colonel Tony Nadal's command. We hadn't been there a minute or two when the fight started. It went from being dead quiet to absolute mayhem in just a few seconds. I think we kind of fooled the enemy. The NVA had been watching us and had seen a single company in a landing zone, but other U.S. troops had been tromping around in the jungle near the LZ for awhile. When troops were boarding the helicopters to leave, they (NVA) saw us—the first 16 helicopters with B Company—they must have thought, *Let's go get them!*"

 ❝ It went from being dead quiet to absolute mayhem in just a few seconds. ❞

"This started their movement. The first thing they hit was a platoon; B Company was well forward. They attacked it, but they also continued to attack toward the creek bed. Then we showed up! Eight helicopters landed first with half of the company, and right behind them were the other eight. Suddenly, this North Vietnamese battalion commander, who likely thought he was attacking one company, found himself attacking two! We were in the creek bed, which was a good defensive position, and we were able to stop them. In my opinion, if we (A Company) had not arrived, B Company would've been decimated.

There's no question in my mind. Tony Nadal was commander of A Company. I believe, in theory, the NVA had the strength to overrun us, even the second lift in between the two companies. The NVA was probably stunned by the ferocity of our defense, and they had also bled away a bunch of troops to address a platoon that had gotten too far away and cut off. The enemy probably should've ignored this lost platoon and put those forces in the main assault against those of us in the creek bed. It was a very, very tenuous situation. And the outcome of the whole battle at LZ X-Ray was decided in those couple of minutes. If we had been five minutes later—had it taken us five more minutes to get to the LZ—the whole outcome of the battle would have been different."

On the first day of the battle, when we were so vulnerable, the enemy never made an attack on the LZ proper. They never made an effort to control the LZ. And that was a big mistake on their part.

"It really came down to the fact that sides were balanced, and we prevailed. The NVA attacked us again, then we attacked the NVA. We went out of the creek bed twice on assaults, and we were repulsed. Next to arrive was Charlie Company. Then B Company, 2nd of the 7th, came in. And then my company, Delta Company, came in."

One of the biggest mistakes the enemy made was not attacking the landing zone. The landing zone was essentially undefended at the very beginning. All our forces were facing toward the west, toward the direction of the enemy attack. If the enemy had maneuvered, they could have taken the landing zone. As the other companies were landing, they were coming under fire, the fire mostly from the west. The enemy, throughout the whole fight, never made the LZ a priority. Hanson reported, "On the first day of the battle, when we were so vulnerable, the enemy never made an attack on the LZ proper. They never made an effort to control the LZ. And that was a big mistake on their part."

"They did attack us through the C Company sector and attacked the landing zone on the morning of the second day, 15 November. They almost prevailed, nearly got through. Charlie Company was decimated, and we actually had NVA soldiers inside the perimeter and on the landing zone. We were able to counterattack with a reconnaissance platoon, and I think B Company 2nd of the 7th may have played a role. When we repulsed them that time, the morning of the fifteenth, that essentially was the end of the battle in terms of decisiveness. From that point on, we kept getting stronger and stronger.

❝ Hansen saw incredible risks routinely taken. One of his good friends, Joe Marm, received the Medal of Honor. ❞

"The first man I ever saw die in combat was Lieutenant [Robert] Taft, who was leader of the platoon I was attached to and worked with. When we got off the helicopter, the fighting hadn't started, but Nadal had been there maybe two or three minutes, not more than five; he had sized up the situation. When the firing started, Nadal ordered Lieutenant Taft to move to the left and attack toward the creek bed. We actually got to the creek bed and went through it to the other side. I couldn't keep up with Lieutenant Taft; I don't think anybody could. Then, all of a sudden, Taft went down. I saw it. He'd gotten shot in the throat—instantly killed—dead before he hit the ground. There were people being shot all around me! We went back into the creek bed and gathered all of the wounded. As time permitted, we took them back to the battalion command post (CP). The battalion CP was maybe 50 yards away, where the medics were set up. A number of wounded soldiers had to be taken out. We all worked together to get them transported. When you land by helicopter in the middle of nowhere, there's no turning back, you're committed. Potentially, you have a lot of help. You have artillery and helicopters and all that other stuff, but you have to fight your way out, and that's what we did!"

Lt. Col. Hansen recollects the first NVA soldier he killed: "I remember the dust coming out of his uniform when I hit him in the chest. He had a surprised look on his face and just collapsed. Sergeant John Rangel, who was also in A Company, to our right, actually bayoneted a North Vietnamese soldier; that's how close Rangel got. I wasn't that close to them this time.

What happened to me is that as a forward observer I went out there with all of this great anticipation. By the time B Company came in, my radio operator (with my radio) had replaced one of Tony's radio operators, who had been killed. I had no radio, and it wasn't until later in the fight that I actually got a radio and was able to call some fire missions. During the hairiest part of the battle, I was a rifleman, just like everybody else."

Hansen saw incredible risks routinely taken. One of his good friends, Joe Marm, received the Medal of Honor. Hansen recounts, "Joe Marm was a very good friend of mine. Joe was not killed, but he was shot through the jaw and spent quite a bit of time at Valley Forge Hospital being put back together. He was a young second lieutenant, had just graduated from Officer Candidate School (OCS) about the time we were leaving the States, and he was assigned as a replacement. When we organized to go to Vietnam, a lot of the junior officers, real short-timers, were pulled out, and we got some excellent officers who had just graduated from OCS. Joe was one of them. He was a platoon leader. When we made our assault out of the creek bed at X-Ray, we couldn't advance. We were having a real problem and heavily engaged. One of the problems was a machine gun that was really tearing everybody up. It was partially covered by an anthill some distance in front of us. We tried everything to take it out, but nothing worked. Finally, Joe grabbed an LAW (light anti-armor weapon), which looks a little like a bazooka but short. He fired this LAW at the machine gun position, and then he got up and attacked by throwing a couple of hand grenades behind the anthill. He took out the NVA machine gun crew. If you could have seen the volume of fire that he weathered, you would find it hard to believe that he lived through it. I had the opportunity to work with Joe in the *Happy Valley Operation* and a couple other operations. So, I knew him well, and we remain friends until this day."

 I knew that day I was lucky to be alive. The difference between victory and defeat was a small, small window.

At the end of the Battle at LZ X-Ray, Hansen remembered: "I recall getting on the helicopter. As we lifted off, the further away from X-Ray we got, the further away we got from the smell. It just faded out. I looked back, and I'm not a particularly religious person, but I thanked God for my deliverance. I knew that day I was lucky to be alive. The difference between victory and defeat was a small, small window. Most of the close friends I lost were with C Company. We shared a barracks with C Company, and I knew everyone in C Company. We all ate in the same mess hall. They took the brunt of the casualties when they were overrun on the second morning. I knew them all."

After a brief reorganization at An Khe, Hansen headed to Bong Son. Upon arrival at Bong Son, Hansen explained, "I was brought by my mentor, First Sergeant Adams, back to the company headquarters, where my job was logistics, making sure we were supplied. The second part of my job was to keep track of what was going on in the rest of the battalion, because our little company command section was the alternate command post for the battalion. If we lost the battalion command post, in either an aerial accident or as a result of enemy fire, we would still have all of the information, so the headquarters could be quickly reestablished. It was unbelievable. I was just a few hundred yards away from where the action was but not directly involved in it. The radios were cracking; I'd hear things, and I knew where everybody was going and what they were doing. But for me, it was almost like I was floating in a cloud. This was all going on around me, and yet, I didn't have any direct contact. It wasn't personal."

"One of the things I remember very distinctly at Bong Son is picking up some replacements who had flown in, and they were to be added to the company. A quick auxiliary lesson—in 1965, while all of this was going on in Vietnam, there was a revolution of some sort in the Dominican Republic. The United States military sent the 82nd Airborne to the Dominican Republic, and they did a good job there; but it wasn't comparable to what we were encountering in Bong Son. When I went to get these replacements, virtually all of these men had been paratroopers on jump-status for the 82nd Airborne. They all had their combat infantry badges and considered themselves combat veterans. Well, when we arrived at our medical unit, there were more casualties—more dead people—from one day of combat at Bong Son than their whole division had suffered in the Dominican Republic. When I pointed that out to them, they went from being upset about not being on jump-status to frustrated about assignment to a leg unit and not an airborne unit. After that, they were not very vocal."

"We lost some of those guys right at Bong Son. One in particular, a mortar gunner, was hit by a hand grenade. As he lay dying, he mumbled something that sounded like, *Tell my wife I love her*. When people are gravely injured, they do say things like, *Tell my mother I love her*. Well, anyway, they say things that are not selfish; it's really quite amazing. I hope none of you ever have to go through that, and I hope I never have to experience it again."

"My strongest recollection of Bong Son is all the sand. The Bong Son plain is mostly sand. We had sand everywhere! We had it in our underwear, rubbing on our skin. It was in our food because helicopters stirred it up, and it was miserable. You couldn't dig a good fighting hole in the sand. We could get down in it, but we couldn't do much more than that. The sand was nasty. I don't think I was ever as dirty in Vietnam as I was when we were operating at Bong Son."

"Many of the veterans of the Ia Drang said that, for them, the fighting at Bong Son was worse than the fighting at X-Ray. Principal reason, I think, is because it kept going on and on, and on, and on. Typically, on our operations at X-Ray, there was a whole lot of excitement for a few minutes and a whole lot of boredom for the rest of the time. At Bong Son, we continually made contact. It was a tough, difficult operation. For us, the 1st of the 7th, the two Bong Son campaigns just about wiped out the original guys who came over on the ship. Most of the troops were sent out as wounded or sick. Some came back to us, but most of them died."

"When we came back for the second operation in Bong Son, I was sitting with some of my friends in the small mess hall, and when we looked around, we didn't know anybody. All of the guys we had known, our circle, were now sitting at one table. I hesitate to use the term *survival guilt*, but I felt very strongly about what I'd been through and how lucky I am."

Hansen recounts his last day in Vietnam: "When my day came to go home, I was the fifth and last soldier from my company to leave in the organized rotation. There was nobody else left from my company who had been there from the very beginning. When I got back to the U.S., I was a little upset with my orders because I wanted to be close to home, within reach of Los Angeles, where I was from. The Army cut orders sending me through Fort Louis, Washington, where I was going to be pushing troops!"

One can quickly understand Hansen's debacle; he was coming off the battlefield and learning his new assignment was to be recruiting. Hansen remembers, "I got off the airplane at Travis Air Force Base, and I got intercepted by a team from the Army Recruiting Command looking for recruiters. They said, *Sergeant, how would you like to be the Army Recruiter in your hometown?* That's exactly what the guy said. I replied, *You can't do that.* I should have said, *I'm not interested,* but instead my response was, *You can't do that,* and sure enough, I wound up recruiting in my hometown. I lived at home, and worked in an Army Recruiting Station. I hated it; I absolutely despised it! There were kids coming in all the time who wanted to be cooks, truck drivers, rocket missile launchers, and jobs like that. I understood that we needed those kind of people and that joining the Army with that kind of option is perfectly permissible; but when I looked at them I'd often think, *This guy's a draft dodger, combat dodging, and I'm ...* That just didn't work with me. After a while I said, *Get me out of here, please!*"

"My prayer was answered with a telephone call from my headquarters at the L.A. Recruiting Command, saying, *You're going to be commissioned, you're going to go to the basic course, and then you're going to go to Fort Huachuca, Arizona.* So, I did that. When I got to Fort Huachuca, I managed the rifle range. I knew I would be going back to Vietnam, and I knew that running a rifle range was not good preparation. So, I called my infantry branch assignments officer thinking he would say, *You can have Vietnam or Korea.* Instead he said, *We've got a leadership problem in Europe. Would you like to go to Europe?* So, I went to Europe. The day I turned first lieutenant, I assumed command of a mechanized infantry company in Germany. Subsequently, I assumed command of the battalion headquarters for a while."

Lt. Col. Hansen soon found himself coming full circle: "Before long, I found myself back in Vietnam at Camp Alpha, on the grounds of Tan Son Nhut Airport, just outside Saigon. (Figure 28) I had no input on where I was going or what I would be doing. In short order, I was at Sa Huynh, in command of a rifle company. My first fire fight as a company commander was over a bridge."

"To defend the little bridge, I had 10-15 guys, about half a platoon, and one machine gun. We had concertina wire around the outsides of the bridge and more concertina wire that we could pull across the road when we closed it. One of the things that always upset me was the quality of the placements we made; we eventually wound up with something. But with no plan, and that's what happened here, it was too tough to dig in the sides of the road. So, most of the fighting positions were made out of sandbags piled up on the surface. There was one little block house (bunker); it wasn't very high, but it definitely was our bunker. It stood out, and you could tell right away where the boss was going to be!"

"About two o'clock in the morning, the bridge came under machine gun fire. That fire was designed to distract attention and make people get down. The next thing that happened was the Viet Cong (VC, indigenous guerrilla warriors) stood up and fired a rocket-propelled grenade (RPG) into the block house. The RPG was originally a German design that the Russians adapted. It was nasty—really, really nasty. The RPG hit and penetrated the bunker, setting off a flash-fire inside which burned away all of the sandbags. Inside the bunker, it was just dirt. The sandbags were gone; the fire was that violent. The platoon sergeant was in there, and he was very, very badly injured. There were two other soldiers on the bridge who received peripheral shrapnel but weren't incapacitated. About that time, the sappers who were working on the wire across the road came in; the guys (U.S.) on the bridge shot three of them."

"When A Cavalry got there, they loaded up the platoon sergeant and took him back. As I arrived with a relief platoon, I heard the medevac chopper land. I can't express how good that (chopper sound) makes you feel. You hope not to ever hear it, but when you do and know it's for one of your guys, it's really exceptional!"

It was time for a plan, and Hansen had one: "When we got to the bridge, we interspersed the relief troops with the troops who were already there. I used an Indian trick that Hal Moore taught us at X-Ray. Moore had us all fire a magazine in the direction of the enemy and keep it low.

Guess what? We pre-empted (possibly) an assault. I ordered all of the men out there to fire one magazine into every dark spot and every low spot that they could not actually see into. After all of this commotion, three more guys (VC) popped up, and we got them. At day break, we pulled the bodies up, and we laid them out on the road. The brigade commander flew in, landing on the highway. He got out, walked over, took a look at the bodies, shook my hand, and got back in his helicopter without saying anything."

"I sent word to the village chief that we would not interfere if the families wanted to come and collect the bodies. During the day, women—not men—came out, collected the bodies and took them back. That was the *little fire (or bridge) fight*—my first true engagement as a company commander."

STUDENT RESPONSE

The trip journal of Blane Bias, Lt. Col. Hansen's student host, is revealing. In it he expresses some of the feelings or emotions felt by all in the group. It would be hard to travel around in the Ia Drang Valley or the Bong Son Plain without sensing the difficulty of fighting under such conditions.

Upon reflection Blane said, "It was very emotional for Mr. Hansen to be back in this area. We were able to visit some of the fire bases where he served. He did not recognize things as they had looked in the War. The terrain was very uneven. As I was standing there attempting to imagine what it was like to navigate and fight in this area, I became more grateful for what these soldiers had done."

❝As I was standing there attempting to imagine what it was like to navigate and fight in this area, I became more grateful for what these soldiers had done. ❞

Many conversations between Lt. Col. Hansen and Blane went far beyond discussions of Hansen's job as a forward observer (FO) in a mortar company in combat. Blane recalls, "Mr. Hansen told me that the most difficult thing he struggled with, while in the military, was feeling *worthy* to lead his men. That admission resonated with me because I have wondered if I am and will be an effective leader in various areas of my life. After spending many hours with Mr. Hansen, I have realized that being a good leader takes time and that you must listen to those around you who know more than you do. He told me that in a platoon there is a platoon sergeant who must teach the officer everything that he needs to know so that he can effectively lead his platoon. At some point, the platoon sergeant steps back and allows the lieutenant to lead, but he remains ever present for advice and guidance. Mr. Hansen carried this principle into civilian life as well—if you need help, seek out those around you, whose opinions you value and respect."[5]

> **"** After spending many hours with Mr. Hansen, I have realized that being a good leader takes time and that you must listen to those around you who know more than you do. **"**

"Mr. Hansen left the Army when he was thirty years old and took a temporary job with the Air Force as a personnel management intern. This ended up being a long-term job for 26 years, and he was a specialist/officer for the Air Force. During this time with the Air Force, he met his wife Belinda, and they were married when he was 42 years old."

Blane concluded, "Lt. Col. Steve Hansen is an incredible man who served his country with distinction. I have learned much from him, and I am very grateful for this opportunity to learn from all the veterans. Most of all, I will never forget the sacrifice of the soldiers who fought in Vietnam and will always honor them."[6]

TOPIC SUMMARY

The Battle of Bong Son was fought in Binh Dinh province, one of twelve provinces in Combat Tactical Zone II. (Figure 28) This province included the mountain range in the west and sandy soil on the

Figure 28: II-Corps map.

plain adjacent to the South China Sea. Lt. Col. Hansen distinctly remembers the sandy terrain, "walking in sand, sleeping in sand, eating sand, trying to dig in the sand, and hating sand!" Another difference between LZ X-Ray and Bong Son was the availability of helicopters at Bong Son, which negated the need for reserve forces. Also, one unique part of preparing for battle with access to helicopters was dropping leaflets to appeal to the enemy. This type of warfare, called *Chieu Hoi*, was often effective, though General Westmoreland was not a fan of such activity.

Nevertheless, without this tactic, the battle could have been much worse.

Hansen did not participate in the actual Bong Son combat, as he had been reassigned to Headquarters Company. However, he was close enough to hear the fighting just outside or over the radio. Fighting at Bong Son was exhausting and brutal. There were 140 Americans reported killed-in-action (KIA) compared to an estimate of over 700 North Vietnamese KIA. Hansen recalled, "For a time we were located at the airstrip, and I saw the casualties come in. For me it was kind of surreal. I was there, but I was somewhat detached."

"We operated on the Bong Son Plain twice. No matter what the higher-ups called these operatives, we called them *Bong Son One* and *Bong Son Two*. Most agree that the actual combat was worse than anything at X-Ray, even though the tactical situation was not."

Lt. Col. Hansen brought some vivid memories of the battles with him. He recalled the following:

Riding by truck all night from An Khe, down Highway 19 to Qui Nhon and then up Highway 1 to Bong Son, immediately boarding Hueys and making a combat assault. My understanding is we did this because Bong Son was too far from An Khe to stage the assault from there. But the Hueys could fly empty from An Khe and arrive with enough fuel to stage the assault. In so doing, we achieved tactical surprise. It was a well-conceived and brilliantly executed maneuver.

Watching a Charlie model Huey gunship coming in with fuel streaming out of it. The left side opened up like a shark bite and the gunner dead and hanging by a strap. Apparently one or more of the rockets in the missing pod had detonated on launch or been hit by ground fire.

Going to the S1 (administrative) tent to pick up replacements. Most were 82nd Airborne veterans of the Dominican Republic. On the way back, we passed by Charlie Med, and there were more dead GIs wrapped in ponchos there than the 82nd had lost during their entire mission in the Dominican Republic.

Learning that Sergeant First Class [Glenn A.] Kennedy, a C Company hero in the Ia Drang, had been killed by friendly fire from a 106 in our own anti-tank platoon.

Hearing an explosion nearby and finding out one of our 82nd Airborne replacements had snagged a grenade when he was setting his 81mm mortar bipod down. It blew his arm off, and he died almost immediately in front of me.

Seeing a senior NCO (not a D Company man) throw his boots down a well and report them stolen while he slept.

Seeing Vietnamese Prime Minister Nguyen Cao Ky and his wife in matching black flight suits walking among the ordinary soldiers and thanking them for their service.

Showing no interest in seeing Nancy Sinatra put on a USO show.[7]

When Hansen returned to Vietnam for a second tour, he saw that a lot had changed and not much for the better: "I had two very strong observations. One was that I didn't sense any zeal anywhere. That *on the edge* wasn't there; you didn't see it anywhere. And the second was we really had two armies in Vietnam. On one hand, we had the army that was on the compounds, living behind wire, and they had flush toilets and fresh milk, fresh eggs—all the best. Some had air conditioning; it was really nice. On the other hand, there was a very different scene *outside* the wire. There you were basically a statistic on a chalkboard. You had nothing. We had nothing when I was there the first tour; but this time it was like the guys actually fighting the War were somehow a distant lower class—a discrepancy I sensed and that bothered me a little bit."

"I quickly came to understand that the way we were fighting the War was pretty stupid, tactically anyway. We rarely found the enemy unless the enemy wanted us to find him. When I left at the end of my first tour, we had done a pretty good job. Things were going our way. And when I went back for the second tour, we'd go up on hills that GIs had been on ten or fifteen times or more, muck out the fox holes and clean them up and spend a night or two there and move on. Even though for the time there was considerable dissent, the soldiers did everything we asked them to do. The soldiers were great, but we had problems. We had leadership problems. We went through all the leaders in the Army, the really good leaders, in about two years. And then after that, we were making it up, with junior officers with limited experience; they were reaching down into the belly of the beast and sending people, promoting people who shouldn't have been promoted and sending them out to do very responsible jobs for which they were incompetent. The fact that we were able to make it work is amazing to me, because we weren't really functioning the way a military should function. And we got into this business of minimizing casualties. As soon as we tried to minimize casualties and talk about tactics that would minimize casualties, the enemy would turn right on us and eat us up. It didn't do any good."

"We did return to the Ia Drang. In fact, we air assaulted back into X-Ray. It was quiet. The mission was to search for and retrieve the remains of some that were missing in action (MIA). We found them. The battlefield had been cleaned up pretty good by both sides. We found a scattering of stuff, and I noticed the remains of one NVA soldier near the anthill that sheltered the command post during the battle."

Lt.Col. Hansen's military experiences were many, and he has been able to apply Army principles to his civilian life. Perhaps the most telling comment Hansen made to Blane Bias was, "Everthing that I am today is because of the Army."

CLASS TOPIC 3:
IRON TRIANGLE (III-CORPS)

*The wounded could be heard moaning and
groaning all night; there was
very little we could do ...*

INSTRUCTOR: SP4 PAUL FRAMPTON, USA[1]

Paul Frampton literally came "off the farm" into the Vietnam War, to which he was drafted. Like so many young Americans at the time, he answered his country's call, serving with the Army and doing it with honor. Frampton's student host, Jonathan Minner, wrote a brief essay on Frampton's life. Much of the following was taken from this essay (edited), along with interviews and trip observations.

At an early age, Paul Frampton moved to Maryville, Missouri. He lived in the same house with his parents, brothers, and sisters until he was drafted in February of 1964. Paul attended basic training at Fort Leonard Wood, Missouri. He was transferred to Fort Riley, Kansas, where he spent 18 months training as a driver and RTO (radio telephone operator) for the company commander of B Company, 1st Battalion, 28th Infantry, the *Black Lions*. The 28th Infantry got its name in 1917 at the battle of Cantigny (Figure 29) in WWI.

In August of 1965, the soldiers in Frampton's battalion loaded their vehicles

Figure 29: Entrance to Battalion HQ. Photo courtesy of Paul Frampton, PETP 2014.

onto a train at Fort Riley and headed for Long Beach, California. At Long Beach, the train was unloaded and much was reloaded onto ships headed for Vietnam. Some of the infantrymen went on the ships, while others stayed behind in California loading additional ships for two weeks, until eventually they left on commercial airplanes. They flew out of San Francisco, the last of August, with a destination of Saigon, Vietnam. In Saigon, Paul's company regrouped and joined up with the division commander. Paul's battalion headed for a small airstrip and special forces base in and around Phuoc Vinh. Once there, the battalion cleared the vegetation and set up a base camp of suitable size. With the surrounding areas secure, a battery of eight-inch artillery guns and a battery of 175mm artillery guns moved into place, providing sufficient support for troops in the field. As an RTO,

Figure 30: Iron Triangle and surrounding area. Map adapted from public domain.

Frampton was in charge of all of the outgoing and incoming communications from the battalion commander, as well as any support that the company needed, such as air strikes and evacuations. The majority of Frampton's time was spent running security for convoys and night ambush patrols in the *Iron Triangle* and *Zone D*. (Figure 30)

After spending nearly five months in the Phuoc Vinh area, Frampton was sent to the 90th replacement center in Saigon to await his transfer back to the U.S. On January 26, 1966, Paul flew to Oakland, California, and spent the following two days debriefing and processing out. Once finished, he and four brothers-in-arms hired a taxi to take them to the San Francisco airport where they flew to Kansas City. Paul's decorations include the Vietnam Service Medal, Expert Rifle, Good Conduct, and Combat Infantry Badge.

Paul wasn't home from war for more than a week before he started working for A & P (The Great Atlantic and Pacific Tea Company) as a produce manager. He worked his way up the ladder, and in 1972 he took the reigns as general manager for one of A & P's grocery stores in Maryville, Missouri. In 1972, Paul met Lucille, through a mutual friend. Lucille lived in the neighboring town of Clyde, Missouri. They were married in 1973 and moved to St. Joseph, where they had their son, Steve. Paul and his family moved to Chillicothe in 1978, where he managed another A & P grocery store. He continued to work for A & P until 1982, when they sold out of the Kansas City area.

From 1982 to 2004, Paul's successful experiences kept him managing grocery stores in the Kansas City area, in a civilian career of nearly forty years. He and his wife, Lucille, moved to Branson, Missouri, in 2011, and have since moved to Platte City, Missouri.

Paul has twin brothers, Ron and Don, who also served in Vietnam. Ron was an MP (military police) for the U.S. Army, and Don was an airman in the U.S. Air Force, from which he retired. Don passed away from cancer in 2013.

After his retirement in 2004, Paul joined the VFW (Veterans of Foreign Wars) and became the post commander in Parkville, Missouri. He later became the veteran service information officer for the state, where he oversaw the services being provided to veterans. In 2009, he became the district commander for a year and was offered the position of state inspector in 2010, which he still holds. Paul is in charge of the annual inspection of over 200 posts and 13 districts.

Figure 31: Veteran Paul Frampton and student host Jonathan Minner. Photo by John Luck.

 ## STUDENT HOST: JONATHAN MINNER

Jonathan Minner's motivation to apply for the College's Patriotic Education trip to Vietnam was very personal: "My number one reason for wanting to go is to let those who served in Vietnam know that I have not forgotten about them and what they did." Jonathan wrote, "This patriotic trip will help me better understand the trials my uncle went through." He further stated, "I want the Vietnam veterans to know they are my heroes." When Jonathan met Paul (Figure 31) and all the Vietnam veterans on the trip, he knew he was in the midst of heroes.

Jonathan's uncle, Maurice, served for six years in the U.S. Navy. According to Jonathan, his uncle came back to an ungrateful country, only to be spat on and called a baby killer. Uncle Maurice died of cancer four years before Jonathan was born, but not before telling his family of his ordeal in Vietnam. Maurice had shown up for deployment by way of the *U.S.S. Independence*. He said his goodbyes and boarded the ship with almost five thousand sailors, soldiers, and airmen. During its one hundred days in the South China Sea, the *Independence* launched thousands of flights and played an important role in operations against the military and logistical supply facilities in North Vietnam. He could not avoid tragedies—planes going down right before his eyes, friends dying from deck explosions. No wonder Jonathan's uncle was anxious to go home. In a debriefing before disembarkation, the commanders warned the crew what to expect. Jonathan recalls: "Maurice couldn't believe his own ears. All he had done was serve his country; all he had done was his duty."

Jonathan came from a very patriotic family; his father and everyone in his family (including his mother) were in the military. He is among a large family with a farming background, the seventh of eight children born to Bruce and Michelle Minner. Jonathan says, "I have spent most of my life in Southwest Missouri. My seven siblings and I were all home-schooled from grade school through high school, and I am the sixth to go on to higher education. I was blessed enough to study classical cello and vocals for most of my life. My hometown of Walnut Grove has a fire department where I have volunteered since I was 16. Sports were never my strong suit; nevertheless, I played baseball and football for over six years. I am a chemistry/pre-med major with aspirations to join the military and serve my country, eventually settling down and starting a family. Hobbies aren't something I have had a lot of time for while in college, but I have always enjoyed the outdoors: fishing, hiking, snowboarding, water skiing, etc." While attending College of the Ozarks, Jonathan's workstations included landscaping, The Keeter Center guest services, warehouse, chemistry, laundry, custodial, and recycling.

IRON TRIANGLE BACKGROUND

Located near the heart of the Corps Tactical Zone III (III-Corps) was a triangular-shaped area known as the Iron Triangle. (Figure 30) Its shape forms from the Saigon River on the west and the Tinh River on the east. The apex or southern tip is just a few miles north of Phu Cong, the capital of Binh Duong Province. The eastern border is adjacent to Highway 13, a major north-south road.

Composed of about 125 square miles, the Iron Triangle was always regarded as a stronghold, first for the Viet Minh communists and subsequently for the Viet Cong (VC). Like many of the other ten provinces of III-Corps, the terrain was covered with jungle (a two-or three-canopy layer). Also, the region was full of caves and tunnels which had been fortified over a number of years. As Frampton remembered, "It was mostly a region of thick forests, full of rubber plantations." Apparently, the rubber plantations provided a decent field of view, but off the plantations there were just dense forests.

Just a few miles southwest of the Iron Triangle is the village of Cu Chi (Figure 30), an area of caves and tunnels which have been turned into tourist spots. Demonstrations of booby traps (Figure 32) are on display, and there are opportunities to go down into some of the tunnels. Some veterans (and most students) took a turn in the tunnels. Additionally, there was a firing range, and the crack of AK-47s was commonly heard and disconcerting to some. A few huts, benches were provided to watch old black and white films, which students immediately figured out to be communist propaganda.

Figure 32: Booby traps (Viet Cong). Photo by John Luck.

The Iron Triangle provided an ideal *jumping off* point for VC attacks on Saigon. These attacks were similar to a "hit and run," with the VC quickly retreating to the tunnels. Some didn't make it, and those that did often found themselves chased by GIs who were called *tunnel rats*— infantrymen armed only with a pistol and a flashlight. Basically, a VC would crawl out at night, slip into town, wreak havoc, run back to the hole, and try to get down in the tunnels in time. It was almost like a game of "Whac-A-Mole" but with potentially lethal consequences.

The Iron Triangle was so troublesome that American and ARVN forces consistently tried to root out the enemy. The 1st and 2nd Battalions of the 28th Infantry Regiment *(Black Lions)* were usually on the move conducting sweeps and night ambush patrols. The 1st Infantry Division, of which Frampton was a part, conducted several major operations while he was there. These operations occurred in various parts of III-Corps and took a high toll on the enemy. Operations Hump, Bushmaster I and II recorded almost one thousand enemies killed-in-action (KIA). Clearly, during the early part of the War, the enemy endured terrible losses. While major operations were going on, smaller units, such as the *Black Lions,* fought in the shadows with success and valor.

 ## INSTRUCTOR REFLECTIONS

When Paul Frampton touched down on Vietnam soil, the buildup of American troops was barely underway. "When I went over, there were fifty thousand troops in the whole country," he recalled. "And we were stationed the farthest north of any Army troops. There were Marines north of us, but no Army personnel north of us." Like most of the earliest deployed American troops, they simply did what they were told and went where they were told to go. "It wasn't our place to question what we were doing over there," Paul said. Such a positive attitude waned as the War continued, but in those early years of war, it was common.

Going to Vietnam didn't seem to bother the troops. Paul remembers, "We'd been training and training and training! It had gotten so monotonous that just about everybody was ready to go." The trip still stands out in Paul Frampton's memory. "First, we loaded all the equipment on trains at Fort Riley, Kansas. Every 10 or 12 cars was a caboose that included three guys as guards. We rode the train all the way to San Francisco and then down to Long Beach. We unloaded all of our equipment onto ships at Long Beach. After we loaded the ships, we left six guys with each ship, and the rest of us flew over to Vietnam. So, I flew over on a 707, stopping in Hawaii and then straight to Saigon."

"Scary!" That's how Paul described the very first night he spent in Vietnam. "We went up north to Di An (Figure 30), where the division headquarters were located along with the division advance party, and we spent the night out in tents. Actually, the first night I spent on guard duty. I was an interior perimeter guard. We stood guard all night long with our M14s."

The next day Paul received another jolt. "Somebody found out I had a driver's license and wanted me to take some lieutenants into Saigon. I'd never been on the streets of Saigon, so I asked about security and was told I'd have to come back by myself! I'd already heard about the VCs wearing black pajamas, but everybody over there wore black pajamas. Believe me, it was more than a little scary coming back. I went to the middle of Saigon and came straight back."

The next morning the soldiers awoke to a typical GI breakfast. According to Paul, it was the same thing they had during most of their time in-country, "C-rations that were canned back in the 1940s!" Sleeping in tents with them were security guards wearing M14's, but Paul also explicitly remembers other nearby security. "A battery of eight-inch artillery guns and a battery of 175mm artillery guns were located about a city block away. Their power was so great that the sides of the tents would suck in every time they were fired. It's hard to believe, but they're the same guns as you find on battleships. The 175mm had a 20- or 25-feet long barrel. The eight-inch didn't have that long of a barrel, but it shot a bigger round."

Frampton had many duties, and one was *popping* smoke. "When an airstrike, a request for supply, or a dust-off was called in, the pilot would radio for our location. I would throw a colored smoke grenade, and the pilot would radio me telling me what color he saw. If it was the correct color, they would either come in or start their attack. We had an artillery FO (forward observer) with us who would call in the artillery strikes."

Much of Frampton's time was spent running security for convoys and on night ambush patrols in the Iron Triangle or in War Zone D. (Figure 30, page 76) He explained how that usually happened. "We'd have a trail already in mind or a location where we wanted to go (i.e., 600 meters from Base Camp). We had a point man who kept track of how far we walked. He plotted this and then reported back by radio, *We're in location.* If for some reason or another, backup fire was needed, we would call artillery or mortars and give them the proper coordinates. They would fire one round, and based on where it hit, we would say, *Fire for effect,* and fire would ensue in a circle, an iron circle if you will.

Sometimes this would go on all night long."

Frampton learned a lot about enemy tactics: "Sometimes a VC would be captured in a village, and we had an interpreter with us that could question him. The VC seemed to always have great intelligence; they'd know we were coming before we got there. Then they'd just disappear (in a spider hole or tunnel, most likely). But sometimes we would find a cache of food, ammunition, etc. We rarely saw them. If they fired at us, we would shoot them. Otherwise we'd just capture them. The first one I saw captured was in the middle of a rubber plantation. We had a platoon down at the Song Be River Bridge, guarding the bridge. The commander and I went down there, and the platoon had caught a VC. He was dressed in one of our uniforms! I have a picture of him tied up and laying down in the back of a three-quarter ton truck." (Figure 33)

One of the most troubling fights that Frampton and his squad got into occurred around Thanksgiving 1965. "We never did have much trouble on ambush patrol. It was the sweeps (lasting two or three days) where we had the most problems, in this case near Thanksgiving. We lost something like 35 KIA or wounded in action (WIA). The VC hit us during the night, and if you were standing up you got it [KIA]. Mortar hit us and even some hand grenades; they were very close. We didn't have time to set up a perimeter. As soon as all the stuff started coming in on us, we started returning fire all around, because we couldn't tell how close they were. We had to keep them off of us and make sure they didn't get inside the perimeter."

Figure 33: White circle is of a captured VC wearing an American military uniform. Photo courtesy of Paul Frampton, PETP 2014.

"I called the battalion commander to tell him how many we had lost and what we needed. Each squad had a squad leader, and with the help of a platoon leader, they compiled how many were missing or how many were wounded or dead."

Frampton recalls what they faced: "The wounded could be heard moaning and groaning all night; there was very little we could do for them until daylight, when we could call in the medevac. A lot of them were ripped to shreds. If they were standing up, they didn't survive. When a grenade or mortar round went off, it didn't go straight up. It goes up in a V-shape, it expands out as it rises. You could be laying down fairly close to where it hit, and you might get a concussion, but you wouldn't get any shrapnel. If you were standing up, you wouldn't be so lucky. Some of our troops had been getting ready to bed down. I'd already laid down, along with the other two RTOs, and we had all taken off our socks. They were wet from the day's marching, so we had hung our socks in a tree just above me, not far off the ground. When I went to get them the next morning, they were shredded. The hit was that close!"

❝ The medic did what he could for them, but he couldn't deal with a lot of it. Some of the situations were beyond his control. Some of the guys who were standing up had shrapnel from their toes to their head. Some were killed immediately. ❞

It's ironic that most of these soldiers were killed inside the perimeter. As Frampton recalls, "The medic did what he could for them, but he couldn't deal with a lot of it. Some of the situations were beyond his control. Some of the guys who were standing up had shrapnel from their toes to their head. Some were killed immediately. As soon as the battalion commander heard we were hit, he was on the radio wanting body counts, etc. Two minutes after something happens it's hard to know much. The company commander got pretty upset when I told him, *As soon as we can get a count, we'll let you know.* It just takes time; you couldn't do it in five minutes. Our perimeter was often small because we were just marching or sweeping through the jungle, and then at night we'd congregate with our guards around us in a circle."

"During the battle the night before Thanksgiving, we had three units—A Company, B Company, and Headquarters Company. We got hit a time or two during the day as we kept trying to squeeze the VC to the middle. They kept getting away because they knew where the tunnels were. They just dropped out of sight."

" Watching your buddies get killed or injured affected us all. "

Some GIs handled dead Americans better than others. "It's pretty gruesome," Frampton said. "Something you don't want to go through. Watching your buddies get killed or injured affected us all. Just imagine if 20 or 30 people that you work with everyday were walking down the street, and there was an explosion. Half of them got killed and half got wounded, just imagine how you would feel. Many soldiers wondered, *Why him and not me?*"

Searching villages was another risky assignment for Paul Frampton and his company. "During the daytime, villagers were glad to see us, and at night they'd turn on us. We didn't allow many of them to come inside the perimeter. Later, when we allowed the villagers in, they would sometimes be observed pacing from one building or one tent to the other, plotting where they were going to send their mortars or artillery in on us at night."

Needless to say, Frampton and his buddies in B Company, 28th Infantry Regiment were glad to get out and come home. But they couldn't erase the experience from their minds. "I followed the War," he said, "because I still had friends over there. We went over as a unit; we didn't go as individual replacements. Several in my unit got out about the same time I did. Also, I have kept in touch with my commander, a quartermaster, who now lives in Minnesota. Additionally, there is another Black Lion who lives in St. Louis, an NCO (non-commissioned officer) down in Texas, and a second lieutenant who lives out in Phoenix."

Even early in the War there was a stigma attached to those who had served. "I lived in a small town. I never broadcasted the fact I had been in the service. I wouldn't wear green shirts for years. When I got married, my wife had a green car. One of the first things I did was trade it off. I didn't want to be associated with the military. I can remember after

I had worked for A & P for a couple of years, the district manager had heard I'd been in Vietnam. One day he called me to the back of the store and asked, *Are you really a Vietnam veteran?* It was a big shock to him. He just couldn't believe that I'd been in Vietnam, and I just shrugged it off and went on. It was too much to deal with, too much pressure. For years and years, the only people I associated with were guys that came back from service. When we were coming back, they were still asking us to wear our uniforms. Soon thereafter, they told us *not* to wear our uniforms. We veterans are making sure that never happens again." But uniforms weren't the only source of contention. Demonstrations against the War were common in some parts of the country. And dishonorable acts by public figures—such as Jane Fonda—engendered bitterness in those that had served. "She was a traitor; she should have been brought up on charges," said Frampton. "She hasn't changed. You won't find a veteran who will give her the time of day, *Hanoi Jane.*"

STUDENT RESPONSE

"I had met Paul a month previous to our trip. Since having lunch with him that day, I had been in constant contact with him. He seemed as excited about this trip as I was, but there were definitely some underlying feelings that he had not yet voiced."

Figure 34: Jonathan experiencing a spider hole. Photo by John Luck.

Jonathan's perception was correct in wondering if Paul really wanted to go back to Vietnam. After thinking about it, Paul said, "Had it not been for John Clark and Bill Bailey (both former six-year POWs), I probably wouldn't have gone. But I figured, knowing they had been POWs, if they could handle it, I could too. And, I had been told by a friend that he'd been back and felt safer walking down the streets of Saigon than walking down the streets of Kansas City."

Jonathan and Paul got along well together. "Paul seemed well-adjusted to being in Vietnam, although it had taken him a day or two. He was his normal, chipper self. Though it was his first time back in almost fifty

It was the ARVN, and not Americans, that held and tortured prisoners at this base…the NVA treated the Americans worse than the ARVN treated the NVA.

years, he was quite open about talking of his time there. We started out in the Mekong Delta by shopping at the Mekong Floating Market. We saw many fruits and vegetables being sold and traded. Paul said he didn't do a lot of shopping during his deployment; however, he did say that right before his tour ended, he made a trip to Saigon's open-air market and bought silk for his mother and sister."

Jonathan (Figure 34) was especially excited about visiting the Cu Chi tunnels, which are in III-Corps and close to where Paul spent most of his time. "While we were there, Paul mentioned the great respect he had for the corpsmen and how all the infantrymen would do anything to keep them alive. He also mentioned the *tunnel rats* who would crawl down into the tunnels and plant explosives to cause cave-ins."

"After seeing the tunnels (Figure 35), we toured a museum where Paul came across the artillery, mortars, planes, and helicopters similar to the ones he used to contact by radio. We toured the ARVN (Army of the Republic of Vietnam, South) prison, where they held and tortured NVA (North Vietnamese Army) soldiers. The prison was filled with pictures of how poorly the Americans treated the prisoners.

Figure 35 : Molly Matney at the entrance of a tunnel. Photo by John Luck.

Paul corrected them by saying, *It was the ARVN, and not Americans, that held and tortured prisoners at this base.* He also added, *the NVA treated the Americans worse than the ARVN treated the NVA.* There were a lot of Agent Orange exhibits outlining the bad effects it had on the locals, but there was no reference to the effect it had on Americans."

Paul and Jonathan saw much of Vietnam together. Khe Sanh made quite an impression on Jonathan, though this was far north of where Paul experienced his combat. There they met several Swedes. When asked why they had come, the Swedes responded, "Because the Americans were here fighting for the freedom of the Vietnamese."

Jonathan Minner and Paul Frampton left America together and came back together. Jonathan recalled in his journal, "We finally landed at the Kansas City Airport to find a welcome party of about fifty people and a full brass band waiting! It was amazing to see the support that showed up at twelve o'clock at night to give these veterans the *welcome home* they deserved."

Fifty years late, yet meaningful.

TOPIC SUMMARY

The III-Corps Tactical Zone was the site of numerous battles and combat operations. The fighting was virtually continuous as the zone was the conduit for men, supplies, and armaments flowing down from the Ho Chi Minh Trail. This was especially true for the area often avoided by most ARVN units—the notorious *Iron Triangle*. As it turned out, this area in which Paul spent a lot of his time was of continuous concern

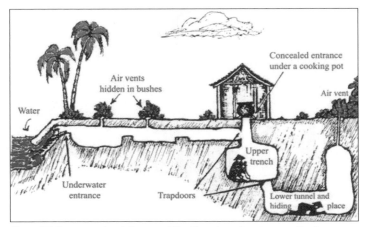

Figure 36: Cross-sectional diagram of Viet Cong tunnel system used by the communist insurgents during the Vietnam War. Diagram from public domain.

to General Westmoreland, for a variety of reasons. In his book, *A Soldier Reports* Westmoreland wrote, "The regular VC units had to have safe base areas or *sanctuaries*. There they could rest, conduct training and indoctrination, and prepare for operations. The bases were usually located within a reasonable distance of densely populated areas and often had elaborate underground facilities, such as hospitals, command posts, kitchens, and printing plants, all connected by vast tunnel systems. (Figure 36) No one has ever demonstrated more ability to hide his installations than did the Viet Cong; they were *human moles*. "Some base areas dated from the days of the Viet Minh and were vast and well-fortified. For example, War Zone C was located northwest of Saigon in the Tay Ninh Province, where the headquarters of the Central Office of South Vietnam (COSVN) was reportedly located. War Zone D was situated in a vast wooded area north of Saigon and the *Iron Triangle* had a base formed by two rivers a few miles northwest of Saigon, convenient for operations against the capital."[2]

It is easy to see why the zones and river areas around Saigon were so important. Even after heavy bombing from B-52s later in the War, the NVA and VC managed to reinfest the region. They always seemed to reappear, often at the worst possible time.

After Frampton served his tour of duty, he returned to the United States. He closely followed the III-Corps region where he had served because many of his friends were still in combat. The War continued to escalate in all four zones. Some of the War's major operations took place in III-Corps (i.e. *Operations Junction City, Cedar Falls, Attleboro,* and many others).[3] Later in the War, some of the battles received wide attention. Frampton's buddies in the 1st Division, 1st and 2nd Battalion, 28th Infantry Regiment, *Black Lions,* continued to serve with honor. One of these, Second Lieutenant Robert J. Hibbs, received the Congressional Medal of Honor.[4]

Likewise, the Battle of Ong Thanh was fought in this region and was the subject of two books: *The Beast Was Out There* by Brigadier General James E. Shelton, USA (Ret.) and *They Marched Into Sunlight* by David Maranis. Many Black Lions died in this battle, later called an ambush; they were, "missing and presumed dead. Half regular army, half draftees, white, black, and brown—all dead."[5]

Additionally, many other units made up the American force fighting these battles. Few have been properly recognized and some weren't acknowledged for decades, such as the famed Blackhorse Regiment (Alpha Troop, 1st Squadron, 11th Armored Cavalry) that rescued the Charlie Company of the 2nd Battalion, 8th Cavalry in the "Anonymous Battle" in the Tay Ninh Province. Almost 50 years later, soldiers (Figure 37) of the Blackhorse Regiment were presented a Presidential Unit Citation (PUC).

Figure 37: Members of the Blackhorse Regiment (Troop A, First Squadron, 11th Armored Cavalry Regiment) being recognized with the Presidential Unit Citation, 50 years later. Adapted from public domain.

CLASS TOPIC 4:
CON THIEN (I-CORPS)

We will carry our wounded, and we'll carry our dead, but we don't intend to be airlifted...

🍎 INSTRUCTOR: COL BILLY R. (BILL) DUNCAN, USMC (RET.)[1]

For 31 years, Bill Duncan served America. He said he had a "warrior's heart." He definitely had a heart for a small-town Texas teenager, Arlene. At 17, Bill (and Arlene) graduated from high school, and he joined the United States Marine Corps. Bill and Arlene were thereafter married (after she finally agreed), and their marriage has been exemplary, now 65 plus years and going strong!

Duncan's warrior lifestyle began in 1948 when he was assigned to Korea. He received a special battlefield commission in March 1953, when the 5th Marines were assigned tactical control of a corridor in the western Korean front. Following this, in 1963-64, Bill was assigned to the United Kingdom Royal Marines (RM) and attended RM commando training and served in Central Africa, North Borneo, Malaysia, and the Kota Tinga jungle area west of Singapore. Bill Duncan was the second American to be awarded the Royal Marine Commando Medal for Distinguished Service with the RM and Gurka Battle Forces in Borneo.

Lieutenant Colonel Duncan (hereafter referred to as Colonel Duncan) began his tour of Vietnam in 1967. His initial assignment was Assistant G-2 (assistant chief of staff, intelligence). He spent time in Da Nang, Con Thien, and Khe Sanh, as well as other locations. He was well-respected, even became known as *mayor* of Con Thien and Khe Sanh! As a commander, he became very close to all his men, establishing a brotherhood bond.

Shortly after the War began, Colonel Duncan was put in some very stressful and heartbreaking situations. For example, he was given the task of triaging the wounded, determining who would live and who would die. At the battle of Con Thien, there were many wounded Marines. One Marine left a lifelong impression on him. This very seriously wounded Marine stopped him and asked, "Am I going to make it?" Colonel Duncan had to tell the young Marine that he would not be going home. The Marine asked Duncan if he would have one last cigarette with him. Colonel Duncan found a cigarette and sat there with the young Marine until he took his last breath. Duncan had many such experiences, and each made him a better leader and commander. He loved his men and did everything he could to save them. Colonel Duncan left Vietnam in 1968 and returned home to his wife, Arlene, and two daughters.

Throughout his 31 years of military service, Colonel Duncan served in more than 80 countries and received many decorations, including the Silver Star, two Legion of Merits with Combat V., two Purple Hearts, a Royal Marine Commando Medal, and 22 area and combat decorations from his service in Korea, Borneo, Federation of Malaysia, Africa, and Vietnam. He retired from the Marines in 1979 as a colonel of infantry and special reconnaissance operations. Since the War, Colonel Duncan worked as a weapons specialist and a commercial contractor. After retiring, he founded the Commonwealth of Independent States (CIS) Church Development Foundation and, along with his family, spent 18 years in the former Soviet Union working in Christian ministry. CIS is a foundation focused on reaching the people of Russia with Jesus' love and compassion. It operates a variety of ministries such as prison ministry, children's camp ministries, educational institutions and women's ministry. He is also co-founder of Veterans Against Jihadism.

Throughout Colonel Bill Duncan's life, he has led and been respected by many people. He has been a faithful servant, continuing to share the Lord's name with the world. Colonel Duncan's passion for people is evident; you can see it in his gentle smile and peaceful presence. He served this country proudly as a United States Marine and is an ultimate American hero. *Semper fidelis* definitely describes this patriot.

Figure 38: Veteran Bill Duncan and student host Taylor Johnson.
Photo by John Luck.

 ## STUDENT HOST: TAYLOR JOHNSON

"I have never been outside the United States," wrote Taylor Johnson (Figure 38) when applying for the Patriotic Education Travel Program. Her reasons for going on the Vietnam trip were family driven. "My interest is fueled by my uncle who fought in Vietnam," she said. "Actually I had a couple of uncles who fought, but my uncle Colonel Robert W. Watkins is one of my heroes. He was a Marine Corps Colonel and served for 30 years. During those years, my uncle was President Ronald Reagan's command pilot for *Marine One*. In Vietnam, he flew rescue missions and would take the wounded to hospital ships off the coast. He was affected by Agent Orange but continued to fight."

Taylor grew up hearing about her uncle's war stories and career. He was a Marine who took pride in his service and country and said he would go back if he had to. During her uncle's career, he was the first to ever fly and land within the walls of the palace in Japan, with the President on board. He flew and worked with General Terrence R. Dake, alumnus of the College of the Ozarks and Chairman of the Board of Trustees. Taylor noted, "My uncle and aunt had a personal relationship with General Dake and his wife, and they spent a lot of time together throughout the years." Taylor is rightfully proud of all her uncle accomplished during his military career and feels honored to have known him. Colonel Watkins earned a Silver Star, Meritorious Service Medal, Air Medal, and Navy

Unit Commendation. He earned a Silver Star in Vietnam for a rescue mission under combat conditions. He was a very accomplished man, well-respected by all he came in contact with, and loved by all.

Taylor wrote, "Having the opportunity to travel overseas to Vietnam was such a blessing; seeing the ground where my uncle and other men fought was an honor. My uncle was never able to travel back to Vietnam after the War. I know he would have liked the opportunity to do so. I wish he were still alive and could have gone with me, but he passed away seven years ago from leukemia. He was buried in Arlington National Cemetery with full military honors. I know it would have meant a lot to his wife, children, and the rest of my family if he could have known that I had the chance to represent my family on such a trip. I have three other uncles (brothers of Colonel Watkins) who served in Vietnam, too. My family was lucky to have each of them return home alive. I recently spoke with my Uncle Bob's wife, and she told me that he would have been incredibly proud of me for taking such interest in the War and its history. She told me that he would be honored that the College is taking the time and opportunity to educate us about our past and the patriots who fought for us. I'm aware that this trip was a once-in-a-lifetime opportunity to travel with Vietnam veterans. It was a privilege and honor to participate and represent my uncle. Experiencing Vietnam firsthand is something I have wanted to do for a long time and this was the perfect opportunity."

CON THIEN BACKGROUND

Con Thien (Figure 39) is situated just two miles south of the Demilitarized Zone (DMZ) and 12 miles from the coast. It was the site of heavy combat, especially during late autumn before the Tet Offensive. In fact, the fighting had gone on virtually all year long, and Marine casualties were high. Con Thien was a dismal, depressing locale but served an important purpose. It overlooked one of the routes the NVA used to sneak across the DMZ and then down into I-Corps. Despite major shelling by the North Vietnamese Army (NVA), Con Thien had the benefit of Arc Light B-52s, artillery, and naval gunfire.

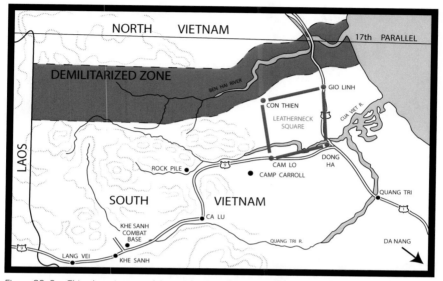

Figure 39: Con Thien location map. Adapted from public domain.

Located in the Quang Tri Province, Con Thien was in an area of high strategic importance. It was part (the northwest corner) of a "square" formed by Gio Linh (to the east), Dong Ha (south of Gio Linh) and Cam Lo (west of Dong Ha & south of Con Thien). This was Marine territory, which they dubbed "Leatherneck Square." (Figure 39) Additionally, the DMZ became known as the *Dead Marine Zone* because so many Marines were killed in action.

Con Thien was part of a first line of defense. (Figures 39, 40) It was to be part of the McNamara Line, an electronic observation line south of the DMZ that ran from Laos to the east coast.

Colonel Duncan spent time in Da Nang, Con Thien, Khe Sanh, and many other parts of Quang Tri Province. It is no surprise that he was asked to play a leadership role and often tasked with making life-and-death decisions.

Figure 40: Aerial photo of base at Con Thien. Photo courtesy of Bill Duncan, PETP 2014.

 INSTRUCTOR REFLECTIONS

It was obvious to the students and other veterans that Bill Duncan took his responsibilities seriously, and he expected those who served under him to do the same. This simply cannot be overstated. Students were asked to recite the Oath of Office as Colonel Duncan requested. "Put your hand up and say, *I (state your full name), do solemnly swear that I will support and defend the Constitution of the United States against all enemies, foreign and domestic; that I will bear true faith and allegiance to the same; and that I will obey the orders of the President of the United States and the orders of the officers appointed over me, according to the regulations of the Uniform Code of Military Justice, so help me God.* That's the oath I took; I've taken it twice, and I required all of the officers who served under me to take it every time they were promoted—same thing for the enlisted."

Having served in many combat situations, Colonel Duncan said: "There's no way I can stand here now, uninjured, having fought in over five different areas—starting off in Korea, going through Africa, through Borneo to Malaysia, then to Vietnam—without having asked for the Lord's help." He then proceeded to have another veteran read what he referred to as the "Commander's Prayer."

> The Lord is my light and my salvation; whom shall I fear? the Lord is the strength of my life; of whom shall I be afraid?
>
> When the wicked, even mine enemies and my foes, came upon me to eat up my flesh, they stumbled and fell.
>
> Though an host should encamp against me, my heart shall not fear: though war should rise against me, in this will I be confident.
>
> One thing have I desired of the Lord, that will I seek after; that I may dwell in the house of the Lord all the days of my life, to behold the beauty of the Lord, and to enquire in his temple.
>
> For in the time of trouble he shall hide me in his pavilion: in the secret of his tabernacle shall he hide me; he shall set me up upon a rock.
>
> And now shall mine head be lifted up above mine enemies round about me: therefore will I offer in his tabernacle sacrifices of joy; I will sing, yea, I will sing praises unto the Lord.
>
> Psalm 27:1-6, KJV

Duncan knew from his start in Vietnam that he was heading into a heavy combat area (I-Corps). He shared, "I didn't have any reservations. I knew it was what I was trained to do." His group flew straight into Da Nang, and then he was assigned as the assistant G-2 (an intelligence officer). "I was responsible for trying to track the path and trace all enemy movement in our TAOR (tactical area of responsibility), which included all of I-Corps." (Figure 41) Duncan's responsibilities began quickly, and he explained what happened next: "I knew two battalion commanders had been wounded. One of them was in the approach route getting ready to go into Hué and the other one was up at Con Thien. The one at Con Thien was just standing outside his bunker area, and there was a lot of heavy shelling taking place. He didn't have his flak vest on. He was hit hard with enemy projectiles and had to be evacuated. The general called me in and said, *We've got two battalions that need new commanders, and you have your option. I know you, and I've learned to know how you process things. You want to be in Hué, or you want to go to Con Thien?* I answered, *I think the real challenge right now is Con Thien.* The general agreed, saying, *I do too.*"

"At Con Thien, our threat was an enemy that used very heavy weapons, not just 105 artillery. We got hit with larger shells, must have been 152s. Some observers complained, *No, they don't have them in the country.* I responded, *I think otherwise, 105s can't do the damage we are getting.*"

"We had a triage set up outside a medical bunker and had one round that came straight in. It hit in the overhead of the medical facility, near the doctors. When I arrived to take over, I asked for an assessment from the company commanders, *Where are you on this? Give me your position.* We talked about holding Con Thien and how we had held another area on the way to Dong Ha, about a mile from us, where we had company reinforcements positioned. I gathered the troops to get an assessment of what they were doing, what kind of casualties they had, and to find out the major factors affecting morale. Of course, the big thing was, they were sitting ducks. I instructed them to start moving out and try to take over enemy mortar and artillery positions."

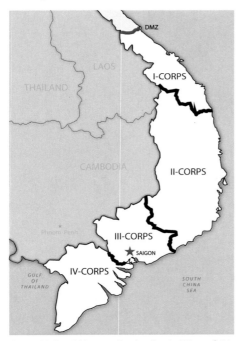

Figure 41: South Vietnam Combat Tactical Zones (I-IV Corps). Adapted from public domain.

The rules of engagement were often a hindrance to Marines. Duncan explained, "We could see the enemy moving and would direct fire their way. As they got over into Laos, I knew that the code of warfare said, *if engaged in an ongoing fight and the enemy receded into the territory of another country, as long as we were in constant fire, we could legally go after them.* Without constant fire, we couldn't chase them very far. I filled out daily reports, documenting we had a platoon, a company, or even a major battalion at the edge of and/or entering into Laos. These details would raise red flags." Duncan believed that in dire circumstances like these, changing the rules of engagement "would have saved lives."

On the other hand, at Con Thien, the Marines were not without sufficient support. "If we had contact with the enemy, a laser was sometimes used," Duncan remembered.

Figure 42: Duncan and his RTO on mission. Photo courtesy of Bill Duncan, PETP 2014.

He explained, "At Con Thien we knew what was happening. We knew when the enemy units were coming down the Ho Chi Minh trail. We had platoon-size patrols; we would drop off four or five people in an area and proceed. Their identity would pretty much be unknown, unless they were foolish and got visible during daylight hours."

Day or night, Duncan put the welfare of his men (Figure 42) first, even to the point of turning away a commanding general. "He (Westmoreland) wanted to come up from Saigon and visit. He wanted to come into our bunker, and I said, *No!* In short order, I told the radio operator on the command line, *I want no new helicopters in here. We only want to be evacuating wounded, and Westmoreland (I used his code name) is denied clearance.* This really irritated people; he was the guy in charge of everything!" My RTO (radio telephone operator) came running over to me while an artillery barrage was going on and said,

I'm kind of scared of what the general might do; they intend to land anyway. I took the phone and said, *This is Texas Pete 6. I want to speak directly to the officer for Westmoreland*, whose code number I used. I told Westmoreland's Marine assistant to relay the message, *They are denied landing; they can land at Dong Ha, if they wish. They can get into vehicles, and from Dong Ha they can drive about eight miles up to Con Thien.* The assistant's response was, *Well, he doesn't want to do that. He's trying to get his ticket punched, where a lot of fighting is going on. We are*

Figure 43: Northwest aerial view of Con Thien, handwritten annotation by Col. Duncan. Photo courtesy of Bill Duncan, PETP 2014.

receiving major artillery! I reiterated, *He's denied landing. We will not have him coming in here.* That put an end to that for me, but it didn't put an end to it for the Marine Corps!"

Bill Duncan had to deal with one crisis after another. A priority was trying to save lives so that injured Marines could be flown out. He explained, "First, we didn't have medical tents there, but we had a medical hospital (Figure 43) and three doctors. They were in a bunker, called a dye-marker bunker. The casualties were heavy, and the NVA were relentless. They were not like the Viet Cong (VC) down south. The NVA were hard-core soldiers—good uniforms and good helmets, in good physical condition, all with AK-47s—and they knew how to use artillery!"

"The kill-ratio was very high, and we buried many of the bodies. Down near IV-Corps, they (leadership) thought we should have a higher body count. At one point, over the radio, we were instructed to, *Dig up what you have and give us an exact count.* I interjected, *This is Texas Pete speaking; who am I talking to?* I found out it was the Graves Registration Service (now known as Mortuary Affairs), and I replied, *If you want to know the exact number, we'll give it to you. You gather a bunch of people and get on a helicopter and get up here; we'll tell you where to dig.* We'd buried enemy bodies in bomb craters, because that was the easiest way to get rid of the animal infestations. We were overrun with rats and there were small dogs running wild, and even tigers were in the area. My final response was: *You want to find them, then come dig them up!* It would have been a horrible scene."

Colonel Duncan had other recollections of the War: "I remember helicopters moving in and out with people. Some helicopters brought people from operational units stationed down south, toward Dong Ha. Most of them came from OPs (observation posts), and other locales. We tried our best to direct the stretcher-bearers to the bunker area and triage, so the wounded could get treatment. In our bunker complex, triage was in the center. Off the OP was a double dye-marker bunker that was about 10 feet wide and 30 feet long; it was a big place. I think we had five tables and three operating room doctors. For lights, we had a normal 75 KVA (kilovolt ampere) mobile transformer, which covered a number of bunkers, and size 37 KVA transformers for back-up; we had good electricity. The base (Figure 44) was circled by a trench and sandbags and concertina wire with mines."

"My sergeant major and I had to do something neither of us wanted to do. We had to select those we thought were wounded too badly to save. We had to move fast because triage was overcapacity with people in bad shape." Duncan took a senior doctor to do triage, but one doctor blatantly refused, arguing, "*I don't care what you do; we're going to operate on whoever you send in. I'm not going to make a judgment call. I'm not going to be your god; you do what you want.* He just wouldn't do it." It was a nightmare scenario, and this wasn't the last time Duncan would see this doctor.

Colonel Duncan never forgot one Marine in particular, with both legs blown off. "I really felt sorry for him. He had lost both limbs and he waved at me and said, *Just move me over. I know that I can't be repaired, isn't that right?* I confirmed. He had lost both legs and his bowels were blown out. The upper part of his body, his heart and lungs were okay; he could talk. His injury had blocked the pain out of his brain, which sometimes happened. He wanted a cigarette before he died. He said, *Texas Pete, could we have a cigarette together?* I told him I'd go get one. I knew they were still packing cigarettes in C-rations, and most people would carry an extra. One of the corpsman gave me a cigarette. I got it lit and gave it to the Marine. Then, I remember him asking me, 'Will I see you again?' I responded, *Not in this world, but I know you told me earlier and we discussed it, that you have accepted Christ into your heart. It's okay. That's all part of the fight we are in together; we're all brothers.* I've used this example at Marine reunions. I always say, *The strength we have now as surviving warriors is to teach others what war is about.*"

❝ The first questions I often got asked by a new recruit were, *What's it like to kill somebody? What's it like to be that close? What's it like to know if I'm going to die?* ❞

"The first questions I often got asked by a new recruit were, *What's it like to kill somebody? What's it like to be that close? What's it like to know if I'm going to die? How will my body be taken out? If we got mixed up in Napalm, and bodies were burned beyond recognition, how would we know if they were American or Vietnamese? How do they send the body back?* I try to reassure, *We will do the best we can with Graves Registration and make identifications the best way we know how.*"

"I would take the time to learn about my Marines. I knew where they were from, and I wrote to the families of all who died. I wrote

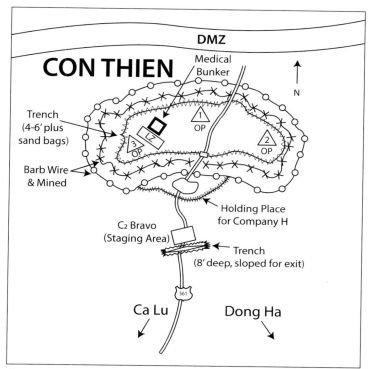

Figure 44: Sketch of the American military base at Con Thien. Drawing by Col. Bill Duncan, PETP 2014, Jerry C. Davis, and Sara Franks.

condolence letters for every one, and there were a whole bunch of casualties (116)."

"My command at that time included reinforcements of other Marines, Army units, and some Navy and civilian personnel—close to 3,000 people. The triage would have a double-digit census at any one time. Sometimes we'd have a guy in triage who we knew would make it, but he'd have an arm off; everything else looked good. With the helicopter waiting, we'd put a tourniquet on his arm, then get him on a bird and send him out. Other times, they'd die before they got help. It was grueling, day in and day out."

Duncan recalled, "I remember one time finding the chaplain huddled in a corner of the bunker. He had continuously been trying to help in any way he could. At a breaking point, he said, *I'm no good, Texas Pete. I'm no good; get me out of here!* I thought, *You're on the next bird out.* About a month after this occurred, the division senior chaplain, a Navy captain, called and requested for me to let the chaplain come back. When he reported for duty, I told this young chaplain, *You and I both know you're back up here because your big boss down in Da Nang says that he wants you back up here, and maybe this will work and maybe it won't.* I was proactive and laid out some clear instructions with the chaplain. I told him, *I want to never see you in the compound if we have people fighting. When we have helicopters moving in and out, and you can't take it anymore, you find a helicopter and get on it. Otherwise, you get where people are being wounded; they need prayers.* We worked with him, and that chaplain became known as *the battlefield commander with the Bibles.* He'd take the M14 and M16 mortar slings (that the rounds go in) and he'd stuff them with Gideon New Testaments. He became very well respected."

At C2 Bravo (observation post), Duncan vividly recalled making nightly inspections. "We still had a lot of wounded being treated. Some didn't have much time; hunks of meat might be gone. The doctors were trying to patch them up and then get them out. One night, I conducted a nighttime inspection, because I couldn't sleep. I walked with a doctor into one of the new doctor facilities at C2 Bravo and noticed something strange. I asked, *What is this?* I saw one pair of feet; then I saw another pair of feet. Both were doctors who had tried to commit suicide, one was in serious condition and one was less so. I looked at the doctor with me and said, *I know you know what happened. Can we go in the leg, in the arm and flood the body, get a catheter in and wash the system out? There's a chance we could save their lives; they need not leave here in this fashion.* It worked! The doctor worked for over two hours and we got them out on helicopters—alive!"

Under these trying circumstances, Duncan was compassionate, and he understood the toll of war. He knew some couldn't take the stress, not even doctors. But the suicide incident didn't go unnoticed. "Somebody asked me to write a letter, since the two doctors were under my command. I just simply stated, *They were underperforming.* I didn't want to ruin their whole careers. Doctors are not trained to deal with those kinds of conditions. When you bring a medical doctor out to the battlefield outside his hospital environment, and he sees so many badly wounded and wrecked people, he sometimes can't handle it. The stress is too much."

Duncan certainly endured stress himself. "At times I had to select who was going to be seen by a doctor. We would do separation of bodies and, other Marines would see who got moved. They would ask, *Do you think I'm going to die?*" It was a common question that Duncan answered in a special way. "I told them, *At this time you may, but I hope you will have found favor with God and that you have accepted Him.* I didn't require a death bed confession or anything like that. I just talked to them out of my heart."

In March 1968, Duncan (2nd Battalion, 1st Marine Division) was ordered to depart Con Thien and proceed toward Cam Lo through C2 Bravo. Duncan explained, "It had been reported that the 1st Air Cavalry was engaged in *Operation Pegasus*, along Rte. 9 toward Khe Sanh, and we were their left flank relief." *Operation Pegasus* lasted through April.

"In May, we (2nd Battalion 1st Marines) joined with the 1st Air Cav around Hill 881-N, and our job was to destroy the threat to Khe Sanh." The battle at Hill 881-N (Figure 45) will long be remembered by the Marines like Bill Duncan, who fought there. "When we first went there, we didn't have a major fight. But not long after, we had a hot contest with heavy artillery coming out of Co Roc." (Figure 45)

Along the way, at a place called Cam Lo, Duncan had yet another unusual experience. "When we came out of C2 Bravo, we went to a place

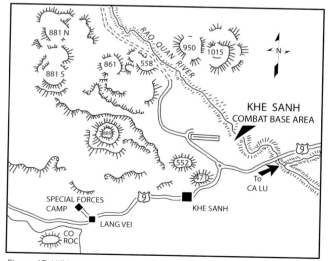

Figure 45: Hill Locations. Adapted from public domain.

called Cam Lo (Figure 39, page 95), where the 1st Air Cav was positioned. I presented a problem since I was now a part of the command structure. General Tomlinson asked, *Is Texas Pete here? I didn't select Texas Pete."* He (General Tomlinson) said to Colonel Duncan, *"I understand you don't fly?* I replied, *I've flown, Sir, but I'm not helicopter qualified.* He said, *Our commanders must be. We will assign you one of our command helicopters, which is a modified Huey, and you're going to fly in combat.* Turning to his ADC (assistant division commander), Brigadier General Davis, General Tomlinson said, *Okay, Texas Pete, we're going to set up our times.* We set up times for take-off and landing and everything else. I had five days of training as we were bulking up our forces, getting ready to go forward. I had two MC (Seabees—mobile construction) battalions assigned to us, and we were to build and repair bridges all the way into Khe Sanh, where the river was crippled. *I think you can handle it,* the general said."

"We made our way to Khe Sanh and took a lot of heavy fire, artillery and some small arms fire. We were working out of bomb holes and craters, and we had been hit twice with heavy artillery. One round that came in killed my night observation officer; he was standing next to me, and I took part of the shrapnel. I lost my equilibrium. I remember saying, *I'm ok.* We were getting people evacuated out on choppers, and the corpsman said, *You're going.* I replied, *No, I'm okay, I think, but I can't stand and walk.* And he said, *You're a hazard to us.* And I said, *Look corpsman!* And he said, *Sir, I know my rights, and I want to put you on that helicopter. Can you walk to the helicopter?* And I finally responded, *No, but I can crawl.* He said, *We're going to throw you on a stretcher and put you on that helicopter."*

"So, I temporarily lost command, and my XO (executive officer) had been notified. I went to the hospital ship, though I really didn't think I was hurt badly. I had a bad concussion and a lot of shrapnel. I didn't have any focus and couldn't stand. On the hospital ship they confirmed I didn't need to go in the operating room. I just needed to have an exam to see if I had anything really damaging. I knew some shrapnel was in my upper body. They said I could be taped up and would be able to return the next day. I went straight to the flight deck, and a dear friend of mine said, *We heard you'd been hit, Texas Pete; it was all over the net.* Then he asked, *Are you free?* and I said, *Yeah, I'm free. (I freed myself.)* I got out of the Navy hospital ship, got in a helicopter, and we took off. I was in the jump seat between two of them, and so that's the way I got out."

Upon return, Duncan checked in at Khe Sanh and went to Hill 881-N. He knew timing was crucial. "If I didn't go fast they would order somebody else up, and I would not have my command. A friend told me about chatter coming over the radio, *We are missing an officer listed as Texas Pete from the hospital ship. Anybody know him?* My friend asked, *What's my response?* I said, *Don't answer.* He said, *You'll probably get in trouble,* and I said, *You'll get in trouble along with me.*"

"We got all the way up to Khe Sanh and started fighting again. Then shortly, we got the order that we would be evacuated. They wanted to send helicopters in to pull us out, but I sent word back down to the Division, to Major General [Carl] Hoffman. (I didn't know him then; I got to know him much better after that.) Hoffman inquired, *You mean you have refused helicopter evacuation?* I said, *Yes, sir. We're going to walk out of here.* The men were exhausted; we'd been fighting for three days. I didn't like that I had lost time going out and being evaluated on that ship. I was absent less than eight hours. I messaged back to him and said, *We will walk out – all of us – and we are starting now. We will carry our wounded, and we'll carry our dead, but we don't intend to be airlifted, nor will we take a hospital lift.*"

> **❝ When we reached the division headquarters, we were greeted and asked, *Do you know that you were named the Ghost Battalion by the Vietnamese?* ❞**

Duncan knew that sending helicopters would be risky: "The enemy would take out any helicopter they saw landing. It took us about nine hours through the night to make our escape. When we reached the division headquarters, we were greeted and asked, *Do you know that you were named the Ghost Battalion by the Vietnamese?* I said, *No.* I was so tired I couldn't understand. I said, *Tell me what you're saying.* Division responded, *We've been monitoring the enemy's radio traffic, and the lead general is over there because 881-N has not been returned to their control.*

And he (the enemy general) said, *They are not here.* He was told by General Giap, *Search again, don't let them leave.* And he came back on the line and said, *Sir, they are not on this hill. They vanished as if they were ghosts! They're gone!* The NVA officer was relieved of his command. He had disgraced the fighting units by losing our battalion!"

The Marines persevered through many different circumstances. "Coming out of Khe Sanh, casualties piled up. It was two days later, and we were still fighting. It seemed like months, but it was only three days, and everybody was pretty much dead on their feet. We were traveling down Route 9 and got to an area that was a big, open field. There were a bunch of girls – 10, 15, or maybe 20 girls – coming forward, and they had little ribbons in their hair. When I saw them, I stopped. I had one tank; we'd just lost three tanks while fighting. The first thing we noticed was these young girls were marching out and forward. Someone shouted, *They're all loaded (armed), Colonel, they're not girls! They're loaded, get down! Get down!* Some of them were girls and some of them were not. They were dressed up like girls, and they were waving flowers and everything. We used a canister round to clear the field. A canister round is just like having one hundred shooters. It's like you're firing shotguns one hundred times over using a double-aught barrel; it's so damaging!"

"As I said, some could be girls, most were not, but you couldn't tell them apart. I couldn't tell them apart. They wanted peace; that's what they said, but all of them had machine guns behind them or with them. When one would fall forward, another one would come over and grab the gun off their back and start firing at our troops, who were exposed like spectators watching a parade. In order to shoot those who were close by, we had to clear the field. It could have been handled a bit differently, but I think the tiredness of everybody affected us. A different approach might have saved, maybe a dozen, a dozen and a half young kids' lives. The point man knew (or saw) what was happening because he was in front of me. He had walked toward them, and he had turned and was coming back quickly and had said, *No, no, Texas Pete! Get out, get out!* He noticed one of them and must have seen what was going on. When the kids dropped down to their knees, there were a lot of guns being fired, and that's when the canister round was fired by our tank. We fired several shots."

The Marines frequently took prisoners, often at great risks to themselves. But because of incidents like the aforementioned *girls*, caution was paramount. "We had taken some prisoners at Khe Sanh, usually the NVA. We would take their shoes off and look at them; the condition of their feet would tell us a lot, because they'd been wearing boots for a long time. We had to watch them all the time. If they saw somebody with a weapon, they'd try to get the weapon and shoot whoever had it. It was a hard way to survive, and I didn't like it. I don't like to see people killed. In fact, I have not fired a gun in over thirty years, maybe thirty-five, and I'm a good shot."

Not everything Duncan participated in led to death or destruction. "I think about us going in and freeing some of the areas, places like Cam Lo and outside Khe Sanh, and the Rock Pile. The locals didn't want to die; their whole families were there. When we were running patrols and we had opportunities, we'd try to get food to them and we'd try to get medical treatment to them." Marines were tough, but compassionate, warriors.

STUDENT RESPONSE

Taylor Johnson remembers her first encounter with Bill Duncan: "I was surprised and pleased to have the opportunity to meet Colonel Duncan two days before we left for Vietnam. The group was having a last-minute trip meeting when I walked into the room and was greeted by the Colonel. I had no idea who he was, but he knew me. *Are you Taylor?* A little confused, I responded with a *Yes, Sir!* His face lit up. *I do believe you're my host for this trip!* Right away I walked over and stuck out my hand for a proper shake but was pulled in by a warm embrace that was much like a grandpa's. We hit it off from the start, as we were both excited to start this journey together. On the trip, I learned more than I could have possibly imagined. Colonel Duncan was an overflowing fount of knowledge. He is one of the sweetest, most gentle and loving men I have ever met, making it hard to picture him as a rough and tough Marine colonel. At the beginning of this trip, he explained to me that he didn't want to revisit Vietnam, but after praying and seeking God's help, he felt like he was supposed to return to teach us— his replacements— the importance of the War, as well as to honor the men who died while serving."

"We had the opportunity to visit several sites where Colonel Duncan fought. The moment that will forever be etched in my mind was when we were at Con Thien, north of Hué, near the former DMZ, and he told us a beautifully haunting story about fighting, honor, and brotherhood. This was by far the most emotional part of the trip for me. Colonel Duncan's men were engaged in a fierce fight and NVA artillery fire inflicted many casualties upon them. The battalion doctor refused to take responsibility for which men were too wounded to be saved, leaving that decision to Duncan. As he retold the story and his voice quivered, my heart broke, as was true for most others in our group. He had been placed in an impossible situation of having to pick one brother over another. Despite the circumstances, the Lord used him to love and show compassion to those in their last minutes of life as he stayed with them until each had drawn his last breath."[2]

 ❝ I did whatever I had to do to save my men, myself, and my country. ❞

"Colonel Duncan shared, *I did whatever I had to do to save my men, myself, and my country.* These are the words of a true hero, a man who put his life on the line to secure the freedoms for future generations around the world."

"I was able to learn and hear stories from a military standpoint that my grandpa or uncle never felt the need to share. It's a special feeling when the veterans open up and unpack some of the details of what they went through."

"Colonel Duncan explained some of his missions. He spoke with me about one of his injuries. He told me that he was once hit by shrapnel; it went through his cheek and knocked out a couple of his teeth. He explained some military rankings to me, and also we talked about where certain units would have been. We discussed whether he would have had any contact with my uncle. He believes he probably would have, but he's not certain. I was grateful for being teamed with Colonel Bill Duncan and for his willingness to answer my questions."

Taylor recalled both the excitement and terror of visiting the underground tunnels: "When we reached the tunnels at Cu Chi, all of the students were pretty excited to see where the North Vietnamese so cleverly hid. Colonel Duncan even joined us! The entrance was larger than it used to be; they widened it so average-sized people could go in and get the full experience. Once we got down under the ground, I could not believe how little the tunnels actually were. I had to crawl on my hands and knees. And that was in the larger part of the tunnels. I certainly didn't understand how the Vietnamese were able to run as quickly as they did and fight in that small of a space. I had to get out as soon as I could because it was just so small and dark. When I climbed out, I was surprised to find Colonel Duncan being held up by two students and another veteran. My heart stopped with fear that something had happened. He was short of breath and couldn't stand up. His face was covered in sweat and his eyes were heavy. I ran to get Nurse Lori, and she helped get some water in him, but it really scared me. He told me that it was just too tight and he got dehydrated down there."

"There was one part of the tour where you could actually shoot AK-47s. The tourists who were not connected to the War thought it was cool to shoot the guns. As soon as the first gun went off, we all jumped. For me, it was because it scared me; but for the veterans, I think it took them back to those long nights of warfare and crisis. We could tell that several of the veterans were disturbed by the noise. Colonel Duncan immediately started telling me about the different sounds the guns make, but I think he was honestly trying to cope with the sounds and memories."

Taylor was able to see firsthand the Vietnamese slant to the War: "A lot of the battlegrounds in Vietnam have not been maintained. It's very different from how we care for our U.S. battlefields. When you visit a Vietnam War battle site, you have to picture it in your mind, because there are not many remains. We visited the war museum in Saigon. From what I could tell, some of the veterans didn't really seem all that interested in it. Most likely that was because it was all coming from the Vietnamese viewpoint, making the Vietnamese look good and the Americans look evil. Colonel Duncan and I started on the main floor, and there were a lot of Vietnamese posters and advertisements. The posters were awful and ugly towards Americans. When I first asked which part he really wanted to see, he said he didn't really care; when I asked him again, he said he would like to look at the Agent Orange section. After making our way there, we looked at the history of Agent Orange, and it was very disturbing seeing the before and after pictures. Additionally, the birth defects and images of the people with disfigurements made my heart break. It's incomprehensible that a chemical has the power to change the appearance and genetic makeup of human beings for generations. Colonel Duncan told me, *I am seeing pictures I've never seen before of the effects of Agent Orange.* I can't even imagine what he was feeling. He talked about the fact that they had no idea it would impact the people the way it did. Agent Orange was not intended to break down the people groups; rather, its use was to alter the enemy's source of shelter and food. Colonel and the other soldiers didn't have any other option than to spray Agent Orange. It was their order and they had to do it."

"It was an honor being able to walk through that exhibit with Colonel Duncan as he processed the effect. As we were ending our time in the Agent Orange room, he explained something to me and a woman from South Africa interjected. She overheard him telling me about his experience, and she began to ask him many questions. I could tell he was proud of his service. He was touched that someone from a different country had that much interest in the War. We spoke to her for about 15 minutes. It was neat to hear their conversation. Again, I was honored to be with Colonel Duncan in that moment."

 ❝ …words of a true hero, a man who put his life on the line to secure the freedoms for future generations around the world. ❞

"I asked Colonel how many battles he thought he had been in, and he said that in the I-Corps region, it was really just one long continuous battle. He explained they had a few hours or a day or two of rest, but other than that, they were in the heat of it. He told me it was that way because near the DMZ is where the NVA would cross the border. His battalion was responsible for shutting down this access. It was tough for him and his men because they were constantly on the move. He wanted to keep his men safe."

Figure 46: China Beach. Photo by John Luck.

Taylor reported a very poignant moment with Colonel Duncan: "Out of curiosity, I asked him if he lost a lot of men. I mainly asked this because he hadn't really mentioned it. When I asked, the look on his face changed. He solemnly responded, *Too many.* I turned my head because I knew I had asked him a touchy question. He was silent for about a minute and then got more specific: *Well, over a hundred.* His response was in a different voice, had a deeper tone. I glanced over at him, and he was looking at me with his light blue eyes that were beginning to fill up with tears; in his deep voice he restated, *Well, over a hundred men.* I had to keep my emotions in check because that really hit me. My grandpa was never willing to talk about his experience in Vietnam, but a man that I have known for a week is able to. I could not imagine going off to another country and losing the only friends I had, and some were even losing brothers. Colonel Duncan was a commander, a leader, and was responsible for many men. I can only imagine that when he lost one, a part of him left with them."

"We drove through Da Nang. From what I saw, it was a beautiful city. Colonel Duncan gave some information about Da Nang because he served there for three months. He said nothing there looked the same; it had been very developed in the last 45 to 50 years. He recognized the beach, China Beach (Figure 46) to be exact. We stopped, and it was beautiful. The times when we got out of the bus, taking a little time soaking it all in, were some of my favorite. Colonel pointed out several of the mountains that he remembered. He told me that the mountains used to be full of tigers. They learned to use the tigers as weapons against the NVA. Right after we passed through Da Nang, we reached Marble Mountain. It was beautiful. Marble Mountain was near where my uncle earned his Silver Star, and it was neat to see that area."

Taylor was able to actually see the battle sites she had read about: "We visited Con Thien, the Rockpile, and Khe Sanh (Figure 39, page 95), a few of the major sites where Colonel Duncan had fought. I didn't know what to expect. I didn't know how he would react or how his emotions would hold up. He had asked me to be praying for him."

"We first visited the Rockpile. (Figure 47) It's precisely named because it's just a large pile of rocks. Colonel said that they used to blow up the mountains, and there were tunnels in them. Our next stop was Khe Sanh, and it was beautiful, like a plateau. The surrounding mountains were outstanding. When we arrived at Khe Sanh, nearby was a little museum, and Colonel wanted to take a look at the old planes and tanks

Figure 47: Rockpile. Photo by John Luck.

that were on display outside. We stood on the grounds where the old runway would have been. He told me that when planes would drop supplies, they wouldn't land. They would get close enough to the ground to drop, but they had only about 26 seconds to pull back up or the plane would crash. He told me that one time a plane didn't get up in time and ended up crashing at the end of the runway. I was able to picture that because I was standing on the same ground that Colonel Bill Duncan had stood on during the War."

"I have been so blessed by this trip opportunity. I couldn't have been paired with a better veteran. I have come to think of Colonel Duncan as a grandpa, and I'm so blessed by that. Thank you!"

TOPIC SUMMARY

As Colonel Duncan described his experiences during the bitter fighting at Con Thien to Taylor Johnson and the rest of the group, it was difficult to envision the turmoil of the battle. They were standing on a slight hill,

Figure 48: Col. Duncan explaining battle at Con Thien (note greenery). Photo by John Luck.

not far from where the medical bunker was located. Surrounding this spot were trees of bright green. (Figure 48) No one would have guessed that a violent battle had occurred under their feet. However, fifty years ago, there were no trees on this little hill. (Figure 48) The sound of artillery and mortar fire must have been deafening. Worst of all, death and fear were undoubtedly the only things in plentiful supply.

Marines at Con Thien had to spend much of their time living like moles. Underground bunkers were cold, damp, and muddy. Some Marines occasionally slept (or tried to) outside their bunkers because of the almost constant presence of rats—BIG RATS! Some were said to be as large as rabbits, and these monsters would often drag the traps with them to escape the wrath of annoyed Marines.

Colonel Duncan and his fellow Marines were at greater risk during monsoon season because air support was limited or nonexistent. Mostly, they exchanged artillery, mortar, and rocket fire with the NVA, who were not far away. At night, enemy soldiers would cross the DMZ trying to get inside the perimeter at Con Thien. This was not easy to do, as they had to get through a mine field, concertina wire, and listening posts. According to Colonel Duncan, it was not uncommon to send a patrol out in the early morning and find NVA bodies.

The importance of holding Con Thien was not readily apparent to Marines who were just trying to stay alive and keep the NVA on their side of the DMZ. It was just a despondent place to be, with no end in sight, even though battalions were replaced on a three- to eight-month rotation. As Colonel Duncan confirmed, the Marines prevailed, but the price was high.

Meanwhile, back in the States a much less honorable effort was going on. While Marines were dying, college students took a break from what many saw as an obsession with sex, drugs, and partying to demonstrate against DOW Chemical (maker of napalm) on their campus at the University of Wisconsin, Madison. Additionally, a march of one hundred thousand people happened at the Pentagon via the Lincoln Memorial in October 1967.[3]

The fighting at Con Thien received quite a bit of media attention. CBS ran a special on October 1, 1967, titled *The Ordeal of Con Thien*, and *Time* magazine carried a feature story describing the fighting at Con Thien.

By the end of 1967, the fighting at Con Thien continued at a slower pace. President Johnson was unhappy and frustrated. Perhaps his political style (building a consensus) was a detriment. At any rate, in late fall, while the "hill battles" continued to rage, President Johnson initiated a campaign to make the War more appealing to the public and Congress. General Westmoreland and Ambassador Ellsworth Bunker were called to Washington. General Westmoreland stated on a *Meet the Press* show that it was "conceivable that within two years or less the enemy will be so weakened that the Vietnamese (ARVN) will be able to cope with a greater share of the war burden." To this end, author Robert Dallek notes what journalist David Brinkley recounted of President Johnson saying, "I'm not going to be the first American president to lose a war."[4]

Given the attitude of the President and his top commander, it is easy to understand why they felt that battles in I-Corps, like Con Thien and Khe Sanh, must be won at whatever the price. If the NVA could overrun either one, it would be viewed as another Dien Bien Phu (site of French defeat in 1954). The media was already making these comparisons.

Clearly, the Marines persevered and prevailed, thanks to leaders like Colonel Bill Duncan. Unfortunately, the attitudes of the public and politicians did not match the commitment and sacrifice of the Marines they had sent into battle at such a place.

PART II
MIDDLE YEARS (1968-70)

OVERVIEW

The Middle Years (1968-70) of the Vietnam War encompassed both the peak of American troops and the beginning of withdrawals. They also included a major battle, the Tet Offensive, that was a turning point in the War. Oddly, the Tet Offensive, in which dozens of South Vietnamese villages, towns, and cities were attacked (Figure 49), turned out to be a major military defeat for the North Vietnamese, in spite of catching the United States and South Vietnamese somewhat by surprise. The Viet Cong, who came out in force for the Tet Offensive, were virtually annihilated.

The Tet Offensive occurred during the Tet holiday, a Vietnamese celebration of the New Year. A truce was pledged but ignored by North Vietnam. The Military Assistance Command Vietnam (MACV) Commander, General William Westmoreland, had received seemingly trustworthy information from captured prisoners and documentation that a "general offensive and general uprising"[1] was planned. The North Vietnamese believed that it would be supported by the people of the South. To the contrary, no popular uprising occurred.

Strangely, although the Tet Offensive was a military disaster for the North Vietnamese, the media portrayed the situation differently. The media's negative reporting undermined both public confidence and support of the War, leaving most Americans to believe we had actually lost! One newsman, Walter Cronkite, stated, "the only rational way out of the War will be to negotiate, not as victors, but as an honorable people…"[2] Additionally, very little had been said about the fact that several thousand people were murdered or executed during the Tet

Offensive by NVA death squads. The NVA had acquired and brought with them lists of targets to be eliminated. The following year, the Mỹ Lai massacre—where an entire village was wiped out—was uncovered. Again, the media's reporting of this unfortunate deed was unrelenting, while the Tet massacre was largely underreported.

Figure 49: Tet Offensive (major attack sites). Adapted from public domain.

In the wake of negative reporting of the War and declining public confidence, President Johnson announced in March 1968 that he would not run for reelection. He was, no doubt, disillusioned about the War and worried about his "Great Society" plans.[3] Prior to this announcement, Johnson's advisors had talked him into restricting the bombing of North Vietnam to the area just north of the Demilitarized Zone (DMZ).[4]

President Johnson relied on a group discreetly called the "Wise Men."[5] Perhaps, they were so named because many held Ivy League degrees. No doubt others thought this a misnomer and that these advisors should have been called "unwise men" as a more appropriate label.

The North Vietnamese violated the bombing agreement, as they often did during the War. The only substantial outcome of the halt was that it made the presidential election results a little closer. Richard Nixon won anyway.

The year 1968 was pivotal in both the history of the War and the history of our nation. Following the Tet Offensive, General Westmoreland was replaced by General Creighton Abrams, who had a new strategy for fighting the War. This year was made more difficult with the assassinations of Dr. Martin Luther King, Jr. in April and Robert F. Kennedy in June.

The Paris Peace talks started in January 1969, Nixon's first year in office. Battles continued to rage, but useful strategy like "Vietnamization"[6] took root, an effort to help the villages with their own defense and governance. Ho Chi Minh's death in September was unexpected. The War was at a low point in public support, thanks to the irresponsible American media. Additionally, in the fall of 1969, massive demonstrations and "teach-ins" across the United States called for a moratorium on funding of the Vietnam War, which put political pressure on President Nixon. This followed a restless summer that included the Woodstock concert in upstate New York.

Spring of 1970 produced more turmoil, due to a riot and shooting at Kent State University; this came after Nixon allowed an invasion of Cambodia to clear out sanctuaries. Congress repealed the Gulf of Tonkin Resolution in June, which was likely encouragement to the North Vietnamese.

By then, American POWs had been languishing in North Vietnam prisons for several years. In November 1970, a specially trained group of Green Berets, under the command of Colonel "Bull" Simons, developed a well-planned attack on the Son Tay Prison, about 23 miles from Hanoi.[7] Reconnaissance had shown that POWs were being held there. However, a flood had obscured any more observations, causing some to think the raid should have been called off. A decision was made to go in anyway. Unfortunately, no prisoners were found, but there were other good outcomes: the POWs were now concentrated in the Hanoi Hilton, the attempted rescue had dramatically increased morale among prisoners.

In the middle years of the War, much was happening on many different fronts simultaneously. The next three class topics highlight some of these. Khe Sanh was south of the DMZ, located in Quang Tri Province in the northwest corner of I-Corps; Hué City was a coastal town in Hué Province; and Chu Lai had a coastal location in Quang Nam Province. These locales (Figure 49) were spread throughout I-Corps. Khe Sanh and Hué City were sites of two major battles during the Tet Offensive. Chu Lai was the site of the 91st Evacuation Hospital where American and Vietnamese soldiers and civilians were treated. The battles of Khe Sanh and Hué were the longest battles during the Tet Offensive; Hué lasted 33 days and Khe Sanh lasted over 5 months. These were the sites of tremendous losses on both sides, but the Americans and ARVN (Army of the Republic of Vietnam) troops prevailed.

CLASS TOPIC 5: KHE SANH (I-CORPS)

I cried. I lost a lot of friends.
I had survivor's guilt.

⬤ INSTRUCTOR: COL DONALD E. (DON) "DOC" BALLARD, USA (RET.)[1]

Who would be better to instruct students on the horrors of war than a veteran who served as a combat medic? This was the assignment of Colonel Don "Doc" Ballard, whose sacrifice and service resulted in this nation's highest honor for valor, the Medal of Honor. Neither Ballard, nor anyone else, could have known what he would experience on the battlefields of Vietnam.

Don Ballard enlisted in the U.S. Navy in 1965 and attended basic recruit training in Great Lakes, Illinois. After graduation he attended hospital corps school, also in Great Lakes, followed by an assignment in the surgery department of the Naval Hospital located in Memphis, Tennessee. As a Navy corpsman, civilians would call him a paramedic.

In December 1966, Ballard was selected to serve with the Marines. He attended his second basic training, this time at Camp Lejeune, North Carolina. After completion of the basic field medical service training, he was assigned to the 1st Battalion, 6th Marines aboard the *U.S.S. Cambridge*, a troop transport ship in the 6th Fleet, and set sail for the Mediterranean.

From the fall of 1967 to late summer of 1968, Ballard served as a frontline combat corpsman with Mike Company, 3rd Battalion, 4th Marines in Vietnam. As a grunt corpsman, his job was to save the lives of Marines in combat and to get them home to their loved ones.

Colonel Ballard was credited with saving several Marines' lives and was himself wounded eight times. He was transported by medevac to Japan for treatment and was later returned to duty as the corpsman for the brigade at Camp McTureous, Okinawa, where he was awarded his third Purple Heart medal.

Ballard's life changed significantly on May 16, 1968, in Quang Tri Province, in the Republic of Vietnam. Colonel Ballard was then a second-class hospital corpsman, also called "Doc" by the Marines who greatly respected the corpsman. His actions that day resulted in receiving the Medal of Honor (MOH). The Citation makes clear the risks he took while administering and saving the lives of several U.S. Marines. On May 14, 1970, Doc Ballard was awarded the Medal of Honor by President Nixon in a White House ceremony.

CITATION

For conspicuous gallantry and intrepidity at the risk of his life and beyond the call of duty while serving as a HC2c. with Company M, in connection with operations against enemy aggressor forces. During the afternoon hours, Company M was moving to join the remainder of the 3d Battalion in Quang Tri Province. After treating and evacuating 2 heat casualties, HC2c. Ballard was returning to his platoon from the evacuation landing zone when the company was ambushed by a North Vietnamese Army unit employing automatic weapons and mortars, and sustained numerous casualties. Observing a wounded Marine, HC2c. Ballard unhesitatingly moved across the fire-swept terrain to the injured man and swiftly rendered medical assistance to his comrade. HC2c. Ballard then directed four Marines to carry the casualty to a position of relative safety. As the four men prepared to move the wounded Marine, an enemy soldier suddenly left his concealed position and, after hurling a hand grenade which landed near the casualty, commenced firing upon the small group of men. Instantly shouting a warning to the Marines, HC2c. Ballard fearlessly threw himself upon the lethal explosive device to protect his comrades from the deadly blast. When the grenade failed to detonate, he calmly arose from his dangerous position and resolutely continued his determined efforts in treating other Marine casualties. HC2c. Ballard's heroic actions and selfless concern for the welfare of his companions served to inspire all who observed him and prevented possible injury or death to his fellow marines. His courage, daring initiative, and unwavering devotion to duty in the face of extreme personal danger, sustain and enhance the finest traditions of the U.S. Naval Service.[2]

Ballard returned to the States after his service. He left the Navy and joined the Kansas Army National Guard in 1970. He led an ambulance platoon, served as a company commander, and was tasked with creating the Medical Detachment 5, a unit that performs physicals for Guard members.

In 1998, he was promoted to the rank of Colonel, and he retired in 2000, after a distinguished 35-year career. Upon retirement from military service, Ballard joined the Fire Department in North Kansas City, Missouri, where he later retired as a captain after twenty years of service.

Ballard is one of three Navy corpsmen still alive who received the Medal of Honor. Out of 44 million veterans who have served our great country, only 3,526 Medals of Honor have been issued, and today, there are only 69 living. He is the only recipient living in the state of Missouri.

At the age of sixty, Ballard wanted to become a funeral director in order to help veterans who could not pay for their funerals. He currently owns two funeral homes and cemeteries. Swan Lake Memorial Park Cemetery in Grain Valley, Missouri, is the host site for the National Combat Medical Memorial and Youth Education Center.

In addition to the Medal of Honor, Ballard received three Purple Hearts with 5/16-inch Gold Stars; a Navy Combat Action Ribbon; a Navy Good Conduct Medal; National Defense Service Medal; the Vietnam Service Medal with FMF Combat Operation Insignia and two 3/16-inch Bronze Stars; the Republic of Vietnam Meritorious Unit Citation (Gallantry Cross) with Palm and Frame; the Republic of Vietnam Meritorious Unit Citation (Civil Actions) with Palm and Frame; and the Republic of Vietnam Campaign Medal with 1960 device.

The name of Donald E. Ballard will always be remembered by those who served alongside him. He has dedicated his life to serving the military and the general public.

Figure 50 : Student host Sara Cochran and veteran Don "Doc" Ballard.
Photo by John Luck

 ## STUDENT HOST: SARA COCHRAN

Student host Sara Cochran (Figure 50) had a very personal reason for wanting to go to Vietnam: "The Vietnam Era is a time with which I am most familiar when it comes to wars. I don't remember the stories my grandpa told my brother and me as kids; he fought in World War II. But I do remember my father's stories about his time in Vietnam. I would never want to experience anything like that. However, to travel and see where my dad stood and fought for me, leaving everything he loved behind him, was a privilege.

Cochran continues, "My dad served as a medic in the U.S Army. I still have lots of souvenirs he brought back from Vietnam. One souvenir that is closest to my heart is a folded military flag I keep in a shadow box in my room. Life has its battles and everyone carries scars. I believe it is part of the human experience. But soldiers carry deep scars with them forever. I believe this statement because I heard someone I love more than anyone or anything else share these stories. My struggle is that I never get to hear these military stories from him anymore. I just have the memories to cherish and share."

"My dad once told me a story about Vietnam that I will never forget. He and the soldiers he had trained with were leaving and moving to a different site, being transported via ships. My dad mistakenly was on the wrong ship. He was watching when the ship that all his brothers were on was blown up. They were gone, and this was only the beginning for him. I thank God everyday my dad was not on that ship. But he lost everyone he knew at that point. I have many more stories from him, but that one was the one that impacted me most."

"My father served four to five years in the Army. He was ranked as SP5, which is not considered a ranking anymore. He was a specialist who received the same pay as a sergeant but didn't give commands. He then went to Texas and worked at a burn facility. He returned home a couple years later and worked in surgery at our hometown hospital. People tell me how great my father was working in surgery. He was always on top of things and many people have said they learned more from working with him than with the doctors. That is the military in my father. My mother also worked in surgery and has shared memories about working alongside my father. She attributes much of what she learned in surgery to my father. It makes me proud to hear this about my father and to know our country made him who he was. He was my number one role model, supporter and best friend. I hope I help and touch as many people as he did."

"My dad told me how people reacted to the Vietnam soldiers when they returned. I am offended by how those soldiers were treated. As they came home, people called them names and frowned upon them. I will forever be respectful of these veterans. I wanted to see the battle-fields they walked on and the streets, the scenery and everything about Vietnam. I know Dad would be smiling, loving that I was learning about what he, and others, did for this country."

KHE SANH BACKGROUND

In the buildup to the Tet offensive (January – March 1968), numerous battles took place in the upper regions of I-Corps, just south of the demilitarized zone (DMZ). Some of the bloodiest battles of the War were fought primarily between U.S. Marines and a division of the NVA. Colonel Don Ballard, assigned to the 3rd Battalion, 4th Marines, faced the possibility of death almost daily.

The Khe Sanh combat base was the focal point of much, but certainly not all, of the fighting. Standing on the old runway (Figure 51) at Khe Sanh, Colonel Ballard pointed to the surrounding terrain and said, "These hills are bathed in American blood." Numerous small villages were scattered near the Khe Sanh Combat Base.

Figure 51: Don Ballard at old runway, Khe Sanh. Photo by John Luck.

If one stands on the old runway and looks in most any direction, the distinct hills (Figure 45, page 105) are obvious. They are numbered according to their height in meters (i.e. Hill 881-N, 881-S, 861, 558, etc.). Securing these hills, especially those west of the base, was of the highest priority for our military. Otherwise, the base would have been vulnerable to attack from NVA troops who were coming down the Ho Chi Minh Trail (Figure 52) and infiltrating the upper northwest corner of South Vietnam. Marines secured these hills but at a high price; it was one of the bloodiest fights in the War. These "hill fights" went on for a number of months prior to the launching of the Tet Offensive on January 30, 1968.

Much of the priority on holding these obscure outposts was due to the fact that General Westmoreland thought the hills would be the main target of an expected Tet Offensive. He must have convinced President Johnson, who was worried Khe Sanh would be overrun like the French were at Dien Bien Phu. The President even had a sandbox model of Khe Sanh built and placed in the basement of the White House so he could follow the battle. The Joint Chiefs were required to put in writing a guarantee that Khe Sanh would not fall. Naturally, the media couldn't resist the temptation to compare Khe Sanh and Dien Bien Phu, even though they didn't have much in common.

As it turns out, General Westmoreland and President Johnson were wrong about the strategy of the North Vietnamese, which apparently was an effort to divert attention away from urban areas, including Saigon, An Loc, and Tay Ninh.

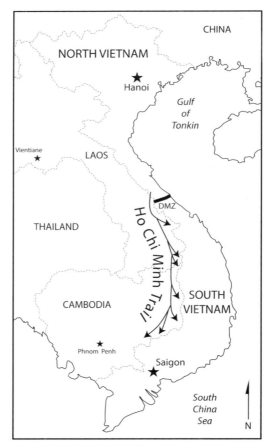

Figure 52: Ho Chi Minh Trail. Adapted from public domain.

INSTRUCTOR REFLECTIONS

Standing near the former battleground of Khe Sanh, Colonel Ballard addressed the students: "I never thought I'd be back here. I never wanted to come back. I never had a desire to come over here and find something that I never could find. I was about as shocked as any of my friends when I told them I was going back to Vietnam. They said, *You've got to be crazy!* But, I want to thank the College for making this trip available and for the opportunity to make new friends and impart some history of the Vietnam War. First, I owe a lot of people a lot of things, and I'd like to have a couple of moments of silence for our brothers that never came home. If you'll join me, you can have your own prayer and a couple moments of silence to remember our veterans. Their spirit is still here, even if their bodies are back home. Two minutes of silence, please."

> **❝ I never had a day that I could laugh. I never had a day that didn't end up with somebody's blood on my hands, and I would pray at night that I could go to sleep. ❞**

"Two minutes seems like an awful long time when you sit there and wonder what's going to happen. But two minutes is a relatively insignificant number when you talk about the amount of respect and the amount of reflection that you can have on your buddies. There's no greater love than combat buddies. You're in a different type of warfare up here in I-Corps; this is Marine Corps country. The Marines did everything differently from the Army. There were more grunts, more hand-to-hand combat, and more survival skills needed on a daily basis. I never had a day that I felt like I enjoyed it. I never had a day that I could laugh. I never had a day that didn't end up with somebody's blood on my hands, and I would pray at night that I could go to sleep. We didn't actually have a fire fight every day, but we always had casualties of some sort. When we visited that village down south, you got to see some of the weaponry that was crude. You got to see some of the tactics that were employed against us. We just had a different experience up here."

"There was no security. There was no real perimeter. They would just stick you in the field of fire and you would protect each other. When we got inside the base camp, it was like going home to Kansas City for a while, until the siege. For the most part we felt like we were pretty secure. We were the path finders. We never walked on anybody else's path. We always figured that there were booby traps." (Figure 53)

Figure 53: Example of a trap. Photo by John Luck.

"The guys who had been living here for months sometimes became complacent. The 26th Marines were here when we arrived. This was their home, so they invited us in. We didn't provide any security; we were simply a reactionary force. When a reactionary force was needed, we would load up on the helicopters and take off. We would go do our duty, and then come back. At no time did we ever maintain any kind of perimeter defense here. Even when the siege happened during the Tet Offensive, they flew us out to get behind enemy positions and try to pin them between the two Marine units."

"When I joined the service in 1965, I didn't join because I wanted to go fight or contribute anything. I was trying to go to college and ran out of money, and I was looking for tuition assistance. The Navy had the best liars. I joined the Navy because they convinced me that I would have a pretty good quality of life. I didn't want to get into the Army because I'd heard about the Army, fighting in foxholes and living a dirty life. Therefore, I joined the Navy. I could see myself out on the high seas or in a Navy hospital. However, about a year and a half into my Navy experience, I was drafted into the Marine Corps. And I mean drafted. I did not volunteer to go be with the Marines. I tell everybody that I fought it, but I had to go anyway. Once there, I had an opportunity to join a team, and it was different from any team I had ever experienced. In the Navy, when the alarm sounded, you would go to your battle stations, but really it was just showing up and acting like you knew what you were doing. The Marine Corps actually made life miserable for the guys. I have a shirt at home that reads, *Marine Officers: Making Life Miserable Since 1775*. Marines have a different attitude. Look at their song. The *Marines' Hymn* summarizes what the Marine Corps is all about. *We fight our country's battles* and that's what they're taught to do."

Speaking to our Vietnam tour guide, Colonel Ballard said, "We came to help South Vietnam because our country was asked to come and help fight communism. Your country asked us to come over, and our young men (like you) came over to help free you and keep you free, so the South Vietnamese could be independent and have their own life. That was our only goal. We didn't have any enemies; I didn't know the North from the South. There was no way of knowing who the hell our enemies were. Up here in the north, most of the NVA were well-equipped, well-trained, and had uniforms. So, we had a little better target acquisition. We somewhat knew what our *friendlies* looked like. But we had none, since we didn't go into the villages very often."

"As grunts, the only thing we had was what we carried on our backs, in our pots, our pockets, and our pants. They gave us *rubber ladies* (air mattresses) when we first got there. We wouldn't carry them because they were worthless. I got rid of everything that I couldn't carry in order to lighten my load. I also had to carry medical equipment and water for the patients. The corpsman's duty was to be there to take care of the Marines and any other Americans that we ran across."

"We would sometimes medically treat the civilians, especially the kids. They would stumble into some of our exposed ordinances (i.e. bombs, claymores, or booby-trapped mines) that we had set ourselves. But a lot of the times they weren't stumbling. They were intentionally following us, trying to find stuff they could salvage. We'd leave food lying around and anything half eaten would become a meal. Some of our things that we threw away became recycled and recirculated. So, they were in and out of our area all of the time, trying to find a way to improve the quality of life that they had."

❝ We would take a hill or take a mountain, and then we'd give it up because we didn't have enough personnel to hold it. ❞

"I had no animosity or hard feelings. I didn't hate the Vietnamese. My job was one of a caregiver instead of a killer. The Marines had the ability to understand the mission. And the mission was to use survival skills, take the objectives, eliminate the problem and do it all over again."

One of the biggest problems, as Ballard explained, was sustainment. "We would take a hill or take a mountain, and then we'd give it up because we didn't have enough personnel to hold it. We might hold it for a few days, after fighting three to four days to take it, care for casualties, raise the flag, and then move on. Likely, the North Vietnamese would come in right behind us and take over the same ground. See, in combat there are strategic initiatives, and one of them was to maintain the high ground. If you can control the high ground, you can control everything around you. We knew we needed to maintain it, and unfortunately, we walked off."

After some broad explanation, Ballard got more specific with the class: "I'm going to share with you what an average day looked like for a combat grunt in northern I-Corps. Typically, Marines were constantly in a defensive posture. In order to maintain a good defense, you had to be aggressive sometimes, so we would go out in patrols. We'd gather intelligence and then pass it on to other units, especially if they were in the same area of operations. If we could capture somebody, our mission was interrogation. Really, we didn't have *friendlies*. We had some ARVNs with us, but most of the time they proved to be unreliable Northern sympathizers. Often they came with us to learn what we did and how we did it; then, they used it against us."

"Most of the time we operated without much of a perimeter. We would set up a hasty perimeter without concertina wire, without any security, so there was nothing between us and them. Nothing. We would establish fields of fire and were self-sustaining. We used everything we had available to us including aircraft and support with naval gunfire. The only mission that I ever saw was basic survival. I was the medical asset, to be used for medical treatment or medical advice."

"Besides communication, one of the things that we desperately needed was water. From the perspective of the corpsman, we needed the water to cool bodies down. We had heat casualties, heat stroke and heat exhaustion. Believe it or not, we found the best treatment was to vomit in the lake or river. And, of course, everyone wanted to get in the water. However, this posed a problem, because we would fill our canteens out of the same river; it was the water that we drank! We had halazone tablets and iodine tablets that we would put in the canteen to treat the water. Boy, that was some foul-tasting stuff! But after a while, you wouldn't drink it without a tablet. In fact, we were leery of any water that didn't taste like halazone."

"Another obstacle of being in the lake and crossing the rivers was the leeches. They would attach themselves to our bodies. We were told to tuck our trousers into our boots to keep the leeches out, but you couldn't get everybody to follow orders. We'd find leeches in private areas and anywhere there was skin. A leech would attach itself, and they were very hard to manage. Near Khe Sanh, there were different kinds of leeches depending on the water source. We often found really fat leeches; some were long and some were short and stubby, but they were all healthy. They had, perhaps, dined on other Marines as they passed through the waters!"

Ballard remembered how to get rid of leeches: "We had different techniques for getting rid of leeches. A lot of times we would light them to burn them out, much like dealing with a tick. We would try to irritate the leech so it would pull its head out and extract itself. Then we would kill it. We couldn't just yank them and leave the head in the body, because there would be a major infection. With the heat, the possibility of infection was extremely high, along with the likelihood of gangrene."

All of this fighting took place in an unforgiving environment. "The hills look pretty, but they're tough to climb." Pointing out places he remembered, Ballard continued, "That was our holding area up there. We had to seize the high ground, and we didn't use helicopters to get up there; we had to climb! Sometimes it would take us two or three days to climb one hill, and this depended on the vegetation growth, the enemy activity, the Marines' strength, and the heat. The climate up here was a little different from down South. In the morning, it was clear and cold, gradually heating up. By noon, we were almost at heat exhaustion stages. Our bodies would lose fluids, and we would start dehydrating. Staying hydrated was very much a problem. It would start cooling off after the sun went down and got extremely cold at night. There was such a swing in temperatures that the body couldn't get acclimated. The terrain caused another problem as we walked down a road. The enemy could be 10 feet or even just 5 feet inside the jungle growth on each side of the road, and you couldn't see them."

The VC had an advantage, as Ballard explained: "This was *their* country. They lived here and adapted to it a lot better than we did. They had been fighting all their lives, so they were well-trained in jungle warfare."

Living conditions didn't improve with time. Keeping the days straight took real ingenuity. Ballard noted, "We never had a doctor, and we never had a chaplain, so we had to fend for ourselves. Sunday became the day that we handed out orange malaria pills. Monday was a very important day—we changed underwear! We took a bath when we passed through the river or a creek. We had no luxury of extra water. All the water we had was what we could carry. I carried four canteens, which added a lot of weight."

"All we ever did was walk; we hardly ever got a ride. Once in a while we'd run into the tanks, and every one of us wanted to jump on. We were young, so it was a novelty to get on the tank and ride around on it. A whole lot easier than walking, we thought, but it became a big target, so there was a tradeoff. If they were going to shoot anything, it was going to be that tank, especially with a bunch of Marines hanging all over it."

Ballard explained to the group why footcare was a high priority: "We never had more than one pair of boots and usually no change of socks. When we could get socks, we kept everybody changing according to instructions, which was to keep your feet dry, aired out, and your socks changed. When we were sitting in a fixed area, we encouraged everyone to take their boots off and let their feet dry out. We had a lot of jungle rot; because we didn't have a place that we could call home for any period of time, we kept our boots on. Also, we were a reactionary force, so we never knew when we were going, and we didn't have time to get our boots on. It was always *hurry up, move out*."

In battle after battle, Ballard lost a lot of buddies, but he saved several, too. When asked what he had done to receive the Medal of Honor, he modestly told the student group, "The actual event took place right there in the hill fights around Khe Sanh. The day that I earned the medal was no different than any other day. That particular day I was bringing a Marine in over my shoulders, when a grenade came toward us. I hadn't realized that we were that close to a spider hole. (Figure 54) We were close enough for the enemy to throw a grenade in our path. I laid the Marine down, and I laid on top of him when it blew. The explosion took the pack off of my back, shredding

Figure 54: Spider hole. Photo by John Luck.

136

all my medical equipment, but I did not get injured. But there was a Marine lying there whose legs had been blown off. And then another Marine whose face had been torn open. I had more casualties there, so I immediately started working on the airway and tried to control the hemorrhage."

"I had never used a tourniquet. I was a surgical tech, and I actually went in with Kelly forceps and hemostats and tied off the arteries instead of trying to use compression bandages. I never found that compression bandages worked all that well. The first time I had to cut them off of the dead in order to put them on the living, I realized this wasn't working. When I went back for supplies one time, I went over to central supply, and I *borrowed* some equipment. I made up my own surgical kit. *What would you do if you have a battle casualty coming in, and there are no battle dressings?* You try to figure out what's going on, and you have to get arteries tied off. Our job was to do whatever we could to save their lives, then get them back to the nurses and medical assets, whatever that might have been."

"Once, when I had started working on the patient that had his leg blown off, another grenade came in, and it hit me on the right side of my helmet and fell down beside me. It was a ChiCom grenade, which looked like a potato masher with a wooden handle; it didn't look like any of our grenades. I grabbed it and flung it back out of the bomb crater in the direction it came from. I got rid of it. Well, it wasn't very much longer until the Marine that was behind me, one of my patients, hollered at me *Doc, grenade!* I turned around and there was another ChiCom grenade lying there. So, I yelled *grenade,* and I dove for it. The grenade was just outside my reach. I grabbed it and pulled it up underneath my chest. I was thinking, *I can save their lives.* I knew that if it blew it would kill all of us."

"I had really never seen the cause and effect of a chest wound by a grenade. I had seen bodies blown apart, but it was usually the limbs. My moves were more reactionary than prior planning. I don't know what went through my brain, except that *I had to take some other action.* So, I rolled up on my patient, and I flung the grenade out from the bomb crater. When it went out of the bomb crater, it detonated with an air burst. The concussion part came down, and all the shrapnel was outside of the bomb crater. No American was injured, for which I'm grateful. I admit when I threw the grenade up, my second thought was, *Hell, I might have thrown it on my own guys!* The official citation says what I did: *I reached out and jumped on the grenade, it failed to go off, and so I continued to treat the Marines.*"

Figure 55: President Nixon and Don Ballard at Medal of Honor ceremony. Photo courtesy of Don Ballard, PETP 2014.

"I was a young kid when I stood by President Nixon at the White House. (Figure 55) I cried. I had lost a lot of friends. I had survivor's guilt. I felt bad that I had lived and that so many of my other corpsmen didn't. When I put that medal on, I wear it for the other corpsmen who didn't come home. I wear it for the Marines who served with me, who saved my life several times. I wear it for all veterans who served; whether they got wounded or not, they placed themselves in harm's way. I don't really feel like I did anything heroic. Rather, I think it was something borderline stupid, but I realized that I was the only one capable of doing anything for the rest of the guys. At that moment, I felt we were all going to die. I've analyzed it for several years, thinking, *Why did you give me a medal for doing this?* I didn't even know why I was getting a medal, until they read it in front of the President. I had to do what I could do because nobody else could do anything. I was just doing my job. The most important thing to me is that I served with a group of Marines who thought enough of me that they would recommend me for the Medal of Honor."

"A lot of times, we knew we had killed more bodies than we could find. At one point, we found where the enemy soldiers were carrying their dead. They would tie the dead man's hands and feet to a pole. Then with a person at the front and one at the back, with the pole on their shoulders, they would carry off their dead. We hoped we'd find out that we were more effective than first reported because, at that time, the Marines were very interested in headcount. We had to justify our existence and effectiveness. If we weren't getting the body counts, then we had to go out and do more."

"Right across from where we stopped at Camp Carroll, we had killed about eighty North Vietnamese. I don't know that I can find it again, but I think it's probably right that we do share that information. We wanted to know about our POWs, MIAs, and KIAs, and I think they probably would want to know, too. Right in that area, we buried about eighty casualties, North Vietnamese."

With all the casualty information, Ballard shared insight: "By the way, it was never our objective to win the War. Isn't that terrible? You come over here, thinking you're going to fight, but none of us could control the War. We were just a small part of it. If you're getting shot at, it doesn't matter if it's called a police action or anything else. It was war to the individuals on the ground."

"I want to give credit right now to any aviators we have on this bus, because no matter what their call sign, what their duty, or what their assignment was that day, if we got on the horn and asked for medevac, every bird flying out there would drop in and (if they could) pick up our casualties. They weren't always medevacs; they were anything that was flying. I have a lot of respect for any of the helicopter pilots who were up there helping us."

Ballard offered a comparison lesson: "During the Vietnam War, our whole effort of medical treatment changed. In the Korean War, they would try to medevac as soon as they could, with ground ambulances to the rear. Well, we had no ground ambulances and had to wait on the helicopter. If we didn't have helicopters flying, we had to keep the patients not only alive, but in as good of a condition as we could, while waiting for medevac. The sooner you could get a patient back to normal, within that first hour—*The Golden Hour*—the better the survival rate. We had to sustain life and keep them overnight or maybe two days. Overall, we had a better survival rate than they did in Korea and World War II. These kids today have an even better survival rate than we had, with better training and better equipment. They have a lot of stuff that we never envisioned or had available to us."

Ballard explained the risks of being a corpsman: "It was my job to go get the patient, the Marine, and either treat him there or drag him back to the bomb crater or some place fairly safe. A lot of the corpsmen got killed because they ran up to where the Marine was shot and started treating him right there. The problem with that is that you can't protect yourself if you've got your head up. I've never been able to lay down beside a man and treat him. You have to be up over him to treat the guy. Most of the corpsmen got killed with head shots. It was safer to either fireman's carry or drag the wounded away from where he was shot and treat him at an alternate location. The extent of the injury, whether an airway compromise or uncontrolled hemorrhage or whatever, dictated how far away we could go from the site. Most certainly, we would move from where he was shot, hoping that we could hide from the enemy."

"If you remember, they (enemy) had spider holes. Many times it was just a lid on the tunnel. *Can you imagine someone sticking a gun out of this terrain here, shooting you, and then dropping back down in?* You'd be trying to figure out where the hell the round came from, you know? It was a new kind of warfare for us. We welcomed Agent Orange at the time because it got rid of the foliage, and we could see the enemy better. We didn't realize that if it could kill animals, bugs, and plants, that it was probably going to kill us. We would rub it all over ourselves, just trying to make sure we didn't get any bugs on us."

"I think it is important for kids to understand what war is all about: blood, guts, pain, suffering, and real-world activities. I will tell you of one horrific incident for me. We were moving from point A to point Z, going through Bravo and Charlie checkpoints. We were climbing a mountain and had to set up for overnight with a hasty defense perimeter. We were clustered back to back, so that we could see each side of the ridgeline. We had visual contact of the guys on the other ridges. I positioned myself on the very top of the ridge, so that if anyone was wounded, I could run either way. The battle cry for a wounded Marine was *corpsman up!* We also had our food and water and basic supplies stacked there for overnight, ready to pick up the next day as we moved out. We were all tired, and it was a quiet night, no activity. But we were also mindful that each of us must have watch duty in case the enemy slipped up on us."

> **" I think it is important for kids to understand what war is all about: blood, guts, pain, suffering, and real-world activities. "**

"The next morning we awoke to small arms fire, like an AK-47, different than our M16s. I couldn't tell where it was coming from and began looking around to see if anyone in my area of operation needed me. The man down in front of me had a machine gun, and he was shot. I saw him fall over as I grabbed my bag and started running. When I got to him, another Marine had pushed him out of the way and taken over his gun, returning fire. I knew there was an enemy right in front of us, so I jumped in a hole to treat the guy. Almost instantly, the other Marine was shot right square in the forehead. The shot was a small hole, but it blew the back of his brains out. He fell over on me, and when he did, all the blood and brains came out of his helmet and hit me right in the face. Both the Marine under me and on top of me were dead."

"Very soon the six North Vietnamese soldiers who were firing on us were standing over our position. One of them stood with a weapon ready to shoot, while the other five were picking up our machine gun and ammo. I laid there playing dead. I had my flack jacket on, which helped me to make my breath really shallow. My eyes were mostly closed, but I could still see through my eyelids. I was so scared and didn't know what to do. I just laid there, waiting for what would happen next. When they turned to leave, one of them shot all three of us. I got shot in the abdomen. The other guys were already dead, and I think that because I had blood and guts on me, they thought I was, too. They wanted to see if any of us would react, and none of us moved."

"After they had left and walked up the hill, I thought, *I've got to do something; I can't just lay here. And there are probably guys who need me.* I pushed the Marine off me. I had no weapon except the K-bar (Marine Corps knife) strapped inside my boot. When I got to the top of the hill, the guy who had shot us was going through our food. He hadn't heard me. I knocked him to the ground, jumped on him, held his mouth, and slit his throat, laying on him until he bled out. I wanted to make sure he was dead. Once he was dead, I drug him off his rifle and took his blood-covered AK-47 and went up the hill to get involved in the fight. I killed other people up there. And many of our brave soldiers died, too. They deserve recognition; they deserve the Medal of Honor!"

STUDENT RESPONSE

Sara Cochran reflected on her experiences: "I knew I would gain a better understanding of the Vietnam War and that I would get close to my veteran. But I had no idea that my interest in the War would soar and that the friendship developed with my veteran and all veterans would be lifelong. I'll never be able to explain to anyone those feelings I experienced in Vietnam. But I can talk about the man I accompanied back to Vietnam," wrote Sara Cochran. "Colonel Donald E.—*Doc*—Ballard enlisted in the Navy in 1965 but was soon drafted into the Marine Corps in 1966. Doc had no idea at the time he enlisted that he would be going to Vietnam. He had been told at a young age, *To live in a free country, you must pay the price.* So, he did as he was taught and went to serve his country and work for freedom."

"When we first arrived in Saigon, I was stunned by the humidity. Entering the city, I remember the smell being different than I was accustomed to in the Ozarks. The culture, life, and people were also different.

People rode mopeds with surgical masks around their faces, telephone lines were tangled in big messes, and the traffic had no rules. I would describe it as chaos, but to them it is normal."

"While being on a plane for almost 38 hours, I did not have much time with my veteran, Doc Ballard. However, while waiting to board the airplane in Kansas City, I got to sit down with him, have a nice conversation, and know him better. I had first met Doc the prior spring semester at the College. He had spoken at a convocation with two other veterans, and I had enjoyed the privilege of meeting him and having dinner with him. However, this time it was just the two of us on a more personal level. He told me how he did not want to return to Vietnam because of the severe post-traumatic stress disorder (PTSD) he has suffered most of his life. He asked me, *Why return to a place you have spent your whole life trying to forget?*"

"As we sat there together, I learned how much Doc and I have in common. For instance, my connection to the Vietnam War is that my father served as a medic. When my father was deployed to Vietnam, he was separated from his unit and, unfortunately, the ship he was supposed to be on got blown up. So, they shipped my dad back to Fort Sam Houston, Texas, where he was a supervisor at Brooke Army Medical Center. Doc also served as a medic in the War, specializing in orthopedic and neurological surgeries. My dad focused on surgeries his whole life. To be matched up with a veteran so similar to my dad was amazing, and I knew I would have the best time with him. When I entered the streets of Saigon with Doc and all the other veterans, students, staff, and administrators, I knew I never wanted the experience to end."

 Most of what the press reported was not accurate about the War and our veterans confirmed that.

Sara continued, "Vietnam was beautiful—the trees, the animals. The people loved to look at us and wave; most were very friendly and excited to see us. At our hotel welcome dinner, Doc wore his Medal of Honor and explained to everyone the meaning, history, and privilege of wearing the Medal. It was amazing to listen to and learn from this man; he was extremely knowledgeable. That night I realized I had found my true hero and was so blessed to accompany him for two whole weeks."

"After we explored the region of the Mekong Delta, we traveled back to Saigon to stay at The Rex Hotel. The Rex is historic, and it is where the CIA and the media stayed during the Vietnam War. This is where the *Five O'Clock Follies* were held. Most of what the press reported was not accurate about the War, and our veterans confirmed that."

"As we traveled from place to place, Doc and I would discuss what had happened. He informed me, but he mentioned that *he was also being educated.* He was never in the southern part during the war, so he was learning with me. Doc made sure to have humor in most every situation. He told me *he had to learn to laugh because he spent so much time in tears during the War.* Laughing is Doc's specialty; everywhere we went we were laughing together."

"In Vietnam there were not many historical buildings or war sites that had been retained or restored. At the Cu Chi tunnels (Figure 56), we got to see what the VC did on a daily basis—what they used for

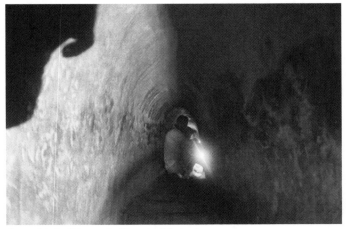

Figure 56 : Cu Chi tunnels. Photo by John Luck.

attacks. As we traveled through the area, the sound of AK-47s and M16s got louder and louder. There was a shooting range where people could experience what it was like to fire such weapons. *Those weapons are what we mainly used on enemy attacks,* Doc explained to me. He also stood by me and explained differences in these enemy attacks compared to the enemy attacks up North. He told me, *Traps* (Figure 57) *were very much real, but these traps were never to kill you, just to infect you.* I had asked Doc how he felt about the gunfire going off and he calmly responded, *It's the same feeling, except I'm not hitting the deck for safety.* I knew war was awful, but just to hear those noises was disturbing to us students. I could never imagine being in an actual firefight and surviving to tell the story. I'm sure these veterans all felt the same emotion when they heard them, but they still kept going. They are true heroes."

Figure 57: Traps. Photo by John Luck.

Sara Cochran continued her experience in great detail: "We went to a war museum. Doc helped me as we walked through the museum and explained everything we saw. He reminded me, *This museum is the Vietnamese side of the story.* There was a lot of propaganda in the museum, as well as everywhere else in Vietnam. Doc explained the story of how our servicemen never knew friend from foe. He told me about a cottage the Marines occupied. A little Vietnamese boy came in to shine the Marines' boots for them, and Doc and the rest treated him with candy. The children had not eaten American candy, so they really enjoyed that. However, one day the boy came in with a satchel (which carried a charge), threw it, and ran. The Marines ran out for safety and shot the boy. *You could not trust anyone,* he explained to me."

"I'm confident every war has two sides of the story, especially this war. Some of the veterans asked our guide what he was taught in school about the War. Unfortunately, he never gave us a clear response. Doc explained that, like a Democrat versus a Republican, you could not tell a communist from a South Vietnamese."

"We drove to Da Nang, and it was gorgeous; it surprised me how pretty it was. Da Nang is where Doc came into the country, stayed three nights in a plywood tent, and ate monkey from Monkey Mountain! We all got the chance to experience the beach, which Doc shared was much more enjoyable than the last time he was there."

"Doc explained the brotherhood that was created in Vietnam. He told me that he can say there's no brotherhood like the Marines because he'd been in the Navy and Army as well. He never failed to mention the jobs of other servicemen. He reminded me that people take things for granted. He said, *We fail to acknowledge great people, and your generation needs to learn to recognize them.* On one specific day during the War, Doc treated his Marines in a bomb crater that was deep enough to protect them. However, the enemy was apparently close to where he was located. He shared that one of his Marines yelled his name, and as he looked over he noticed a grenade close by. Doc immediately dove for the grenade, and his plan was not to throw the grenade, simply because he didn't think he had the time. He tucked the grenade under his chest, assuming it would go off. When it didn't immediately detonate, he threw the grenade away from his unit. Because of his heroic action (in 1968), on May 14, 1970, President Richard Nixon presented Colonel Ballard with our nation's highest honor, the Medal of Honor. Doc also received three purple hearts and was wounded eight times in combat. Doc explained to us that *he wears the Medal of Honor for every brother and sister who never came home from Vietnam and for the people that saved his own life.*"

"Doc is a special person. Being a corpsman, one would have to be," Sara believes. She continues, "Because Doc's main job was to save lives, it was hard to protect his own, so he depended on and trusted his Marines for protection. He loved his military brothers and sisters; in Vietnam, they grew as close as a family. Having to treat one of them was hard, but he did his best and depended on God to help him. Doc is a true hero. He did things I could never imagine doing, and he did it for everyone back home in America. As Doc explained, *My ordinary day turned extraordinary; doing my job made all the difference that day."*

Like most veterans, Doc suffered from the War. Vietnam was hard and I will never be able to put myself in his shoes. However, I can listen to, learn from, and show concern for all veterans. As civilians, we fail to realize how much these simple acts mean to veterans. After the Vietnam War, Doc joined the Army, spending most of his time in the States and retiring as a full Colonel. Doc explained to me that difficult situations make you stronger and that no man left Vietnam the same as when he arrived. As Nathalia Crane's poem "The Colors" puts it, *You can't choose your battlefield, God does that for you, but you can plant a standard where a standard never flew."*[3]

❝ Doc is a true hero. He did things I could never imagine doing, and he did it for everyone back home in America. ❞

TOPIC SUMMARY

Doc Ballard, as well as Colonel Duncan and John Ligato, fought in the northern-most region (I-Corps) of South Vietnam. These battles were bloody and difficult. Places like Khe Sanh, Con Thien, and Hué received worldwide media attention. As a combat medic in the hill country around Khe Sanh, Ballard had to daily deal with death or even face death himself. Battles in the hills (Figure 45, page 105) around Khe Sanh started months before the Tet Offensive and continued until April of the following year, 1968.

About ten days before Tet, Khe Sanh came under heavy mortar and rocket attack. In the United States, Washington, D.C. was on edge; many politicians were actually discussing the possibility of Khe Sanh becoming like another Dien Bien Phu. Reporters eager for a scoop surveyed copies of two books that had been written about this battle, where the French had been defeated by the communists. Peter Braestrup in the *Big Story*, described how the press kept irritating the Marines by bringing attention to Dien Bien Phu and Khe Sanh. Actually, there were major differences between the two battles and the military forces of each country. The United States had far superior air power, closer proximity to friendly forces, a better aerial supply, and better evacuation procedures by way of helicopters. Dien Bien Phu had become a fascinating subject for the media, because a loss to the NVA would have repercussions for American policy and politics. The "Dien Bien Phu Syndrome" took on a life of its own. None of it worked for the NVA as they suffered horrendous casualties. General Westmoreland reported in an April 12, 1968, issue of *TIME* magazine, that the NVA suffered 15,000 KIA.

For his selfless service around Khe Sanh, Doc Ballard received the Medal of Honor. Sara Cochran, the student who accompanied him to Vietnam said, "To hear Doc tell it, he and the other veterans were *just doing their jobs.* Doc told me that he wears the Medal of Honor for every brother who was lost in Vietnam and for those who saved his own life. He is a modest man and was reluctant in telling us all of his heroic story. Doc said very little about his *three* purple hearts."[4]

Don Ballard is an ordinary man who rendered extraordinary service beyond the call of duty. He more than deserves the nation's highest award for valor, the Medal of Honor.

CLASS TOPIC 6: HUÉ 1968 (I-CORPS)

Goodbye, Marine...he woke up on a truck with body parts...

INSTRUCTOR: SGT JOHN LIGATO, USMC[1]

John Ligato recalls: "I was the first person in my large, Italian family to go to college, and I was the first person in my large, Italian family to get expelled from college!" Having been born in Philadelphia, Pennsylvania, he grew up poor in material things but rich in childhood wonder; in his eyes, he was the happiest kid in the world. Ligato had a warrior's heart. Although he didn't want to be drafted, at age 19, he surprised everyone when he joined the United States Marine Corps. His life would never be the same.

John led his platoon, fighting in the I-Corps Tactical Zone of Vietnam. After going to language school to learn Vietnamese for interrogation purposes, he was sent to Con Thien, near the location where Colonel Bill Duncan was serving. It was in the upper reaches of I-Corps (Figure 61) that John Ligato saw heavy combat. Being so close to the DMZ exposed Ligato and his fellow Marines to 200-300 rounds per day of enemy rockets, artillery, and mortars. For several weeks, they endured heavy NVA attacks. Finally, half of John's company (150 Marines) was lifted off in choppers and taken to Phu Bai, where they showered and got hot food for the first time in months. But the respite didn't last very long. Shortly thereafter, the captain, who was company commander, loaded all the Marines on trucks to help another unit in distress. When John asked the captain how long it would take, the captain replied, "You'll be back by noon."

Many Marines who went north to Hué City never came back. The battle that ensued was one of the most vicious and deadly of the Tet

Offensive, if not the entire Vietnam War. The Marines did prevail in reaching the U.S. Military Assistance Command (MACV) compound, (Figure 58) but at a high cost. The battle of Hué unfolded as follows: on the outskirts of the city, Ligato's Company was attacked and surrounded by NVA regulars. Even though they were surrounded, Ligato and his men fought their way out and continued up HWY 1 to Hué City.

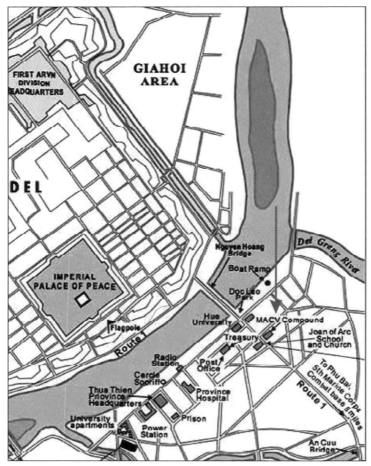

Figure 58: MACV Compound city map. Adapted from public domain.

Unbeknownst to Ligato, any hope of returning to Phu Bai faded quickly, as a 31-day battle unfolded. It was one ugly scene after another. When they got to the MACV compound, dead bodies littered the landscape.

The Marines were told to proceed to the Citadel, where an ARVN general and his troops were holed up and being overrun. Intelligence received from Da Nang had reported that the NVA was just an "oversized company," but Ligato could see NVA soldiers all over the place. Still, the battalion commander ordered the Marines to cover a small, nearly 40-foot wide bridge, while the NVA was firing every weapon they had down on the Marines. This intelligence lapse cost many Marines their lives, but Ligato survived; the Marines prevailed, albeit at a heavy price. In the end, it had been some two hundred Marines against several thousand NVA. Hué was just one of the cities attacked during the Tet Offensive. Da Nang, Saigon, and most major cities came under fire, as did scores of smaller towns and outposts, but the NVA was repelled.

Figure 59: The 6th NVA Regimental Flag, captured by John Ligato at the Battle of Hué. Photo courtesy of John Ligato, PETP 2014.

John Ligato received his first Purple Heart at Con Thien. He proceeded to earn more honors with the Cross of Gallantry, two Presidential Unit Citations, a Combat Action Ribbon, and several Vietnam Campaign Ribbons before he was done. John has recently been nominated for the Silver Star for his actions at Hué, some 53 years ago. He was also responsible for capturing the 6th NVA Regimental Flag, which is on display in the Marine Corps Museum. (Figure 59)

After his discharge from the Marine Corps, Ligato went back to school and earned a bachelor's degree in secondary education and a master's degree in educational psychology. He then spent ten years working with developmentally disabled children and 23 years as a special agent for the FBI. Eight years of his career with the FBI were spent in deep cover and five years in a pilot special operations group. He now teaches homeland security classes at Campbell University in North Carolina, while at the same time writing novels.

John Ligato and his wife of fifty years, Lorraine, have two daughters, Gia and Dani, who are adopted from Korea.

Figure 60: Veteran John Ligato and student host Devan Spady. Photo by John Luck.

STUDENT HOST: DEVAN SPADY

Student host Devan Spady (Figure 60) was born in Chesapeake, Virginia. She describes herself as "artsy," and this is reflected in her studies: "I am majoring in both musical theatre and studio art, with an emphasis on computer art. I work on campus with the Jones Theatre Company and off campus at The Disney Store. I love acting, singing, drawing, painting, and simply being able to express myself through visual arts. My ultimate dream is to animate movies for the Walt Disney Animation Studios."

Spady continues: "I am a child of the United States Marine Corps, as both of my fathers (biological and step) are Marines. All the men on both my mother's and my fathers' side of the family (and step family) have been fighting for this country since the American War for Independence."

Applying for the Patriotic Education Travel Program was a natural step for Devan Spady. She was especially motivated by her granddad, Danny Darden, a Purple Heart recipient, who was disabled due to his military service. Spady recalls, "He died at age 53, and I want his legacy to survive. Granddad loved God, country, family, and music."

"When my granddad was getting ready to graduate from high school, the draft was beginning. Knowing that he would for certain be drafted, he raised his hand and joined the United States Marine Corps. As far as he was concerned, *If I'm going to be forced to fight, I'm going to fight alongside the very best.* He left very shortly for boot camp at Parris Island, followed by the long trip to Vietnam. The 18-year-old hit the ground running as a Howitzer operator/loader, and his world changed forever. Tet was somewhat of a surprise for my granddad, and Khe Sanh seemed like a never-ending battle. He was injured by shrapnel and nearly deafened by an exploding Howitzer, losing all of his friends along the way. When he woke up in a military hospital, he thought to himself, *Why did I live when they died?* Guilt would remain his constant companion for the rest of his life. Even when he came home from the War, after being spat upon, he refused to sleep in his own bed. Instead, he slept on the floor of his bedroom, believing that he was unworthy of comfort when his friends had paid the ultimate price. He eventually allowed himself to love and to marry. Still, he suffered."

Devon explained, "Not much was known about post-traumatic stress disorder (PTSD) back then. Allow me to tell you what it was like growing up in my grandmother's house. Granddad often screamed out in the night. On more than one occasion, he tried to strangle Granny in her sleep, not knowing who she was. His pain was so severe that he was eventually awarded disability from the Veterans Administration since he could no longer work. My mom watched as her father, the vibrant man she had once known, turned more and more into someone she no longer recognized. He became an alcoholic, and eventually there was no turning back. Danny Darden died of a massive heart attack on the kitchen floor at the age of 53."

"Granddad used to call me, *Partner.* The man who only cared about God, family, country, and music has left behind a granddaughter who also loves God, family, and country and whose major at College of the Ozarks involves music. I will be the first person in my family to graduate from college, and I'm here all because of one man who survived Vietnam."

HUÉ BACKGROUND

Hué was one of the largest cities in Vietnam and strategically located. One of a long string of coastal cities (Figure 61), Hué was the long-standing cultural hub of Vietnam, as well as its capital for nearly 150

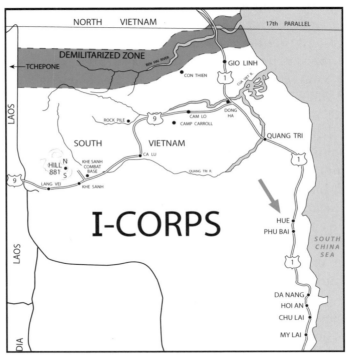

Figure 61: I-Corps and coastal areas. Adapted from public domain.

years. North from Hué, along Highway 1, were Quang Tri, Dong Ha, Gio Linh and the DMZ. South from Hué, via Highway 1, were Phu Bai, Da Nang, Chu Lai, Mỹ Lai, Quang Ngai—all sandy, coastal locations in I-Corps. Most of these locales played an important role in the War. But it was the Battle of Hué that turned out to be the deadliest of the Tet Offensive battles, lasting from January 30, 1968, through March

2, 1968, when Hué was declared secure.[2] In fact, the fighting for control of Hué, as well as Khe Sanh, was the focal point of media interest and—many believe—media irresponsibility. The Tet Offensive was communicated to the American public to be a great surprise and a great loss. In a military sense, it was neither.

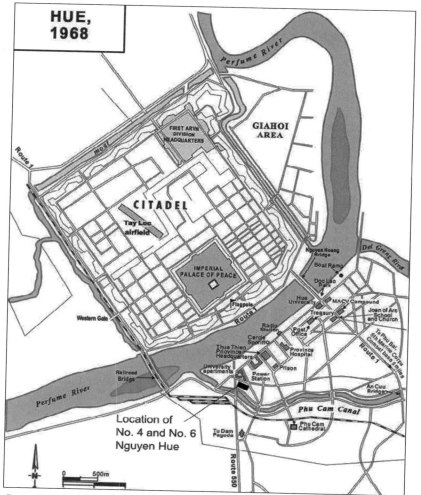

Figure 62: Hué. Adapted from public domain.

Hué was under the command of the ARVN 1st Division in the northwest corner of the Citadel, located north of the Perfume River, which divided the city in halves. (Figure 62) The Citadel was a 19th century fortress surrounded by a moat and protected by a thick outer wall. The MACV was located south of the Perfume River. Early in the morning of January 31, Hué was attacked by two North Vietnam Regiments. The ARVN compound in the Citadel was hit by the 6th Regiment, and the MACV compound was hit by the 4th. Neither was prepared for the magnitude of the attack. But the U.S. and ARVN defenders held on and radioed for help. Hearing this distress, the USMC back in Phu Bai sent a relief column, but it was far too small.[3] Company A, 1st Battalion, 1st Marines faced heavy combat with almost insurmountable odds. Point man in this first group of Marines was John Ligato, who shared his story with student hosts and veterans from College of the Ozarks.

The Marines fighting for their lives in Hué did not know about the North Vietnamese attacks occurring throughout Vietnam. The extent of these attacks, most of which were over in a few hours or a few days, was no doubt a surprise. General William C. Westmoreland (MACV Commander) later quoted a document that the 101st Airborne Division captured in November 1967 from the North Vietnamese Central Headquarters. It stated, "the time might be near for a general offensive and general uprising."[4] This document provided no date but did describe what was later reflected in the Tet Offensive. According to General Westmoreland, few officials or media paid much attention to it.

The buildup of enemy troops at Khe Sanh in late 1967 suggested the communists wanted to turn Khe Sanh into a Dien Bien Phu II. President Johnson became obsessed with this thought, so Khe Sanh became the focus of American concern. General Westmoreland supported the President's position for quite some time, which affected the distribution of troops elsewhere (such as Hué). Many U.S. troops were already on high alert in I-Corps and other zones. The idea that the attacks of the Tet Offensive were a total shock is disingenuous, if not downright dishonest. General Westmoreland specifically recalled that General Fred Weyand had detected more enemy movements toward Saigon and asked Westmoreland to shift more American troops toward the city, which he did. In short, General Westmoreland had reason to expect a major enemy offensive was coming, but he thought it would actually occur right before the Tet celebration started. Meanwhile, back in the States, Senators Kennedy and Fulbright were promoting a bombing halt because of NVA hints of peace talks, likely a diversionary tactic. General Westmoreland objected because he judged the enemy to be planning a major effort to win a spectacular battlefield success on the eve of Tet.[5] What turned out to be a real surprise was the ability of the North Vietnamese to infiltrate so many NVA/VC troops into most of the major towns and cities in the south. This was one of their few successes. Other than the major battles at Khe Sanh and Hué, the Tet Offensive was more of a Tet Flop, with the communists suffering tremendous losses on the battlefields countrywide. The major casualty of the Tet Offensive was public opinion in the United States. The true victories during Tet remained untold for a long time.

 ## INSTRUCTOR REFLECTIONS

Veteran John Ligato recalled: "My company was within the 1st Marine Division, 1st Marine Regiment, 1st Marine Battalion, Alpha Company, 1st Platoon, 1st Squad, and I walked point. So a lot of ones!" As point man, John Ligato was also the number one target.

He told his story to students and veterans alike, and it was riveting: "We had been at Con Thien in October of '67, where we had conducted a lot of operations in rice paddies. So, we were used to combat in jungles, mountains, and rice paddies."

"On January 30, we had taken casualties in Quang Tri, so we were flown to Phu Bai (Figure 61), south of Hué, for some rest and relaxation. We had neither taken showers nor had hot chow in weeks. So half of the company—a Marine Corps company is around 300—lifted off in choppers and landed in Phu Bai. The other half of the company remained in Quang Tri province. I happened to be in the first bunch that went to Phu Bai. I took a shower, and we had a hooch (a tent with a plywood floor), and this was like the Hilton or Ritz Carlton to us."

"Around midnight Phu Bai got rocketed, which for us was no big deal. We had already been in Con Thien where we had encountered thousands over a month's time. It was the start of the Vietnamese Lunar New Year, Tet. It's like the Mardi Gras in the United States, a countrywide celebration and a big deal with lots of fireworks. When we got rocketed, we jumped in the holes there. We were making jokes because we were supposed to be in a secure base. We were salty; we were mud Marines, in the literal and figurative sense. My socks were wet so I took my socks off. I had two bandoliers of ammo. All the officers had remained in Quang Tri except for our company commander, Gordon Batcheller. At approximately 4:00 a.m., Batcheller told us we were going to load up on trucks and help a military assistance command (MAC) unit. I had asked him, *How long are we going to be, Skipper?* He said, *We will be back by noon.* So, being salty, I didn't put my socks on, and I took one bandolier of ammo, no canteen."

"We loaded up in trucks, we waited, we sat in the sun, and as good Marines do, we complained. The company commander said, *Well, there's a MACV compound at Hué City and it's in a little bit of trouble. You'll be back by noon.* I'll never forget that…yeah, by noon…I never got back!"

"Well, we got into the outskirts of Hué City and met six Marine Corps tanks. We were ordered to get on the tanks, and some trucks followed. About a mile outside of Hué City, we got rocketed and hit with small arms fire. The tank in front of me blew up. I jumped off the right side of my tank, and our gunnery sergeant jumped off the left side. I could see that my friend Pat Fraleigh was hit. I grabbed the radio man, who had been on the front of the first tank. He had taken a direct hit and his legs were gone; he just had stumps! He didn't know when I dragged him into a courtyard. He wasn't bleeding much; his legs seemed cauterized. He kept wanting to boost up, and I kept saying, *You're ok.* He was very lucid. He was a lot more lucid than I was. *We've got to move now; we've got to move.* The corpsmen came, and they were tagging guys all over the place with no time for normal triage. My friend, Pat, was dragged by the gunny into a hooch where he tried to pack the bleeding. Pat was bleeding severely. According to Pat years later, all he remembered is the gunny couldn't stop the bleeding and he said, *Goodbye, Marine,* and he put a poncho over him. Then, the next thing he remembered was he woke up on a truck with body parts and dead Marines."

"We continued north on Highway 1, and there was a little creek that had a bridge over it. As soon as we hit the other side of that waterway, we got hit again with everything—automatic weapons and rockets. There was a ditch running alongside the road, and it had maybe two feet of water in it. The firing that came at us was from the left, the west side. We were firing back and proceeding along the ditch, trying to get to and save the MACV compound. What made matters worse was that to the right side were open rice paddies. Then, we got word that the NVA had cut off Highway 1 back to Phu Bai. So, try to understand our dilemma: we were going north and getting hit from the west. We couldn't go east, and we couldn't go back south. (Figure 61) We proceeded on toward Hué City, and right outside of Hué there were some houses, like suburbs, and more houses the further in we went. There was nowhere to go."

"Our captain, Captain Batcheller, the only officer with us, saw a Marine lying on the street. We were in a ditch beside the street. The Marine was dead, and Captain Batcheller ran out and put his body over the Marine. Then Batcheller got hit so hard he flew up in the air. So three of us went out and got him. As we were carrying him back, the guy across from me got hit in the leg. Captain Batcheller, losing blood, stuck his head up and announced, *Don't drop me.* We didn't, and to this day, he's alive. He was my best man and attended my 25th wedding anniversary. He was horribly, horribly wounded and still walks with a limp."

John Ligato shared details of another's exemplary efforts during the Battle at Hué: "A company is commanded by a captain. We had no lieutenants, no captains, no majors. Therefore, Gunnery Sergeant John Canley became the commanding officer. Finally, about fifty years later, retired Sergeant Major Canley (Figure 63) was awarded the Medal of Honor by President Donald J. Trump. This recognition was an exhaustive process;

Figure 63 (left to right): Dr. Marci Linson, Sgt. Maj. Eddie Neas, MOH recipient Sgt. Maj. John Canley, Dr. Jerry C. Davis, Sgt. John Ligato, MOH recipient Col. Don Ballard. Photo courtesy of Bryan Cizek.

his paperwork got lost. He had a Navy Cross; I have been working 13 years to upgrade his Navy Cross, and it finally did happen."

John further explained the scene at Hué: "Canley took command of Alpha Company, and his executive officer (XO) was an E-5 by the name of Alfredo Gonzalez, a young, quiet kid from Mexico. Because of so many casualties, we had lance corporals who were squad leaders; we had corporals who were platoon leaders. We had 150 Marines, but now we were more like 110. So the gunnery sergeant, with Sergeant Gonzalez, charged the machine gun positions and threw grenades, and we got through into Hué. After that, there was a lull in the fighting. In my mind I was thinking, *That was the worst firefight I've been in, and I'm glad it's over.* I had no idea there were 10,000 North Vietnamese there. That was the beginning of a 31-day battle, and that was one of the better days at Hué!"

"We proceeded to the MACV compound. There were very few Americans there. There were Australians; they had one doctor, civilians, and intelligence personnel. They had withstood a lot, with their walls having been breached three times. There were dead bodies all over and around MACV. When we got there, those inside the compound came out and were cheering us. Again, I had no idea there were 10,000 NVA around us! We then fought to the Perfume River. (Figure 64) Golf Company came in behind us—Golf 2/5 with 150 Marines, also under-sized. They were assigned to cross the bridge first. They were headed toward the Citadel, and there was a big NVA flag flying with hundreds and hundreds and hundreds, I mean probably thousands of NVA troops on the other side. The River (Figure 62) was pretty big. I had never seen that many of the enemy, and they had all the weapons we did. I asked the gunnery sergeant, *Gunny, are we going to get any air or artillery support?* His response, *No, Ligato. It's a historical city. They don't want to damage it.* He said, *Intel thinks there's just an oversized company of NVA here.* That points to one of the greatest intelligence failures of the War—how the communists moved thousands of NVA into South Vietnam on Tet and no one knew it. And they just didn't attack Hué; they attacked Da Nang, Saigon, and every other major city in Vietnam. Hué was just sort of their prized jewel, Hué City."

"I found out later that Colonel Marcus Gravel tried to tell Da Nang,

Figure 64: John Ligato walking along the Perfume River. Photo by John Luck.

our Intel Center, that there were more than just a few hundred NVA on the north side of the bridge. Intel was getting pressure from an ARVN general on the other side, who was surrounded. So there was political pressure to go help this general. They ordered Golf Company to cross the bridge. At this point, I was right by the bridge, with the gunny. I remember thinking to myself, *This is a narrow bridge.* Coming down on the bridge were rockets, mortars, and automatic weapons fire. They were throwing everything at us. Colonel Gravel twice tried to tell Da Nang, *You don't want to do this, I'm here!* They demanded, *Either you order that company across, or we'll relieve you.* I talked to Marcus Gravel before he died, and that was one of the things he regretted most—that he ordered Golf Company 2/5 to cross the bridge. Try to imagine a narrow pathway and nowhere to go. They went across, and it was terrible. We were running to the bridge and dragging bodies back. They had no way of getting across that bridge!"

"I'm not a tactical guy, but I do know the NVA had the advantage. Chaplain [Richard M.] Lyons was going around giving last rites. At one point, he grabbed an M16 and our Chaplain, a Catholic priest, became a combatant. Chaplain Lyons got shot in the leg on the bridge, and Major [Walter M.] Murphy got shot. We kept dragging all these guys back to the MACV compound. We only had one Army doctor, named Dr. Bernard. He had been wounded and continued to work with a big gauze bandage, which was leaking blood as he was doing surgery. We

161

also had corpsmen with us. As we were dragging the guys back, fifty to one hundred Marines, the corpsmen were doing amputations, sticking guts back in, and doing major surgery. Guys were moaning all around. It was just awful."

"When Major Murphy got shot, he was lying on the cement floor, screaming encouragement to the Marines. He asked for a pen and paper, and he wrote his wife a note. He signaled to Father Lyons, who had been shot in the leg, and Father Lyons gave Murphy his last rites. Major Murphy's last words were *May God save my Marines,* and he died."

Ligato talked about how the enemy would taunt them: "The first night, we had to protect the MACV compound, so they put us in some surrounding houses, little French houses. Across the street, no more than 30 yards away, were the NVA in houses. All night long they shouted at us. We would hear, *You die, Marines! You die!* The first hour, it kind of freaks you out. This would go on all night long. Since I had gone to Vietnamese language school, Sergeant Gonzalez told me, *Ligato, give them a response.* I knew about ten phrases. I can't tell you what I told them, but Sergeant Gonzalez was very proud that we answered them."

 ❝ When Major Murphy got shot, he was lying on the cement floor, screaming encouragement to the Marines. ❞

"In Hué City, the next 31 days were crazy. We were scattered; we had no front. We saw the enemy up close. In fact, there were times when we would get detached from our unit. There was a chain of command, but it was very loose. We were like pack animals. I stole socks from a dead guy. We were scavenging both food and ammunition. We had no air or artillery support, none. It was one-on-one, 150 Marines against 10,000. *That's even odds for a Marine!* as my friend Doc Ballard would say!"

"It was so bad that, by the fourth day, several other Marine companies were being airlifted in. One of the commanders was General [Michael P.] Downs. As he came in on the fourth day, they had told him, *You've got to go to Hué. It's just some minor NVA problem; you'll be back by tomorrow!*"

"Each day was different. For example, the fourth day our lieutenants rejoined us, but they had to run the gauntlet from Phu Bai. The NVA had cut off the road, and anybody that went to Phu Bai got hit with automatic weapons fire. We kept getting reinforcements, but we also kept losing guys. At one point, they brought in two squads of cooks and

 " There were dead bodies all over the city. The NVA had killed 2,500 civilians, just slaughtered them, murdered them. "

clerks from Phu Bai. They were Marines and riflemen, but they had not been in combat. The poor cooks. So I told them, *We're going to run across the street.* Then I took off and ran across the street. I kept having to say, *Come on!* They wouldn't move. I ran back across the street and said again, *We must run across the street now.* At this point, I'm pushing Marines across the street!"

"We would have replacements come in for a day, get shot and then leave. We had one lieutenant who said, *My name is Lieutenant Rockman.* About a minute later he got shot and was med-evacuated and we said, *Goodbye, Lieutenant Rockman.* It was that kind of battle."

"There were dead bodies all over the city. The NVA had killed 2,500 civilians, just slaughtered them, murdered them. Although many of them were in mass graves, some were scattered around; there were limbs all around the city. There were dogs eating on bodies, just tearing up the flesh. I will never forget that."

"The Marines had never been trained in house-to-house urban warfare. We had zero training. After the War, I was trained as a SWAT team member by the FBI. They had sophisticated training methods on how to clear rooms and how to breach buildings and walls. After one or two rooms, we were doing the same techniques that FBI, SWAT, and hostage rescue teams were trained to do. We learned how to clear a room. The enemy was so close."

"A famous battle at Hué took place on February 4 at the St. Joan of Arc School. That was the headquarters of the 6th NVA regiment, which planned the battle. It was a convent, a church, and a school. We were ordered to take the building, but they had the high ground and were shooting down on us. Sergeant Gonzales made four or five individual attacks with low-air rockets and eventually Gonzales got hit with an RPG. He received the Medal of Honor, but should have received two. So, we lost Sergeant Gonzales."

"The fighting was so furious that my one friend and I got detached. We went to the compound and courtyard. As we were walking, the door opened across the courtyard and four NVA walked out. We looked at them, and they looked at us. We both ran back into our corners. It was that kind of battle, house-to-house and room-to-room. Civilians were just slaughtered all over the place as the enemy scavenged for food and ammunition. We had few officers during the battle, but we never complained about not having any officers. We were perfectly content to have the gunny run the company."

"Someone asked me, *How did it end?* Well, it took us (Figure 65) 31 days to declare the city ours. When we went into the St. Joan of Arc, where the 6th NVA headquarters had been, there was a big NVA flag on the wall. I'll never forget it. I grabbed the flag and stuck it in my utility pocket. I didn't think much of it until I realized, thirty years later, that Hué was so significant. That flag (Figure 59, page 151) now hangs in the Marine Corps Museum. By the end of that battle, there were a ton of casualties, including thousands of NVA, thousands of civilians, and hundreds of Marines."

Figure 65: Group of Marines after Vietnamese flag was surrendered to the museum. Photo courtesy of John Ligato, PETP 2014.

"There's a documentary called *Against the Odds: The Marines at Hué*. The definitive book (there have been about four or five books written about Alpha Company) is *The Marines Under Fire* by Ken Jordan; it came out about two years ago. We were always outnumbered. *What happened? What turned the tide?* Both are good questions. It was about the tenth day, when we took the gloves off of the Rules of Engagement. We had the 7th Fleet firing from the sea; we had air support, artillery support, and that kind of turned the tide."

When visiting Hué City, there was one thing John wanted to find, an ESSO gas station. "I've told you going in to Hué was awful. Remembering the sounds of machine guns, Hué was as bad of a firefight as I was ever in. When we got into Hué there was a lull, and I remember thinking, *This is great.* There was an ESSO station; I think it's still around—maybe we can find it. Anyway, after fighting, I ran behind the ESSO station, and I threw up for about two to three minutes. Then, I was okay. I did fine during the firefight, but when it was over, I felt like *I've got to vomit this out!* There wasn't much remaining of Hué City when I left."

When a student in the group inquired about keeping up with the news, John responded with candor, "This is funny—one guy had a transistor radio. Back then, they had two stations we could get. One was *Armed Forces Radio* with Chris Noel, who played terrible music. The other station featured *Hanoi Hannah*, who played great rock and roll—our favorite—but we had to listen to her propaganda. One night we were listening, and she said, *I have sad news. The Marines of Alpha Company 1/1 have been defeated by the glorious North Vietnamese Army.* You could hear guys laughing in the dark, *You dead?*"

STUDENT RESPONSE

Devon Spady was impressed from the start: "I could not have been more excited to meet Mr. John Ligato. After weeks of email correspondence, we finally met face-to-face in the airport in San Francisco. At first, I failed to recognize him, because in the participants directory picture he had a mustache, but he had shaved it completely off just before the trip."

Devon felt her first interaction was very telling about how their relationship was going to be: "John was very funny, but his humor was also very dry, and he started joking around with me right away. When we sat down to eat, we had a little Q&A back and forth. He told me about his 23 years in the FBI and that, though he was born in Philadelphia, he was currently living in Jacksonville, North Carolina, which was very close to the city where I went to high school. In fact, I have some friends who live in Jacksonville. We had so many things in common that I felt like it was a direct act of God that I was assigned as host to John."

"Once we landed at Tan Son Nhut airport and collected our luggage, John disappeared to go talk to a local Vietnamese kid who worked there. As I got closer to see what he was up to, I realized I couldn't understand what he was saying. John was speaking to the kid in his native tongue. He later told me he was very interested in talking to the kid about the current economic climate in Vietnam. He asked the kid if it were true that Vietnam was leaning more towards capitalism. He said that the kid looked around nervously and said, *Not talk about here.*"

By the time the veterans and students started visiting battle locations, Devan Spady was very comfortable with her veteran. "It felt like meeting my grandfather for the first time," she said. "First, we went on a cruise on the Mekong River to the Floating Market. As soon as we got on the boat, John got right down to teaching me about all the different names for the parts of the boat and even tricks on how to remember each name. I looked around at all the other veterans who were telling their students war stories and sharing their past, and there was mine teaching me about boats and Vietnamese phrases. I was not upset about this fact. It seemed to fit with the fact that he is a college professor. I grew up in a home where we didn't talk about what my father did overseas, serving with the Marine Corps. We did not ask, and he did not tell. We wanted him to know that when he was home, he was away from all of that. So, the fact that John was not talking about the War yet did not bother me. The most important thing was for him to know that, if he ever did want to talk about it, there was someone right next to him willing to listen. I felt like that was really what these veterans needed."

Devan got a window into John's amazing worldview: "While we were on the Mekong, I was looking at the people in the little boats all around us, and I commented out loud that it was humbling. In my head I added, *to see all these dirty people wearing rags with no shoes, crouching in boats that barely float, in houses with walls made of mud and roofs made of grass, working outside in the elements all day toiling for the bare minimum.* John said, *Try not to think too much like that.* He further explained as he pointed, *That man crouching in that boat could be the happiest man in the world, as far as he is concerned.* He had a very valid point. Without all the material possessions that we take for granted, all that really matters in that man's life is his family, his source of faith, and a way to make a living. John told me that he grew up in a ghetto in Philadelphia, and, though he had little in the way of playthings as a kid, he could not have been happier or had a better childhood."

"John thought we should walk around Vietnam more, in order to better experience the culture and its people. He said one of the reasons he came on this trip was to see how the country has changed over the years. He was greatly interested in the people themselves."

Devan tried asking John some things about the War, and he confessed that, unlike a lot of veterans, he did not want to learn anything about the war after he got out of the Marine Corps. He tried his best to just put it behind him and forget. That was how he dealt with the PTSD.

As John spoke more and more about his time as a Marine, Devan learned more and more about this patriot: "He told me a lot of facts regarding his time here in Vietnam. He told me where he had been stationed, and a little about the battles he fought in. He even drew me a little map in my notebook."

"He really does have a soft spot for children. At the museum he did not want to look at the pictures of the kids with the Agent Orange disfigurements. He told me that he could handle a lot of horrific things, no problem, but children and animals just tear at his heart."

While riding on the bus one day, John made an unusual request of Devan Spady: "John asked me to sing the Marine Corps Hymn in front of everyone on the bus, which I agreed to do while he stood at attention. Colonel Duncan thanked me repeatedly for doing this. Devan continued, "We got off the bus at Con Thien, which is very near the DMZ. This is where John told me that they got hundreds of rounds a day of rockets and mortars and enemy artillery. When we got off the bus, he said to me, *This smell is very familiar. It is the smell of Vietnam, of the villages.* He said that Con Thien did not look at all the same as he remembers. Before, it was *just a mud hole. There was no road. NVA everywhere.* Apparently, the Vietnamese had filled in a lot of the bomb craters; however, there were still a lot of land mines around."

"I noticed a change in John as we inched closer and closer to the places where his fighting experience was heaviest. He was quieter. When I approached him, he said that everything was finally starting to look familiar. He smiled and, looking around at the beautiful beaches surrounded by sloping moutains, said that this was more his kind of terrain. He also told me that all of this had not been a dirt road. It had been a rock road, and ambushes happened all the time as they tried to make their way up."

"At the museum in Khe Sanh, there was a large map of the country of Vietnam. John and Doc Ballard showed me where they had been and what hills they were trying to defend at that time. As John looked out over the perimeter from the museum balcony, he told me how, tactically, you would want to be in the highest point. He illustrated the entire base for me so clearly that I could picture it in my head."

"In Hué, we took a cruise on the Perfume River on a dragon barge. John pointed out a bridge that he had helped to blow up. He was stunned to see, in the exact same spot as those many years ago, a bridge that looked precisely like the one before. John said that bridge and that river centralized the War for him. It was the first thing he really recognized and the first thing to make him realize where he was. He said he remembered everything just fine—that when he looked at the river, it was like he was there. He could see it all around him once again. But he seemed more awed by this than distressed."

"As we passed the Citadel where an ARVN General had been terribly outnumbered, John looked out the window and commented that it had been almost entirely rebuilt. As we drove through Hué, John was disappointed by the fact that he did not recognize any of the buildings. Then it hit him. Riding in the bus, we could only see the first floor of each building, which had all been turned into very open shops, where people can just walk in off the street. All those shops used to be beautiful French homes, but you could only see the European architecture when you looked up to the higher levels."

"When we left the hotel in Hué, we rode a cyclos (a three-wheeled bicycle taxi) into the Citadel. John had been here over forty years ago, and he explained to us, *An ARVN General had called into Da Nang and told them he was surrounded. Due to an intelligence error, Da Nang thought it was simply an oversized company of the enemy. It turned out to be 10,000 NVA.* The Citadel (Figure 62, page 155) was where a lot of Marines were killed. John was pretty amazed at the size of the perimeter of the Citadel."

Devan explained, "John pointed out, *That's the Perfume River, but we had another name for it. Of course, it didn't smell like perfume. One hundred and fifty Marines from Golf 2/5 crossed that bridge. Within about an hour, 50 were dead or wounded. When I got to the river, I looked across it and we thought there were 1,000 to 2,000 NVA. They had an NVA flag flying, and what we didn't know, in fact, was that there were 10,000 NVA! The first Marine contingent that came in, Alpha 1/1, had 150 Marines. The number 10,000 is not my estimate; it is Marine Corps history. Golf Company went across there about two in the afternoon, and by two-forty, we had to drag them off the bridge and bring them to the MACV compound. The Citadel was for the ARVN General, and what happened was that he called to say he was being overrun. Our intelligence was that it was just an oversized company. Hué City, well the Tet Offensive, was the third biggest U.S. Intelligence failure in our history, behind Pearl Harbor. The Perfume River was the first sight that jogged my memory of all these details.*"

Devan continued, "We departed from Phu Bai on our way to Hanoi. Phu Bai was where John and half of his company were able to shower and eat a hot meal for the first time in weeks after leaving Con Thien. From there, the Tet Offensive began, and John's company was swiftly moved to Hué to help another."

In looking back on a once-in-a-lifetime experience, Devan Spady reflected on her grandfather's life: "My grandfather was a Marine. He came home from Vietnam physically, but not mentally. He died when I was very young. I never had a chance to talk to him about his experiences. I have been honored beyond words to host a Marine as my veteran. John often said to me, *I have trouble thinking of Vietnam as history!* To him, he was simply going there to do a job and to fulfill his duty as an American citizen. On this trip I have wondered what constitutes a hero. To me, a hero is someone who sacrifices everything for someone or something outside of themselves. And to me, that defines my veteran, Mr. John Ligato."[6]

TOPIC SUMMARY

Hardly two months prior to the Battle of Hué, President Johnson initiated a major effort to communicate more clearly to the American public, and especially to Congress, the progress and necessity of the War. This was against the backdrop of diminishing support from those who had supported his cause. Demonstrations against the War and a rise in combat deaths kept the issue on the public's mind. Even Secretary of Defense McNamara began to lose confidence in President Johnson's policies, which McNamara had helped formulate.

 « To me, a hero is someone who sacrifices everything for someone or something outside of themselves. **»**

In order to reduce the increasing pressure surrounding the War, General Westmoreland and Ambassador Bunker were called to Washington. General Westmoreland spoke to the National Press Club in Washington and gave an upbeat, optimistic appraisal of the current situation in Southeast Asia, telling them we were at a point "when the end begins to come into view."[7] He had no idea that what was shortly coming into view was his lost command of MACV. Appearing on *Meet the Press*, General Westmoreland said it was "conceivable that within two years or less the enemy will be so weakened that the Vietnamese will be able to cope with a greater share of the war burden."[8]

Such rosy pronouncements calmed the public, but the calm was short-lived. There were multiple indications that the NVA/VC were planning an offensive around the start of the Tet New Year, January 31. General Westmoreland and President Johnson believed that increased fighting in the upper I-Corps, places such as Con Thien and Khe Sanh, affirmed their suspicions. However, when Tet began, the communists were attacking most of the provincial capitals, district capitals, and villages. Hué was one of the least prepared for such an attack. The ARVN 1st

Infantry Division (ID) was headquartered in the Citadel at Hué (Figure 62, page 155). A small MACV compound was located in the southern part of Hué, with only Marine guards covering the third largest city in South Vietnam. This changed rapidly after the VC/NVA attacked the city early on the first day of Tet. The closest Marine reinforcements were at Phu Bai. The first company sent to help was John Ligato's unit. A long, bloody fight for Hué ensued and lasted for about a month.

Most of the battles during the nationwide Tet Offensive lasted only a few hours or a few days. This was not the case in the old provincial capital of Hué. The plan was for the people to rise up and join the invaders, but this didn't happen. What did "rise up" was the United States Marine Corps, who resorted to house-to-house and street combat to run the NVA/VC out. Eventually, the Marines were allowed to "take the gloves off" and use artillery, mortars and bombing—any necessary force. Not much of the city was left standing and even fewer enemy soldiers.

This victory was accomplished at a high price. Some 200 Marines were killed in action along with 3,000-5,000 NVA. When the Marines took over, they discovered that during the 25 days of fighting, some 3,000 teachers, public officials, police, and priests were executed or buried alive. Unfortunately, many NVA were able to escape in darkness to avoid the Marines.[9]

After the Battle of Hué and the end of the Tet Offensive, Americans questioned General Westmoreland's optimistic appraisals. Although the enemy had suffered a massive military defeat, the communists had gained in public opinion in the United States. Several things contributed to this, and President Johnson gave few public speeches to explain what was going on. The public needed to hear from their leader, the President, for reassurance.

Max Hastings vividly describes in his book, *Vietnam*, that when a picture of a VC prisoner being shot in the head by a Saigon police officer was picked up by the media and appeared on television, the country and world recoiled in horror. However, the media did not comment on what the Viet Cong prisoner had allegedly done (i.e. cutting the throats of an nine-member family), which was far worse.[10] The media coverage portrayed the Tet Offensive as a disaster for the United States and its allies, a report totally wrong from a military standpoint.

Many Americans were disheartened by the reports on the War. Contributing to this was none other than CBS sage Walter Cronkite (Figure 66), who had made a brief visit to Vietnam. Cronkite's pretense of objectivity was stripped away by his reporting on the battle at Hué. Max Hastings comments on this in his book on Vietnam: "In February, he [Cronkite] visited Hué, then told [General] Fred Weyand, *I've seen those thousands of bodies. And I have decided that...I'm going to do everything possible in this war to bring it to an end.* The General said, *It was particularly troubling...because of the incredible respect Walter had from the American people.* Weyand was disgusted that Cronkite spoke as if the Americans and South Vietnamese had been responsible for the Hué massacres!"[11] It seems as though Cronkite had forgotten it was communist NVA troops that had invaded Hué and commenced to kill thousands of its inhabitants. Many U.S. Marines had died liberating the city.

Figure 66: Walter Cronkite (with microphone) at Hué. Photo from public domain.

Not long after the Battle of Hué, Cronkite is reported by Ernest Lefever in his book, *TV and National Defense*, to have said, "We [media] should not decide what is good and what is bad for people...Because then people are denied the information that democracy entitles them to have."[12] It seems obvious that Cronkite was inconsistent in matching his actions with his words. One of the media's most admired had become a self-appointed architect for American policy.

Mark Bowden later wrote, "Before his TV audience of millions, he [Cronkite] would present his first try at what he termed *advocacy journalism.*"[13] Intentionally or not, Walter Cronkite, along with many other newsmen, followed their own narrative—something that many Americans now call "fake news"—which did not go away after the Vietnam War.

Walter Cronkite may be best remembered with his signature closing, "…and that's the way it is."[14] Instead, he should have said, *and that's the way it is according to me.*

The fact is, U.S. Marines were fighting for their lives and the lives of others. While at the same time, there were those in the media, in the streets, and in Congress who—knowingly or not—were undermining our country's sacrifices.

Clearly, the Marines persevered at Hué and sacrificed at a high price. They were indeed *Semper Fidelis.*

The media was not.

CLASS TOPIC 7: CHU LAI, 91ST EVAC HOSPITAL (I-CORPS)

...she would sit and hold his hand and talk to him until he died.

INSTRUCTOR: 1LT LOUISE (LOU) EISENBRANDT, USA[1]

"I wanted to see the world,"[2] was always the response Lou Eisenbrandt gave when asked why she joined the Army. However, she could never have imagined how much she would see, let alone the conditions under which she would experience much of it. Growing up in the small town of Mascoutah, Illinois, near Scott Air Force base, she had the opportunity to mingle with classmates whose families had served around the world. No doubt this had a profound impact on a bright, young lady who was eager for an adventure beyond the confines of small-town America. Coming from a blue-collar family and the oldest of five, she had little in the way of financial means. She chose the Army because she saw it as her big chance. First, she had to convince her father to let her go away for more education. Her mother helped convince her dad that it was okay.[3]

At St. Joseph's School of Nursing, Lou excelled, and she graduated in 1968 with the Florence Nightingale Award for the highest academic grade. She had volunteered for a special Army program that placed her on active duty reserve, gave her a stipend, and required a future two-year active duty commitment.[4]

Nurse Eisenbrandt attended officer's basic training at Fort Sam Houston, Texas. Upon completion, she was given her first duty assignment in Fort Dix, New Jersey. At Fort Dix, Eisenbrandt immediately discovered what it was like to be in the Army, and what it was like to be a nurse. Lou was in charge of returning veterans whose wounds still needed attention. She was also in charge of the stockade ward, where all of the soldiers who could not behave were held, and numerous other soldiers with cases of minor infections. At any one time, she could have had 100 to 200 patients. Nurse Lou had been there nine months when she received a manila envelope with contents that read, *Congratulations, you're going to Vietnam.* She took thirty days of leave time before flying out to Vietnam.[5]

Her first stop in Vietnam was Long Binh. When she first arrived, Lou was asked where she would like to go. She knew nothing about the country, so she randomly put her finger on the map and said, "This looks like a pretty good place." Lou picked the 91st Evacuation Hospital in Chu Lai. It was monsoon season in Vietnam, and Lou arrived at the hospital, wet and without luggage, because it was lost. She was assigned to a medical ward for her first three months in Chu Lai. Her time in the medical ward was spent treating malaria, hepatitis, parasites, and jungle rot—everything except war wounds. After three months, Lou was asked if she would like to serve in the ER, and she accepted. Lou spent the rest of her time in Vietnam treating many different types of war injuries and saving as many lives as possible.[6]

After her year in Vietnam, Lou was out of the Army. She and a friend took a trip to see more of the USA. Their trip came to an end when they stopped in Denver, Colorado, six weeks later. In Denver, Lou decided to apply for a civil service position at Fitzsimons Army Hospital, and she was hired. Fitzsimons was one of the top hospitals where nurses wanted to work. It was at Fitzsimons that she met her future husband. Jim, a medic in the Army Reserves, had just started to work at Fitzsimons and was assigned to the same floor as Lou. She was in charge of overseeing him![7]

Nowadays, Mrs. Eisenbrandt lives in Leawood, Kansas, with her husband Jim. Unfortunately, Lou, like so many others who served in the War, copes with health issues as a result of exposure to Agent Orange, and now lives life having to deal with Parkinson's disease.[8] But Lou does not let the disease get her down. She has taken up many hobbies to combat Parkinson's such as Tai Chi, golf, and yoga. She has also become a sought-after speaker on Vietnam and her experiences there.

In 2015, Lou Eisenbrandt published a book entitled, *Vietnam Nurse: Mending & Remembering*. Her story is a telling one for those who don't realize that women served in the Vietnam War. During the Vietnam era, some 265,000 young women served in various capacities during the War.[9] And some paid with their lives; eight names of women are inscribed on the Vietnam Memorial Wall in Washington, D.C. The Vietnam Women's Memorial (Figure 75, page 194) has been added to recognize those nurses who played a critical role by serving Americans, Vietnamese, and others. Many soldiers, Marines, and airmen, as well as children and adults caught up in the War, owe their lives to the skills of these nurses.

Figure 67: Student host Chase Davis and veteran Lou Eisenbrandt. Photo by John Luck.

STUDENT HOST: CHASE DAVIS

Like other students chosen to serve as a host for a Vietnam veteran, Chase Davis (Figure 67) saw such an adventure as a great opportunity: "The Patriotic Travel Program is one of many great opportunities students have at College of the Ozarks," Chase wrote in his trip application. "I was interested in this particular trip to Vietnam for a couple of reasons."

Chase's reasons for going on such a trip were clear: "I have never been overseas. This would be a great opportunity to visit an important site of American history for a first-time trip out of the United States. To experience places our veterans served is completely different from just reading about them. Having the chance to spend time with our heroes and hear them tell stories of their service, including many details of the War that no one talks about, would be priceless. I also have family who served in Vietnam."

Chase's grandfather, Jim Davis, as well as a great uncle, Dan Davis, served in the War. "My grandpa was in the Navy and my great uncle was in the Army. Jim was an aircraft mechanic on aircraft carriers, the *U.S.S. Ranger*, and the *U.S.S. America*, and served other aircraft carriers in the South China Sea. Dan was one of the Black Lions, a combat infantry battalion of the First Infantry Division. Dan was awarded a Bronze Star for actions near the Iron Triangle, a hotly contested area between Saigon and the Cambodian border. Having the opportunity to go and see where they served would be an amazing experience that many people never have."

Chase came to College of the Ozarks from Georgia. He said he always enjoyed playing around with computers. Although he worked in a number of workstations on campus, most of his assignments were in the Computer Center. Chase was a good student, majoring in computer science. The main thing Chase wanted to take away from the Vietnam trip was to "experience history firsthand."

Figure 68: View of the beach at the 91st taken from the officers' club. Photo courtesy of Lou Eisenbrandt, PETP 2014.

91ST EVACUATION HOSPITAL BACKGROUND

Without a raging war going on, the location of the 91st EVAC Hospital at Chu Lai would have been an attractive location, situated on a bluff overlooking (Figure 68) the South China Sea. Chu Lai (Figure 69) was a seaport town southeast of Da Nang and a few miles north of Quang Ngai. Highway 1 ran north and south through Chu Lai, which was in the southern part of I-Corps.

Living and working conditions at the hospital were simple, not vastly different from any other medical center. But its construction set it apart: "The operating rooms, the mess hall, the officers' club, and the sleeping quarters consisted of boards or canvas from ground to waist-high and then screen to the sloping roof. Shopping was available at the military

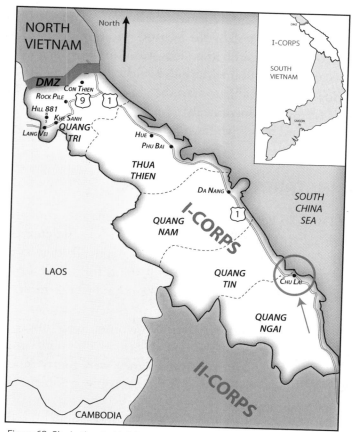

Figure 69: Chu Lai located in I-Corps. Adapted from public domain.

base with limited products as well as limited supply," Lou remembers.

The helicopter landing pad was built by Navy Seabees. The hospital had space for an emergency room, an intensive care unit, wards for military patients, a section for Vietnamese patients, and a POW ward. As far as the captured or injured NVA or VC were concerned, recovering at this facility was a desirable location. Medical personnel dealt with everything from malaria to mass casualties. A commanding officer of the 91st EVAC in 1970, Colonel Keawyn Nehoa, said the facility was "the most active hospital in Vietnam with the greatest turnover.....of patients."[10]

Not far up the coast from the hospital was a South Korean base. Their soldiers were regarded as fierce fighters. The U.S. 23rd Infantry Division also had its headquarters in Chu Lai, after Marines established a combat base and helicopter facility.

Chu Lai and the surrounding area was an important site during the War. It was secured in 1965 by the Marines and solidified by *Operation Starlite*, a regimental-sized battle. This was a bitter fight in which the VC suffered 688 KIA and the Marines 45. This battle was very unusual, since Marines had been able to trap the VC so they couldn't slip away, as was their custom. Unfortunately, a high number of locals were killed, because it was hard to tell which villages were VC and which were not.

 INSTRUCTOR REFLECTIONS

Nurse Lou told her story to attentive veterans and students: "Most of you realize that I have Parkinson's disease. It's been determined this is probably a direct result of exposure to Agent Orange, a defoliate commonly used in Vietnam. So, I will stand for a little bit, but my balance is off. If the road is anything like it has been, I think I'll finish my talk sitting down."

"People ask me if I was drafted. No women were drafted at that time. I also did not volunteer to go to Vietnam, although some nurses did. Let's face it, the odds of men to women were pretty much in our favor. But I really joined the Army for a terribly ignoble reason, and that was *to see the world!*"

"I grew up in Southern Illinois in a small town about 30 miles across the river from St. Louis. It was very close to Scott Air Force Base, which is a huge base. Most of my high school friends were Air Force brats. Their dads—almost exclusively dads, since back then there weren't very many women—had been stationed in Germany and England and Italy. I was the oldest of five children and from a blue-collar family, so there was little money to travel. I thought this would be my chance to see the world. When you sign on the dotted line, you go where Uncle Sam says you're going to go. I signed up before my senior year in nursing school, so my first year I was considered active reserve status, and my job was to go to school and finish school, which I did. Then I went to Fort Sam Houston, Texas, in November and December of 1968, took my officer's basic training, and got my first duty assignment, which was Fort Dix, New Jersey. Actually, it worked out well for me because I really jumped in with both feet to what the military was all about, as well as what nursing was all about."

"The ward that I took care of had returning GIs who still had wounds that needed a little more attention. I also was in charge of the stockade ward where we had guys who had seriously misbehaved and were behind bars. I'd have to go in each morning and check for syringes and knives and anything else they might have. In a separate area (where new recruits came in), if anybody got an upper respiratory infection, it spread like wildfire. So I might have 200 guys coughing and sneezing. One of the most interesting things was a program that the Army had which we called the *fatties* and the *skinnies*. You had to be a certain weight, even if you were drafted. They tried to fatten up the *skinnies* and slim down the *fatties*. The problem was that they put them on the same floor together. So the *fatties* beat up the *skinnies* and drank their milkshakes. The *fatties* got fatter and the *skinnies* got skinnier. At any given time, I might have 150-250 patients in my care. I learned very quickly about time management."

"I was there nine months when I got a manila envelope in the mail containing the message, *Congratulations, you're going to Vietnam.* My first roommate at Fort Dix had gotten orders six months prior, so I guess I wasn't terribly shocked. I took 30 days of leave, went back to my home in Illinois, and then flew out. I flew out of San Francisco on American Airlines through Hawaii, and after a stop in Okinawa, ended up in Long Binh." (Figure 70)

"I remember arriving in Long Binh and being asked, *Where would you like to go?* Now, I knew nothing about Vietnam. But I have to be honest with you, even if I had known more, I could have not have picked a better spot to be. The Chu Lai 91st EVAC Hospital sat on a cliff

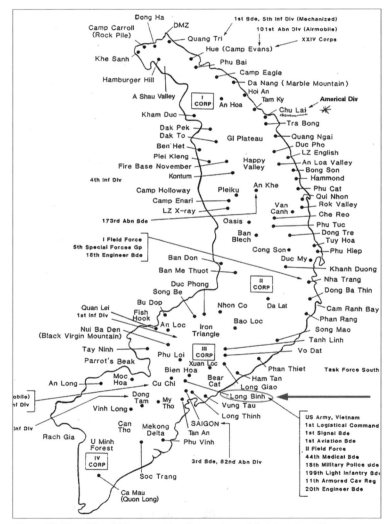

Figure 70: Map of South Vietnam with military units and their locations. Photo courtesy of *Vietnam Nurse* by Lou Eisenbrandt, PETP 2014.

overlooking the South China Sea. Even when it got blistering hot, you had a little breeze off the sea and that really made a huge difference. Plus you had access to water and water sports, which most people don't think about."

"I arrived at the hospital four days after I had come in to the country at Long Binh. They had lost my luggage on the way up, so I arrived in the middle of the monsoon season with no luggage, not even a toothbrush, and everything wet. I think I cried for the first day or two, and then things started to fall into place."

"I spent all my time at the 91st EVAC Hospital. Some nurses were moved around, but I was not. There were actually 25 hospitals throughout Vietnam that I would say were major hospitals like mine."

"There were 109 officers on the roster when I arrived, and that included doctors, nurses, and administrative people. There were also enlisted men, most of whom were corpsmen. When I first arrived, I was assigned to a medical ward. What that means was that we did not take care of patients who were wounded. These were guys that were dealing with malaria, hepatitis, intestinal worms and parasites from drinking dirty water and eating dirty food, and then there was jungle rot. You've heard about wearing the same boots for three or four days on end, plus not giving your feet a chance to dry out. You rub big sores on your legs, and they get infected. And some of them were pretty nasty. So those were the main things. I actually had a colonel who had a heart attack, and I took care of him. Generally, these were ailments that had little to do with combat. We would treat them, and when they were well enough, they would go back to their units."

> **" I'm here to save lives. I can't be falling apart. "**

"After three months of doing this, I was invited—asked—to go to the emergency room if I wished to do that, and I took on the challenge. Here I did nursing that I will never ever do again, thank goodness. When I moved to the emergency room, my very first patient was a double amputee. From his knees down, one leg was missing, the other was dangling. It took about five minutes to stand and compose myself. Then I said to myself, *I'm here to save lives. I can't be falling apart.* That was the one adjustment that I had. I had about five minutes to think about what I was going to do, and then get on with it."

"A little bit of background about the hospital and its operation: Our days were 12-hour days, six days a week. If we had low casualties or no casualties for a little while, we could have a three-hour break. Everybody always wanted the first break in the morning because it was 7:00 to 10:00, which meant you could sleep in for three hours. But there was a rule for working in the emergency room. If you heard more than two choppers come in and land, you knew you needed to get over there, because two meant there could be at least four wounded on the choppers. So you quit whatever you were doing and went into the emergency room. Things generally were a little quieter at night, but not necessarily. The enemy seemed to not attack as much at night as they did during the day."

Figure 71: Emergency Room, 91st EVAC Hospital. Photo courtesy of *Vietnam Nurse* by Lou Eisenbrandt, PETP 2014.

"At the 91st, we used glass IV bottles, which you don't see anymore. Nobody wore gloves. This was pre-AIDS. The only people who wore surgical gloves were the surgeons in the operating room. The floor of the emergency room was just concrete with big drains. (Figure 71) So, we stabilized the patients, did our triage, and moved them on to the operating room or wherever they were going. Afterward, we were able to just get the hose out and wash down the floor."

"Let me describe some of what I saw, without being too graphic. There were various ways of being wounded. One was a mine. The guys who stepped on mines that were hidden in the turf or in the ground frequently lost legs. That's the usual injury that we saw. Sometimes I saw triple amputees, both legs and an arm gone. Another category was gunshot wounds. For those of you who aren't familiar with a gunshot wound, the bullet makes a small entrance wound, but it makes a massive exit wound when it leaves your body. I will never forget a young man who came in with a gunshot wound and various other issues. He really was wounded badly. You always cut off all the clothes so you could assess the situation, because you never knew if there was a piece of shrapnel—

that little metal stuff that flies off when you blow things up. You never knew if one of those hit a really essential place on your body. We started to roll this young man over, and his back stayed on the litter (stretcher with sides). He survived at least long enough for us to patch him up and ship him to Tokyo, where many of our patients went that were too badly wounded to go back to their unit. I think about him a lot and wonder if he actually survived."

"Occasionally, our hospital got rocketed. Fortunately, for me, they did not hit the hospital. You could hear the rockets fly over the hospital and land in the South China Sea. But three months before I arrived at the 91st, Sharon Lane (Figure 72), whose name is on the Wall, was killed at our hospital. She was a nurse working on the Vietnamese Ward when a rocket

Figure 72: Memorial statue of Lt. Sharon A. Lane. Photo courtesy of *Vietnam Nurse* by Lou Eisenbrandt, PETP 2014.

hit the hospital, and she died. She is one of eight women on the Wall. When we had rocket attacks, you would hear a siren go off, and you'd have to get out of bed and go to the nearest bunker. There was a large bunker right in front of the building that I stayed in. I would grab my steel pot [helmet] and flak jacket and just wait there until the attack was over. There were two long rows of benches on each side. You didn't want to be the first one in, because the rats lived there when we weren't there. And they were big rats!"

"The beach was lined with fuel storage tanks. We used to watch the tankers pull in, barely being above the water because they were full of fuel, and then watch them rise out of the water as they pumped the fuel into the tanks. These tanks were very important to the war effort, because if you take away a country's fuel you can't run the jeeps. You can't do a whole lot of anything. Those were major targets for the VC and the NVA to hit. So, we had to deal with those sorts of wounds from just general massive explosions. Rocket attacks aren't easily forgotten. Since my room was right in front of the bunker, a corrugated metal piled with sand bags, I didn't have to go very far. If we were under rocket fire, after the first one, the sirens would go off. And as I remember them, they were usually early in the morning."

❝ Many times in triage, those young men were the ones that we determined were not going to make it. ❞

Nurse Lou recalled how difficult it was to care for terminal patients: "I think the hardest type of patients to take care of were those with head wounds, massive head wounds. Many times in triage, those young men were the ones that we determined were not going to make it. I can still remember several and what we tried to do in the emergency room with little or no privacy. When you go into an ordinary emergency room, you pull the little curtain around you. We had a couple of screens, and if we had someone in terminal condition, we would put him on the litter behind the screen. And if one of us nurses was free, she would sit and hold his hand and talk to him until he died. He would think either you were his mother or his girlfriend. Also, we used the screens if we would get green body bags, meaning someone was KIA, which is killed in action, or DOA, dead on arrival. We put the screens up in front of those. That was the only form of privacy that you had in the emergency room."

"Not all wounds were devastating. Occasionally, you would get things like ingrown toenails or something. Sometimes they were a bit humorous. I was working nights when this young man came in with a silly grin on his face. In halting language, he let me know that he had been to the village and spent some time with a lady, and he was coming in for a penicillin shot. So I drew up the shot and said, *Ok, you need to drop your drawers and bend over.* And he was really shy about doing this. For once I had the right thing to say, *You know if you hadn't dropped them earlier, you wouldn't need to be dropping them now.* I never saw him back again. But that's an issue in a war period that is not particular to Vietnam."

"Some people ask, *Were you on the front lines?* There were no front lines in Vietnam. The mama-san (Vietnamese woman in a position of authority over other Vietnamese women) who swept out my hooch during the day could be a sniper trying to get in through the concertina wire at night. So you did not know who the enemy was and who the enemy was not. I think that's another reason there was so much PTSD, not knowing if the person next to you is friendly or not. And the guys out in the field couldn't get in for even a shower. Multiply that times a hundred, and that's what it's like to be out in the bush. The GIs we would get were usually not very clean."

"Occasionally, we would get patients from these underground hospitals, like the ones at Cu Chi. The NVA and VC really did have hospitals in the tunnels. The conditions were atrocious. I have one picture of a Vietnamese woman who came in, and they had put an inflatable see-through cast on her leg. It was full of maggots, just crawling from one end to the other. You have to have a pretty good stomach to handle something like that, both the sight and the smell."

"One other type of injury that I haven't talked about, but we saw some pictures, I think, in the war museum, was white phosphorus. White phosphorus doesn't ever quit burning if you get it on your skin. It just keeps eating away down to the bone. There is a smell that goes with white phosphorus that I have never forgotten. It's a horrendous weapon of war, I guess I would say—especially if you saw children that were exposed to white phosphorus. It was very tragic. We did see a lot of orphans, Vietnamese orphans, kids who had lost their parents. There was an orphanage not far from the hospital. We would go visit and take things for the kids. That is another reality of war. You end up orphaning children, on both sides, with missing moms and dads."

"We also had recreation, down time. We had a beach. You can't see it now because it was washed away by a typhoon about three months after I left. We also had a motor boat and skis. I have no idea where the motor boat came from. If any of you have ever watched any episodes of MASH, you know that they're always swapping something for something else. *I have a case of penicillin, but we need canned peaches; I'll trade you.* So I don't know if that's how we came to have the boat, but it allowed some of us to go water skiing. And I actually got very good at slalom skiing. You couldn't go in the water after one o'clock, because that's when the sharks came in. We also had something called red tide, which is this algae that just eats through your body. Depending on the weather there were days that the red tide would come in, so we stayed out of the water on those days."

"Sometimes we had to make up our own games. There was no video place; there were no televisions. There was nothing. So you would just do whatever came along. I was a singer and played guitar. I did not take my guitar with me, because I wasn't sure that was something I should do. But early on, one of the doctors went to Tokyo, and he bought a guitar for me. And I still have it, still play it. It's in great shape. I spent a lot of time playing guitar and leading songs. There was a group of guys who were musicians, and when they came to Vietnam, their job was to form a band.

Figure 73: Chinook helicopter. Photo by John Luck.

They would go out to different LZs [landing zones] and provide a little entertainment for the guys. And since I sang, I got to go along a couple of times as the girl singer. Talk about getting attention…I got lots of attention doing that! I remember one trip in particular. We flew in a Chinook, (Figure 73) and we were carrying cargo underneath the Chinook in a giant mesh bag. The floor in the Chinook was open, so we just sat around the edges; I don't even remember if we had seatbelts or not. It was quite interesting. I took some really cool pictures out of the bottom of that Chinook."

Figure 74: 91st EVAC Hospital from LOH, and amphitheater. Photo courtesy of *Vietnam Nurse* by Lou Eisenbrandt, PETP 2014.

"Anything that I could do to get away for a little bit from the War, that's what kept me going. People ask about PTSD. I journaled; I wrote every day. I tried to forget the War when I wasn't on duty. You can't ever forget the images. I mean they float through my head all the time. But you can learn to manage them. So, you did anything that you could when you were not on duty to forget the War."

"Every day, there was much going on around us. I have a picture (Figure 74) that I took from a *loach*, (LOH), which stands for Light Observation Helicopter. It was like the police or weather helicopter, with a little clear bubble thing and no doors. I went up with a friend who was a pilot and took my camera up with me. I hung out with one arm and took some great aerial shots. I have a wonderful aerial shot of the hospital, which was part of the American Division."

"There was an amphitheater there. (Figure 74) I think it was built in the '50s, and I don't know what the reason was for building it, but the good news was I got to see Bob Hope. I speak to students a lot, and have been for about 30 years, and when I say *Bob Hope*, I get this blank look. There's usually only one lonely soul who's heard of Bob Hope, so then I have to say, *Talk to your parents, or better yet, talk to your grandparents, because they would know Bob Hope.* This was a major thing in the war zones, because he entertained the troops for years and years. It was quite a big deal. It was monsoon season, so two minutes into the show it started pouring. He always brought lovely beauty queens with him because the guys out in the field hadn't seen women who weren't Asian for months on end. So he would bring Miss World and some fancy movie star, and they just stood there and got wet like the rest of us. I saw a few other USO shows, but the Bob Hope one will stick with me for a long time."

"I did take one R&R, which meant ten days out of Vietnam. I went to Hong Kong, and I've been back once. It's a fascinating city, if you ever have a chance to go, but very crowded."

"I've learned something about myself that I didn't know before. I've been thinking about the day we were in Cu Chi in the tunnels. I firmly believe that anyone who comes to Vietnam and wants to understand the War and what we were up against needs to do the tunnels. There are several complexes of them. Obviously, when we got patients from the tunnels it was not from Cu Chi, because the tunnels were further north. But you have to appreciate the endurance of the people who lived in those tunnels. On one of my visits, I learned that the tour of duty in a tunnel was three months. And you try to picture living in that existence. You can't win over someone like that. This was their territory; they knew what they were doing. We were not prepared for guerrilla warfare."

STUDENT RESPONSE

"Just What the Nurse Ordered" was the headline of the student blog post by Chase Davis early in the trip. He continued, "When I learned that I was going to be paired with the only female veteran on the trip, I was excited beyond words, because I knew she would provide a completely different perspective of the War. I was not disappointed. Unlike most of the other veterans, Mrs. Lou Eisenbrandt (Mrs. Lou) had been back to

Vietnam on several occasions. With that in mind, both of us understood that our experience would most likely be different from most of the other veteran-student pairs and agreed that we were both interested in observing the other veterans' reactions to being back in Vietnam.[11]

"We were not sure what to expect from the veterans who had not been back since the War, but we were astonished at the composure of these men. As far as we could tell, all of the veterans were overjoyed to have this experience. We observed that they were willing to share story after story with us. We also observed how amazed the veterans were at the dramatic urbanization of the places where they fought over forty years ago. Finally, we observed that for some of the veterans, being on this trip and seeing how much this country has changed has provided a sense of calm for their minds and hearts."[12]

"Even more interesting has been the opportunity to see how the veterans reacted to one another. Some served in the Marines, some in the Air Force or Navy, and others were in the Army. They all seemed to have something in common, an almost brother-like bond. For most of the veterans on the trip, this was their first time back to Vietnam since the War ended. It must have been very emotional for them, since we visited the actual sites where they served."

A trip to a floating market was something unexpected by Chase, and he was fascinated by what he saw. "We took a boat to the floating market on the Mekong River. There were a lot of boats that were a part of the market. Most were small, old, and dilapidated looking, but they were functional. The tour guide told us that each boat was actually owned by a family, and, in most cases, the boat was the family's home. We stopped by one boat selling drinks, and almost everyone bought from him. He was selling two water bottles for one dollar. It was humbling to see the conditions of these families and to see the smiles on their faces as we waved at them."

"We turned off of the river and maneuvered down a canal. The canal was small with trash littering the sides, which was true of most of the city. The tour guide stopped us at a place with a huge Pepsi sign hanging above it. The front of it was almost like a small convenience store. There were pointy hats, water bottles, sodas, and noodles for sale. I was really surprised that there were all those things for sale in a little, dirty canal off a river. In the back of the store there was a man and a woman making rice noodles. It was an interesting process. Many students and veterans took pictures and videos. Everyone went back to the front, purchased some drinks and pointy hats, and got back on the boat."

Perhaps the most impressionable part of the trip for Chase and Lou was a visit to some of the tunnels north of Saigon. Chase's description of this is noteworthy: "We visited the Cu Chi tunnels. These were a system of tunnels that extended from Cu Chi all the way to the Saigon River. The tunnels were extremely small, or at least they were before the area was commercialized for tourism. To give an idea of how small, I'm about 5 foot 10 inches, and I was on my hands and knees! The entrances were incredibly small, camouflaged, and scattered throughout the jungle. The Viet Cong would use these tunnels to confuse the ARVN and our troops. One veteran said that sometimes we would waste thousands of dollars in artillery because one or two Viet Cong would be able to create the illusion of a large force by using the tunnels."

"This was an emotional day for Mrs. Lou. At this tourist site, people were able to shoot some of the guns that were used in the War. Because of this attraction, there was a steady sound of gunfire. Mrs. Lou had been to this place multiple times before, but, for whatever reason, this time the gunfire struck a different nerve. At the start of the tour, when the sounds were distant, the gunfire only seemed to startle her a little. The gunfire became louder and louder as we approached the firing range, and, consequently, Mrs. Lou became more and more unsettled. When we reached the firing range, Mrs. Lou was in tears and trembling. At first, I was shocked. She had been here before, so why was the gunfire affecting her now? I was not sure what I should do. Luckily, there was a vendor there selling drinks. We purchased a coke, and Nurse Lori, myself, and a couple of others sat down with Mrs. Lou on some nearby benches. After a short time, refreshments, and a little bit of laughter, Mrs. Lou was alright again."

Another meaningful stop was at an old ARVN base at Phu Loi. This was in the area where Chase's great uncle served. Chase wrote in his journal. "Apparently, this was where Viet Cong POWs were kept by the ARVN. It looked somewhat restored. Each prison room held 300 to 500 Viet Cong POWs at one time. We went into one of the rooms, and it was lined with mannequins. The mannequins really made the place have an awful feel to it. President Davis and I were able to take a meaningful picture there. The old prison was probably one of the sites where Great Uncle Dan, President Davis' brother, served during his time in the military. We planted an American flag on the ground in front of us and snapped a few photos. My family will be happy to see these pictures."

Unfortunately, the group didn't see much of where the 91st EVAC Hospital at Chu Lai was located. Like so many other remnants of the War, it had been destroyed. Steve Hansen had also served in the area and shared some things with Lou and the group about a strategic battle that took place nearby.

 " Since we had two veterans who were actually there, we were able to sift through all of the propaganda present in the exhibits. "

Chase felt like the "Hanoi Hilton" was one of the most anticipated sites visited on the trip. He explained, "The Hilton was first built by the French, but during the Vietnam War, it was where the POWs were held. We were blessed to have two former POWs with our group [Bill Bailey and John Clark] who were held in the Hilton. We snapped a few photos at the entrance and split up into two groups, each following one of the two former POWs. There were two stories being told by all of the exhibits. The first was the story of French mistreatment of the Vietnamese. This story is true from all of the facts that we have. The second story was where things got interesting. It was the story of the American POWs and their treatment. Since we had two veterans who were actually there, we were able to sift through all of the propaganda present in the exhibits. One thing that really caught my attention was a video that was playing on repeat in one of the exhibits. The video sought to sell the message that the POWs were treated with extreme kindness and were allowed many different forms of leisure. The video also said that as time passed, the Americans had a *change of heart* and *realized the wrongs they had done*. This made me laugh. There were some things that were true, and the veterans pointed those out well. After this visit, I only had more respect for the veterans.

Being able to go back to a place where they were held prisoner for over six years showed extreme courage and bravery. Not only that, they were willing to share their stories. Originally, we were only going to spend about 45 minutes there and then leave, but we decided to stay longer and forget about going to a water puppet show. I am glad we did."

Chase Davis and Lou Eisenbrandt came back to the USA and found one more surprise. Chase recalled what happened: "People were lined up with *welcome home* signs and a live orchestra playing military tunes. There could not have been a more proper ending to our adventure.

> **❝ Thank you for your companionship on this trip, thank you for your service, and thank you for the lives you saved. ❞**

Veterans deserve all of that and much more than we could ever give them." He then turned to his veteran companion and said, "Thank you for your companionship on this trip, thank you for your service, and thank you for the lives you saved."[13]

TOPIC SUMMARY

Women who served during the Vietnam War served honorably and under the most difficult conditions. Unfortunately, they were not recognized for their sacrifices until years after the War ended. The Vietnam Women's Memorial in Washington, D.C., now has a bronze

Figure 75: Vietnam Women's Memorial in Washington, D.C. Photo courtesy of *Vietnam Nurse* by Lou Eisenbrandt, PETP 2014.

statue (Figure 75) of nurses ministering to a wounded soldier. Eight names of nurses who lost their lives are found on the Wall, including Lt. Sharon Lane (Figure 72, page 185), who lost her life in 1969 due to hostile fire.

Lou Eisenbrandt was one of a select group of American women who served in Vietnam. As a trained nurse she had a front-row experience of what the War was like. She and other professionals played a critical role at the 91st EVAC Hospital at Chu Lai (Figure 74, page 189), surviving rocket attacks (Figure 76) and dealing with injuries she never expected to see. This gave Lou a perspective on the War like few others have. Retired Lieutenant Colonel Ruth Sidisin described how there was no way to prepare:

Figure 76: Rocket attack smoke and debris outside the 91st EVAC Hospital at Chu Lai. Photo courtesy of *Vietnam Nurse* by Lou Eisenbrandt, PETP 2014.

"Because everyday was a disaster day.... There was a whole variety of just plain trauma. There were belly wounds, amputations, head injuries, burns. On top of that, they had infiltrations and complications. They had things we'd never heard about in school, [for example], dengue fever, malaria, hepatitis, and bubonic plague which they got from rats. It was exhausting; some days you felt you'd lived a lifetime in just weeks."[14] Ruth went on to conclude, "I consider it an honor to have served in Vietnam."[15]

The Vietnam Women's Memorial Foundation estimates that about 11,000 women were stationed in Vietnam during the conflict. Most of them volunteered and nearly 90 percent served as nurses, like Lou. However, it is important to note that women worked as physicians, air traffic controllers, clerks and in many other positions. Many women served with the Red Cross, Peace Corps, Catholic Relief Services, and other service organizations.

In her book, *Vietnam Nurse*, Lou Eisenbrandt puts her life in perspective for all to see:

> I would never wish for another war but would not change the experience that I had for anything. It is deeply entwined within the fiber of who I am. I chose not to ignore my past but rather to embrace it and share it in order that others may learn by the mistakes of Vietnam. I have addressed civic groups, hundreds of students from middle school level and above, veterans' organizations, and more. I have met some amazing individuals, made new friends, continued to travel, and even published photos and writings about the war. My effort to keep the tragedy of war in the public psyche will continue.
>
> I will also fight for a cure for Parkinson's disease by sharing my story, while offering insight and listening to those also affected by this crippling condition. Whether a result of exposure to the herbicides like Agent Orange (as in my case) or the result of some other factor, better treatment and a cure may soon be on the horizon. In the meantime, those of us who have adjusted to living with tremors, stiffness, poor balance, and depression, must assist others to live the best life that they can. That is a commitment that I made years ago and strive to fulfill every day.[16]

Lou Eisenbrandt's life reflects a commitment to helping others. In her travels with students from College of the Ozarks, she served as a role model to those who, like her as a young college student, don't know where life will lead or what the future holds.

PART III
LATER YEARS (1971-73)

OVERVIEW

As the new decade of the '70s unfolded, the influence of General Creighton Abrams was having an effect. Abrams adhered to the "one war" theory, based on the idea that the War was not just a guerrilla war, a big unit war, a search and destroy operation, a body count war, an infiltration route war, or ARVN (Army of the Republic of Vietnam, South) training only. The War was all interrelated as Abrams saw it. Therefore, in the last years of the War, there was less "search and destroy" and a lot more "clear and hold." A process President Nixon called "Vietnamization" was also implemented to better equip, train, and transfer responsibility and direction to the South Vietnamese government. Even North Vietnam Commander General Giap saw the change in the tactics.[1] Things seemed to be getting better. Nixon had survived the decision to invade Cambodia, which he authorized to clear out communist sanctuaries, a tactic that the military felt was long overdue.

In early 1971, Nixon authorized a raid of Laos, planned by General Abrams. This was a major challenge as ARVN could only depend on American air support. Unfortunately, in 1970 the Congress had passed the Cooper–Church Amendment that prevented American troops from going into Laos or Cambodia. Heavy casualties were inflicted on both sides, but the North Vietnamese Army (NVA) troops paid an especially high price as American air support inflicted heavy losses on enemy troops and made the difference.

It seemed that American planners had again misjudged the NVA's willingness to persevere. If nothing else, *Operation Lam Son 719* in March 1971 showed that Vietnamization was disappointing in that the U.S. had been supporting ARVN for over a decade. ARVN simply was not yet ready to take care of itself. The reporting back to America was less than encouraging. Nixon's problems at home were heightened when *The New York Times* published leaked Pentagon Papers in June of 1971. These documents were a result of a top-secret Department of Defense study of the United States' political and military involvement in Vietnam from 1945–1968. They had been turned over to the media by Daniel Ellsberg, a senior research associate at MIT (Massachusetts Institute of Technology) and former student of Henry Kissinger. The Report described the involvement of presidents Truman, Eisenhower, and Kennedy in planning actions to keep the communists from taking over the country.[2] The public learned that Johnson was planning for war before the nation knew about it. It was embarrassing for President Nixon, who took actions to discredit Ellsberg. President Nixon was paranoid about potential leaks like the *Pentagon Papers*. During his administration, a break-in occured at the DNC (Democratic National Convention) headquarters, in the Watergate building in Washington, D.C. This resulted in five burglars being caught, yet another unhelpful distraction to Nixon's efforts to bring the War to an end.

By early 1972, the Paris Peace Treaty talks had resumed, and Nixon visited China. This caused tension between China and the USSR. Shortly after Nixon's visit to China, General Giap took a risk and launched the Easter Offensive, figuring the NVA could launch a successful invasion since most American combat troops had departed. This was a miscalculation as American air power wreaked havoc on the NVA, which was exposed to an air attack.

By fall, an early breakthrough in negotiations appeared to have occurred with North Vietnam. However, President Thieu (ARVN) objected. The bombing of North Vietnam stopped for "secret talks" yet again. The last few months before the treaty was signed were tense. When Nixon suspected the North Vietnamese's strategy was to continue the War, he ordered *Operation Linebacker II*—the heaviest bombing Hanoi and Haiphong Harbor had ever seen. It was unrelenting from December 17-30 until North Vietnam accepted an American offer to resume talks.

Helicopters were everywhere—in all four combat zones and flying missions over North Vietnam. From the Delta area to the Central

Highlands, the Coastal Plains to the mountains of I-Corps and beyond, helicopters served in numerous capacities.

On the College of the Ozarks' very first Patriotic Education trip to Vietnam, the students were fortunate to hear instruction from three helicopter pilots, as well as two fighter pilots who were shot down and taken as prisoners of war (POWs). The POWs on this trip were willing to share their unbelievable stories of torture, perseverance and determination. The three helicopter pilots had extensive flight time in III- and IV-Corps. Later in the War, with most American combat troops gone, the Mekong Delta was left to be protected by pilots and advisors. Helicopter crews flew long hours to keep the NVA out of the southern tip of South Vietnam.

After years of imprisonment, freedom was in sight for POWs. President Nixon later wrote, "Our POWs knew they were coming home even if our editorial writers did not."[3] On February 12, 1973, *Operation Homecoming* started with the first POWs released by North Vietnam.

CLASS TOPIC 8: SCOUTS (III-CORPS)

...our mission was called hunter-killer....we were bait....he shot at you and you shot back.

INSTRUCTOR: CW4 JAMES (JIM) GREER, USA (RET.)[1]

"High school to flight school," is how James (Jim) Greer described the route that led him to the cockpit of an OH-6A, scout helicopter (Figure 79, page 211), and over the skies of South Vietnam. It was his best option since he had already decided at age 19 he wanted to fly, and because a college degree was not required to fly airplanes and helicopters. Mr. Greer told his student host, Jessica Turner: "Looking back, I believe it was the best decision I could have made at the time for my future career." He must have had second thoughts when he touched down on a crater-riddled runway at Bien Hoa AFB during the summer of 1969. He couldn't possibly have thought that he had made the safest decision by joining the Army in 1968 to learn to fly!

Mr. Greer served two combat tours in Vietnam. His first tour was in III-Corps; his missions were based out of Tay Ninh (Figure 77), flying for Alpha Troop, 1st Squadron of the 9th Cavalry. During this period of the War, Mr. Greer was flying in the aftermath of the Tet Offensive. Flying a scout helicopter, his job was to "scare 'em up," as he stated it. This was done by flying specified coordinates above suspected North Vietnamese Army (NVA) activity. Once the locale of the enemy was pinpointed, gunships flying 1500 feet above the scouts were called in to engage and protect the scout's retreat. Student host Jessica Turner wrote a journal entry asking how Mr. Greer could spot the enemy in such a thick canopy of forest. "They shot at you!" was his short answer. Specifically, "We were the bait!" But most of Mr. Greer's service time he described using the late Harry Reasoner's quote, "hours and hours of boredom punctuated by moments of stark terror."

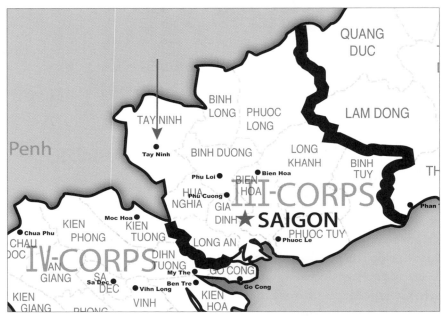

Figure 77: Tay Ninh, site from which Greer flew an OH-6A (LOH). Adapted from public domain.

Chief Warrant Officer Jim Greer was one of many who fought admirably while in harm's way. His decorations list includes two Bronze Stars, three Meritorious Service Medals, 31 Air Medals with one "V" device, two Army Commendation Medals with one "V" Device, a Purple Heart, two Vietnamese Service Medals, and four Vietnamese Campaign Medals.

Figure 78: Veteran Jim Greer and student host Jessica Turner. Photo by John Luck.

 STUDENT HOST: JESSICA TURNER

Jessica Turner (Figure 78) wanted to visit Vietnam for very personal reasons. Although she had never been outside of the United States, she was eager to travel because of the influence of her grandpa, a Vietnam veteran who had served as a medic with an aviation battalion near the demilitarized zone (DMZ). Jessica interviewed her grandpa before applying to go on this trip. What he told her laid the foundation for a once-in-a-lifetime experience.

"Grandpa told me that *the hardest part was just living*," said Jessica. "He was partially referring to the scorching 135-degree heat and unquenchable thirst he endured for thirteen months, but more so to the numerous deaths of his fellow soldiers and friends. It was not a triumphant fight for American freedom, but a controversial conflict that led to the deaths of over 58,000 American fathers, sons, daughters, brothers, and husbands. Most soldiers who served, including my grandpa, wondered why they were fighting a war for such a depraved place. Instead of gathering in celebration of the soldiers' return, Americans assembled to proclaim them *baby killers*. It was a dark time in our nation, making it my obligation to understand the hardships our soldiers suffered in both the unbearable Vietnamese jungle and the country they loved."

"My grandpa, Baxter Lee Turner, Sr., was in the 522nd Aviation Battalion, where he rappelled out of helicopters into enemy territory, providing medical aid to soldiers. He worked most of the time at a hospital in the DMZ, where he performed emergency surgery on wounded soldiers. It was heartbreaking to hear that of the 37 medics under his command, only two were still living after his first six months in Vietnam. He also provided medical treatment to orphans and refugees. In his interview, my grandpa lingered on one story in particular. He had spent a few hours treating an 11-year-old Vietnamese girl who had been beaten by men in her village. He left her with medicines and some candy. A week later, he was informed that North Vietnamese soldiers had brutally slaughtered the girl and her entire family because they had accepted treatment and supplies from a U.S. soldier, my grandpa. *That made me hate human beings, period,* confided my grandpa, when I asked him his initial thoughts on the tragedy. The stories did not end there. He remembered when he was called upon to treat thirty men whose feet were so raw from wading through wet sand that they had begun to walk on their knees. There was also a time when his backpack and boots were riddled with bullet holes while rappelling out of a helicopter. I asked him about the difficulty of leaving his two very young sons and his wife behind, *You have a heck of a time turning your back and getting on a plane,* he explained."

> **❝ It was a dark time in our nation, making it my obligation to understand the hardships our soldiers suffered in both the unbearable Vietnamese jungle and the country they loved. ❞**

Such testimony gave Jessica a newfound hunger to understand the sufferings of American soldiers in a personal way. When she told her grandpa she was applying for the trip, he was thrilled that she would want to visit the places where he gave so much of himself for his beloved country—a country that scorned him for his service at the time. Jessica could not comprehend the wickedness of those who killed that little girl or the weight that her grandpa carried when he blamed himself. She wrote, "I will never know the grief my grandpa experienced when, one-by-one, his friends were killed off, far before it was their time. I cannot fathom the fear my grandfather experienced when he rappelled out of that helicopter while bullets whizzed by. The only way I could begin to grasp his story would be to share in an experience like this trip."

Jessica Turner was born on Offutt Air Force Base in Nebraska and grew up in Sedalia, Missouri. Once enrolled at College of the Ozarks, she majored in business marketing and management. Along the way she was an active student, competing in Phi Beta Lambda competitions and participating in the College of the Ozarks Chorale. It is impressive that she wanted to honor her grandpa and other veterans. It has, no doubt, changed her perspective on the War and life.

HELICOPTER SCOUTS BACKGROUND

The Vietnam War is often referred to as the "helicopter war" for good reason. Helicopters came in many varieties and were used for a multitude of missions: some were small egg-shaped scouts named OH-6As; some were heavy-lift, twin-rotor Chinooks (CH-47s); another large, heavy-lift helicopter was named CH-53; fast, deadly gunships were named Cobras (AH-1s); and the troop lifts were named Hueys (UH-1s). Jim Greer experienced both extremes, the small scout and the large Chinooks. It was the scout that almost cost him his life.

During his first tour, Jim flew out of Tay Ninh. Tay Ninh (Figure 77) is located northwest of Saigon and is now a modest-sized city. During the Vietnam War, the Tay Ninh combat base was a busy place. Built early in the War, it was finally turned over to the ARVN in 1970, which controlled it until April of 1975, when the North Vietnamese occupied it. Unlike the Tay Ninh base, Phu Loi had a long history going back to the time of Japanese occupation during WWII. The U.S. base was used heavily between 1965 and 1972. It was Tay Ninh and Phu Loi that Jim Greer flew from during his first tour.

Jim Greer's experiences flying scout helicopters were not unlike that of many other American pilots. Donald Porter wrote about scouts seeing "combat up close" in *Air & Space* magazine: Upon reflecting on over 1,000 hours flying scout missions over Vietnam, Warrant Officer Clyde Romero said, "You were right in the enemy's face with a helicopter and had to know what you were doing."[2] Porter explained these fighting forces:

Army troops called the OH-6As Loaches, a contraction of "light observation helicopters." The ship was unusually light and had plenty of power, perfect for flying nap-of-the-earth missions, and its 26-foot-diameter main rotor made getting into tight landing zones a snap. It had no hydraulic system and its electrical setup was used primarily to start up the engine—simple even by 1960's standards, which for practical purposes meant it was easier to maintain and harder to shoot down than other helicopters. But the light aluminum skin could be easily pierced by rifle bullets, and it also crumpled and absorbed energy in a crash, and a strong structural truss protected critical systems—like the people inside. Loach crews regularly walked away from crashes that would doom others.

Missions began every day at dawn, when crews were briefed on where to fly and what to look for. To hunt for encampments, bunkers, or other signs of the enemy, commanders would deploy a flight of one scouting Loach and one supporting Cobra, called a Pink Team. (Scouts were known as White Teams and Cobras as Red; the two colors combine to become pink. In some areas, Purple Teams—one Loach, one Cobra and one Huey— were also common, as were other variations.) "We were so close to the elephant grass that we'd blow the grass apart to see if anyone was hiding in there," observer Bob Moses says. Moses, a nineteen-year-old draftee, arrived in Vietnam in July 1970 for the first of two year-long tours, and later worked for the Department of Veterans Affairs as a therapist and administrator. Even trampled grass was a clue; it meant that enemy troops had passed through the area within eight hours, the time it took for grass to dry upright. Since units were all but permanently assigned to particular areas, they came to know the local geography intimately and could spot anything out of the ordinary. "We were combat trackers," says [Hugh] Mills [a Vietnam helicopter pilot]. "I followed footsteps. I could see a cigarette butt still burning. I could tell how old a footprint was by how it looked.

"Most of our engagements [we] were 25 to 50 feet [away] when we opened up on [the Viet Cong]," Mills continues. "I've seen them, whites of the eyes, and they've seen me, whites of the eyes.... I have come home with blood on my windshield. A little gory but that's how close we were." As the Loach flew among the trees, the rear-seat pilot in the Snake (Cobra) circling above kept a close eye on the little Scout, and the front-seat gunner jotted down whatever the Loach observers radioed. Upon encountering enemy fire, Loaches were to leave immediately, dropping smoke grenades to mark the target so that within seconds, the Cobra could roll in. Loach crews were equipped with small arms and returned fire as they fled. They could also use grenades and on occasion even homebuilt explosives; more aggressive units mounted forward-firing miniguns. Cobras generally attacked with rockets, preferred for long-range accuracy, switching to the less-accurate chin-mounted machine gun and grenade launcher only if they were far enough away from friendly troops or if the rockets—AH-1s could carry as many as 76 rockets—ran out. Four troop-carrying Hueys (called a Blue Team) often sat idle somewhere nearby, ready to insert troops if the Pink Team discovered an interesting target—or were shot down and needed rescuing.

For most of the war, there was no formal Army training to prepare Scout pilots and observers. Army headquarters developed doctrine by building on what worked in the field, rather than the other way around, and each unit in-country did things slightly differently. Though Cobra pilots were trained stateside, most Loach pilots didn't take control of OH-6As until arriving in Vietnam. After around 10 hours at the controls of a Loach, the pilots were deemed worthy of flying in combat.[3]

INSTRUCTOR REFLECTIONS

Jim Greer served twenty years in the 1st Cavalry Division and was discharged as CW4 (Chief Warrant Officer). This included two tours in Vietnam, serving mostly as pilot of an OH-6A scout helicopter in III-Corps region. His second tour included piloting a Chinook helicopter. He gave students and veterans a quick overview: "I graduated from flight school on June 15, 1969, went on 30-day leave, and was in Vietnam by mid-July. I was hit by rocket fire January 26, 1970, while sitting in the cockpit waiting for take off. I was medevacked out of the country sometime toward the end of February or early March, through Japan to Scott Air Force Base and then Fort Bragg. I got home around late March. After convalescent leave, I was back on flying duty in May!"

"My second tour commenced in June of 1971, but I came back in April 1972 and was sent to Korea. When I left Vietnam, the NVA was preparing for their Easter Offensive, a massive effort by the enemy to crush the ARVN. Most American combat troops had departed. For a second time, intelligence was lacking regarding the timing of the attack. Also, the NVA devised a three-pronged assault (upper South Vietnam, central and southern). At first, the ARVN suffered losses, but in the end American air power prevailed. The NVA again absorbed tremendous losses. For the first time the NVA was beginning to see that they should negotiate an American withdrawal, leaving President Thieu in power in the South (no doubt to be dealt with later)."

Right before Mr. Greer was to leave, he was injured again, but this time from a different kind of combat—volleyball! He explained, "I broke my right arm and was grounded. I was within my DROS date (date eligible for return from overseas) and the drawdown was continuous. If you were an aviator and you were grounded, you obviously were not flying, so you go home."

Chief Warrant Officer Greer's overview was followed by his explanation of what his tours were really like. First of all, upon arrival in Vietnam he was sent to Bien Hoa, where the 1st Cavalry Division "charm school" was held. All officers who came into the 1st Cav Division had to go there to be indoctrinated and learn their SOPs (standard operating procedures). Mr. Greer got an early welcome to combat before he touched down: "Our plane was not allowed to land but was instructed to *go around* because there was a mortar attack on Bien Hoa Air Base at that time. You could see explosions splashing out around the runway, and we had to wait till they stopped so we could be cleared to land. I was riding with a guy I went to flight school with, so we knew enough that we looked at each other and thought, *What are we doing here?*"

Mr. Greer continued his recollections with an explanation of mission assignments: "Generally, our mission was called *hunter-killer*. We had an OH-6A helicopter and we used a crew of three, a pilot plus two; some only used a pilot plus one. In our unit, scout crews consisted of the pilot, right seat; an observer (OSCAR), left seat; and a door gunner (TORQUE), rear seat right side. We flew treetop level and in right-hand circles looking for the enemy, with a Cobra helicopter at about 1,500 feet circling above us. A Cobra was a gunship, and he was our cover. We had a machine gun, and we carried grenades and things like that, but we were not offensive by any stretch. We called it *trolling*; we were bait. When we came upon the enemy, they would hear us coming; but if you're on the ground and the helicopter is at treetop level, you can't tell where it is coming from until you see it. You hear the noise, but it's hard to determine its location, so you didn't always get shot at first. Sometimes you saw the enemy and you shot at him, or you threw a smoke grenade out to mark the area. As soon as you did that, he shot at you and you shot back. When these engagements happened, the Cobra gunship covered our escape."

"The Cobra had all the contact with the Air Force forward air controllers (FACS). So, if you found something significant, then you had the F-4s or F-5s come in. Of course, the hope always was that you didn't have to mark the spot with a smoking helicopter."

"There were three basic rules of engagement for flying scouts to survive: number one – never hover, so don't stop; number two – don't fly parallel to a tree line, always fly 90 degrees, because if the enemy is out there in the open, in the clearing, and you fly parallel to the tree line, you've lost your cover; and number three – never land, not intentionally. If you got shot up and had to land, then you didn't have any choice, but don't do it intentionally. So, you follow those three rules of engagement or survival techniques."

Scout's Rules of Engagement

1. Never slow down and hover
2. Never fly parallel to a tree line
3. Never (intentionally) land

"There was a gentleman who was my platoon leader when I first got there, and he told me those rules of engagement. He retired as a Lieutenant Colonel in the National Guard. He also gave me the kind of information I needed to have—once you got engaged, once somebody was shooting at you, what to do to make yourself less of a target. I learned quickly that you listen to those guys. When I first got there my platoon leader had nine or ten months in-country. He was getting ready to move out of scouts and go home after a ground assignment within the squadron. I remember thinking, *That's the guy I want to talk to—the fellow who has done this for months, and he is still alive!* I wanted to know, *How did he do it?* I'd reflect on those rules often. I wanted the rules to be second nature. When you fly in the left seat with the seasoned guys, you're doing right-hand circles and the pilot flies in the right seat. The scout is the only helicopter in which the command pilot flies in the right seat. You listen, watch, and pay attention to what is going on, because you know soon they will cut you loose and let you be the pilot in command."

"Sometimes we stumbled into things. One incident stands out in my mind. Of all things, we stumbled onto a Viet Cong (VC) soldier cooking rice! This encounter happened at what we called the Northwest Reconnaissance Zone. The city we flew out of was Tay Ninh, and the zone was located about 25 or 30 miles north and west, up toward what we called the Dog's Head. My crew chief spotted the man making rice as we made a right-hand circle, and the chief said, *Come right; I've got an enemy cooking rice by a fire!* So we came around, and the crew chief zeroed in and started shooting at the guy. The next thing we knew, we had Quad 50s and 30 calibers coming at us. We had run across an anti-aircraft battalion of NVA. We couldn't get out of there fast enough!"

"The crew chief said, *I have no idea how you did that.* I had tree limbs that were hitting the side of the helicopter. We were down in the trees, trying to stay out of sight. We had basketball-sized tracers, or they appeared that big, coming past us. When a Quad 50 shoots a 50 caliber, it makes a distinct *BOOM, BOOM, BOOM, BOOM*—that's what it sounds like when you are on the receiving end! I'm sure it's faster than that on the ground, but that's what it sounded like. Tracers were coming past the cockpit on both sides and they didn't hit us—they didn't hit us at all! We got out of that one and my crew chief still tells that story; he always says, *To this day, I still don't understand how Greer got us out of that!*"

"Well, as a scout pilot, getting shot at was fairly routine. We would take rounds. Then, we would go land, because the engine was damaged or to assess what damage had been done. We would just try to get to someplace that was secure. This happened a lot to us, because we were there to be shot at, and more times than not, we'd get hit. They knew as much about what they were doing as we did about what we were doing. They were pretty good at hitting us too!"

Even though his helicopter was shot down six or seven times, it was rocket fire (Figure 79) on the ground that gave Chief Warrant Officer Greer a "million dollar wound" and a trip home. "They use that terminology, because that means you got a wound but it didn't kill you, and you're going home. It was one of the euphemisms that evolved over the years, probably in the crew chief hooches."

Figure 79: Greer's OH-6A after mortar exploded nearby. Photo courtesy of Jim Greer, PETP 2014.

"The crew members were the ones I always felt the closest to because they really didn't have a single thing to say about their destiny. They would climb in the back of a helicopter with you, and they were yours. From that point to when you came back and landed, that young man had nothing to say about anything. That, to me, was a heavy responsibility. It was one thing for me to be stupid and do something silly, but if I was going to take him or that guy in the left seat with me, it was different because they weren't pilots. We taught the guys in the left seat how to fly on a scout mission in case we got shot. They would learn how to recover the aircraft and fly straight and level and how to land. We taught them that."

Training and communication were important. Jim recalls, "When we first got to charm school, they gave us a piece of paper with instructions on how we wanted our parents or next of kin notified in the event that something occurred or you're killed. They also gave you an intermediate choice if you're just wounded. *Do you want your parents notified?* and I checked the box for *No*. I would call them the first chance I got. They didn't need to know any of that stuff. Well, they bypassed that and sent a letter home when I got injured. My father was a World War II veteran, a B-17 crewman. One of my family members on the other side was on the *U.S.S. Nevada* during Pearl Harbor. They had some idea about what was going on. When Daddy got that letter—I was told this story by John's daughter—he took it to John, who was an engineer with Westinghouse, for an explanation about the injuries. She said my father was white as a ghost when he came up and knocked on the door. I imagine my mother was on the bed crying her eyes out because she had no earthly idea what had happened. That is what I was trying to avoid with that piece of paper when I said *No*—probably one of the only smart things I tried to do while I was over there. But the military did what it did best and took the shortest distance between two points so that they didn't have to explain anything. In the letters that I wrote home, never once did I talk about our mission."

Mr. Greer was out of commission for several months. As he explains, "I was either in the hospital recuperating or getting over the stitches. They sewed you up with bailing wire if you had a big gash someplace, because they could get more meat than they did using catgut. I didn't feel any of it going in, but I'll tell you what, having those stitches removed was an experience; it's not like pulling the catgut. But anyway, I was grounded for about two months." Upon recovery, Mr. Greer ended up in Washington, D.C.

"I was young; I hadn't even made CW-2 (Chief Warrant Officer 2) yet because you had to wait a year. I got to Washington in May and made CW-2 in June. We were flying people from the State Department and practiced the White House Evacuation Mission, but we never actually had to use it."

"I flew once with Kissinger, and I think I almost knocked General Westmoreland down in the hangar one day by accident. We flew Alexander Haig, and we flew all the chiefs of staff for all four services."

It didn't take Mr. Greer long to get bored. He explained, "I went down to the branch office and talked to a fellow named Don Houston. I told Don, *Look, I want to transition. I want to fly something bigger than a Huey; I want to fly Cranes.*" (Figure 80)

"A [skycrane] crane is a helicopter that resembles a mosquito," Mr. Greer described, "It's a CH-54, but they don't fly them anymore. The National Guard got rid of their last ones about 15 years ago. Sikorsky built them, and the Army bought them. They were built as ship-to-shore aircraft to move cargo back and forth between big cargo ships. The Army bought them and for what reason I'm not sure, because they

Figure 80: Sikorsky CH-54 Tarhe (skycrane) helicopter. Photo from public domain.

only had about a 25-minute fuel range when they were at max gross weight. Don, at the branch office, said, *I don't know. We are toning down our crane usage, but if you want to fly Chinooks I can get you into Chinook school.* I said, *Oh, okay, that sounds alright.*"

"A Chinook is a twin engine, CH-47. A CH-46 was the Marine version; it had one engine and a little bit of a bow in it. The Army version had twin engines. The Army didn't have any CH-53 Sea Stallions. The Navy, Air Force, and Marines had them. They were pretty big, but they weren't as big as a Chinook. They had one rotor, but they had six blades. I flew the 47s which are still flying to this day. They were bought in 1958, and they will be operating through 2060! The Army got its money out of that helicopter. Don Houston said, *I can get you into 47 school, but you will have to volunteer to go back for another tour in Vietnam.*"

"The Army had a price for everything. *Okay, I can understand that, if you're going to spend money on me to send me to school....okay.* Houston said *Oh, there's another catch.* And I said, *Okay, what is that?* He said, *I have a quota for safety school, and you need to go there on your way.* Safety school at the time was at the University of Southern California in Los Angeles, and it was three months long. In January of 1971, I went to the University of Southern California, and in April, I went to Fort Rucker and went through CH-47 transition. Then in June, I went back to Vietnam. I was a CH-47 safety officer in a combat zone. I was trying to reconcile in my head exactly what all of that meant. I asked my major when I got there, *What the heck do you want me to do as your safety officer?* He said, *We'll both figure that out as we go along.* That's how I ended up going back to Vietnam for tour number two."

 **" These helicopters were always being shot up, shot down or blown up. The Army never replaced lost aircraft with new ones; we just always got old ones, all the hand-me-downs! "**

"In my second tour, I never heard a round fired. I was more concerned with that helicopter killing us than anything else, because there were countless different ways for that to occur. The helicopters were old A-model CH-47s that were all built back in the early '60s. The 1st Cavalry never got new anything. These helicopters were always being shot up, shot down or blown up. The Army never replaced lost aircraft with new ones; we just always got old ones, all the hand-me-downs!"

Upon Mr. Greer's return to the U.S., he found the country unfriendly to veterans. "I thought it was unpatriotic, at a minimum, and I thought to myself, *I'd sure like to be locked up in a room with these two (Jane Fonda and Tom Hayden) for about fifteen minutes and have nobody bother us and forget the noises you would hear coming out of there!* I had plenty to keep me busy, but I remember the protests quite well, because they were in the news and on *60 Minutes.* Everybody was talking about it, and we all knew of it."

Like many veterans, Jim Greer resented micromanagement of the

War by those in Washington, D.C.: "I am saying micromanagement or management by those who didn't know anything about it. They were making decisions based on their own opinions. They must have had good information, but it was information that didn't fit."

Mr. Greer wanted to help the Vietnamese orphans. He remembered, "I ran into a Sister Celia when I was working for Sikorsky, years and years later. I had to go out to the Catholic University in Washington, D.C. She was the nun who was in charge of seeing to it that the orphans from Vietnam were relocated back into this country after the War. We had lunch together, and as a result of that meeting I became a donor to her cause for about 10 to 15 years. I would get letters from her every year at Christmastime."

Jim Greer did not fly as far south as IV-Corps: "I did not have much contact with ARVN on either tour, because my missions were different. I was not involved with troop insertions or extractions. When I flew Chinooks, it was a cargo resupply of fire bases, for the most part."

"When we were there in '69, the Dog's Head (Figure 30, page 76) primarily belonged to two organizations in the U.S. Army: one was the 25th Division, which worked out of Cu Chi. The other was the 5th special forces, with a fire base where the Dog's Head abutted Vietnam. The fire bases were shaped like a star, not a circle, and that's how you knew it was a special forces fire base. They had pits, artillery pits at each point of the star. Other Army firebases were circular with artillery placed at points around the perimeter."

> **" I am saying micromanagement...They were making decisions based on their own opinions....information that didn't fit. "**

"We also flew long-range reconnaissance patrols (LRRPs, pronounced "lurps") for the long-range patrol guys: We would insert those guys and then go back and pick them up. They normally ran a seven-day mission. We had no idea where they were going or what they were doing, and then we would get the call to go pick them back up. Almost always, we would get enemy contact when we picked them up. When we put them in, we did not have air cover. We could just send a Huey out to insert them, but we always had Cobras and a scout go out with the Huey to pick them up."

Like many veterans, Jim Greer resented the media. He recalled, "I saw Mike Wallace. I never interviewed with CBS, but they spent one day talking to our commander, the first sergeant, and folks like that. Our guys despised them; they hated them because of what we/they saw on *60 Minutes*. We saw *60 Minutes* and heard broadcasts on AFVN (Armed Forces Vietnam Network)."

Mr. Greer felt like American soldiers were misrepresented by the media: "Well, it wasn't just *a troop*, it was the *whole War*. We felt like it was being told from a different point of view, and it was a biased viewpoint. We didn't have much use for them. There's never been such a thing as a pretty war. There are always bad things that happen in war. The Mỹ Lai massacre was a good example of what can happen when things come off the rails, but then it ends up being poster-worthy for the entire War."

❝ We felt like it was being told from a different point of view, and it was a biased viewpoint. ❞

Greer's personal life was also affected by media bias. He remembered, "I dated a girl from Fredericksburg before I left Washington to return to Vietnam. When I came back for the second time, she was still single and still around. I found her and went out with her once. We were halfway up Route 1, going to a movie someplace, when she brought up Vietnam. She said something about me being a *baby killer,* and that was when I turned the car around and took her back home. I said, *You and I have just parted company.* Those were the kinds of seeds that were being planted back here in the United States by the media."

"Not too long ago. I saw an interview of John Kerry on television. He said something about his experience in Vietnam, and I immediately sat up in my chair, thinking of when he threw his ribbons at the White House fence. Boy, we would have liked to have gotten our hands on him. I found out from John Kerry that *if you get three Purple Hearts, you can leave.* I didn't know that was in the regulations. So when he got three Purple Hearts, he went home."

"The one visitation that I remember most vividly was when a B-52 crew came to join us, and I believe there were four of them—three captains and a major. They came over from Thailand. They wanted to see how we operated because they knew we did bomb damage assessments for arc lights. Their bombing missions were referred to as arc lights. Arc light was the terminology we used for the massive destruction in a particular grid square or target box of B-52s. The bombs were dropped from about 35,000 to 40,000 feet and would go *BOOM, BOOM, BOOM, BOOM, BOOM, BOOM!* The bombing noise was massive and could be heard from halfway across the country. The North Vietnamese were scared of B-52s. When the last bombs went in, we went in behind them and gave a report of the damage—any kills or any of that kind of stuff."

"Well, the visiting crew wanted to go out with us. We put one captain in the front seat of each of the OH-6As and one in the front seat of each Cobra. You almost always came in contact with the enemy, because they knew that we would be coming after the last bombs were dropped. They would wait for you underground, and then they would come up and start shooting. Well, sure enough, we made enemy contact, and one of those Air Force captains got a kill with an M16. Boy, you should have been in the officers' club that night. You'd have thought he was Audie Murphy! He actually got a kill. They all wanted to come fly our mission. Everyone of us was pulling our wings off saying, *Give me yours, and you take mine. I'll go back to where you came from, and you come here.* If one of them would have gotten killed or if one of their helicopters had been shot down, it would have been a different story."

Jim was asked to explain the helicopter we'd seen in the yard of the museum where the Peace Treaty was signed in Saigon. He told the students, "It's a UH-1, referred to as a *hog*. Hog was another term used for a Huey, because the first ones that came over had the rocket launchers on the side." Also in the museum, a big deal was made about Agent Orange. Jim Greer recalled, "Well, that was another thing. We didn't distribute Agent Orange in our missions. That whole area of operation, called the Northwest Reconnaissance Zone, was the whole northern area of III-Corps going up to the Cambodian border. It went all the way up the west side and across the north. The whole area had been treated with

Agent Orange. We hated to go around that area because it had been defoliated to the point that you didn't have the canopy cover. So if the enemy popped up while you were there, then you were uncovered and extremely vulnerable."

STUDENT RESPONSE

"This brings back memories," Jim Greer told student host, Jessica Turner (Figure 78, page 203), upon arriving in Saigon. Jessica listened as Mr. Greer recalled his first landing, almost 50 years ago, circling because of mortar fire and finally landing on a runway full of mortar potholes. Jessica recalled, "It was quite an introduction to the past! Although it was painful for the veterans to relive frightful memories, it was necessary for us to learn the impact of the Vietnam War."[4]

From day one of the trip, Jessica learned more and more about her own life in America and her responsibilities of citizenship. She remembered Jim telling her, "The government *is* the people." Jessica said it was enlightening to hear her veteran speak about this because, as she observed, "We are often caught up in blaming political leaders, rather than the people." She felt as if her many conversations with Jim Greer prompted her to reflect on her roles and responsibilities as a citizen of the U.S.

The visit to Cu Chi (Figure 30, page 76) was a memorable experience for Jessica, as it was for all students on the trip. She remembered, "Jim mentioned that the tunnels in Cu Chi were helpful in understanding why the NVA was so effective. They had an extremely strong will to fight and were willing to suffer in poor conditions. The Americans, Jim said, were not as passionate about their fight as the Viet Cong. Americans were not willing to live underground for months at a time in order to win South Vietnamese independence."

Jessica recalled, "While walking the trails at Cu Chi, we heard rapid AK-47 fire from a firing range at the site. It would be an understatement to say it was haunting. I immediately thought of the veterans and what terrible memories the sound had triggered. Jim told me that AK-47 fire was the *scariest sound in the world!* I would be dishonest if I said it didn't make me emotional. I couldn't help but think of how terrifying it would be to have that sound surrounding me, harming my friends and endangering our crew in the middle of a jungle where I couldn't even see the enemy. The sound made me sick, and I saw many emotions expressed by the veterans. Some tried to tune out the sound with conversation; some were silent. One was crying, clearly affected by flashbacks. I gained a completely new understanding of just how haunting the War is to the veterans."

All stories from Jim Greer were not sad. "He told me this humorous story about a time when he was a private rushing around and found himself staring General Westmoreland in the face, almost knocking him down. Westmoreland told him to *slow down there*. It gave me a good laugh."

"I learned so much from Jim and really enjoyed hearing his stories. We also encountered a Russian man in his twenties. He asked us where we were from and, when we said America, he told us we were lucky to live in the greatest country on earth. This really surprised me. I often get the impression that other countries dislike America, especially with Russia's history with America. The conversation revealed to me how thankful I should be to have been born in America."

"I enjoyed my conversations on the bus with Jim. He compared the developing Vietnamese economy with Korea's economy. Vietnam is following in the footsteps of South Korea, encouraging trade and foreign investment."

We marked the enemy's location with a burning helicopter.

"Something Jim said brought the War into perspective. I asked him more about his experiences as a scout helicopter pilot. He said that a common phrase among the scout pilots was, *We marked the enemy's location with a burning helicopter*. According to Jim, this phrase was true all too often. Scouting helicopters were often shot down. Jim mentioned one incident where he barely missed that fate. He was flying a scout mission and flew straight into an NVA anti-aircraft battalion. We were aggressively attacked and barely made it out. *Someone up there was watching over us that day; we shouldn't have made it out alive*, said Jim."

Jim explained details about his day to Jessica: "Jim told me his war consisted of daily flying into danger and then back out again. *The ground troops, he said, had a different experience. They would have a very rough battle, but then it would be over for a short while. They were hit harder and with a more one-on-one personal intent."*

The visit to Hanoi stood out in Jessica's mind: "I could definitely tell we were in North Vietnam. The tour guide would not carry the American flag. Every business and home had a Vietnamese flag hanging outside, almost as if it were a requirement. We also had to censor what we said about the "Hanoi Hilton" and its propaganda."

"It was inspiring to hear John Clark and Bill Bailey's experiences as POWs. John Clark explained the tap code he used to communicate through the walls of his prison cell. Both veterans described the *sewer grass* and *pumpkin soups* as *barely sustaining*. The guilt of revealing information during torture was almost as bad as the torture itself. I cannot imagine living six years in the conditions the POWs described."

"The Hanoi Hilton itself was sickening. We saw the leg irons used on American POWs for punishment, as well as the tiny, dark, cold concrete cells. The wall keeping the prisoners in was topped with broken glass and electrical fencing. I can't imagine trying to escape."

"The part of the museum that disturbed me the most was a small room dedicated to the living conditions of the Americans. According to POW Bill Bailey, *the beds, Christmas dinners, and wonderful treatment described in the video and pictures was complete propaganda.* There was no mention that the prisoners hardly saw the light of day and nearly starved to death. What made the whole experience real for me was seeing Bailey search through a book of American POWs to find the names of his friends. My veteran, Jim, asked Mr. Bailey how he could possibly come back to this place. Bill said, *I guess I can come back because I left.* I will never forget this experience at the Hanoi Hilton. Its technical name, *Hỏa Lò*, translating to *Hell Hole*, is very fitting."

At the end of the trip, Jessica reflected on her time with Jim and the other veterans: "I had bittersweet feelings about leaving Vietnam. I will miss these amazing veterans, especially Jim. We have shared many serious conversations about the tragedies of the War and an equal amount of laughs. He has also shown me the importance of the free enterprise system, in addition to his Vietnam experiences. I have learned so much, and I cannot wait to share my experience with others. However, there is no way I can fully convey what this trip has meant to me. In my essay, I wrote that I wanted to be able to connect with my grandpa in a way no one else in my family can. I can honestly say I have surpassed that goal."

❝ I am overjoyed to see that they were able to experience the welcome home that they were hideously deprived of after the Vietnam War. God bless America! ❞

"I was so glad to return to America. It was a surprise to see an amazing *welcome home* for the veterans. The band played, and many people were holding supportive signs. Both the students and the veterans were very touched. I am overjoyed to see that they were able to experience the welcome home that they were hideously deprived of after the Vietnam War. God bless America!"

TOPIC SUMMARY

Flying a scout helicopter in the Vietnam War was a high-risk assignment. This is confirmed by the fact that one-half of those serving in the conflict were shot down. According to Gary Roush of the Vietnam Helicopter Pilots Association, 1422 of the OH-6A models were in combat and 964 were lost. Specifically, 233 pilots were killed along with 251 crew members. These numbers were second only to the widely-used Hueys.[5]

Chief Warrant Officer Jim Greer accumulated hours flying "hunter-killer" missions in the OH-6A. Known as a LOACH, it was a small scout helicopter, made primarily of plexi glass and metal—thin metal. The incident on the ground that sent Mr. Greer home demonstrates the damage (Figure 79, page 211) that even nearby rockets can do. While Mr. Greer sustained injuries, he likely would not have survived had the mortar directly hit the "bubble."

On Mr. Greer's second tour in III-Corps ('71-72) he flew a Chinook (Figure 73, page 188), a large, heavy-lift helicopter. Ironically, Jim said of his second tour, "I never heard a round fired!"

Mr. Greer left the Army a decorated (and blessed) soldier, applying much of what he learned in the military to a career in the business world.

He has never forgotten those with whom he served and the country they all served with honor.

Jim Greer was intrigued to hear that a college would spend its money to send Vietnam veterans and students on a trip such as this. He said, "I was surprised about it and I was grateful for the opportunity, because I had been promising myself for years I would go back. With a wife and family and a job and all, it just kept sliding off the priorities and back into a *when I get around to it* category. When a friend of the College called and shared that this opportunity could be available to me, I thought he was kidding at first. I didn't know what the heck he was talking about!"

Jim wasn't suspicious or apprehensive about traveling with college students and was rather encouraged: "As a matter of fact, I've told many of the students on the trip and numerous people since that the students at College of the Ozarks have ignited my faith that there is still hope left. I mean, every parent must be glad as punch that the College has programs like this. After talking with my grandson about my impression of the College, he said he's *definitely interested*. Of course, he's only in fifth grade!"

❝ I've told many of the students on the trip and numerous people since that the students at College of the Ozarks have ignited my faith that there is still hope left. ❞

Mr. Greer was surprised and pleased to have had the chance to instruct the students from College of the Ozarks about his treetop-level combat perspective in Vietnam. He and others took great risks flying observation helicopters.

Many of these pilots and crews lost their lives, but never their honor.

CLASS TOPIC 9: "DELTA EMERGENCY" (IV-CORPS)

We killed the entire command element.

⬤ INSTRUCTOR: CPT THOMAS (TOM) EGLESTON, USA (RET.)[1]

Thomas Egleston was a baby boomer. Born in 1946, he grew up under the care of parents from the "Greatest Generation" in northeast New Jersey. Though Tom's father had been identified as unfit for military service because of deafness, there were plenty of war-hardened individuals around. So veterans were always a part of Tom's life. Even as a Boy Scout, Tom and his fellow scouts were influenced by the stories of their scoutmaster, who spoke of his exploits in the Pacific as a Seabee.

Somewhere along the way Tom got interested in flying. He graduated from high school and entered Norwich University, an all-male, military institution in Vermont. While in college, Tom finally settled on Army ROTC, to be commissioned upon graduation. Although Tom passed a flight physical, the Army overlooked his flight school qualifications and sent him for a field artillery basic course, one week after he got married. After finishing this program, he notified his chain of command that he was supposed to have gone to flight school.

Finally, Tom attended flight school and learned to fly the UH-1 (Huey). In February of 1970, Egleston arrived in Vinh Long, South Vietnam, as part of "D" Troop 3/5 Cavalry; it was to be his base of operations for the next 365 days, and Vietnam was to become one of the defining periods in Tom's life. By the time Tom arrived in the Mekong

Delta region, President Nixon had declared IV-Corps pacified, which meant that American ground troops had been withdrawn. That is, except for aviation and engineer units who conducted support operations for the ARVN (Army of the Republic of Vietnam). For the duration of his tour, Tom operated under an American officer for air command and an ARVN officer for mission command.

Tom recalled several instances from the beginning of his tour when he and his comrades were restrained from landing their troops to engage the enemy due to incompetence of ARVN commanders. In the Mekong Delta, the element of surprise was vital, and the reaction time of commanders to give the go-ahead was critical. However, the reaction time of ARVN commanders undermined mission effectiveness. The Viet Cong would slip away in an instant, if allowed. Tom quickly realized that he was going to be fighting the War with one hand tied behind his back. Despite the unassertive nature of certain ARVN commanders, today Tom remains objective: "Some were good and some were not, just like our military." Regardless, questionable decisions made by his superiors made it clear to Tom that he was not there to win this war, at least not for the South Vietnamese people. He was there to fly missions for his fellow pilots and crew chiefs. An inexplicable bond was forged and remains today between Tom and his comrades. One such bond that remains alive and well is with John Sorensen, a pilot with whom Tom flew during his tour in Vietnam. After logging thousands of hours of flight time all over the Mekong Delta, into Cambodia, inserting and extracting ARVN, special forces, RFPF (Regional Force Popular Force or "Ruff Puffs"), and Navy SEALs, Tom returned stateside in February of 1971. He was honorably discharged from the Army in April 1972. He joined the New Jersey National Guard in 1979 as a pilot and platoon leader but reverted to warrant officer a few years later. In the civilian theater, Tom worked as the head of administrative operations for multiple corporations in New Jersey and New York City.

One of the most memorable experiences of his life, however, would be during his time in the National Guard when the World Trade Center towers were attacked on September 11, 2001. "If you've never been to New York, you don't know how enormous they were," he said of the twin towers. He recalls New York shutting down completely: "It was an eerie feeling to be the only person walking down the street in midtown Manhattan." His ARNG (Army National Guard) unit activated Tom in order to fly support operations for the next six days, as they were the closest military heliport to NYC. Tom transported many FBI personnel and VIPs from location to location throughout the week.

Subsequently, Tom moved to Florida to get remarried and start a new segment of his life where he could make a difference as a 911 operator/dispatcher for the Broward Sheriff's Office. Tom commuted to New Jersey for drills and in 2003, finally retired after four years of active duty in the Army and 24 years in the Army National Guard.

Tom received many decorations: the Bronze Star, with one Oak Leaf Cluster for Meritorious Service; 32 awards of the Air Medal and two Awards of the Air Medal for Valor; the National Defense Service Medal; the Vietnam Service Medal; the Vietnam Campaign Medal; and the Cold War Victory Medal. Additionally, he is entitled to wear the Republic of Viet Nam Cross of Gallantry w/Gold Palm because it was awarded to his unit while he was serving. He is also entitled to wear Master Army Aviator wings for his military service.

After moving back "north" to Tennessee in 2007, Tom's "soul mate," Diane, passed away. Tom has remained active in civic life. As his student host Jacob Mullet (Figure 81) said: "Thomas Egleston has lived an incredible life of service. He is one of those men to whom my generation can look up to and recognize the debt we owe."

Figure 81: Student host Jacob Mullet and veteran Thomas Egleston. Photo by John Luck.

 STUDENT HOST: JACOB MULLET

When applying for the Patriotic Education trip to Vietnam, Jacob Mullet (Figure 81) said, "I want to be on this trip not to travel, but to revere the men who went to war, knowing that if they survived and came back home they might not be welcome. That takes something special." This young man was taking his education seriously. As a sophomore, he had already made up his mind to major in history and business administration with a minor in military science. Jacob's application reflected the impressions made on him by previous generations of those who served. He said, "With a lot of service members in my family, my parents brought me up to have the utmost respect for the military."

"My parents are Brad and Kari Mullet and I am the youngest of four children. My siblings, Whitney, Kelsey, and Peter have all graduated from College of the Ozarks. When I was six years old, my parents entered the mission field to do church planting in Budapest, Hungary. I spent the next 12 years of my life as a third-culture kid in central Europe. First through 12th grades were spent at the International Christian School of Budapest. Basketball and soccer consumed my time. Upon high school graduation, I enrolled at College of the Ozarks. My job assignments included resident assistant, custodian, and dining room server in the College of the Ozarks work program. At the College, patriotism is taken seriously and embraced as a civic duty."

"I feel the strongest emotions at social events when veterans are asked to rise, and my father and other relatives stand. They are the kind of emotions that I cannot put a finger on, a mixture of pride, respect, and intense humility. When I was younger, I always wanted to be like those men standing. Seeing an older veteran saluting his flag makes me think twice about what I have done with my life. Men who now struggle with everyday tasks spent their prime years clinging to life. The average age of soldiers in the Vietnam War was 19, so life was supposed to be just beginning, but it was taken away from many of them. Among other relatives who are veterans, my Great Uncle Gord was drafted into the Army at the time of the Vietnam War. *The drill sergeants hated us draftees; we didn't want to go to Vietnam,* I remember him saying. At College of the Ozarks, my respect for veterans is nurtured. Last year, I joined the Missouri National Guard and contracted Army ROTC. I am confident I was able to 'sign on the dotted line' because I remembered the heroes, the elderly men with their WWII or Vietnam vet ball caps. Seeing an older man who can hardly walk but musters the strength to stand in respect of the nation he and his friends bled for grips something in you. The Vietnam War was a horrific conflict, one that took a kind of courage I could never hope to possess. It is difficult to accept, *Thank you for your service* from a man wearing a Vietnam veteran hat, knowing that I will never be half the man he is."

HUEYS "DELTA EMERGENCY" IV-CORPS BACKGROUND

Tom Egleston had been in South Vietnam for about ten days when he found out just what a "Delta Emergency" meant—and he'd only been flying a few days! According to Tom, he was serving in the Delta (Figure 82), which was broken down into four sections with each section being assigned to a Vietnamese commander. He pointed out that one section belonged to the 9th ARVN Division, one belonged to the 21st Division, one belonged to the 7th ARVN Division, and then there was one area out in the middle of nowhere toward the Cambodian border called the 44th Special Tactical Zone. The latter was manned by the equivalent of the National Guard or RFPF Troops ("Ruff Puffs"). All of these were South Vietnamese units, because in 1969, President Nixon had declared that the Delta was pacified, and all American troops were pulled out.

Egleston recalled, "When I got over in February 1970, the only Americans were advisors and helicopter pilots, basically. Since there were no American ground troops, we worked with the Vietnamese. We

Figure 82: IV-Corps map. Adapted from public domain.

worked for a different Vietnamese commander every day. During my first mission, we were located in an area called *The Tram*—a wide, open, unpopulated area. It was on the Cambodian side of Can Tho, close to Chau Doc. (Figure 82) *The Tram* was a vast area of nothing—no villages, no rice paddies—just a wide-open area."

"Every day the commander would send out 13 helicopters for our mission: four scout helicopters, four Cobra gunships, four Hueys, and one command and control Huey. Basically, our job was to go out and find the enemy and see if we could stir something up. And, if it got too big to handle, we would turn it over to a unit that had more assets than we did, an air mobile or an assault helicopter company."

Captain Egleston explained to students and other veterans the details of a mission that culminated in an emergency: "Our air mission commander one day was actually the Cobra platoon leader. He had the eyes of a hawk. When we flew our missions, the command and control helicopter (Figure 83) was usually 800-900 feet above the ground. They were between the scouts at treetop level and the Cobras, who were 1500 feet above the ground. The commander told the lead scout about this area of trees in the middle of nowhere. He said he thought he saw some *blue* down through the trees. The NVA sometimes wore light blue uniforms. He had seen a flash of blue from 800-900 feet in the air and sent the scouts to check this out. As soon as they flew over the area, they started taking fire. The lead scout called up and said, *We have NVA troops all over the place!* So they started calling the gunships in."

Tom continued, "We had stirred up a hornet's nest. Other units and assets were called in to help out. The overall aviation commander in IV-Corps, call sign Delta 6, declared a DELTA EMERGENCY, which meant every asset was to come to where we were. They started putting troops in around this large area of trees. They brought troops from wherever they had them, and they were all ARVN troops with American advisors."

"After dark, we were released and went back to Vinh Long (Figure 82), our home airfield. We went back out first thing the next morning. They assigned me as co-pilot to the air mission commander. We learned that the NVA unit we had found was an artillery battalion that was infiltrating from Cambodia down to the U Minh Forest (Figure 82), the southernmost point in Vietnam controlled by the VC and NVA. They were sleeping that day in this copse of trees to prevent detection. What we had stumbled across the first afternoon was the commander and all his key officers planning for their night movement. We killed

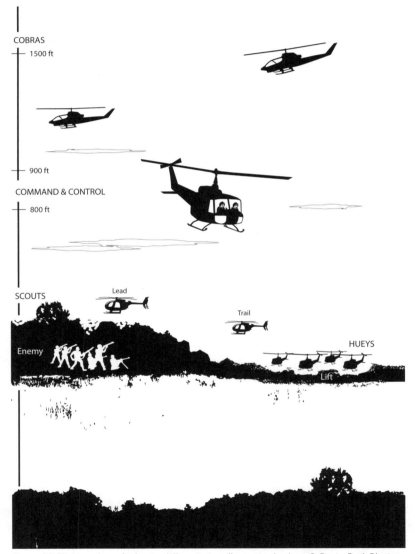

Figure 83: Flight package for hunter-killer mission. Illustration by Jerry C. Davis, Beth Blevins, Sara Franks, and JaMarie Thompson.

the entire command element." Egleston's unit was credited with 110 kills, but most advisors thought the number much higher.

The next day, attempts were made to help locate the NVA unit. Some had gotten away, maybe back to Cambodia. The Delta Emergency ended in disaster for the VC and NVA units. Others couldn't be found. As Tom Egleston reported, "They were pretty good at disappearing!"

 ## INSTRUCTOR REFLECTIONS

Tom Egleston recalls that the first days he flew in South Vietnam were anything but easy: "I flew something like 12 hours the first day! However, this was not unusual. The second day, we took off before dawn and got out there and worked all day long. That time of the year in the Delta, they're burning off the rice paddies, getting ready to plant a new crop. Visibility was obscured by a lot of low-hanging smoke. At the end of the second day, our troop commander sent the scouts home. Then he released the Hueys to go back and finally released the guns to go back. By this time, it was eight o'clock at night and dark. One of the Cobras crashed not too far from Chi Lang, where we were stationed at the closest safe area. The Cobra had experienced *settling with power.* You don't realize it, but you just fall out of the sky. The air speed got too low and the visibility was poor. I'm sure they weren't looking at their instruments to keep track. Nobody knew they had crashed until they hit the ground. A friend of mine just happened to be in the front seat. We had gone to flight school together."

"The crash didn't kill either pilot, but they were both injured. The co-pilot, my friend, was thought to have been killed. When one of the Cobras landed, they noted the main rotor blade and transmissions were on the front cockpit, so they figured my friend was dead. Then they saw his arm move because of the illuminated dials on his watch. We were the only Huey around, so they called us out there to bring some troops to mark the crash site and take the two pilots out. I didn't know who had crashed. But then I saw them bring my friend over to our Huey, and his face was just covered with blood…" Egleston said it made him wonder about his own mortality. He thought, *How the heck do we tell Frankie (his friend's wife) what had happened?*

"We had to go back out to the crash site more than once. It was about nine o'clock at night. The troop commander instructed, *Take us back to Vinh Long.* The first time I'd ever been out there was the day before. I looked at my charts and noticed up toward Saigon a radio transmitter, which I tuned in. Well, I followed the radio beacon, and we had flown about maybe an hour or so when the crew chief said on the intercom, *We should be seeing some lights now for Vinh Long or Can Tho. I don't see anything out there.* I dropped in altitude to see if they could spot anything on the ground. The next thing I heard the crew chief say was, *I'm from California. I spent a lot of time surfing. Those are white caps under us!*"

"We had been flying in the wrong direction for close to an hour! We were out over the Gulf of Thailand. So we turned and took another heading to Ca Mau, which was right on the edge of the U Minh Forest. We landed there at about 11 o'clock at night. Nobody around. Just us at this little refueling point. We took on all the fuel we needed while waiting for somebody to shoot us, because we stood out like a sore thumb! Back at the airfield someone in Operations wanted to know where the heck we had been. They laughed at us, saying *Can't you find your way home?!* That was the longest day I ever flew, not only in Vietnam but anywhere. I put in 18 hours flying that day!"

Egleston especially liked working with the Navy SEALs (Sea, Air and Land). He recalled, "The first time we worked with them it was a snatch mission. We flew out and met up with them at a little village near the Cambodian border. It was great working with them because they simply said, *Show up around 10 or 11 a.m.* So we got to sleep in! When we met up with them, they had everything laid out for us. They had a diagram of the village; we were going to cross the border to snatch some North Vietnamese. They said, *Here's the village!* and they said, *We're gonna bring one ship here!* They told us exactly where they wanted the ship to go and what they were going to do. They had even marked the building where this person was going to be. It was 'in and out.' So, we went in. They did their thing. They got back on the helicopter with the person they were looking for. We went back to this little village and dropped them off, and we were done for the day! It had gone off according to plan."

The second time Egleston worked with the SEALs was elsewhere in the Delta, not near the border, but near Dong Tam, which had been a base camp for the 9th Division (U.S.). Close by was an island called, Ben Tre (Figure 82), where there was supposedly a cache of weapons. He told us, "So, we put the SEALs (both American and Vietnamese) onto the island, where they quickly located the cache and blew it up. Then we picked up the SEALs and took them out."

Egleston distinctly remembers the Cambodian incursion that attracted so much attention. And he certainly remembers the orders they were given: "I can tell you, when the troop commander called all the pilots together in his room in late April and told us we were going into Cambodia the next day, everybody cheered!"

"Whenever we got shot at from Cambodia, we were not allowed to shoot back. So, the fact that we were going to be allowed to go after them and try to distrupt them was a good thing for us. Going in with a 25-mile limit was better than not being allowed to chase them across the border at all. Sometimes there was some really intense fire and they wouldn't let the Scouts over the border at all. Instead, we used a super heavy gun team—three Cobras flying together. A friend was flying at treetop level in his Cobra and spotted an NVA soldier on a bicycle, pedaling for all he was worth to get away. The pilot in the back seat punched off a pair of rockets, and they came together right at the guy...who shortly disappeared."

The rules of engagement often cost American lives. As Captain Egleston revealed:

> It was frustrating. We were not allowed to shoot back if we didn't have a Vietnamese commander telling us it was okay to shoot back, unless we could identify exactly where the fire was coming from. It slows things down; it puts you in danger, too. Here's an example. We used to fly airfield security at night around Vinh Long. We called it a firefly mission. We used a Huey with what's called a *bug light*, a high-intensity light on it and a barrel of flares. There was always a Cobra circling over the airfield at night, just in case something happened. On occasion we would get mortared. For a few months, every payday night (at the end of the month) we would get mortared. Nothing really serious happened very often. Frequently, we would take off, come back around, and usually fly three circles around the airfield—each circle growing farther out from

the airfield—down low and slow, looking to see if we could find anybody sneaking up to the perimeter. Afterward, we'd go out looking for trouble for the rest of our fuel load, another hour and a half or so. A Cobra overhead would keep an eye on us; we had our lights on, and he'd keep a close eye on us while we were doing our surveillance. One night while we were out, my crew chief said, *I've got somebody!* I circled around and, sure enough, this guy had jumped into a flooded rice paddy. We found him under the water, breathing through a reed. I called back to squadron operations and told them where we were, what we'd found, and asked for permission to shoot the guy. We circled for close to an hour. Finally, the squadron commander replied over the radio, telling us to back off! He said the ARVN headquarters in Vinh Long had determined that this is an AWOL ARVN soldier going back to his compound. How they determined that while sitting in a building, no one knows. So we had to break it off and go back to the airfield. Whether the guy was an ARVN soldier or not, he didn't belong out there. We knew he was up to no good, because a lot of the ARVNs were Viet Cong, but we could not get permission to shoot at him.

> **❝** We knew he was up to no good, because a lot of the ARVNs were Viet Cong, but we could not get permission to shoot at him. **❞**

Helicopter duty in the Mekong Delta was frustrating and certainly risky. One of Egleston's roommates was returning to his base in marginal weather. Flying along a canal straight for Can Tho, he flew through a helicopter trap, which is essentially four machine guns set up in a box. They would just shoot up at the helicopter as it flew through. On this occasion, however, the VC let the scouts through, then the gunships, saving their fire for the Hueys. While trying to keep the Huey from crashing, Tom's friend took a shot to the head. According to Tom, "He lived about five days and died in a hospital in Bien Hoa or Saigon."

Egleston's experience bonded him with his fellow soldiers for life. He reflected, "I think a number of things created this bonding. One, is that for a year, day in and day out, you were with those guys. You ate with them, fought with them, and flew with them. It was just a very, very close-knit group."

Another factor Captain Egleston pointed out was what it was like when a soldier returned from Vietnam. "I was never spat upon," Tom said. "Basically, you were just ignored. I certainly was. When I came back I was still in the Army, assigned to Fort Jackson, near Columbia, South Carolina. *Don't wear your uniform in Columbia,* we were told. And that's in the South, a college town. Whether you were in uniform or not, they knew you were in the military just from the way you looked. We didn't fit in—close haircut, clean shaven."

> **" While trying to keep the Huey from crashing, Tom's friend took a shot to the head....He lived about five days and died in a hospital in Bien Hoa or Saigon. "**

The first job Egleston had was with Prudential Insurance, a program to train sales management people. He explained, "In my first class were four veterans, all officers. I think every three months a new group would start. The class before me was not veterans. One was even a McGovern supporter. He used to greet me every morning with, *Here come the baby killers!* A friend joined me in feeding him tales just to irritate him. So, we received animosity even as we were ignored. I think, as a group, Vietnam veterans tend to be very close just because of their shared experiences both in Vietnam and when they came home."

All the veterans bonded with one another quickly on this trip, as well as with their student hosts. Students asked questions throughout the trip. Jacob asked about how American GIs were equipped. Tom Egleston told Jacob, "By the end of my tour, I could see through my fatigues. They were worn out. When we got to Saigon, most of us (probably 99 percent) didn't know what was going on. We went through to get our basic gear. Everybody did, no matter your rank. Since I was a pilot, I asked about boots. The sergeant said, *Oh, you'll get those in your unit.* Actually, he was taking those leather boots and selling them instead of handing them out. When I got to my unit, they just laughed about getting boots. But we got two sets of Nomex flight suits, supposedly flame resistant. They had been worn so much you could see through them! When I left after a year, I turned those back in, and they were issued to the next person my size. I never got a replacement set of them."

It wasn't just clothing that was worn out. Egleston said, "The unit I was in received one new helicopter right out of the factory, but we had to turn it over to the Vietnamese Air Force after putting about 200 hours on it. We did get two helicopters from the 25th Infantry Division, when their pilots returned home, but they had been plenty used."

For a war that is often called "the helicopter war" the use of hand-me-down helicopters is ironic! "We just made do." Egleston said.

STUDENT RESPONSE

Jacob Mullet, the student host for Tom Egleston, witnessed the veteran bonds: "Tom was deployed to Vinh Long in the Mekong Delta region of IV-Corps just two months ahead of John Sorensen. The two are almost inseparable; there is clearly an unusual bond between them—like brothers. Tom and John flew Hueys together in Vietnam (Figure 84). In addition to learning about veteran bonds, Jacob said Tom gave him a crash course on Hueys, Cobras, Cayuses (scouts), and Chinook helicopters.

Figure 84: John Sorensen and Tom Egleston. Photo courtesy of Tom Egleston, PETP 2014.

"We took a tour of the Can Tho region." Jacob remembers, "It was just as brown as it had been the day before and visibly polluted. A visit to a small family-owned rice/noodle factory evoked a strong reaction from our group, as a lot of hands touched that rice paper and the rice noodles." A visit to a floating market was also startling: "It was both fascinating and sobering to see how the people live. They use the river for laundry, sewage, and dish washing! It really makes one think twice before complaining about any circumstances back home. I can't imagine what is it like for a child to grow up on one of those boats."

The highlight of the tour for Tom was stopping in Vinh Long. This was where Tom and John served their tours. Jacob says, "Tom told me that when he had been stationed here, it had been an airfield. The bus stopped so we could get off, and a garbage pile greeted us. We walked down a tiny dirt road and found that a Vietnamese military installation stands where the airfield had been located. We were told not to take pictures, but a few did! It was a disappointment to find only one filled-in bunker near a gas station."

"Seeing the tunnels at Cu Chi made me reflect on how awful the War really was! The heat, insects, booby traps, malaria, dysentery and the enemy were everyday things. I feel pride for these veterans and what they went through."

"One aspect of the War that the veterans reiterated is that they all had different experiences. The Mekong Delta, to Cu Chi, to the Central Highlands, to the coast—they were all completely different and had their own unique challenges. Nowadays, there is a lot of construction in this country, but they don't maintain infrastructure very well."

The War Remnants Museum in Saigon, which contains many weapons, aircraft, and artillery, made quite an impression on Jacob. "I was able to stick with Tom and have his individual insight for the duration of the Museum visit." Jacob was disappointed that near Pleiku "the Vietnamese government stopped us short of the battlefield, which was the site of the Ia Drang battle at Landing Zone X-Ray, made famous by one of the earliest and most vicious battles of the Vietnam War. But we did hear an explanation from tour veterans who had fought here—Tony Nadal and Steve Hansen."

Another spot that caught a lot of attention was Chu Lai. At the 91st Evac Hospital during the War, one of the veterans, Lou Eisenbrandt, served as a nurse. Jacob was very fascinated with this: "I was interested to hear Lou talk about the medical side of the War. I participated in a color guard for the 24th Medevac Field Hospital reunion, and that sparked my interest and respect for medical personnel. When Lou Eisenbrandt spoke, I was amazed at her humility."

Going from the southern part of Vietnam to the northern part of Vietnam, Jacob was puzzled by much of what he saw: "There is such a disparity between homes. There are modern roads in some areas of the country whereas others consist of mud trails." It all bothered Jacob so much he decided to ask Tom about it: "How is it that these people, these half-starved people, go through hell to fight an enemy that was physically bigger, stronger, and better equipped, yet hold out for almost a decade for their country to look like it does? The country is plastered with huge monuments and modern buildings, but the population allows them to get run down." Tom replied, "There's no pride in the population, no respect for the country."

Jacob experienced more unsettling feelings in Dong Ha. He remembers, "We walked around Dong Ha, but the market was disgusting and smelled rancid. We made a quick loop back to the hotel, which in turn smelled like dog food and cigarette smoke, but much more bearable. On our way back, we got a lot of attention from locals, no doubt wondering what so many 'round eyes' were doing on their streets. An elderly man on a moped stopped Tom, John, Doc, and Bill Duncan. He had been alive during the War and remembered the fighting that took place. He said he was ARVN. Neither Tom nor Doc Ballard believed his story, but they remained courteous."

"There's no pride in the population, no respect for the country."

Jacob was intrigued by the old imperial city of Hué: "The infrastructure and history of this city are reflected in the French and Vietnamese architecture. The huge Citadel was a focal part of the battle of Hué," as veteran John Ligato explained so well. The trip was winding down, but Jacob's interest was still on the upswing: "I want to make the most of the time we have left. Any time I see a group of our veterans going out, I try to tag along. I can sleep when I get back home!"

Jacob had one more important site to visit: "Arriving in Hanoi from Hué, we passed a bunch of MiG fighters (Soviet military aircraft) on our taxi to the terminal. I think the veterans felt a sense of irony at being in the capital of their former enemy. Many had been talking about how much less advanced than the south Hanoi was. We went straight to the "Hanoi Hilton" where two of our veterans, John Clark and Bill Bailey, spent half the War. These men went through horrible conditions. John and Bill both spoke multiple times about their experiences, but they never talked about their torture," Jacob said. "I thought that was interesting. I think it may still be too difficult. I can't even imagine. John Clark spoke to us about how they would communicate with taps on the wall. This was incredible!"

As Jacob closed out his student blog post he wrote, "I do not possess the vocabulary nor the tact to express the gratitude and pride I feel toward these veterans. The only way I have been able to show my respect is by listening and learning. I do not even know what to ask Tom. He is a gold mine of information and stories."

> **"** I do not possess the vocabulary nor the tact to express the gratitude and pride I feel toward these veterans. The only way I have been able to show my respect is by listening and learning. **"**

Jacob continued, "The dilemma on this trip is that I cannot be in 32 places at once. I wish I could give all the veterans my full and individual attention for two weeks each, but I guess that's why we are assigned to one. I feel a responsibility to these veterans to express my gratitude to each by face-to-face time. I am glad that I have been able to gain some knowledge from each one of them. I have met, chatted, and sat next to each of them. The more I talk with them, the more I realize the size of the shoes I am called to fill as an Army officer."

TOPIC SUMMARY

The ubiquitous Huey was believed by many to be the "workhorse" of the Vietnam War. This helicopter absorbed over 5,000 crashes, suffering over 1,000 pilots killed.[2] Captain Egleston was the pilot of a UH-1 helicopter, one of the most prevalent helicopters used during the War.

He served with an Air Cavalry troop flying in IV-Corps (the Mekong Delta). His responsibility was to directly support the South Vietnamese military on a daily basis. Most of his time was spent with troop insertion and extraction, medevac, re-supply, retrieval of downed aircraft and flare ship missions. As flight lead, he was responsible for the aircraft crew that made up the flight, leading the flight to proper locations, and ensuring that the tasks/mission objectives were met. As a command and control pilot, he was responsible for constant observations of scout aircraft operating at treetop level, directing scout teams to areas of interest to the Vietnamese commander.

As air mission commander, Egleston was responsible for the entire aircraft package—13 helicopters and crew. His was with the 1st Aviation Brigade, 3rd Squadron, 5th Cavalry.

After the War, Tom worked in administrative management for various corporations. As a member of the New Jersey National Guard, he flew rescue and recovery operations in support of military and civilian authorities in New York after the 9-11 attacks on the World Trade Center.

Tom Egleston believes the best part of his time in the military was the bond that he built with the men he was with every day.

About this, there is no doubt.

CLASS TOPIC 10: INSTRUCTOR PILOT (IV-CORPS)

I truly believe God heard those prayers...
I'm here today because He did!

🍎 INSTRUCTOR: CPT JOHN SORENSEN, USA[1]

John Sorensen was a good student, having gone to high school in Jacksonville, Florida, before enrolling at the University of Florida, where he entered the ROTC program. As a distinguished military graduate, John was commissioned as a second lieutenant in the U.S. Army. After completing a couple of specialty courses, he began his flight training in Texas. Thereafter, he moved to Hunter Army Airfield in Savannah, Georgia, for extended training. Again, John graduated with honors, and his mother was able to pin on his Aviation Wings. Next stop, South Vietnam!

Captain Sorensen was deployed to the Mekong Delta and flew over the entire Delta, working with U.S. and ARVN soldiers. John flew on many missions with the purpose of finding and destroying the enemy. As John recalled, "During these missions, scout choppers would fly just over the treetops, attempting to draw fire from the VC or NVA. If hostile soldiers fired on the choppers, the scout helicopters would drop a few grenades and leave the area. Cobra helicopters would come in and use their rockets and guns on the enemy. Sometimes Huey choppers would come in and put in ARVN troops."

John remembered one mission where the scout choppers were flying so low and slow to draw fire that one of them reported "smelling bacon cooking." Captain Sorensen was often frustrated when enemy contact occurred: "We couldn't get the authority from ARVN officers to clear the area of VC soldiers. By the time ARVN gave permission to engage the enemy, the VC were gone. The lack of efficiency from ARVN officers is the reason many more lives than necessary were lost in Vietnam."

John's student host, Caleb McElvain (Figure 85), reported details he learned: "Due to a lack of decisiveness from the ARVN officers, John and his buddies built relationships that were very close and have lasted a lifetime—relationships that have superseded most all other relationships. These relationships were formed because they didn't fight so much to stop the spread of communism or to win independence and freedom for South Vietnam; rather, they fought for each other." John also told Caleb the reason they were able to form relationships at this level was because, "We did not have the support of our population, but we certainly knew we had the support of one another."

John Sorensen became an instructor pilot five months into his tour in Vietnam. In this leadership role, he gave six-month proficiency check rides to the pilots in his platoon. When he returned to the U.S., he became an instructor pilot at the U.S. Aviation School in Alabama and taught there for two and a half years until he was no longer on active duty.

Captain Sorensen received many recognitions and honors: a Bronze Star with one Oak Leaf Cluster (second award); Air Medal—49 awards for combat flight time; Vietnamese Cross of Gallantry with a Bronze Star (individual award); and a unit award—the Vietnamese Cross of Gallantry with Palm leaf. He has continued his service, having served as president of the Vietnam Helicopter Pilots Association (VHPA), co-founder and past president of the South Missouri Chapter of VHPA, and as a member of the Patriot's Guard.

Sorensen has been married for 36 years to Liz, with four children and six grandchildren.

Figure 85: Veteran John Sorensen and student host Caleb McElvain. Photo by John Luck.

 ## STUDENT HOST: CALEB McELVAIN

According to Caleb McElvain, his reason for wanting to go on the Patriotic Education trip to Vietnam was that he believed it would help him "gain gratitude for living in America and also deepen [his] appreciation for veterans." He also believed such a trip would "inspire him to influence the community as a patriotic leader, to value Vietnam veterans as many of their generation failed to do."

Caleb also stated a very personal reason for going to Vietnam: "Donald Darden, my uncle, served in Vietnam as a pilot flying a Cessna 0-1 Bird Dog. One of his primary jobs as a pilot was to fly close to the battlefield, observe exploding shells, and adjust artillery fire via his radio. Another one of his jobs was to fly low reconnaissance missions to find VC and to report their locations. Because these missions were flown in close proximity to the ground and were in direct contact with the enemy, many of these planes and pilots were lost. I remember my mom recalling being scared for her brother and telling me we were lucky to have Uncle Don still alive."

Caleb is a very patriotic young man, and he hasn't forgotten who influenced him: "Respect and patriotism were developed in my uncle while he was in Vietnam, and as a veteran he was able to teach them to me. From a young age, my uncle taught me respect. I was expected to answer his questions with a *yes, sir* or *no, sir*. I believe the respect he anticipated from me was a result of not experiencing the same respect when he returned from Vietnam." Caleb continued, "Uncle Don taught me true patriotism. From when I was young until the last time I saw him, my uncle ended his prayers with, *God, please bless and protect the service members everywhere.* My uncle taught me that patriotism is the willingness to stand up and even die for the biblical principles of equality and freedom, the foundations of America, so that future generations may enjoy the same opportunity that I have had. This Patriotic Travel trip allowed me to see how and why these character traits were developed in my uncle and many other Vietnam veterans."

 This Patriotic Travel trip allowed me to see how and why these character traits were developed in my uncle and many other Vietnam veterans.

Caleb had obviously been affected by his uncle's life in a very personal way. He relayed, "Although Uncle Don has not talked to me much about his time in Vietnam, I can see how it has affected the way he lives. After taking for granted that my uncle would always be around, I learned he had a rare form of Lou Gehrig's disease caused by exposure to Agent Orange in Vietnam and had been given less than two years to live. I realize that now is the time for me to express my gratitude, let him know he has been my hero, and convey to others how much he has taught me."

Caleb made good use of his time at College of the Ozarks. A math major with a minor in computer science, he wants to become an engineer. His work assignments at the College were diversified—first in the technology department, then maintenance for Youngman Residence Hall, followed by Camp Lookout, and his final workstation was resident assistant in Youngman Hall. He also worked off campus as time permitted. Amidst all of this, Caleb found time to pursue a private pilot's license through the General Terrence R. Dake Aviation Scholarship at the College.

Caleb wanted to learn as much as he could about the War in Vietnam and those who fought it. His goal was to: "Share my experiences with my uncle, a Vietnam veteran, once I return."

INSTRUCTOR PILOT "IP" IV CORPS BACKGROUND

John Sorensen was assigned to a unit in IV-Corps. He accepted his assigned location of Can Tho, in IV-Corps (Figure 86), without

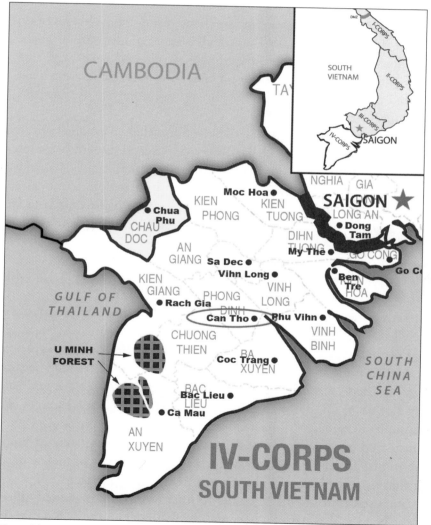

Figure 86: IV-Corps map. Adapted from public domain.

reservation and with a good sense of humor. He told this story: "A fellow pilot's dad had been in Vietnam and had explained that *the place to be was in IV-Corps, because there were very few mountains, mostly rice paddies, and if you have an engine failure, it's just like landing on a table…it's all flat, a nice place to crash.* Fortunately, I didn't have to experience that!"

IV-Corps (Figure 86) was the southernmost part of Vietnam. It is a very large area that forms the Mekong Delta Region, noted for the Mekong River with its many tributaries and wet flood plains, rice paddies, and small villages. Its main city is Can Tho, which is an economic hub.

Sorensen and fellow veteran Tom Egleston covered a very large area of the Mekong Delta. (Figure 86) John said, "Our area of operation literally covered the entirety of the IV-Corps, working alongside the 7th ARVN division, the 9th and the 21st."

Many veterans on the trip had served in other corps areas and had never been in the Mekong Delta. These veterans and students were interested to see the many little villages and open-air markets. IV-Corps was mostly agricultural, but also a noteworthy fishing region. Some call the region the *Bread Basket* of Vietnam; it also warrants being called the *Rice Bowl.* It is becoming more diversified financially, profiting from tourism.

 ## INSTRUCTOR REFLECTIONS

John Sorensen's patriotic roots run deep. He recalled, "My dad was a civil service employee at the Naval Air Station when I was born. He had been a boat builder. He was born in Denmark, so he was a boat builder by trade and worked on a boat for Henry Ford. My dad became a naturalized citizen five days after the Pearl Harbor attack and told my mother he loved our country enough to go serve, even though, as a naturalized citizen, he didn't really have to. He went to the South Pacific and served our country in that theater. My mom was a stay-at-home mom until my dad passed away during my senior year of high school. At that time she became a full-time secretary for our pastor."

Sorensen continued, "My older brother was a commissioned officer in the Navy and a charter officer and plank holder on the *U.S.S. Carrier*

Enterprise, the first nuclear-powered aircraft carrier. Of course, growing up in this time, I had thought that, eventually, I would follow in his shoes and go in the Navy. After graduating from high school, I'd been accepted to the University of Florida, where the first two years of ROTC were mandatory. They only offered the Army and Air Force ROTC programs. Meeting with my advisor, I was hopeful of being a pre-med student, but chemistry told me to look elsewhere! My advisor told me that the schedule for the Army ROTC would lend itself more favorably. So, I completed the first two years of the mandatory ROTC program and signed up for the advanced courses the final two years. I graduated and was commissioned in December of 1968. During my senior year, I took the ROTC flight course. Upon graduation, being a flight student, I was limited to the branches I could consider. My first choice was armor, second choice was artillery, and my third choice was infantry. As a distinguished military graduate, I got my first choice and was commissioned in the armor branch."

In March of 1969, John took the armor officer basic course, which he completed as an honor graduate in the class. In early June he reported for primary helicopter school at Fort Walters, Texas. After the primary instruction portion was completed, John finished advanced helicopter training at Hunter Army Airfield in Savannah, Georgia, getting his wings on February 23, 1970. After a thirty-day leave, he reported to Vietnam on April 8, 1970.

Reflecting on his training, John said, "I think just about everybody knew that we were on orders to go to Vietnam. I didn't have any particular regrets or fears about it. As a distinguished military graduate, I had an opportunity and could've selected and received a regular Army commission, as opposed to a reserve Army commission, but that carried a four-year obligation. The flight school obligation was three years. I didn't opt for the regular commission."

John was willing to accept most any assignment. He said, "I could have been assigned anywhere. We went into, I think, Long Binh and the 90th replacement battalion."

John described his environment at Long Binh: "It was hot; it was dry season; it was dusty; and it smelled. The last stop before arriving in the country was Clark Air Force Base in the Philippines. We deplaned while the aircraft took on some fuel. When we got back on, there were these little customs declaration cards in the seat, along with a little four- to six-page comic book. When you opened it up, right in the middle, there were cartoons on each side of the page. One side was labeled, 'Things to worry about in Vietnam' and the other side labeled, 'Things not to worry about in Vietnam'. I vividly remember both sides of one cartoon. The thing to worry about showed a picture of a GI getting his hair cut and whether or not the Vietnamese barber with a straight razor was a VC. If the barber's a VC, he could very easily cut your throat! The thing not to worry about was if it rains today, is it gonna rain tomorrow, because once it starts raining, it rains for about six months."

John's unit interacted daily with the South Vietnamese: "Once we got into the unit areas, the only people with whom we really interfaced daily were a hooch maid who would come in and do our laundry, polish our boots, and so forth; the Vietnamese waitresses at the officers' club (O-club); and the Vietnamese barbers. In 1970, in the Mekong Delta, our infantry and artillery support was all supplied by the ARVN (Army of the Republic of Vietnam). Every day we would pick up a senior ARVN officer who flew in our command and control aircraft. He was actually in charge of the mission. The air mission commander's responsibility was to make sure that what the mission commander was wanting to accomplish was within our scope and possibility of success. On a rare occasion, the air mission commander and the Vietnamese mission commander would disagree, but overall, those were the people we worked with. As for the actual ground troops, we had very little to do with them."

John vividly remembered his first engagement with the enemy: "The first day I was in the unit, I met with our instructor pilot for lunch. I was slated to do an orientation check ride with him that afternoon, because I had just been on a month's leave and hadn't flown in four or five weeks. This check was to get me back in the aircraft, take control, and go practice a few emergency procedures. The second day, I flew with him again, and I don't remember very much happening. The third day, I was chosen to fly co-pilot for our air mission commander, Captain Roy Sudeck, to whom I give credit for being my mentor. He had taken a direct commission from a warrant officer. He was younger than me, but I never let age enter the picture. There were some very experienced pilots at 19 years old, and I was 24 years old when I got there. You learn from those who have been there, done that. I don't remember much about the morning, but that afternoon our troop was scrambled to help some Navy gun boats that were going up the Mekong River. They had gotten into an ambush and were being attacked from both sides of the river. As air mission commander, we got right in the midst of it. We had our Cobra gunships overhead, and they were suppressing fire with mini-gun fires or grenade launchers, plus the rockets. And our crew chief and door gunners were suppressing fire with M 60 machine guns. Here I was, three days in the unit, and my thought was, *This is for real!* In the midst of all that, Roy Sudeck asks, *What's the score of the ball game?* And I replied, *I don't have any idea.* He looked over and saw that I had turned off the toggle switch for the ADF (automatic direction finding) radio, and he said, *The next time I ask you, I want you to be able to tell me.* So as we had to break away and go refuel, I got a radio lesson."

"As we were refueling, while I was left in the aircraft, Roy told me, *Turn off all the radios.* We had five radios on board on the command and control aircraft. Then he asked me, *Which one is the least important?* I quickly replied, *The ADF because it's just like the radio in your car.* So he instructed, *Turn it on first, and tune it to where it's just barely audible. Now, what's the next least important? And you work your way from that least important up to the most important radio in the aircraft; each one being set with just a little more volume than the one that preceded it.* Then he says, *Now that you've got them all on, you just train your brain to listen for key words and phrases, and based on the volume, you'll be able to know which radio it was.* And so, within a month or so, I was able to tell him that it was the Cardinals 6 – Cubs 5 after seven innings, but I couldn't tell who was pitching, who was batting, or anything. So, I give him credit. I flew with him a number of times as air mission commander, and then toward the end, when I was air mission commander, I would often reflect back on those lessons that he taught me."

On the bus, John mentioned two missions that came to his mind. The first occurred while dropping illuminating flares during a night mission. One of their AH-1G Cobra gunships suffered a tail rotor failure separation; it began to spin uncontrollably, inverted and crashed. Sorensen explained, "I had been dropping flares from six or seven thousand feet, when we got the call. He was going down! Thankfully, I had already been to instructor school and was an instructor pilot. Quickly, I applied strong right pedal, and left cyclic, literally falling out of the sky. My co-pilot read off our altimeter settings, and when he called 1,000, I leveled out. We were on the ground within a matter of seconds after they impacted. The Cobra co-pilot, who flew the front seat, was already out of the aircraft, but the aircraft commander had to be assisted out of the gunship by my crew chief, door gunner, and co-pilot. Both of them had back injuries from the hard landing. We laid them on the floor of our aircraft and flew them to the area hospital. The co-pilot was treated and rejoined our unit. When the aircraft commander got strong enough to leave the hospital, he was sent home—not because of the extent of his injuries, but because he had already finished his full year and was well into his extension period. In 2006, I saw him for the first time at our national reunion in Washington, D.C. Hundreds of us were standing in the lobby of the Marriott Hotel, prepping to march in the Fourth of July parade. Out of nowhere, this man came up to me and asked, *You're John Sorensen, aren't you?* I replied, *Yes, I am.* He stated, *Well, I'm Pete Jordan and you saved my life!* I had wondered what happened to Pete. We gave each other a big hug, and we've maintained contact ever since. I look forward to seeing him every chance we get."

"We were very blessed. I say this because, in the full year that I was there, we lost only three people. One was a scout observer who was shot in the head in May of 1970, right after we had entered the campaign into Cambodia. A couple months later, we lost a Huey crew chief. The aircraft had an engine failure over the River, and it went down in the water. Everybody got out of the aircraft, but he must have gotten sucked down or pulled under with the rotor blades as the aircraft sank, and he drowned. His body was recovered about three days later. The third, the one pilot we lost, took a shot from small-arms fire in the head, and he died a few days later in Japan. Again, I consider myself very blessed in that aspect. I was duty officer one night when we had a mortar attack on the airfield; the enemy was far off target, none of the aircraft were significantly damaged, and we didn't sustain any casualties."

The second memory forever etched in John's mind was a negative experience working with ARVN: "We had picked up an ARVN officer to be our mission commander, and I was flying co-pilot with Roy Sudeck. We had scouts doing reconnaissance, and they called and said, *We can smell bacon, and there is evidence.* They saw VC flags. The scouts wanted to throw some type of grenade into the bunkers, to see if they could get some type of activity from the bunkers, because our mission was to find the enemy. If the scouts got shot at, we had accomplished our mission and found the enemy. But, the ARVN officer who was actually running the operation refused to allow us to use grenades in the bunkers. As a result, Roy pulled scouts back up to altitude, and we all went back to the command post. Roy deplaned and went to see the ARVN commanding officer, who was a full colonel or maybe even a general, and told him what was going on. The CO replaced the original ARVN officer, and we went back to the scene. The fire was barely smoldering, all the VC flags were gone, and the people were nowhere to be found. This was the only really negative experience that I encountered."

Theoretically, the United States was scaling down the number of troops when John went to Vietnam, but he and his buddies did not feel the U.S. had given up trying to win the War. He said, "We were in support of the ARVNs and we supported them with everything we had. And I think that they, honestly, were still trying to win the War. They were fighting for their country. But they were up against other Vietnamese. I think they were fighting for what they believed was right and just."

Captain Sorensen returned home in 1971, before Nixon authorized the bombing that ended the War. He recalled, "In early '71 one of the troops from the 7th of the 1st Air Cav was to be sent up north to participate in Lam Son 719, which was the invasion of Laos. In order to bring the troop up to full status, both personnel and aircraft statuses, they had a lottery from the other troops to see who would be transferred to the one unit. At that point, I was not considered because I was too close to coming home. I was lucky; we lost a lot of aircraft within a very short time."

It was intriguing to learn what information our servicemen and women were privy to. For example, when John was asked if he had heard things like the fact that Congress had revoked the Gulf of Tonkin Resolution, he replied, "Not specifically, no."

"I got back into Travis Air Force Base, in California, at 10:30 at night. We left San Francisco, made a connecting flight in Dallas, and as we were getting on the aircraft, the captain announces, *We'll be pushing back from the gate shortly. We were waiting on a couple servicemen who are returning from Vietnam.* Then, we flew from Dallas to Atlanta, Georgia, which was my buddy's destination, and connected further on to Jacksonville, Florida. As I was at the gate, flying standby, this fellow traveler noticed the aviator wings on my uniform and asked, *I've got a nephew who is a helicopter pilot in Vietnam; do you know him?* Well, I didn't, but there were 45,000 helicopter pilots in Vietnam; you couldn't know every one of them! Anyway, we had a very nice conversation, and he waited around to see whether or not I was picked to be on the flight. As it turned out, I was not given a seat for a 6:30 flight in the morning. He insisted, *Here, take my reserve seat and give me your standby seat. I'll catch the next flight, because I am going on business and you've got family waiting for you.* So, we switched seats and I have often wondered since, *Would I have done that or would I have thought that since I'm in such a hurry, I have to be on the plane?* I arrived home and my mom, my younger brother, and my girlfriend were waiting for me at the gate."

John had a welcoming return. "I had a pleasant return, but I was one of the lucky ones. Others were not treated so well. A number of my buddies were yelled at and accused of being baby killers and murderers. They were accused of raping, pillaging and burning. Some were spit upon or had tomatoes and eggs thrown at them."

ʻʻ A number of my buddies were yelled at and accused of being baby killers and murderers. They were accused of raping, pillaging and burning. ʼʼ

Sorensen and his student host, Caleb, stay in contact. John reported, "We have met on the campus for Honor America, the Fourth of July celebration at College of the Ozarks. We have played phone tag, but I know he's in the area. Last I recall, he's the youth pastor at Branson First Baptist Church."

John happily shared his thoughts about the trip and how he saw it influence the student hosts: "I think it's a wonderful way to learn our history. The Vietnam War was an unpopular war at home. It caused divisiveness not only among the people, but also within Congress and our national leadership. I firmly believe that it is one thing to hate the War, but you don't hate the warrior. What I learned on this trip, and I think all the students did as well, is the fact that there were 12 veterans on this trip, from four different branches, with different experiences. Yet, the tendency, when we hear the phrase *the Vietnam War,* is to singularize it. However, we learned about 12 individualized wars; each one experienced different things than the other. It wasn't uncommon for a helicopter pilot to fly a single ship mission, but it wasn't a combat mission. Maybe it was, as we called it, *ash and trash.* As I recall, on one mission I flew down to the U Minh Forest in the southwestern region of the Delta. I picked up a young second lieutenant and flew him up to Saigon, so he could take his R&R flight. I had an extra helmet in the aircraft and plugged it in, and he remarked, *Man, I wouldn't have your job for anything; these are nothing but bullet magnets!* I kind of turned and looked at him and I said, *Well, I don't see those starched fatigues stopping very many bullets. So, I wouldn't have your job either.* I guess the Army, in its infinite wisdom, got at least two people in the right jobs!"

I was not surprised by Sorensen's response when asked what he thought when he heard about the actions of Jane Fonda, Clark Clifford, John Kerry, and Tom Hayden. John explained, "Obviously, my first thought was, *They're wrong!* It borders on treason! But I think we see a lot of that today, maybe not sitting on an enemy's anti-aircraft gun, but publicly supporting the enemy. Some think because they have celebrity status that they have the right to speak, act, or make a position known that is more important than mine. I can voice my opinion and it carries very little weight, but because someone makes millions of dollars, either being on a big screen, in a ballpark, or on a football field, that gives them credibility and a bigger stage. To me, their voice is still only one. The example of John Kerry, who served during Vietnam and then came back and threw his ribbons away belittles everything that the rest of us ever did. You know, Jane Fonda and Tom Hayden, Hollywood activists...well, I think I've made my point."

"On the other hand, I loved Henry Fonda; I thought he was a great actor. I didn't know him personally, but I loved his movies. To this day, I won't watch anything that Jane Fonda is in. For our nation or the media to consider her as one of the top 100 women in the country is, to me, downright ridiculous—ludicrous really. One word—hypocrisy. That's my opinion and I'm sticking to it."

John humbly acknowledges, "I am blessed, I was blessed, and I don't think I knew the extent of provision at the time. Somebody was watching over me. I mentioned we took a round in the fuel cell of the Huey helicopter. The fuel tank has a self-sealing liner on the inside that would close itself when penetrated from the outside. We knew we had been hit, and then we found out that it was a fuel cell hit. It was ball ammunition, probably an AK-47 or something similar, and we had very little spillage. It was just an enemy taking a pot shot at us. Had it been a tracer round or an incendiary round, we would have blown up in space, so to speak."

"The other time I took a hit, it was on a radio antenna. That's about like going out and breaking the antenna off your car; your car still functions normally, you're just short a radio. Those were the two times that the aircraft I piloted was hit.

"Like I said, I knew that someone was looking out for me."

STUDENT RESPONSE

Reading books, watching documentaries, and writing papers could not have prepared Caleb McElvain for the trip of a lifetime: "Hearing stories from veterans like John Sorensen and seeing their eyes gaze upon the ground where they risked their lives, I began to understand how their time in the War changed who they are, and I began to change as well." Caleb felt like he had a unique opportunity when the group visited the Mekong Delta. "I had been waiting for an opportunity to thank John for his service to our country. This was the time! I took him aside, shook his hand, looked him in the eyes, and thanked him for his service. Instantly, the grip on our handshake tightened. We embraced, and in the hot Vietnam climate, as mopeds flew by, I understood why John Sorensen served. He fought for every man, woman, child, and me."[2]

As the trip progressed, Caleb and John communicated freely. Caleb recalled, "When I sat next to him, he opened up about how he does not understand how he survived. John said there must have been a higher power protecting him." Caleb remembers asking him for advice: "John told me what I have heard so often from all the veterans, *Find something you love and do it! Do not waste your time doing something you do not enjoy. Do not settle for something else.*"

One of the most meaningful stops on the trip for Caleb was the location where one of the veterans, Bill Duncan, conducted triage. It has forever made an impression on young Caleb McElvain. This is where Colonel Bill Duncan (Texas Pete) explained his Vietnam experiences to the group. "He had to make life-and-death choices for his wounded Marines. What shook me to the core," Caleb said, "was seeing the strongest men I know moved to tears as he recalled the death of his friends and the images he has of his friends losing legs, arms, etc. When I saw him break down in tears, and I saw the other veterans begin to cry, I started to understand. I understand more about brotherhood among veterans than I ever did before. As Bill Duncan hugged John Sorensen, both men cried, and so did I."

> **❝ I understand more about brotherhood among veterans than I ever did before. ❞**

As it was for so many of the students on the trip, traveling with the veterans was a deeply satisfying experience. Caleb concluded, "I have made memories that I will cherish for eternity, and I have learned lessons that will change my life. I learned how to develop relationships from the best examples possible, the U.S. veterans and specifically, John Sorensen."[3] (Figure 85, page 243)

TOPIC SUMMARY

John Sorensen, Tom Egleston, and Jim Greer were typical examples of a "Combat Band of Brothers" phenomenon. (Figure 87) This existed not only with helicopter pilots, but with all American combat units during the Vietnam War. John explained some of what contributed to this comradery: "The population at home was not supporting us, and there were riots in the street. We didn't have the support of the home front, but we certainly knew every day we had the support of one another. I've often said through the 40-plus years since I was in Vietnam that the relationships I developed with Tom and others I served with, in my opinion, superseded all other human relationships. Once you're in combat, everything changes. Don't misunderstand me; I love my wife, children, my grandchildren, my nieces, nephews, and brothers. But when you get up in the morning and you crank up that helicopter and you pull pitch, you know that everyone else is willing to lay down their life for you. And they know that you are willing to do the same for them. I'll share that and believe that as long as the Lord blesses me with breath. The relationships are without equal."

Many Vietnam veterans kept a diary which captured some of the rare insights of those who flew helicopters in the War. Some of these have been published. Lawrence H. Johnson, III, has written about Capt. Ray K. Clark. What follows is a day from Clark's diary.

> Somehow the days just don't get any shorter. There is always some major flap that requires personal attention and keeps me from doing all the things I need to do. Such as eat, sleep...One of my captains fired into an area 24 Nov., suppressing for slicks on an extraction. He did not call for permission to fire and though he saw no one, there were three civilians in the tree line and one was killed. He was recommended for an Article 15 for not requesting permission to shoot. So much for a fine officer's career, if he gets it. A fine war and fine support we have from the people at home. We must risk our soldiers' lives and take casualties in order to insure we do not injure any civilian who may or may not be friendly. There has never been a war fought by such rules in the history of warfare. The self-righteous indignant public autonomy over so-called American atrocities makes me sick. How can people be so naïve? When you fight, people get hurt, no one every said war was nice. It surely isn't fun![4]

No doubt, such frustration and resentment was felt by many in combat. Men like John Sorensen were grateful to have survived and believed they knew why. Sorensen said, "My dad served our country as a naturalized citizen. Before I left to go to Vietnam, my mom gave me a small, pocket-sized New Testament that my dad carried during WWII. She said, *I want you to carry this.* So, I stuck it in my shirt pocket every single day that I flew. As we finished our pre-flight, having gotten on the aircraft, fastened our seatbelts and harness, I simply said a small prayer every morning. It became a ritual just like a young child saying before bedtime: *Now I lay me, down to sleep, I pray the Lord, my soul to keep...* or like a blessing: *God is great, God is good..."*

He continued, "My prayer was that the Lord would protect the lives of everyone who was to fly on that aircraft that day. Because of 1200 hours of combat flight time and having been shot down with a round that hit the fuel cell, I truly believe that God heard those prayers, and I think I'm here today because He did!"

Figure 87 (left to right): Student Caleb McElvain, veteran John Sorensen, veteran Thomas Egleston, veteran Jim Greer, student Jessica Turner, and student Jacob Mullet in front of a Huey. Photo by John Luck.

CLASS TOPIC 11: POW – NAM DINH (NORTH VIETNAM)

I spent the next three days undergoing torture....The rope treatment...solitary confinement for six months,...

🍎 INSTRUCTOR: CDR JAMES W. (BILL) BAILEY, USN (RET.)[1]

A prisoner of war (POW), a family man, an example for others, and a hero ... such was the description of Bill Bailey given by his student host, Haly Johnson. Further, she said, "He is a man who has lived an incredible life, and yet, if you met him, you might never realize how truly amazing he is."

Bill Bailey grew up in Mississippi. After attending Holmes Junior College and the University of Southern Mississippi, he entered the Naval Aviation Cadet Program and was commissioned as an ensign in the U.S. Navy. In October 1964, he became a designated Naval Flight Officer. Bailey attended Radar Intercept Officer (RIO) School in South Georgia, subsequently deploying to Southeast Asia aboard the aircraft carrier *U.S.S. Ranger* and, ultimately, the *U.S.S. Constellation*. His plane an F-4 (Figure 94, page 268) was shot down while making an attack on Nam Dinh, North Vietnam, and he was taken prisoner on June 28, 1967.

Haly Johnson was moved by hearing Bill relate the hardships of his time as a POW. She said, "It was incredible and somewhat hard to hear. But one of the things that struck me most about Bill was his attitude, despite his experiences. Some of the things that he went through as a

POW were terrible and, quite frankly, something many could not have survived. As he told his stories, he was completely calm. He showed no bitterness and was able to easily speak about everything he had gone through. He even showed extreme kindness to the Vietnamese people we met. This might seem like a normal thing, but many veterans have a hard time facing the descendants of those who committed horrible crimes against U.S. soldiers."

A highly decorated officer, Bill Bailey was awarded two Silver Stars. One resulted from being shot down over Nam Dinh, Vietnam, (Figure 91, page 265) the secondary target of an alpha strike by a large number of planes, designed to eliminate the enemy's petroleum, oil and storage supplies. Then, Ltjg. Bailey vectored his pilot and plane to hit the target. This was done despite heavy anti-aircraft fire and SAM (surface-to-air missile) activity. Once his plane was hit, he ejected. The North Vietnamese captured him and sent him to the "Hanoi Hilton," where he was tortured before being sent to solitary confinement for six months. Living conditions were poor, and he was in need of medical care. Five years and eight months later, he was released as part of *Operation Homecoming.*

Bill Bailey received many decorations including two Silver Stars, a Legion of Merit, two Distinguished Flying Crosses, a Bronze Star, two Purple Hearts, 12 Air Medals, and the Prisoner of War Medal.

After his military service, Bailey worked as a high school teacher for a year and then as a high school assistant principal for 16 years. Bill met his wife, Suzy, in London in 1973, following the War, and proposed to her two weeks later in Paris. They have been married 43 years and live in South Carolina.

Student host Haly Johnson said, "Bill has lived an incredible life. He is a great man and truly a hero. It was an honor to have been chosen to participate in the Patriotic Travel Program, but the best experience I had was meeting and spending time getting to know Bill Bailey." (Figure 88)

Figure 88: Student host Haly Johnson and veteran Bill Bailey. Photo by John Luck.

 ## STUDENT HOST: HALY JOHNSON

Like so many student hosts on the Vietnam trip, Haly Johnson (Figure 88) had a very personal reason for going. Her uncle William Asmussen is a Vietnam veteran, but Haly knew little about him other than that he had retired from the military. She knew he had received two Purple Hearts but didn't know why. She asked him about his time in Vietnam and was shocked to know that January 31 was the anniversary of the worst day of his life.

Haly's uncle explained to her how he got one of his Purple Hearts. "He was 19 years old that January (1968), a young boy forced to be more of a man than many twice his age. His battalion was supposed to fly at eight o'clock the next morning, but instead was awakened by an attack at four in the morning. My uncle and his buddy ran out of their bunker toward their plane just in time to see it hit by a grenade. They returned to their bunker and, a few minutes later, an enemy suddenly ran in and started firing his rifle all around the room. My uncle was shot in the neck and shoulder, and then watched in horror as his fellow soldier and friend's head was blown off."

Hearing such a story was troubling to Haly. She explained, "He was younger than I am now and went through things I cannot imagine.

It's amazing how so many served in the military and received so little thanks. My uncle made a statement to me that broke my heart. He said, *This may sound weird, but we never got a parade. We never got a "thank you" when we got back.* This made me think about all the veterans even more. The silent treatment they got upon their return both angered and saddened me."

"Silence seems to be the theme that surrounded the Vietnam War. Fellow citizens, friends, and even family often treated returning military personnel with disgust and never thanked them for serving our country. There is also a silence that resounds in schools, where my generation is learning nothing about the Vietnam War and those who fought it."

"I, too, experienced a type of silence when I was able to take part in a play production at College of the Ozarks. This play told the story of one of the school's most distinguished graduates, General Terrence Dake. This experience taught me far more than I ever dreamed I could learn about Vietnam and the sacrifices of those who served there." (Figure 89)

❝ There is also a silence that resounds in schools, where my generation is learning nothing about the Vietnam War and those who fought it. **❞**

Haly recalled a particularly moving production of the show: "It was opening night of the show *Four-Star Country Boy*. The entire cast and I had already had some exciting experiences, such as getting to meet four-star General Terrence Dake and his wife, Sue. Now we had the chance to perform a play honoring the General's life and honoring Vietnam veterans. The audience was responding exactly how we wanted, laughing at the comical parts, and feeling empathy for the touching family moments. I entered the auditorium as an American war protester, yelling and picketing against the soldiers who were returning from Vietnam. Immediately, I felt a change in the air. I delivered my line just as we had rehearsed, yelling out... *No one cares about Vietnam; you should go to Canada instead!* A suffocating sickness came over me. As we screamed horrible things at the soldiers and shoved them to the

Figure 89: Picture from student play, *Four-Star Country Boy*. Photo courtesy of Public Relations, C of O.

ground, I thought of the audience members who were remembering similar experiences. The silence in the audience spoke volumes. As I walked backstage toward the dressing room, I felt breathless, and tears pooled in my eyes."

After the play, Haly was overwhelmed when people approached her and thanked her for being in the play. One lady said to Haly, "No one else is doing this—showing people what it was really like during that war. If you don't do this, no one from your generation will know."

Haly Johnson will always be glad she did.

NAM DINH: POW BACKGROUND

Bill Bailey was one of thousands of American pilots shot down (over North Vietnam, South Vietnam, Laos, or Cambodia) during the Vietnam War. Many survived, and some did not. Of those who survived, most were imprisoned in North Vietnamese camps. (Figure 90) Those imprisoned in South Vietnam, Laos, or Cambodia were kept in different camps from POWs in the North. Many POWs were moved from south to north. Unlike POWs from earlier wars, the majority of Vietnam's POWs were well-educated officers of the Air Force, Navy, or Marines. Most were pilots or aircrew members.[2]

Bill Bailey was no exception, having attended Holmes Junior College and the University of Southern Mississippi prior to assignment in southeast Asia. He flew off the aircraft carrier *U.S.S. Constellation* as the Radar Intercept Officer on an F-4B Phantom jet with Commander Bill Lawrence. They were assigned a target in Haiphong Harbor. This was the major port of North Vietnam where supplies were regularly

PRISONER OF WAR CAMPS IN NORTH VIETNAM

CHINA

NORTH VIETNAM

DOGPATCH

MOUNTAIN CAMP

CAMP HOPE (SON TAY)
BRIARPATCH
FAITH
THE PLANTATION
THE ZOO
DIRTY BIRD
ALCATRAZ
HANOI HILTON
SKID ROW
FARNSWORTH

ROCKPILE

LAOS

GULF OF TONKIN

PORTHOLES

NORTH VIETNAM

★ HANOI

||||| PRISON CAMPS

— DMZ

Figure 90: POW Camps, North Vietnam. Adapted from public domain.

unloaded from China and the Soviet Union. Due to inclement weather, they diverted to a secondary target in the Nam Dinh Province (Figure 91), where they were shot down by 85mm anti-aircraft fire. Shortly, Bailey was captured and wound up in Hỏa Lò prison, also known as the Hanoi Hilton, in central Hanoi. (Figure 92) What ensued was years of abuse—torture, terrible living conditions and constant efforts on behalf of the NVA to use POWs for propaganda purposes. It is ironic that former NVA commander Bui Tin states in his book, *From Enemy to Friend,* "Our battlefield discipline was clearly delineated, and it was strictly forbidden to beat up, kill, or verbally abuse prisoners of war." He goes on to say, "It is my personal belief that no circumstance would justify the killing of even one POW or civilian."[3] Given the well-documented reports of POWs, this type of propaganda borders on absurdity. The facts are that many POWs were beaten (one literally to death), starved, kept in solitary confinement, subjected to rope torture and many other painful indignities.

Although the Hanoi Hilton received the most attention, there were at least a dozen other POW camps. Prisoners were often moved around

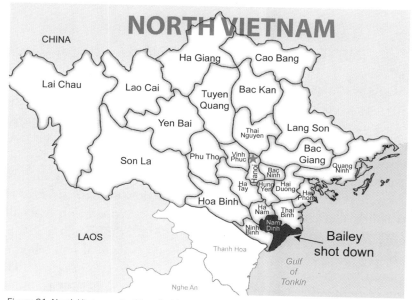

Figure 91: North Vietnam site (Nam Dinh) where Cdr. Bailey was shot down. Map adapted from public domain.

to other camps, as Bill Bailey could attest. Some of these camps were in the Hanoi area, and some were scattered about the country.

Figure 92: The Hanoi Hilton in a 1970 aerial surveillance photo. Photo from public domain.

 ## INSTRUCTOR REFLECTIONS

All of the students and veterans listened intently as Bill Bailey reflected on his experiences in the Vietnam War: "The experience of being there for a period of five years and eight months as a POW is the very pinnacle of all the events that have shaped my life (apologies to my wife!). And subsequently, it was unbelievable in molding my character." He continued, "First, let me explain what John Clark, others, and I were doing. John and I were part of a plan to help reduce the flow of men and materials into South Vietnam from North Vietnam. The operation was called *Rolling Thunder,* and it consisted primarily of bombing attacks upon the lines of communication and transport. Up front, I will tell you it was mostly a wasted effort. Quite simply, as long as you've got a large group of tremendously dedicated people able to move 300 pounds on a bicycle, you can drop all the bombs you want, and it just won't make much of a difference. It wasn't totally useless. I'm sure if we had not bombed at all on the Ho Chi Minh Trail, things would have been more difficult on our ground troops."

According to Bill, the Air Force bore the brunt of carrying out the attacks: "The effort to bomb the Trail was executed by a ratio of roughly two Air Force attacks to one Navy, with some assistance from Marines. The Marines, a self-contained unit, had their hands full providing air support to all the people they had on the ground."

Bailey pointed out that perhaps a dozen Marines were POWs in the North. He added, "This smaller number of Marine POWs is basically a reflection of the number of missions they flew over the North. I made two cruises, flying 183 missions from January through August of '66 and March until 28 June of '67, when I was shot down. In the Navy, we flew from a location we called Yankee Station. (Figure 93) We usually had two aircraft carriers on station—sometimes three or more in special

Figure 93: Yankee Station, *U.S.S. Constellation.* Photo from public domain.

situations. I flew off one of the super carriers, the *U.S.S. Constellation.* Carriers rotated in and out. Sometimes carriers from the East Coast would come in. We also had smaller carriers out there, such as the *U.S.S. Orinsky,* the *U.S.S. Bon Homme Richard* and others."

Bailey further explained, "Typically, an air wing in the Navy is composed of two fighter squadrons, three attack squadrons, and support aircraft. The main job was done by the attack people. I flew the F-4B. (Figure 94) I never had any encounter with MiGs, which is what fighter pilots live for. You don't drop bombs on the ground! Air-to-mud is not exactly what you do, but we did that in the F-4B. Almost every time I went north with an F-4B, we carried either ten 500-pound bombs or four 1000-pound bombs. If we were looking along the coast, we carried five-inch rockets. We did not have a gun in the F-4B, nor did the Air Force have a gun in the F-4C. For the most part it was missiles and bombs."

Figure 94: An F-4, like what Bailey flew. Photo from public domain.

"There were three aircrafts that probably had the bulk of the War on their shoulders. It was the mission of the Air Force to carry a tremendous bomb load. The Air Force also used the F-4 for fighter cover because they had a little more air opposition than the Navy. In the Navy, we used the F-4, but our mainstay was a little thing we called a *tinker-toy*. It's an A-4 (Figure 95), a very small aircraft, extremely reliable, and it carried a lot of bombs."

Bill Bailey calmly explained how he became a "guest" of the Vietnamese government when his F-4B was shot down: "The phantom jet has a pilot and naval flight officer. I was the naval flight officer during my last cruise, or, as we referred to ourselves, the RIO (radar intercept operator). During my last cruise, I always flew with the squadron commander. We were a team. It was a lot easier and more effective to fly with the same person.

"The day we were shot down, the target was to be located in Haiphong Harbor. We were flak-suppression fighters. We were leading an Alpha strike, with about 25 to 30 aircrafts. As we came close to the shore, we realized the target was completely hidden by cloud cover, so we diverted to the secondary target with our ordinance of four, 1000-pound bombs. We were going after a railroad yard. Since we were providing flak suppression, we went ahead of the group to drop our bombs on those shooting at us. We were hit just before we reached the roll-in-point. We were about two and half miles high when the airplane shuddered, and I knew we had taken a big hit."

Bailey and Commander Bill Lawrence thought they were going to make it. Unfortunately, at the bottom of their dive as they were pulling off their target, the plane lost all hydraulics, and it pitched straight up. Bailey remembered, "I blacked out as the plane went into a flat spin. When I regained consciousness, our wingman was yelling *Get out! Get out!* I realized it was all over. I ejected, came down, and probably spent 20 or 30 seconds in the chute."

Figure 95: A *tinker toy* (A-4 Skyhawk). Photo from public domain.

Things did not get better for Bailey. He recalled, "The Vietnamese were waiting for me. I mean, they were waiting for me, probably a dozen with rifles, hoes and sticks. I just kept my hands in the air. I came down in a little water irrigation ditch about one or two feet deep. Captured immediately, I was taken to Hanoi, and we arrived at night." "I spent the next three days undergoing torture. Finally, I reached a point where I couldn't handle it anymore. It had become a routine procedure for them. From 1965 and through mid '66 prisoners were left alone. But in mid '66 they went back and got the earliest ones captured and, with few exceptions, everybody went through the same regime. Typically, you'd arrive and be tied up with hands very tightly behind your back, and your legs would be in leg irons, shackled in leg irons. You'd be sitting on the floor, or sometimes they'd make you a little seat, and you had to sit on it. It would be okay for a while, but after hours have passed, it gets tough. The first part of it is usually softening you up. You weren't beaten, just slapped around a little bit, open-handed blows to the face and maybe a fist to the stomach. You were given no water or food, and you were kept awake. If they were in no particular hurry they'd do that for 24 to 36 hours. That's what they did to me. During that period of time, I was adhering to name, rank, date of birth and serial number. Occasionally, an English speaker would come in, sit in front of me, and question me. They would tell you that you're now their prisoner, you're never going home, you're a war criminal, you indiscriminately bombed old folks, women and children. This was a wearing down time, as much as anything."

> **❝** It was called the rope treatment. You'd be sitting there with your hands tied up behind you and your feet tied together. He'd start pulling your arms over your head. It would dislocate your shoulders. The pain of the rope treatment was pretty unbelievable. For a long time, I had a scar where the ropes had cut into the skin. **❞**

Bailey explained the torture method that usually brought prisoners to the point where they were going to talk. "It was called the rope treatment. You'd be sitting there with your hands tied up behind you and your feet tied together. He'd start pulling your arms over your head. It would dislocate your shoulders. The pain of the rope treatment was pretty unbelievable. For a long time, I had a scar where the ropes had cut into the skin. The rope treatment occurred on the third night. I was working on three days with no sleep and nothing to eat or drink to speak of."

Regarding the interrogation, Bailey recalled, "I realized I had to tell the Vietnamese something. One of their questions was, *Who are the officers of your squadron?* I gave them the names of the people who had rotated out of my squadron. They wanted to know what our targets were. Well, there were two problems with that from my standpoint. One, I was a lowly Lieutenant Junior Grade (Ltjg.), same as a Lieutenant in the Air Force, and I had no idea what the targets were. I wasn't exactly in that loop! Two, it had been three days, and anything that would have been on the target list was probably already hit. So, I just told him every target I had actually hit over the past three weeks, and that satisfied him. After that period, I was moved to another camp and put in solitary confinement for six months, and then I got a couple of roommates."

Bailey discussed with students the POW system. "The thing most of you think of is the Hanoi Hilton. It was the central prison (Figure 92), an old former French complex in downtown Hanoi, and it had a couple of sections to it. The section we called Little Vegas was where, for the first five or six years, American POWs were processed and held in individual cells, for the most part, before they were farmed out to other prisons in the system. After the Son Tay raid (an attempt by Army Special Forces troops to free the POWs), they brought most of us into the Hỏa Lò complex, where they opened up about seven rooms around the outside perimeter. They put anywhere from 40 to 50 POWs per room. However, they tried to keep older, senior leadership separated."

There was another major complex called the Zoo. (Figure 90, page 264) Bailey explained, "I don't remember why it was called the Zoo. There were five different buildings in it. It was an old building. The Zoo annex was right next to it and I was there for about three years."

Bailey spoke to students about another complex called the Plantation from which early releases were made: "It had a great big, old French colonial, two-story house in the middle, and the area around it was where POWs were held. That's where I was in my solitary confinement for the most of six months. And that's where I was in contact with

John McCain. He was there after he was out of the hospital. He was in the room directly across from mine. At that point, McCain was all beat up; he had a cast on. Bud Day, an Air Force Major and Medal of Honor recipient, was in there with him."

Bailey distinctly remembers the other POWs: "There were other new areas that held a few POWs from time to time. We had close to 100 POWs up in North Vietnam who were captured during the Tet Offensive. They pretty much walked to Hanoi from down south. They were a mixed bag and included German nationals and aid workers. Included were enlisted Army and a few enlisted Marines. The NVA moved people from time to time, but one of the things we always tried to do was memorize the names of all the POWs in the system. So over the weeks, months, and years, we got to know pretty much who was in the POW system in the North."

Bailey pointed out numerous little cells to the group: "There were three particular rooms used for torture: a room with acoustical tiles to cut down on the noise when guys were screaming, a green room, and a meat-hook room. I was only in one of them. Naming privileges for these rooms went to the Air Force, since they outnumbered the Navy by about two to one." Bailey remembered *Little Vegas*, *Riviera*, and *Thunderbird* as cell block names. Many cell blocks were named after Las Vegas hotels or casinos.

Bailey brought up the issue of the Code of Conduct for students to consider: "The Code says that *I will make every effort to escape when I'm captured,* among other stuff. This became a very sore point among POWs in Hanoi after we were captured. The reason is very simple. Somewhere there is a line between committing suicide and your duty as a military member to cause as much discomfort to the enemy as you can by escaping. Just where that line is located became a matter of debate. When confined like we were in Hanoi, we had no resources, other than what you could carry with you, to escape."

Some modifications to the Code of Conduct were made. Bailey said, "One of the things we have now is an understanding that you're still going to try to deny aid and comfort to the enemy as much as you can. But you need to understand that there will be a point where you can't resist anymore. Suicide is just not an option. I have no doubt that if all I had to do was take a pill, I wouldn't have done it, but I have no doubt that a lot would have done it. Don't know how many. Even one percent would have been too many. You can put enough pain on people, and they will do something. Most of us lied our fool heads off! I really had nothing of value to tell our NVA captors. Sure, I gave them names of people who had left my squadron from the first deployment. And when they wanted targets, perhaps a semi-legitimate military type of question, I didn't know any targets. All I did was give them every target I could remember I never hit!"

Nevertheless, Bill Bailey regretted telling his captors anything. He said, "I still felt very, very bad about the fact that I was not able to literally keep all of the Code of Conduct. The Code has been changed. Now it doesn't say, *I will,* it says, *I will attempt to…* .Some people think it's dumbing it down, but I don't think so. I think it's a realistic way of coping with where you're at. It doesn't mean that the first time someone looks crossways at you, you say, *Ok, ok, what do you want to know?* I don't think military people are like that."

> ❝ There were three particular rooms used for torture: a room with acoustical tiles to cut down on the noise…, a green room, and a meat-hook room. ❞

The severe treatment of POWs led to attempted escapes. Bailey recalled, "We had a case where a couple guys just wandered off because the Vietnamese left the door unlocked, and it was a place where only a few were being kept. We had men who were captured and escaped right after being captured. Most notable was a guy that wound up being awarded the Medal of Honor for that and more. Col. Bud Day was captured in the south, injured, escaped, and recaptured. We had one escape attempt that was classified, until about ten years ago. I'll tell you about both of them."

"One escape attempt was from the Zoo, a prison on the outskirts of Hanoi, perhaps ten minutes from the Hanoi Hilton. It was a very low-security environment, so there was no problem getting out of the Zoo. We had eight rooms, nine people in each room, and I was in a room next to the room from which these guys (Edwin L. Atterbury and John A. Dramesi) escaped. It was absolutely a piece of cake to go up into the rafters, remove the tiles, and go out. The actual fence around that place was very, very low security. All they had to do was wait until one of the periodic storms when the lights went out and take off. And they did. Our meager contribution was that we knocked out the lights in our courtyard, just in case they came on while the guys were escaping. Their plan was to go down to the river and float down all the way to the Gulf of Tonkin, then hope somebody would pick them up. But they were captured. They escaped one night, and they were captured early the next morning, just as it got light. They were trying to hide under some weeds. The two were brought back to the compound. The Vietnamese beat one of them to death and the other almost to death. Then they went after everybody that was involved with this. Every senior ranking officer (SRO) of each of the rooms was also seriously tortured. They were whipped with chains, radiator belts and other stuff and were kept in leg irons for about a month."

" Every senior ranking officer (SRO) of each of the rooms was also seriously tortured. They were whipped with chains, radiator belts and other stuff and were kept in leg irons for about a month. "

According to Bailey, senior leadership came up with a directive that there would be no more escape attempts without the aid of an outside agency. He added, "There's a difference between getting shot down and captured by two guys who have a pistol, and when one of them goes to sleep, making a break for the woods. There's a big difference between that and trying to escape from downtown Hanoi! The Atterbury-Dramesi escape attempt had no chance. In that situation, the senior officer, who was really just the same rank, could not stop them because the Code said, *I will make every effort to escape...*"

As for the other attempted escape, Bailey learned about it ten years ago and explained it to our group: "Information was passed to the U.S. government that somebody was going to try the same trick again. They were going to float down the river, but by this time, they wanted to coordinate with the Navy SEALS. It was very, very secretive. Under the cover of darkness, the helicopter took the four SEALs in and was going to drop them. The SEALs said the helicopter pilot was incompetent. They said that, instead of dropping them at an almost hovering level at a very low altitude, he came in too fast and too high. The Navy SEAL leader suffered a broken neck and another SEAL was seriously injured. The SEAL I talked to said every piece of his gear was stripped because he was going in so high. So, one SEAL, I think, out of four managed to survive somewhat intact. The SEALs were to be picked up later, and the submarine that was supposed to be around there came in a few days later. There never was an escape attempt. What happened reflects what limited communications we had. So, that attempt fizzled."

Toward the end of the War, Bill Bailey and his fellow prisoners learned more about what was going on in the War and the world: "In late 1971 and throughout 1972, the U.S. started bombing again in large numbers. We had over 100 who were shot down in 1972. These guys were aware of what was going on in the country. They were, in some respects, different from the rest of us. They had gone through several years of hearing protests against the War. While flying missions for us, they were certainly more aware of opposition to the War than we were. Most of the old-timers refused to believe anything, because of the abundance of Vietnamese propaganda. Some of what they told us was true, but we only had one source of information. If it's the enemy, you don't believe it. We didn't know much about what was going on in the country and wouldn't until we got home."

Bailey said the POWs didn't know about peace talks: "We had very little idea about peace talks or anything else. After reading about it later, my conclusion is that we basically got the same agreement as we thought we had in October 1972, when the North Vietnamese walked out of the peace talks. That's when the B-52s started bombing. The B-52s could not operate during the daytime environment. They would have been shot down by fighters. And, we had very specific targets that we were hitting around Hanoi. None of it was in the residential areas. After about ten days, it was over."

When the Peace Agreement was signed in January of 1973, some POWs were skeptical. Bailey recalled, "We named one guy the 'Dark Cloud' because he was so pessimistic. He was a Navy guy and refused to believe anything."

Naturally, the enemy wanted the prisoners to present well, so they fattened up the POWs. Bailey said, "Things had been better for us for a few months prior to the signing of the Peace Agreement. You had to be an idiot to not understand that things were over at that point. When it was time to go, they gave us a pair of khaki-type pants and a pair of black shoes—western garb. Interestingly, when things started getting better after Ho Chi Minh's death in 1969, a protocol was established that called for getting a five-pound package a month from family. And that's what I got. It was kind of a hit-and-miss thing. Some people did, and some people didn't. Once a month we were allowed a letter. (Figure 96) You could write about five lines."

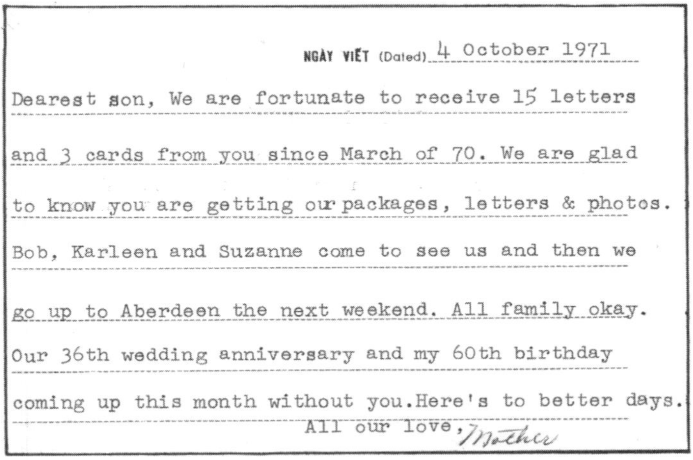

NGÀY VIẾT (Dated) 4 October 1971

Dearest son, We are fortunate to receive 15 letters and 3 cards from you since March of 70. We are glad to know you are getting our packages, letters & photos. Bob, Karleen and Suzanne come to see us and then we go up to Aberdeen the next weekend. All family okay. Our 36th wedding anniversary and my 60th birthday coming up this month without you. Here's to better days. All our love, Mother

Figure 96: Letter from Bill Bailey's mother. Courtesy of Bill Bailey, PETP 2014.

Bailey was no doubt glad to get any communication. He said, "Your letters were censored for sure. For roughly the first three years, I had no communication at all with family or anybody—no letters, no packages, nothing. After that I usually wrote letters and was able to receive maybe 20 or 30 the last year. We also got some pictures. For example, I received a picture from a girl I had dated, a Delta flight attendant. I did not recognize her—short skirt; dyed, long black hair, and she was beautiful. The guys were all sitting around me saying, *Who is that? How come a good-looking girl like this has anything to do with you?*"

At least Ltjg. Bill Bailey had someone to look forward to seeing!

STUDENT RESPONSE

Clearly, Haly Johnson was nearly overwhelmed with this Patriotic Education trip to Vietnam. She wrote, "There are so many words to describe this trip, but none would do it justice. Never in my life did I dream I would have an opportunity like this. As we leave the friends we have come to know and love over the past couple of weeks, I am sad but also excited to share my experiences with others. The love that I have felt on this trip has been special. I came expecting to learn from my veteran about his stays and experiences in the Vietnam War, to travel and learn about the culture, but I have gained so much more. I have made some of the most amazing friends—men and women from whom I can learn so much and who have so much kindness in their hearts. They are willing to teach us students and be there for us when, in reality, we should be the ones being there to support them and to give them the honor they deserve."

From the very first day, Haly bonded with her veteran, Bill Bailey. She explained, "He was a fighter pilot during the War, was shot down, and kept as a prisoner of war (POW). Another Vietnam veteran on the trip was John Clark (Figure 97) and he, too, was shot down and became a POW. They were both willing to get to know us and share their experiences." One of Bill's stories still remains with her: "Bill told me that

Figure 97: Veterans (POWs) John Clark and Bill Bailey in front of Hanoi Hilton. Photo by John Luck.

when he was a POW, the Vietnamese decided to move him to a different compound. As they led him to a different building, he was watching through the door and saw two men who had to be at least 50 years old. He said they had untrimmed, wild hair, and looked like they had been kept there forever. It turns out, they weren't that old, but he said their faces are something he will never forget." No doubt, Bill Bailey wondered if he would end up looking like that.

Haly distinctly remembers Bill telling her about his ordeal of being captured. At the Hanoi Hilton, he was able to see how the communists are still propagandizing the POWs time there. (Figure 98)

Figure 98: Cdr. Bill Bailey examines Hanoi Hilton propaganda. Photo by John Luck.

Haly was in awe of the veterans and what they had endured. "The terrain here is crazy," Haly said. "I can't imagine how hard it was. This place would have been so hard to live in, let alone fight in. Yet, the soldiers willingly gave up so much to fight for this country's freedom. As I heard story after story from the veterans on this trip, I was so amazed. The courage they showed is astounding. Yet, to them, they are totally average people. I am so blessed to have been able to come on this trip. It has truly been amazing. Just amazing."

TOPIC SUMMARY

Operation Homecoming brought about the repatriation of almost 600 prisoners of war (POWs), Bill Bailey and John Clark among them. They were released in groups, starting in early February 1973 and ending in April. No doubt, some POWs were skeptical that the transfer at Gio Linh Airport in Hanoi would actually take place. Though the POWs had gone through extreme hardships, including isolation, beatings, sickness, starvation, and worse, they never gave up. Some died in captivity, some were murdered, a few tried to escape, and the two who tried to escape paid a high price—one beaten to death and one nearly so.

Many POW wives contributed to better treatment for the POWs. They formed an organization, League of Wives, that led to the POW/MIA movement in the United States and around the world. They had been told by government officials to *keep quiet.* Officials thought calling attention to the increasing plight of POWs would be counterproductive. All that changed as the women lobbied all who would listen, from the President on down. POW/MIA bracelets began appearing across America. Bill Bailey shared a bracelet with his student host, Haly Johnson. (Figure 99)

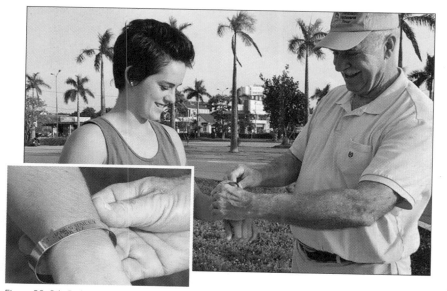

Figure 99: Cdr. Bailey shares POW bracelet with student Haly Johnson. Photo by John Luck.

Bill Bailey and his fellow POW friends maintain a strong bond. This is facilitated by an organization called NAM-POWs. They elect officials and occasionally get together to plan reunions. Bill enjoys telling stories from the War, and this one brings a smile: "A Navy crew (F-4) whom I knew from training (Neils Tanner and Ross Terry) were shot down and captured. The Vietnamese kept pressing them to make statements against the War, anti-war statements. They were tortured into making statements, so they concocted a story about how two pilots had turned in their wings in protest against the War, and they made a tape of this. This tape recording was taken to the War Crimes Tribunal in Stockholm, Sweden, in 1968. The problem was that when the tape was played, one of the guys who turned in his wings was named *Clark Kent,* and the other one was *Ben Casey.* Now, I know all of you know Clark Kent was Superman and Ben Casey was a popular TV medical doctor in those days."

 " We were strangers in our own country, and we didn't like a lot of what we saw. "

"This was a significant propaganda black eye to the North Vietnamese and more than a black eye when word got back to the prison system. They really laid into Neils and Ross. I think they spent a year in leg irons, plus they got the heck smacked out of them. But the biggest punishment was the leg irons...it's tough to live a year in leg irons."

Bill Bailey and John Clark, along with scores of POWs, did their duty. All suffered, and some paid the ultimate price. While visiting what is left of the Hanoi prison, students, staff and veterans alike stood in awe of those who spent years of their lives here long ago, but have been able to move on. They had plenty of adjusting to do when they got home.

George Coker, a six-and-a-half-year captive, remarked about his return to the United States: "We were strangers in our own country, and we didn't like a lot of what we saw."[4]

CLASS TOPIC 12: POW - HOA BINH (NORTH VIETNAM)

...so many fellas like me had died in that prison.
Why should I be the exception?

🍎 INSTRUCTOR: COL JOHN W. "GYRO" CLARK, USAF (RET.)[1]

"I am afraid that this story is only a scratch on the surface of a lifetime full of service and honor," wrote student host, Molly Matney, about her veteran, John Clark. Molly described Clark's inquisitive, energetic childhood: "He preferred drawing pictures of German planes being shot down to practicing his spelling. He always dreamed of flying airplanes. To this day, he fondly remembers zooming around his yard, buzzing like an engine, and acting like an idiot. Although this was all fun and games, it would translate into a lifelong passion for John. Growing up, he spent all of his summers working on his dad's farm in northern Missouri and became familiar with hard work and long hours. In high school, John played football and ran track, while maintaining a permanent spot on the honor roll."

Molly learned much about John Clark's education and training: "After graduating from Hickman High School, he attended the University of Missouri. He majored in mechanical engineering but also got involved with the school's ROTC program. After the completion of his degree, he received his officer's commission and began his military career."

"After college, John went to pilot training at Reese Air Force Base in Lubbock, Texas. Next, he was off to survival school. While there, he received both *cold* and *hot* war training. During the cold war training, he was taught how to endure different types of psychological torture and brainwashing. At this time, the U.S. military was using knowledge of torture based on Korean methods. It proved to be very different from what the Vietnamese used in later years. John completed survival school seamlessly and moved on to his first assignment, which was flying aeromedical evacuations across the U.S. He was based out of the East Coast and thoroughly enjoyed this job, because he was doing something both useful and interesting. During this time, he had the opportunity to see much of the country. John was soon reassigned to Alconbury, England. It was there that he received the fateful news that he would be joining the fight in Vietnam."

"During the War, John was initially assigned to Udorn air base in Thailand. The pilots were sent out on tactical reconnaissance missions and were told that they needed to either accomplish 100 counter-missions or serve for a total of one year. John was motivated to finish early, so he began flying missions with vigor. After only five months, he had completed 80 to 90 missions, with the majority being counter-missions. The end was in sight! Then, on March 12, 1967, his plane, an RF-4C Phantom II, was shot down."

"As his plane tumbled, John knew he had to act fast. The plane was moving around so much that he couldn't tell which direction the canopy was facing. He had a 50/50 chance that it was facing downward, and therefore, ejecting would send him headfirst into the ground. Taking the chance, he released his ejection seat. Luck was on his side, and he made it safely out of the plane. However, he was not in the clear. It only took seconds before he spotted Vietnamese soldiers approaching. He tried to hide in a ditch but ran into two guys with guns pointed directly at his head. They chattered in Vietnamese to him, but he was unable to understand their meaning. Finally, he realized that they wanted him to lay down on the ground. John refused to do so. He was determined to look his killers in the eyes as they pulled the trigger. Finally, a third Vietnamese soldier approached and was able to communicate to John that they only wanted to restrain him, not kill him just yet. In submission, he finally lowered himself to the ground and had his clothes and shoes removed. After this, he was transferred to multiple people and places until he reached what would become his home for most of the next six years, Hỏa Lò Prison, "Hanoi Hilton." Unfortunately, the other pilot was killed trying to shoot it out with the Vietnamese."

"While in prison, John was subjected to physical and emotional torture, including solitary confinement for the first few months of his time there. When he was eventually moved into a cell with another prisoner, he entered a small, damp space with not even enough room to walk back and forth without having to shift sideways. Their diet was meager, consisting of pumpkin or *sewer grass soup*. At first, communication was difficult. Eventually, John was able to learn the tap code used by his fellow prisoners, and it became a lifeline. He was very ill and nearly died, due to a mysterious lung condition. However, through a determined willingness to live and a rekindling of his own personal faith, John was able to recover from his sickness, surprising even the Vietnamese doctors, who thought he would die."

"Following the Paris Peace Accords of January 1973, John and his fellow prisoners saw the day they had only dreamed possible, the day of their freedom. After his release from prison, John returned to college and earned his MBA. He continued to be involved with the military and spent 15 years on active duty and 15 years as an officer in the Missouri Air National Guard. On June 18, 1982, he married Anne Johnson. They met through a mutual friend who forced the pair together, seemingly against their will. For John, it was immediate love when she whipped her head around and declared him the *most chauvinistic man she had ever met*. John and Anne have now been married for 32 years."

"During the course of his 30 years of military service, John earned many different decorations including a Silver Star, two Legions of Merit, the Distinguished Flying Cross, two Purple Hearts, the Meritorious Service Medal, six Air Medals, the Air Force Commendation Medal, the Prisoner of War Medal, and two Republic of Vietnam Gallantry Crosses. His other employments through the years have included holding the position of water engineer for the City of Columbia, Missouri, and co-owning three clothing retail stores with his wife, Anne. They currently reside in Columbia, Missouri."

Molly's comprehensive essay about Colonel John Clark reflects a person she described as "a man of immeasurable courage, strength, and integrity."

Figure 100: Student host Molly Matney and veteran John Clark. Photo by John Luck.

 ## STUDENT HOST: MOLLY MATNEY

Molly Matney (Figure 100) grew up just a few miles from campus with strong family bonds. She is an avid reader and majored in English and history. Molly was especially interested in history, which motivated her to participate in the Patriotic Education Travel Program at College of the Ozarks. She is of strong faith and said, "The most important thing about me lies at the center of my life: my relationship with Jesus Christ…my greatest desire is only to follow His will in all things."

Molly Matney's reasons for wanting to learn more about Vietnam veterans are very well stated: "Vietnam was something my [high school] history teachers did not talk about. They spent weeks discussing Okinawa, Normandy, Bataan, and Pearl Harbor, yet phrases like Ap Bac, Khe Sanh, or Xuan Loc never came up. I was an unabashed history buff through high school, but I am ashamed to admit that I never took the initiative to learn about the War that we didn't discuss. Perhaps I thought it was irrelevant or boring. Perhaps I just didn't understand. What I do know is that Vietnam held no value to me until one impactful encounter that changed everything."

"I was working as a waitress at a small, family-owned restaurant. Like any little restaurant, we had our four or five regular patrons. One, in particular, we simply knew as Art. If there was one thing Art loved, it was telling stories. If it was a slow day, he would sit and talk to the staff for hours on any topic imaginable. However, there was one topic that Art did not talk about. You see, Art was a veteran of the Vietnam War. The more I served Art, the more I began to notice that beneath his happy-go-lucky facade, there was a man holding on to an immeasurable amount of pain. He never seemed to look well-rested and complained of bad dreams. He refused to sit with his back facing out, preferring to see everyone and everything around. He drank far too much but never seemed satisfied. When no one was looking, his careless smile disappeared and a far-off look replaced it. Eventually, my curiosity effectively won over my caution. One day, a few of us workers and Art were sitting around chatting when the topic turned to upcoming Veterans Day celebrations. I asked Art if he planned to attend any of the Vietnam honor ceremonies. The silence in the room became deafening; I had crossed the unspoken line. Art looked at me and responded that he had done nothing worthy of honor in that place. He proceeded to tell us a story unlike any he had ever told before."

 ❝ What I do know is that Vietnam held no value to me until one impactful encounter that changed everything. ❞

"In it, Art was a young man, a soldier, embroiled in unimaginable horrors. It had been a day of intense fighting, and the casualties were more than they had ever witnessed. Art had stood at the edge of a lake with three or four other men, numb from all they had seen and survived. He looked into the water and saw several Vietnamese women and children bathing in the water. A terrible hatred ripped through his entire body, and in one deft motion he pulled a grenade and threw it into their midst. Although the grenade malfunctioned and did not explode, Art said he could still to this day hear the terror-stricken screams of those innocent people as they fled in utter hopelessness. As he finished his story, no one dared to move; we were all struck speechless by what we had heard. Then, out of the corner of my eye, I saw movement. One of those sitting with us was a Vietnamese-born woman named Yen. She stood up, walked over to Art, and simply placed her hand upon his shoulder in a motion of compassionate solidarity."

 "I cannot go back and change what may have happened in the past, but I can have a part in influencing what may happen in the future. "

"In that moment, I witnessed the incredible power of forgiveness. I later learned that Yen's family had suffered terrible consequences in the time of the War. Yet, that day she was able to overcome years of pain and bitterness in order to give a broken hero the chance for redemption. Like Art, many Vietnam veterans endured situations of unimaginable horror, and several made decisions that have haunted them for over 30 years. They returned to a nation that labeled them as monsters and baby killers. No parades were thrown, no banners hung; instead, signs of protest and words of hate greeted them from the very people they had fought to represent. I cannot even fathom the emotional toll that they must have had to endure. One day, Art left our restaurant and never came back. I will always regret that I never had the courage to look him in the eyes and say the words, *Thank you.* I never took the time to explain to him that he was forgiven for his past mistakes by our Lord and Savior and that he was immeasurably loved by Him. I cannot go back and change what may have happened in the past, but I can have a part in influencing what may happen in the future."

"POW" HOA BINH BACKGROUND

Unlike Bill Bailey, John Clark's plane was shot down six months earlier in the War (March 12, 1967). Clark was flying an RF-4C, whereas Bailey was flying in an F-4B. Bailey flew off the *U.S.S. Constellation* aircraft carrier; John Clark flew out of Udorn Royal Thai Air Force Base in Thailand. Bill Bailey, a Navy pilot, was shot down over Nam Dinh province; John Clark, an Air Force pilot, was shot down over Hoa Binh Province (Figure 101), northwest of Nam Dinh Province. They both ended up in Hỏa Lò Prison, located in central Hanoi and known as the Hanoi Hilton. Not unlike Bill Bailey, John Clark did not spend all his time at the Hanoi Hilton. Bailey spent about three years of his time in the Zoo, located about ten minutes from central Hanoi. John Clark was housed briefly in Son Tay Prison, called "Camp Hope" by the POWs. Son Tay was the site of a raid led by Army Colonel Arthur "Bull" Simons. Unfortunately, as Clark could attest, though the raid was well-planned, the POWs were nowhere to be found. They had been moved back to the Hanoi Hilton; John Clark was among them. Nonetheless, the effort of the Son Tay Raid sent an important message to the POWs back at the Hanoi Hilton and the Zoo who could see the fireworks, suggesting something was going on.

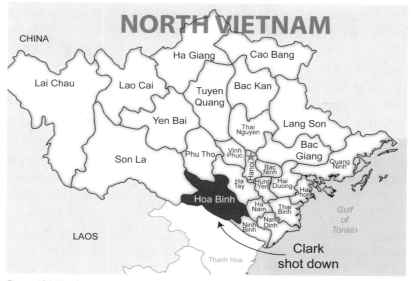

Figure 101: North Vietnam site (Hoa Binh), where Col. John Clark was shot down. Map adapted from public domain.

Benjamin Schemmer, editor and publisher of the *Armed Forces Journal International*, writes of one POW in his book, *The Raid*: "Ed Martin, from his cell…saw the flares overhead, explosions around, and surface-to-air missiles flying above Son Tay. Instinctively, he knew what was up…Martin watched them explode harmlessly only 19 miles away; … He had seen lots of SAMs—at much closer range. One had finally nailed his F-4…he knew all too well what the explosion looked like when an SA-2 slammed into a plane in midair. He broke into tears. He knew that Son Tay was empty; but that didn't really matter, he told himself. America cared."[2]

Clark's host, Molly Matney (Figure 102), along with the entire group, was given background material by those who spent years as POWs in a North Vietnam prison, especially the infamous Hanoi Hilton.

 ## INSTRUCTOR REFLECTIONS

No doubt nicknames were common in POW camps during the Vietnam War, and not just for NVA guards. John Clark was an American POW who was given a peculiar nickname by a fellow POW who was impressed with John's ingenuity. Colonel Clark explained the unusual name: "It was a product of Vietnam, but originated when I was first placed with some other cell mates. Paul Galanti, who was an A-4 Navy pilot and a very creative kind of fellow, was an Academy graduate. I've always been an ideas person. I'm always coming up with ideas for something; they may not be good, but they're ideas. They're always cranking through my head. So when we started living together, I kept coming up with these ideas for different things. In fact, I was sought out for ideas for escape plans or security plans and things like that. Paul said, *You know, you remind me of some cartoon character. I know who it is! It's Gyro Gearloose, the Walt Disney character, the mad scientist.* So, I got the nickname, *Gyro,* just because I was always coming up with some kind of an idea for something, sometimes zany and sometimes not." One of his ideas resulted in figuring out a way to weigh POWs. They all wanted to know how much they had lost since being captured. *Gyro* Clark was quickly accepted for his creativity. The fact that he had majored in engineering while in college became very useful.

John flew the RF-4C Phantom II, which was basically the F4-C Phantom II fighter jet, except it was the brand-new unarmed reconnaissance version—hence the added *R*, and is generally referred to as the RF-4. It was flown by two pilots rather than a pilot and weapons system operator (WSO) as in the fighter version.

But before John characterized the RF-4, he explained for the group another aircraft, the F-105 Thunderchief. It was the primary fighter-bomber used in Vietnam earlier in the conflict. Clark described the bomber: "Affectionately termed *The Thud* by Air Force pilots, it was made by Republic Aircraft, which was famous for its sturdy airplanes—the F-105 was no exception. It had a big jet engine to get it in the air and it was fast. But it had a deficiency of crashing from time to time! Well, one of the things that everybody seemed to notice was that it never seemed to crash with a flourish; it just crashed with a *thud*. Now, there was a range of mountains that divided Laos from North Vietnam, which ran up to the northwest from a few miles west of Hanoi to China. That ridge was nicknamed *Thud Ridge*, and I'm sure you can guess why."

Figure 102 (left to right): Student host Molly Matney, veteran John Clark, veteran Bill Bailey, and student host Haly Johnson. Photo by John Luck.

"Now let me tell you about *my* airplane," John told the students. "Our squadron rotated from England to Udorn, Thailand, taking the RF-4s with us. We were replacing the RF-101s that were all getting shot down. Our new RF-4s were very sophisticated, technologically advanced aircraft, much more so than the RF-101s. We had a great deal of reconnaissance capability: side-looking radar, infrared (IR), low-altitude high-speed photo optics, high-altitude photo optics, and a radio on which we could talk halfway around the earth."

"Let me tell you a little about this low-altitude high-speed photo optic camera. I was always surprised at what it could do. For example, let's just say you're taking some photographs of a race car. The race car goes by, *zoom*. If you've got your camera out in front of you and you click it as the race car goes by, you've probably got a blurred race car. So, now you take your camera, and you say, *Okay, we're going to move the camera as fast as the race car's going.* This time, as the race car goes by, you move your camera with it and click the picture. Now you've got a picture of a race car, but everything in the background is a blur. Well, that's okay, if you're wanting a picture of the race car."

"In this airplane, we had a camera with a glass triangular shaped lens and a prism that spun at about 20,000 revolutions per minute. That is what made the *image-motion compensation*. It adjusted for the speed of the ground passing under the aircraft. It made the ground sit still even though the jet was moving at 500 miles per hour. I have flown that jet 50 to 100 feet above the ground flying over an old barbwire fence with the camera running; when we checked the film later, we could see blades of grass growing out of the top of the old rotted fence posts. It's spectacular. We also had the capability of taking 300 miles of infrared; when turned on, it could give you the infrared track over your entire flight!"

Then, Clark told the group a true story of using the infared: "Flying out of Alconbury in England, we often got tasked to exercise with the U.S. Army in Germany. One day, during an exercise, we went out looking for tanks that had been reported in a certain area. So, we flew the area with our cameras running, but we didn't see a thing. Not a thing. We hunted around a little bit more, which, by the way, in combat you *never do*. You don't give somebody a chance to shoot at you on another pass. But we were still looking for the tanks. We wanted to come back with a tank. When we returned to base we had to report a *no show*. Maybe an hour later, the intel people called and said, *Lieutenant Clark, we want to show you something.* They ran through the panoramic film, that was just regular photo film, showing everything we'd flown over—nothing. It showed a clear, cultivated field with haystacks in the middle. Then Intel said, *Watch this,* and went through the IR film. Well, in the infrared, those haystacks were *hot* (they had white heat spots in them rather than the normal gray hay look). Intel said, *We've got something here!* They went back to the photo film, magnified it, and you could see the muzzles of these tanks sticking out of the haystacks—*WE HAD TANKS!* Those were the kinds of capabilities that were brand new."

"We also had brand-new ground-looking radar (50,000 watts), which would just about curl your hair if you happened to be stupid enough to stand in front of the airplane with the radar on. It would give us a terrain-following or a terrain-avoidance mode. We could follow the terrain up or down or avoid it, which meant we could go around the mountains or over them. Now that might not seem so exceptional, except this was done at night or in the weather on instruments as low as 500 or 1000 feet above the ground. It could make one a bit nervous."

John commented about the bombings: "I would like to present a different slant on one of the things Bill mentioned—the nature of the conduct of the War. Bill said he just didn't think that the bombing really accomplished that much. What I saw was we were blowing the devil out of all kinds of stuff; there was too much competition between the Navy and the Air Force as to who would drop the most bombs, who would fly the most sorties [armed attack from a place surrounded by enemy forces], and who would get the most money."

John continued, "I just got through telling you that infrared could easily fly a 30-mile track. But they would send us out to fly five miles of a 30-mile road target, and then they'd send another airplane out to fly the next five miles of that same 30-mile target, and then again. So you can just imagine what the last guy ran into; the enemy knew where we were coming from, what we were flying, and everybody was ready. So it was just like walking through a nest of stirred-up hornets for the last couple of guys. It was absolutely unnecessary; the first airplane could've gone through there at 600 miles an hour and flown the whole thing and been out of there before the North Vietnamese Army (NVA) even got to their guns. But, we did that to make it look like we had flown a lot of sorties."

John continued, "I remember, in the squadron operations section, there was one photo that one of our jets had taken. It was supposed to be a photo of bridge. Photo terminology: *Target: bridge over water.* But this *bridge* was a log; it was just a log laying on the ground. There was, I guess, a creek at one time that ran down through there, but whatever was there had been totally destroyed. On the photo, it said, *aircraft committed to target, one flight, four F-105s,* however many 500-pound bombs were expended on the target. *Target: bridge over water. Damage to terrain: considerable. Damage to target: none.* The target was the log. Tell me why we were doing that? I have no idea other than our Joint Chiefs of Staff were assigning the targets, and they weren't over in Vietnam. They were in the Pentagon in D.C.!"

"I was in Vietnam from '66, shot down in March of '67 at 27 years old, and was a prisoner there for six years. During that time, one of the greatest events of our time occurred, an event that probably few of you know about. The raid at Son Tay Prison happened. Basically, the raid at Son Tay was a group of Special Forces people who went into the Son Tay Prison after POWs had been taken from Hanoi to Son Tay. We were in that camp for about six months. With intelligence that the military leaders were able to gather, they realized we were at Son Tay, and they planned a raid. Unfortunately, we had been moved to another camp about a month or so before the raid. However, I feel it's important, and I'm going to explain the raid." (Figure 103)

"Starting in early 1970, the Chairman of the Joint Chiefs of Staff asked the Air Force and some people in the chain of command to consider the possibility of extracting some prisoners of war who were reportedly being held at Son Tay, and they started planning. They asked a Special Forces brigade for volunteers, and they got over 100; actually what they got was more than that, but they picked 109. They got these guys together and said, *This is an operation we can't tell you about. We're not going to tell you where we're going; we're not going to tell you what's there; and we're not going to tell you why we're going. We anticipate a reasonable loss would be 50 percent. Now, any of you, with absolutely no repercussions whatsoever, may choose to opt out, and we appreciate you volunteering for this assignment.* Not a single one of those dudes opted out!"

John continued sharing the details, "They cut the number down to 56 Special Forces guys with a whole bunch of air commandos. This was

Figure 103: Aerial image of Son Tay. Photo from public domain.

being planned at Herbert Field, which is the Air Force's special operations base in the United States. They constructed a full-scale model of the prison camp at Son Tay. Now all of this was completely unknown to us POWs."

"They had done some photo reconnaissance and some other intelligence work, so when it came time to execute, they had two windows. They needed to plan for moon phase weather that was advantageous for flying. They picked, I think, a half-moonlit night. They had originally wanted to go in October, but they decided to go in on the night of the 20th of November in 1970. They flew at least two C-130s into Udorn, all black, and they landed on the end of the runway. The operations officer and the commander there knew nothing about what was going on, only that they were coming in and that they wanted several A-1Es, or sandy aircraft, or air rescue aircraft. It's a big and magnificent airplane, single-engine fighter, Korean vintage aircraft. They wanted several of those, all painted black, armed in a certain configuration, and parked on the end of the runway. It was all a bit mysterious."

"It was a complex operation. The Navy would be flying diversion area bombing operations in Haiphong Bay, the Air Force would be flying cover, and then there would be these two 130s coming in from the back (west). So that there wouldn't be any chance of anybody asking any questions about these black A-1Es, they'd have to ferry them all the way from the United States and put them together once they got them over there. They were painted on-site and the pilots were trained. They took off about 10 p.m. and flew from Udorn toward Hanoi. Now, Son Tay, if you want to look on your map (Figure 90, page 264), is west of Hanoi. And Hanoi is, and was, one of the most highly defended cities in the world. They had the latest surface-to-air missile technologies, the latest radar technologies, and the latest radar-laden guns; there was just a lot of stuff around there."

"So these guys were flying right into the dragon's mouth, and about twelve o'clock, they hopped over the mountain. The helicopters flew in a V-formation and trailed behind the C-130s. The prison at Son Tay was too small for them to land a helicopter in it, so the plan was for them to crash a helicopter. These HH-53s were big helicopters; they'd have to be, because they were planning on bringing out about 50 of us. There were 14 guys assigned to *Blue Boy,* which was the aircraft that was supposed to crash in the prison camp. There were 14 or so assigned to *Greenleaf,* which was supposed to land outside the compound and then pull everybody out. Before they did that, they were going to blow a hole in the wall and go in. Then there was *Red Wine,* which was supposed to secure the area from intrusion from the outside. *Red Wine,* which carried Colonel Bull Simons, commander of the exercise, missed its target and landed about a quarter mile away. There were barracks there, and they stirred up a bunch of soldiers in these barracks. They came out of that place like hornets, but we were in position to eliminate somewhere between 100 and 200 of them."

"Anyway, they jumped back in the helicopter and moved over to the position that they were originally intending to occupy. They isolated the area by blowing a couple of bridges and took care of some extraneous threats. By this time, the guys who landed in the compound had gone around and knocked the doors down on all the rooms, or cells, only to find them all empty. The *Greenleaf* guys had already blown a hole in the wall, so they exited through the wall, jumped on *Greenleaf,* headed out and picked up *Red Wine* on the way."

"And this is what's interesting—amazing, actually—that predicted 50 percent loss turned out to be a sprained ankle. That was the only injury they suffered, one sprained ankle, and that was the guy who was standing in the door when the helicopter crashed!"

"Of course, they were very disappointed. We, the POWs, had been moved back to those big rooms in the Hanoi Hilton, because they thought that there would probably be another raid. We didn't find out until a couple days later, because there were some South Vietnamese pilots in the Hanoi Hilton, who naturally understood Vietnamese, and the radio was going nuts. They tapped to us on the wall, and said, *Hey, you know, you guys have just missed the boat!*"

"Even though we were a little put out by the news, the truth of the matter is that our morale went absolutely sky high. If you had been in that situation, what would you have thought? You would've thought, *My gosh, my country cares, and there are a bunch of guys who are going to really hang it out to come get me!* And so, we were just sky-high about the whole thing."

"As it turns out, when we were released, Ross Perot decided *I'm going to get these Son Tay guys together.* So, he gave us all airline tickets out to San Francisco, gave us some money to wander around town and a couple of days to get to know each other. Then he had a big banquet; if there was anybody in Hollywood who was anybody, they were there. They had invited Son Tay raiders and ex-POWs, along with dignitaries like John Wayne, Gary Cooper, and the Lennon Sisters."

"At the banquet, Ross Perot got up and told this story: *Years ago, well not that many years ago, we tried to get some packages from families to you guys. We weren't getting any mail, and you guys weren't getting any mail. We tried to push that point. So, we went around to the various airlines and told them we needed to have their birds take us from Udorn up to Hanoi. Of course, the airlines had been told they couldn't fly into Laos or Vietnam, and the State department had said no, too. So, we found an airline that would do it. This airline started out from (I think it was) Udorn, and they got into Laos, and the embassy gave them a call on the radio; they were ordered to turn around and come back, stating they were not cleared to go into North Vietnam. It just so happened that the CEO of the airline was on board that aircraft; he took the mic, made some static noises, turned the radio off, and the plane went on.* Perot continued, *We didn't get there, but we sure as the devil tried. That was Braniff Airways that did that,* and he said, *the CEO is here with us tonight.* The guy was sitting at our table!"

Efforts like the story above gave the prisoners hope. Like the other POWs, John Clark was tortured. He endured solitary confinement and rope torture, and he recalls, "The pain never passed; they always found new places to torture that were sensitive and tender. I knew that I was not doing very well, that I needed help and strength to get through it. Even though I was raised in a Christian church, I had cut it out of my life through college. I considered myself a lost sheep. I started praying, praying hard and earnestly. I knew I couldn't pray to be back in my airplane or back at Udorn. I knew I had to deal with my situation right there, so I prayed for strength and hope. But there was nothing; it felt obvious to me that I was on my own. It was about that time that I thought about committing suicide. I expected to go home with physical disabilities, but I did not want to go home with a disabled mind. I thought, *This is a little severe, what I'm going to do, but I think I have a forgiving God, or did at one time. I'll have to start praying for a sign. So, I prayed in earnest for a sign, just a little bit of encouragement.*"

"One cold and overcast afternoon, I was laying on my concrete slab covered by a mat, praying. I dozed off and then suddenly woke with a start. The sun was beaming through the window behind me. It was like a powerful flashlight shining through fog and haze. And there on the opposite wall was a tall cross! How could I take that as anything except a sign and encouragement?"

"At one point I felt very alone. I was talking to God, but I didn't feel like He was talking to me. I didn't have faith. There was a 20-watt bulb hanging from the ceiling, which was always on. One day I woke up and for some reason, the light was off. For the first time, I noticed light coming through a tiny crack. When I looked through the crack, I was looking right at the door across the hall. When I woke up the next morning, the light was on. I could hear the opening of doors, clanging and banging, for breakfast. I looked through the crack and there was the ugliest American I had ever seen, Charlie Green. He was my connection to the outside world. I couldn't talk to him, just see him through that little hole."

> **❝** The sun was beaming through the window behind me. It was like a powerful flashlight shining through fog and haze. And there on the opposite wall was a tall cross! How could I take that as anything except a sign and encouragement? **❞**

"My new cell where I still lived in solitary confinement was pretty nice, actually. This cell was a good size and didn't have anything in it; it was shuttered and barred on the back, shuttered door in the front. I had had no communication with anybody other than just looking through a little crack seeing Charlie Green. In this new cell, I'm there the first day looking through the louvers, and here comes somebody out of the cellblock doorway headed to the cell next to me—an ugly guy—tall, thin, really scrawny guy. I'm thinking, *Wow.* He's obviously an American, and I thought, *Oh, I hope I don't look like that in a couple of years.* Later I found out he'd been there for two years; he was an early shoot-down. It turns out, he was a Navy guy."

All this led to Clark learning about the *Tap Code.* (Figure 104) "He started tapping on the wall. He was just tapping like crazy, and I had no idea what he was doing or saying. So I just sat there, and whenever he'd stop, then he'd tap and I'd tap back. And he'd tap again. As it turned out, the guards would have a siesta, which lasts about an hour to an hour and thirty. By the end of the siesta, he'd quit tapping. I'd sit there and listen and look at the wall and sit down. Next day, there he was again. This happened for about two or three days, I think, and finally he had to stop after the siesta. After a couple of days, I noticed that there was a consistency about these taps, and I thought, *You know, I wonder if he's tapping the same thing every time?* So, the next time, he started I counted."

Lee Ellis, another POW in the Hanoi Hilton, later explained in

Leading With Honor, the code in simple terms: "The first tap was for the row, and the second tap was for the column. For example, the word, *Hi*, would be composed of—**down 2 and over 3**—for the letter, *H*, and—**down 2 and over 4**—is the letter, *i*. Thus, tapping, *Hi*, would sound like this: *tap tap* pause; *tap tap tap* pause; *tap tap* pause; *tap tap tap tap*."[3]

Ellis further explained the important role of the tap code: "Over time, because of the code, we were able to find out who was in the camp, connect into the chain of command, and function as a team. Learning the code became an obsession for me."[4]

Clark detailed how they would shortcut the tap code: "Once you understood what a word was, you didn't go ahead and let the person—the

Figure 104: Col. John Clark, assisted by Molly Matney, hold John's rendering of the Tap Code as he shows-and-tells, "down first, across second." Photo by John Luck.

one who was tapping to you—spell a whole word. You tapped them on by going: *tap tap*. Then, they'd go right to the next word, and it was just continuous. So, if they, for example, were sending the quote: *Fourscore and seven years ago...*, and you realized from the context of the previous conversation what was being communicated—the whole thing would just be the first letter of each word. We would anticipate it and tap them right on through."

Colonel Clark continued the lesson: "As time went on, the people who were the communicators would make their own abbreviations, and then it was just virtually impossible for the NVA to break into the code. There were all kinds of ways to keep communication going. For example, instead of taps, one might *cough*, or do eye *flashes*, or make sweep sounds like, *shh shh*; or a communicator could make a chop motion—*chop chop, chop, chop*. Another method of communicating was to take a string out of our blanket and tie little knots and slide it through our fingers. Or, when we were going somewhere blindfolded, we might bump up against our neighbor in the duce and a half (big Army truck); this way, we would find out everybody who was on that duce and a half—we all knew who was going and who wasn't. The tap code was a very, very important piece of communication—a lifeline. With communication came faith, hope, and comradeship with our fellow prisoners of war."

No doubt the various communications made a very difficult situation a little more tolerable. Camp Regulations were strict and never referred to POWs as prisoners. Rather, they were called "criminals"—mentioned 13 different times in the Camp Regulations document of February 1967.[5]

Clark continued, "Later, I moved in with a roommate, Tom Storey. He was a pilot who had been flying F-4s, sent from MacDill Air Force Base, to teach us how to fly the new RF-4C. Tom had a jutting chin, a brusque kind of guy, but he was also very religious. He started delivering to me various parts of the Bible. I remember one he gave to me seemed to fit at the time: *Seek and ye shall find.* I was seeking, and apparently I was finding. Tom and I had *church services* in that cell."

"Not too long after that I became very allergic to something, in addition to having malaria. I would sneeze 30 or 35 times in a row. I tried to hold the sneezes back, but instead of helping, it made me start choking. I constantly felt like I couldn't breathe. My breathing was shallow, and I knew my lungs were in bad shape. Eventually, my lungs started filling up with mucus and I started to gurgle. I was drowning in my own mucus."

"At this point my roommate and I decided that I needed some attention. We yelled, "BAO CAO" (which means attention) and asked for a doctor. Actually, only he yelled; all I could do was whisper. A few days later one of the guards went out and came back with a pretend doctor;

he just wore white. He listened, then closed up his stuff and left. I realized that he couldn't cure me and he was leaving me to die. I would be hauled out and never heard from again. Mostly I was lying down, and fluid was building up in my chest. Once when I was sleeping, I seemed to be zipping through blackness. I thought, *What's going on? Where am I going?* It seemed as if my soul had separated from my body and I thought, *Jesus! I've died!* But I didn't want to die yet, and I kept struggling to pull myself back. Inch by inch, and exhausted, I perceived that I was getting closer to where I started. Then, all of a sudden, I woke up and there I was, barely breathing. I sat up, and I was able to gasp for air just a little better."

"Of course, I was praying a lot. There were so many fellas like me who had died in that prison. Why should I be the exception? If that was my fate, I prayed that my family wouldn't suffer because of it. When I laid down again, I felt a warm sensation, a sensation of relaxation move up through my body, and I just had an overwhelming peace. I fell asleep."

Figure 105: Col. Clark and Molly Matney look at POWs being freed. Photo by John Luck.

"As I slept, I laid over on my side. When I woke up, this syrupy mucus was running off the side of my mouth, off the bunk and onto the floor. I figured I needed to get my chest above my mouth, so I got up on my knees with my head down. Before long, mucus started flowing out of my nose and my mouth. My roommate brought our excrement can over to collect it. I thought that as long as I could keep that stuff from building up in my lungs, I'd be okay. So, I kept up with that regimen for several days, until the mucus finally started to dry up, and I began to get better."

"In the winter it got cold, and there was no way out of it for weeks. I was afraid that breathing the cold air might affect my lungs. I had been praying all this time for God to give me some hope, guidance, and peace, and to show me how to help myself. I came upon a plan to throw my blanket over my head. I was re-breathing my air and it was warm."

❝ But when I got off the plane at home, there wasn't anybody there to meet me. ❞

Operation Homecoming (Figure 105) was the return of POWs—about 600. John Clark was in the second group. It was not a happy time for many POWs. John Clark remembers, "It's a long sordid story. There were a lot of guys who came home to nothing—an ex-wife gone to Mexico, one who had gotten divorced, etc.... Very few guys came back and had their wives actually waiting for them. There were a couple of guys who had girlfriends who had been loyal to them for all those years."

"When we got on the airplane to come home, we flew in to Clark Air Force Base. *Operation Homecoming* had reserved, at their first stopover in the Philippines, telephone lines for soldiers to talk to their families."

"The Air Force was putting everything out, making facilities available to the families, giving the families highest priority, because it was a big deal when we were released. But when I got off the plane at home, there wasn't anybody there to meet me."

"I hadn't yet seen my son. He was born after I was in Southeast Asia, and then I was shot down after that. My daughter was about ten or twelve years old. They weren't at the airport but came to the hospital, maybe an hour later. They just kind of looked at me." Eventually, John would be divorced and estranged from the children he had never gotten to know.

When John reentered the U.S., a lot had changed. He told our group, "There was still a lot of anti-war sentiment evident. There was a lot of that fervor. When we got to Clark AFB, we had our first interrogation and debriefing. It was our first time back with Americans and people who liked us. We wanted to go home and just disappear. We didn't want to be part of the War; we didn't want people to bother us; we just wanted to go home and get back with our families and maybe some of us would get to stay on flying status. But we were in pretty bad shape. So we got to Clark, and ours was a small group of 20. Normally, they were releasing them in groups of 100 or 75, I think. I was in the second, but it was an in-between group, as we were a gift to Henry Kissinger."

> **❝ I was greeted back at home with a sign, COLUMBIA WELCOMES HOME JOHN CLARK....but in the back, up against the wall, were some protesters....one of them [the protesters] made some remark while I was sharing my *thank you* comments with the mayor. A lady in front of him [the protester] turned around and decked him; she dropped him right to his knees! ❞**

"In Hanoi, they had pulled 20 of us out from the rest and put us in another cell. They took out our senior ranking officer (SRO) and, when he came back, he said, *Guys, I think we've got a problem. Here's the deal. They want us to go home.* Normally, you wouldn't think that's a problem! *They want us to go home; Henry Kissinger's coming to visit, and they want to give us to Henry Kissinger as a gift. The problem is, we're out of order.* We all had different shoot-down dates, and we had orders about not going before the people who were shot down before us. He said, *I'm going to leave it up to you guys; what do you think about that?* And to the man, we said, *We are not doing it. I'm not going to be one of the guys who's Henry Kissinger's gift before other people that were shot down before me.* The Camp commander said, *You will go as our gift to Henry Kissinger, or you will spend the rest of your life in a prison in North Vietnam.* We still refused and said, *No, we want to speak to our senior ranking officer.*"

"Well, our SRO didn't show up right then, but I'll tell you who did: he was either a *full bird* colonel or a brigadier general who was part of the contingent, and he said, *Alright guys, you gotta go. We cannot risk you screwing up the release.* Then our SRO showed up and said, *Guys, get the hell out of here!* We asked where Bill Bailey was, and Bill said, *Oh, I'm here.* And so off we went!"

"At Clark AFB in the Philippines, our senior ranking officer announced, *Guys, here's what's going to happen. They want to debrief us and find out who we knew and some of that kind of stuff. We're going to get to talk to our families on the phone. We'll be getting some reorientation, but not a lot; that will all be mostly done when we get home. And they're going to prep us to play the hero when we get back.* And we're like—*Huh?* No. Not going to happen. I am not being any hero."

"We did our best to come back honorably. It was just our job. We didn't deserve any heroics for that. We had another senior officer training us and he said, *Ok, guys here's the deal. We know you don't want to be heroes, and neither did the first group. But our country is terribly divided. Our country seriously needs heroes. And you guys have been out of the fray of burning villages and doing all that kind of stuff, and catching all the heat.* We didn't know they were catching that much heat. He continued, *And guess who the heroes are? You guys are the heroes. Like it or not, that's an order. You're going to be heroes.*"

"I was greeted back at home with a sign, COLUMBIA WELCOMES HOME JOHN CLARK. It was a rainy, nasty day, and people turned out—which was nice. A little girl, who had worn my bracelet, came up and gave me my bracelet and a big kiss. Her actions were very nice, but in the back, up against the wall, were some protesters—maybe three or four, possibly a half-dozen. I was just trying to [mentally] keep a grip on life, and thought I was doing fine, then one of them [the protesters] made some remark while I was sharing my *thank you* comments with the mayor. A lady in front of him [the protester] turned around and decked him; she dropped him right to his knees! He took his signs, and they all left."

Jane Fonda, Hollywood actress and so-called peace activist, evoked bitterness, and her actions still bother veterans. John explained how the POWs knew when she was there, "because they forced these guys to go see her. They wanted her to be told by the American prisoners of war that we were being fed fine food, and all this kind of stuff. They couldn't get any POWs who would do it, unless they tortured them, and then eventually you were going to do it."

Stories about Fonda took on a life of their own, according to Clark. "There's a story about guys giving her their names. We wanted to get as many names out as we could. So, they got some of the toilet paper and little scraps of things you could find and some sort of ink, and they wrote their names. The story goes that when they shook Jane Fonda's hand, they gave her these names. As soon as she was done, she turned all the names over to the North Vietnamese, letting them know. This has since been debunked. The guys who were supposed to have been involved in that said, *No, that never happened.* As much as we hate her, she did not do that!"

"Fonda did do some terrible things." American servicemen will never be convinced otherwise. Her actions, as well as the actions of other celebrities, will always be remembered by millions as dishonorable and harmful.

STUDENT RESPONSE

"My internet isn't working. How will I check Facebook? That traffic jam ruined my schedule for the whole day! This dress is from last year. I have nothing to wear. My hamburger is half pound, not two-thirds. I'm starving! As embarrassing as it is to admit, most Americans make comments like this on a daily basis. We have been conditioned by our culture to believe that these *first-world problems* are a true measure of suffering. However, join me (Molly) for a moment in imagining a world where day-to-day issues bear a heavier consequence. Imagine a world where your very survival is a constant struggle. In this world, you are sequestered from your society, isolated from your comrades, and aware that your life is in the hands of those consumed by a vile hatred for your country. You only eat an unappetizing, slimy broth with very little nutritious value every day; have no proper protection from the bitter cold or stifling heat; and if you get sick, you will be left to die in the small, dismal room you call home. You have been tortured, interrogated, and fed propaganda to rob you of any hope that you have struggled to maintain. If you can possibly force your mind to imagine this world, then you will have a mere glimpse into the life of an American POW in North Vietnam. I have the honor of knowing one such former POW, a man named

John Clark, and he is the bravest person I have ever met."[6]

"As soon as I saw John Clark across the terminal, I recognized him from his photo. He smiled and waved at me and immediately walked over to greet our group of students. I was so anxious to meet him that I tripped and almost fell. Thankfully, he just chuckled and extended his hand to shake mine."

"We found out that [another veteran on the trip] Bill Bailey and John Clark already knew each other from their time in prison at the Hanoi Hilton. I also briefly spoke to another veteran, Jim Greer, for the first time. He was joking around with me about the other veterans' war stories. He told me not to believe everything I hear, *These guys will say anything to top each other.*"

A long flight allowed Molly to refocus her mind from the initial veteran meetings. "After landing in Saigon, I was able to find John, my veteran. The bus ride gave us plenty of time to talk some more. I asked him if he spoke any Vietnamese. He told me, *No, the guards in his prison did a good job of ensuring that we did not learn the language.* They didn't want the POWs to have any chance for communication. I was a little concerned at first about talking to John about his time in prison, but he told me to not feel trepidation about asking questions. He said that he has been asked most everything at this point. I really appreciated his willingness to share with me. It was an honor to hear his stories, and I have nothing but the utmost respect for him. He talked a lot about his wife, Anne. He seems to love her very much. He also briefly mentioned that his first wife had been a peace activist during the War, but he didn't elaborate. John also told me about the Son Tay raid. He told me that he is the only veteran on the trip who knows much about it, and that he would like to share it with the rest of the group at some point. [He did.] He is such a good storyteller."

Molly found the group's first church service, which she led, "surreal." "I got to share a bit of my heart and spoke over Psalm 25. Afterward, John Sorensen approached me, slapped me on the back, and thanked me for my words. He is so kind and encouraging. We talked for a little bit. He mentioned how excited and honored he felt to be a part of this trip. He said that he and Paul Frampton had just been talking about how they felt sort of unworthy to have been chosen, in light of the high profile of some of the other veterans. It broke my heart to hear him say this. I wish I could think of some way to let him know that the respect I feel for him has nothing to do with rank or medals. Each and every one of these men exhibited courage and sacrifice for our country. They are all heroes to me!"

"John told me the story of his capture. He was flying a mission with his co-pilot when they were hit and started to descend quickly. He said it was the first time in his life that he was in a plane and didn't feel in control. He knew time was running out as the plane fell and that he needed to eject. However, he also knew that the plane needed to be upright for him to properly eject. With the plane out of control, he figured there was a 50/50 chance that he would eject the wrong direction and crash into the ground immediately, killing himself. Without much time, he accepted the odds and pulled the lever. He said that it felt like forever before he ejected."

"After landing, he could hear and see Vietnamese approaching. He knew they were most likely unfriendly and that he couldn't outrun them, so he hid in a ditch. After he thought it was clear, he began to move along the ditch but ran into two soldiers holding *the biggest guns I had ever seen*. They took his clothes and shoes and told him to get on his knees and put his head down. Thinking they were about to shoot him, he refused, preferring to die while facing his killers if that was to be the case. They started yelling at him and, finally, a third Vietnamese man approached and explained to him that they were not going to shoot him. With that knowledge, he agreed to lay down, but he still did not kneel. They then moved him to a cave for the rest of the day, tying his hands painfully behind his back. That night, they handed him off to a more 'official' group of NVA. They took him to a village and placed him in a small hut. In the afternoon, while everyone was taking a siesta, a woman approached his hut and began slashing a machete through the wall, hoping to kill him. Her son had been killed by an American air raid, and she wanted revenge on any American pilots she found. She was eventually subdued."

"After that, they moved him by truck to Hanoi. In the truck, he saw a bloody parachute and assumed that his co-pilot had tried to shoot it out with the Vietnamese. He said that he felt very cold to this information. He had been through too much to really feel sad at that point. I cannot even begin to imagine what this must have been like. I just feel so honored to be able to hear his stories."

Molly continued, "John told me about the shoes that they had to wear in prison. The men all called them 'go aheads' because that was the only direction you could go: ahead. They were made out of rubber tires and only had one front strap. Because of the way they were made and fit, it made running (and, therefore, escape) impossible. We also talked about the propaganda videos that the POWs were forced to watch by the NVA. He said that they didn't watch them very often, but it came to be a sort of treat. Even though the information was not to be trusted or believed, it was a nice break from the normal routine. Generally, they would bring the prisoners out and let them watch the movies outside, so they got a little more freedom than normal. This would happen usually every one to two months once they moved out to Son Tay."

A visit to the Reunification Palace and War Remnants Museum made a big impression on Molly: "The museum was especially interesting. It was very much filled with propaganda and misinformation. I was really glad that I got to go through it with John. To me, it was hard to always discern fact from fiction, but he was good about pointing out things to me and explaining them. Some of the exhibits, especially those on Agent Orange, were horrifying. John said that it can't be denied that there were horrible consequences from the chemicals, but he also told me to remember that many of the photos were staged and that the Americans suffered too. I really do respect what he has to say, and I was thankful that he was willing to share with me. We talked a bit about survivor's guilt and some of the more difficult aspects of war. It was heavy conversation, but it was also really good."

"John is such an amazing man. He has sure led a remarkable life! I still can't quite believe that I am here in Vietnam experiencing this indescribable trip. I don't know when it will become real...probably not until I return to C of O. I know what I see and hear here will continue to teach me for many years to come. I am so thankful to have this opportunity!"

Molly and the others listened intently to John's stories: "John and Bill spoke to us a bit on the bus. I was glad that John got to share some of the stories he had told me with the rest of the group. They are fascinating, and he is an excellent storyteller. I think this was the first time there was a speaker on the bus and almost everyone was awake. It's hard not to listen when John is speaking."

John told Molly that he was compiling his POW experiences into a book: "He said that he had been working on it for a while, but he has recently become more serious about it. He doesn't want his stories to be forgotten when he gets too old to tell them anymore. Hearing him share this sentiment made me realize just how important it is to take the time to listen to our veterans before it is too late. They have lived through unbelievable circumstances and have valuable knowledge to impart to us, the younger generation, if we are willing to listen. I want to challenge myself to not let stories of heroic men like John be forgotten. I offered to help him with any editing he needs done. He told me I might regret that offer, but I doubt it. I hope he knows I'm serious! I would love to help him out. He has some awesome stories that need to be shared!"

 “ His advice to *find God in even the smallest of things* really hit home for me. ”

At a second church service, the group listened to John attentively. "He had mentioned to me before about how he had been raised in a Christian home but had moved away from his faith until his imprisonment. However, he had not elaborated on that topic very much. Then, out of the blue, he expressed an interest to share his testimony with not just me, but our entire group. I was surprised but also very excited. He said that he had never fully told this story before, and he wasn't sure how it would go. He said that he felt if there was ever a time to tell it, it was now and with these people. I felt honored that he trusted us and felt that deep of a connection with our group to be able to share such difficult and emotional memories. Hearing him talk this morning was one of the moments that I will carry with me for the rest of my life. His advice to *find God in even the smallest of things* really hit home for me. I feel that I have a tendency to get too hung up on the speed bumps in my day-to-day life. I need to learn to trust in God and to see the evidence of His divine life in even the really difficult situations. I know this in my head, but I must capture it in my heart. John and I have not talked about faith a lot, but what we have shared has been some of the best conversation of the entire trip. There is so much I can learn from his strength and courage and love of God."

"Going into Hanoi was a very emotional time," Molly noted in a journal entry. "It was the day John and I had been thinking of and talking about for the entire trip: Hanoi. We left Hué in the morning and separated from our tour guide, Quan, who had been so great. From Hué, we flew to Hanoi. It was a quick and easy flight. Our photographer kept coming over to me and taking my picture. He said not to be alarmed, that he was just trying to get as many as possible for the blog post. He asked me what I was going to write about and what my purpose with it would be. I had already started my post and typed some of it out, but I hadn't really thought about an answer to his question. What was my purpose? I began to think on this and realized exactly what I wanted my purpose to be. I wanted people to read my post and be filled with the same sense of overwhelming pride that I now felt for every single one of our veterans. I wanted people to understand the depth of their sacrifice, the bounds of their strength, and the power of their courage. I wanted my readers to look at their own life and question what they called—hardship."

 " I wanted people to understand the depth of their sacrifice, the bounds of their strength, and the power of their courage. "

Molly continued in her journal with thought-provoking notes: "I wanted them [readers of her blog post] to look within and determine what their true passion was. What were each and every one of us willing to give up so much for? For our veterans, it was their country...their country and freedom. I don't know what it is that I love that much just yet, but I intend to find out and spend the rest of my life pursuing it, because our veterans have inspired me to do so."

Molly was anxious about the POWs' return to the Hanoi Hilton:

"As we approached Hỏa Lò Prison, the Hanoi Hilton, I asked John how he felt about returning. He said that he didn't feel much of anything really. He had made his peace a long time ago. I was still worried about how this would affect him. Our other POW, Bill Bailey, said that he began to feel a bit of anxiety upon arriving at the former prison. Twelve students split up, each half joining a POW as we toured the facility, so that we could hear what they had to say. I was surprised to see how much of the prison was left. Most of it was a re-creation and filled with propaganda, but it was still interesting to see. (Figure 106) They seemed to focus on the period of time when the prison was used by the French to imprison and torture Vietnamese rebels."

Molly noted about visiting Hỏa Lò: "There was only a very small portion of the American pilots who were held there. It was filled with photos and videos of the—*humane*—treatment that the Americans received there...all horribly fictionalized or staged. I was worried about John, but he still seemed to be handling everything quite well and with the utmost composure. He immediately went into teacher-mode, gathering students and veterans alike around him to hear his perspec-

Figure 106: Col. Clark points out communist propaganda to students. Photo by John Luck.

tive on things. The crowd around him grew to include not only our group but also some of the other tourists present at the museum. John just seems to have that power. People want to listen to him because they know that he knows what he is talking about. He commands a certain respect everywhere he goes. Our procession did not go unnoticed, and an NVA guard followed us for much of the tour. John later told me that he had to keep quiet about a few things he wanted to share because he was afraid that the guard would grow suspicious or even upset."

"After we left the Hanoi Hilton, John and I talked a bit about what we had seen on the old prison grounds. He seemed very surprised by how much of it was left intact. He still didn't recognize all that much though, and he was very apologetic about that fact. I couldn't believe that he would be apologizing to me! Sharing this experience with him has been nothing but an honor. I have learned much more than I ever thought possible. He has become a true hero to me over the last few days, and he is not alone. Each and every one of our veterans have shown me the meaning of courage. They are the bravest men that I have ever met, and I love each of them deeply."

❝ Each and every one of our veterans have shown me the meaning of courage. They are the bravest men that I have ever met, and I love each of them deeply. ❞

Molly revealed, "Tonight I cried, not because of exhaustion or emotional distress, but because I cannot imagine leaving all of our veterans. I don't want this incredible experience to end. I have had an amazing journey, made lifelong relationships and memories, and have grown as a person in deep and powerful ways. These veterans have taught me so much, and I don't think I could ever say or do enough to thank them. However, from now on, I will sure try! I will look at our veterans through new eyes. They are my heroes, each and every one."

TOPIC SUMMARY

When visiting Hỏa Lò Prison, the Hanoi Hilton, it is difficult to imagine the terrible conditions in which American POWs were held for some of their youngest years. The NVA claimed that "humane and lenient" treatment was afforded the POWs. This was pure propaganda. From the isolation, starvation, beatings and other forms of torture, an uncommon bond of brotherhood endured for those held in the Hanoi Hilton.

The POWs attached nicknames to their guards and torturers based on their techniques, appearances, or habits. Names like: Rabbit, Stoneface, Pigeye, Slime, Ears, Bug, Greasy, Weasel, Slopehead, Lump, Smiley, Frenchy, Chihuahua, Fox, Mole, and Pudgy. These names are just some among many others. Returning to Hỏa Lò Prison must have brought back memories of pain inflicted on them by prison guards and officials. Most were hated.

John Clark, Bill Bailey and hundreds of others survived out of determination forged by mistreatment and hardship. Coping day-to-day was difficult, both physically and psychologically. The camp radio or speaker system was a daily nuisance with several hours of propaganda programming. In *Honor Bound*, a book that documents the experiences of the American prisoners of war, the author writes, "Taped appeals from prominent American peace advocates, many of them visitors to North Vietnam—personalities such as Jane Fonda, Joan Baez, Stokely Carmichael, and Ramsay Clark—at once incensed and demoralized the prisoners. ... the most devastating were quotations by [anti-war] Senators Mansfield, Fulbright, and McGovern."[7]

❝Anti-war demonstrators in the United States gave support to North Vietnam and extended the War, two returned war prisoners said. ❞

Some POWs thought protesters extended the War, as the *St. Louis Globe-Democrat* headline confirms. Walter Orthwein wrote, "Anti-war demonstrators in the United States *gave support to North Vietnam and extended the War,* two returned war prisoners said."[8] (Figure 107)

In *Stolen Valor: How the Vietnam Generation Was Robbed of Its Heroes and Its History*, author B.G. Burkett elaborates on the depressing effects of the anti-war visitors, especially Jane Fonda:

Maj. Robert D. Peel, left, and Capt. John W. Clark display garments they wore while prisoners of war in North Vietnam. —Globe-Democrat Photo

Protests extended war, 2 returned POWs say

By WALTER E. ORTHWEIN
Globe-Democrat Staff Writer

Antiwar demonstrations in the United States "gave support to North Vietnam and extended the war," two returned war prisoners said.

Meeting with newsmen Tuesday at Scott Air Force Base for the first time since their release, Maj. Robert D. Peel and Capt. John W. Clark, both 33, also had harsh words for actress Jane Fonda.

They said they were aware of her antiwar activities in Hanoi during their years of imprisonment, and Peel added:

"I certainly did not care for what she was doing."

Figure 107: Newspaper article, courtesy of John Clark, PETP 2014.

To all the GIs in my acquaintance, the anti-war protests were like people doing a rain dance to stop a hurricane. We looked at their activity as treason, actively encouraging the enemy to kill us. The soldiers who suffered most were soldiers in the bush with line companies.

In Vietnam, actress Jane Fonda was the most visible symbol of the anti-war movement. ... She epitomized everything we hated about the anti-war movement: She had wealthy parents and knew nothing of the reality of the war. To me, protesting government policy was legitimate; traveling to North Vietnam and making broadcasts saying you supported the people trying to kill American troops and destroy a democratic nation was nothing short of collaborating with the enemy.

My mother wrote to me twice a week. Those letters were the history of my family for a year. But after I had been there a few months, the military began advising us to read our mail and then burn the letters from home. Why? The Jane Fondas of America.

Military authorities told us that mail found on the bodies of dead Americans had been passed by the North Vietnamese to anti-war protesters back in the states. Parents of the dead men had gotten harassing letters and calls from people using information they had gleaned from personal mail. So we began burning letters from home. When my mother died, I felt the loss of those letters acutely. To this day, I believe Jane Fonda personally stole a piece of my family history. For many Vietnam veterans, the feelings are even more severe; to them, it is as if Fonda murdered a member of their family and then beat the rap.[9]

When POWs came home in *Operation Homecoming,* much had changed in America. John Clark and Bill Bailey were gone long enough to see a change in the cost of living. A stamp was five cents when they went to Vietnam and eight cents when they came home; a gallon of gas had increased from $.27 to $.39 per gallon; a dozen of eggs was now $.78 compared to $.49; to name a few.[10] This was nothing compared to the appearance and conduct of young people, many of whom were openly hostile to their own government. Drugs were prevalent, and the sexual revolution was now in full force.

John and Bill did not regard themselves as heroes, but they were told to play the role anyway because the country was said to be divided and needed heroes. The country was certainly divided, as Clark found out at his welcome home celebration.

A letter (Figure 108) to John Clark from President Nixon expressed the heartfelt gratitude of millions of Americans for the safe return of the POWs.

THE WHITE HOUSE

WASHINGTON

February 20, 1973

Dear Captain Clark:

No words can compensate you for the ordeal you have passed through for your country. The captivity you have undergone for nearly six years required a strength of faith, patience and patriotism which can never be fully comprehended by others. However, I do want to impress on you the heartfelt gratitude that I and millions of other Americans feel toward you on your return home.

Some things about America may appear to have changed since your departure. That is inevitable. But I can assure you that there has been no change in the pride and gratitude the American people feel for what our servicemen have done in Indochina, and the thankfulness we share on your safe return.

My sincerest wish is for your future success and happiness.

Welcome home,

Richard Nixon

Captain John W. Clark, USAF
United States Air Force Medical Center
Scott Air Force Base, Illinois 62225

Figure 108: Letter from President Richard Nixon, courtesy of John Clark, PETP 2014.

PART IV
AFTERMATH (1973-75)

Students on the Patriotic Education trip to Vietnam had the opportunity to learn the unfiltered truth about the Vietnam War from those who were actually there. The American public was not well-informed about this important part of American history. Instead, the public was fed an image that represented a media narrative that presented a biased portrait of the War.

Those who served in Vietnam have never received from the American public the recognition they deserve. Unrecognized valor was prevalent in all branches of service in all combat zones. Retired Lieutenant Colonel George Hobson (Figure 109) has spoken to College of the Ozarks students on more than one occasion about what has been called the *anonymous battle*, fought later in the War (1970) near Parrot's Beak, about 40 miles northwest of Saigon. Hobson was a company commander for Charlie Company, 2nd Battalion, 8th Cavalry Regiment, 1st Cavalry Division, which stumbled on a full NVA battalion. While on a search and destroy mission, Lt. Col. Hobson only had 79 men but was surrounded by over 700 NVA troops of the 227th Regiment. The Americans faced certain death but were prepared to fight to the end. Scarcely two miles away, their radio cries for help were heard by Captain John Poindexter, commanding officer of an armored cavalry squadron. The famous "Blackhorse Riders" risked everything, driving

Figure 109: A young Vietnamese made this sketch of George Hobson upon his arrival in Vietnam. Image courtesy of Lt. Col. George Hobson, (Ret.).

their tanks (Roman Plows) through the heavy forest and rescued the men of Charlie Company. Many, such as company sniper Richard "Rick" Hokenson (Vietnam 2017 Patriotic Education trip participant), credit George Hobson for keeping them alive. The story of this battle appeared on television in the series *Against All Odds*. There were many such battles during the War.

Several celebrities, higher education, media, and politicians were responsible for misleading the American people during the War, dishonoring those who served and certainly those who died. What lingers in the public's mind is an inaccurate image. Details of the War were either confusing or omitted altogether, and correction is long overdue.

In much of what has been reported, one gets the idea that the American military harmed the very people they were trying to help. Very little was ever recounted about the military's significant effort to help the Vietnamese. Establishing security in the small villages and hamlets was a necessary, but risky, business.

Seaman Fred Pfohl, a U.S. Navy volunteer who also participated in the Vietnam 2017 trip, was involved with the NSA (naval support activity) Village Assistance Team 14 near Da Nang. He is a typical example of many pacification teams who worked hard to improve the living conditions of those who lived in the hamlets and villages of South Vietnam. Fred was a *veteran instructor* on the third Patriotic Education trip to Vietnam. He remembers, "My specialty was working with village farmers to introduce new crops, increase yields, and improve irrigation…with help from USAID, we brought power to our village using a cast-off Air Force generator…we recycled dunnage from cargo ships to assist villages in improving their homes…and with the Navy corpsman on our team, we helped with emergency medical conditions for all ages. This gave me great pleasure and a sense of accomplishment."[1] Pfohl received the Navy Achievement Medal by Vice Admiral Elmo Zumwalt for his service. He, along with countless other "bands of brothers" (Figure 110) never received proper recognition for trying to win the hearts and minds of the Vietnamese people.

The humanitarian work of the U.S. military stood in stark contrast to communist strategy and techniques. As President Richard Nixon later wrote of communist death squads, "Those labeled *traitors* faced a grim fate. Once the communists occupied a village whose chief had cooperated with the Saigon government, guerrillas assembled all the villagers outside, including the chief and his family. While everyone watched, they disemboweled the chief's wife and dismembered his children one by one, cutting off their arms and legs despite their screams. ... After witnessing these grisly executions, no one in the village dared cooperate with the central government."[2] It is difficult to believe the media did not have knowledge of such atrocities and the courage to report them.

Figure 110. Lumberyard crew at the Triangle. Far left: Fred Pfohl; in the driver's seat, Ken White (Daisy, AR). Photo courtesy of Fred Pfohl, PETP 2017, from his friend, Bill Andrews.

Ernest Lefever, in his analysis of CBS News from 1972-73, states, "This power of the media to restrict national debate and decision is noted by Charles W. Bray, Press Spokesman for the State Department from 1971 to 1973: *To an extraordinary degree, television and newspapers set the national agenda: by their treatment or nontreatment of issues, they define what is important and, hence, what gets decided and acted upon by our government.*[3] He makes other insightful observations: "There was a constant barrage of criticism against the U.S. military, not only in Vietnam, but across the board...The line between constructive criticism and irresponsible attack is sometimes difficult to draw, but our study concludes that CBS frequently crossed the line...the constant carping against the U.S. military that characterized CBS coverage eroded respect for a vital institution and tended to discredit in advance anything a military spokesman had to say."[4] Lefever points out, "CBS news coverage of North Vietnam stands in sharp contrast to its treatment of South Vietnam. On balance, the enemy tended to be cast in a favorable light and our ally deprecated."[5]

> **((There was a constant barrage of criticism against the U.S. military, not only in Vietnam, but across the board... The line between constructive criticism and irresponsible attack is sometimes difficult to draw, but our study concludes that CBS frequently crossed the line...))**

Finally, Lefever explained, "CBS News failed to provide the basic facts essential to understanding the central national security issues confronting the United States. It ignored many vital facts, overplayed others, and often focused on the trivial at the expense of the significant."[6]

Given the media track record, it appeared the United States military had to fight both the communists and the media.

The Paris Peace Accords came about after years of fighting and talking. Ultimately the Accords were signed in January of 1973 – after the December bombing of Hanoi and Haiphong areas by the United States. President Nixon authorized the bombing because of North Vietnamese intransigence. He refused to order it stopped until Hanoi agreed to return to meaningful peace talks. This they did after about eleven days of bombing. The Paris Peace Agreement was signed on January 23, 1973. Bruce Herschensohn, in his excellent book, *An American Amnesia*, cites the media's reaction to the bombing that likely made the agreement possible. *A Washington Post* editorial characterized the bombing policy as, "so ruthless and so difficult to fathom politically, as to cause millions of Americans to cringe in shame and to wonder at their President's very sanity." *The New York Times* informed its readers that "all of this was occurring in *densely populated areas*." At CBS, Dan Rather, told his audiences that the U.S. "has embarked on a large-scale terror bombing."[7] Accuracy didn't seem to matter to these journalists.

The Paris Peace Accords—known formally as, "The Agreement on Ending the War and Restoring Peace in Vietnam"[8]—were not honored. Hardly two years later as Communist North Vietnam invaded South Vietnam, a disaster for South Vietnam, Cambodia, and Laos ensued.

Chapter IV
THE EXERCISE OF THE SOUTH VIETNAMESE PEOPLE'S RIGHT TO SELF-DETERMINATION

Article 9

The Government of the United States of America and the Government of the Democratic Republic of Vietnam undertake to respect the following principles for the exercise of the South Vietnamese people's right to self-determination:

(a) The South Vietnamese people's right to self-determination is sacred, inalienable, and shall be respected by all countries.

(a) The South Vietnamese people shall decide themselves the political future of South Vietnam through genuinely free and democratic general elections under international supervision.

(a) Foreign countries shall not impose any political tendency or personality on the South Vietnamese people.

Article 10

The two South Vietnamese parties undertake to respect the cease-fire and maintain peace in South Vietnam, settle all matters of contention through negotiations, and avoid all armed conflict.

Figure 111: Excerpt of Paris Peace Accords. Adapted from public domain.

The *dominoes* had indeed started to fall. Many were naïve, believing the Peace Accords would be followed. Chapter IV, Articles 9 and 10 of the Accords (Figure 111), sounded encouraging.

The called-for cease-fire was never completely implemented by either side, but at least POWs like Bill Bailey and John Clark were released. The first POW off the plane at Clark Air Force Base in the Philippines was Navy Captain Jeremiah Denton, who remarked, "We are honored to have had the opportunity to serve our country under difficult circumstances. We are profoundly grateful to our Commander in Chief and to our nation for this day. God Bless America."[9]

Actually, the communists never intended to honor the Accords. Deception was a part of their culture. Colonel Bui Tin, a former North Vietnamese colonel, explained how deception is viewed by communists: "One cannot just subjectively say that the Vietnamese government is lying when it says the documents are fakes, even though they consider *professional lying* and *shameless lying* to be virtues because *to cheat the enemy for the sake of the righteous cause* is inherently a good thing."[10]

No one should have been surprised when the communists violated the Peace Accords. The Peace documents would remind you of our own founding documents—only the Paris Peace Accords were used to deceive, as a cover to repair infrastructure and prepare for the ultimate goal of invading South Vietnam. The NVA needed time without the fear of B-52s overhead! The Ho Chi Minh Trail became a road system, and a pipeline replaced barrels to get gasoline to the lower parts of South Vietnam. In addition, the treaty allowed the NVA troops to remain in place where they were located before the cease fire. Basically, the U.S. got a ticket out of Vietnam—leaving ARVN to fend for itself but not strong enough to succeed. Our ally was abandoned. We had provided them with equipment and supplies that became a "gift" to the communist NVA when they invaded and occupied the South in 1975. The highest price for our efforts is reflected by the names on a black wall on the National Mall in Washington, D.C.

Lack of congressional support is likely to have been the determining factor in this debacle, along with the Watergate fiasco. The burglary that occurred at the Democratic National Committee (DNC) Headquarters at the Watergate Centre in Washington, D.C., on June 17, 1972, burst into public view a year later and led to a distracted President Nixon; he was struggling to save his administration instead of saving South Vietnam from being gobbled up by Communist North Vietnam. Nixon resigned in August of 1974.

> **❝ ...Congress gave North Vietnam the green light to invade South Vietnam, Cambodia, and Laos. These decisions were dishonorable acts which led to tens of thousands of deaths... ❞**

During the Watergate turmoil, Congressional mismanagement increased by attaching riders to bills making their way through Congress. A prime example was the Fulbright-Aiken Amendment which read: *None of the funds herein appropriated under this Act may be expended to support direct or indirect combat activities in or over Cambodia, Laos, North Vietnam, and South Vietnam or off the shores of Cambodia, Laos, North Vietnam, and South Vietnam by United States forces, and after August 15, 1973, no other funds heretofore appropriated under any other Act may be expended for such purposes.*[11] In short, the amendment prohibited the use of U.S. combat forces in Southeast Asia which was an outright betrayal of previous U.S. treaties to assist and defend these nations against the spread of communism. Many in the Nixon administration knew the inevitable. As Bruce Herschensohn recalled, "...The United States was not giving South Vietnam the material we had promised them...we weren't giving them anything. So it was pretty obvious to anyone who knew how you win or how you lose a war that you won't win if you don't give them the equipment you said you were going to provide." He went on to say, "Some of the better politicians are the ones no one ever heard of because they didn't make noise...they wanted to tell the truth."[12]

In essence, Congress gave North Vietnam the green light to invade South Vietnam, Cambodia, and Laos. These decisions were dishonorable acts that contributed to tens of thousands of deaths, and the result left blood on the hands of a shameful Congress.

Congress cut aid to South Vietnam due to increasing budget deficits and broke a U.S. Peace Accord pledge to replace arms and material destroyed or used up by South Vietnamese forces after the cease-fire. Republican presidents Nixon and Ford had to reduce spending to attempt (unsuccessfully) to keep inflation in check. According to Richard Nixon, aid was "reduced from $2,270 million in fiscal year 1973 to $1,010 million for fiscal year 1974 and $700 million in fiscal year 1975."[13] All of this brought severe restrictions on South Vietnamese forces. Even medical supplies were cut, no doubt causing needless suffering and even death.[14] All of this was taking place as China and the Soviet Union were increasing their help to fellow communists. The results were Communist USSR and China were more loyal to their ally North Vietnam than the U.S. was to South Vietnam.

The final days for South Vietnam (Figure 112) came quickly as the North Vietnamese had planned for a two-year campaign for the invasion—it only took two months. First, the North Vietnamese attacked and overran Phuoc Long Province.[15] This was followed by an attack on Ban Me Thout (Darlac Province), which could only hold out for a day.[16] Panic eventually surfaced in Hué City, Da Nang, and Saigon itself; civilians of all ages, military, and others fled. A "convoy of tears" was ascribed to the long columns of those trying to escape. After a crucial battle at Xuan Loc (east of Saigon), hand-to-hand combat was evident. Things were so bad that President Ford met with Congress in a joint session and begged for help, but none was forthcoming.[17]

On April 21, 1975, President Thieu resigned. That night he bitterly addressed his nation, telling them the U.S. didn't keep its word or promises and was inhumane, untrustworthy, and irresponsible. He then left for Taiwan. Perhaps his speech should have been directed at the Congress. After all, over 58,000 Americans had died trying to help the South Vietnamese. On April 30, NVA tanks rolled into Saigon, and South Vietnam surrendered. It appeared that the U.S. Congress had turned America's back.[18]

What happened next is a black mark on American history. For those who doubted the "domino theory," they didn't have to wait long to see it in action. The fall of South Vietnam was followed quickly by horrifying brutalities in Cambodia and Laos. President Nixon later wrote about what the world saw. First was Cambodia; "Wanton executions soon followed. Khmer Rouge soldiers immediately killed army personnel,

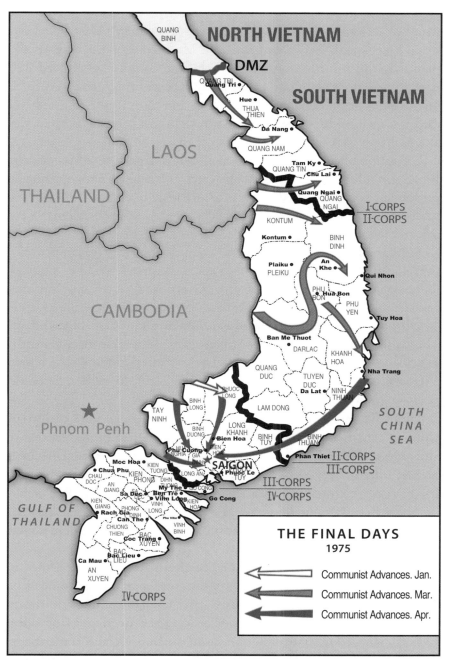

Figure 112: Final days, NVA infiltration routes. Public domain map.

government employees, intellectuals, teachers, students, and anyone who was seriously ill. In Siem Reap, over 100 patients were murdered in their beds with knives and clubs. In Mongkol Borei, after carefully planting land mines throughout a field, the communists forced 200 Army officers to walk into it. In Do Nauy, Khmer Rouge troops crucified one colonel on a tree after beating him and cutting off his nose and ears; it took him three days to die. And after these executions, the wives and children of the victims were led off to be killed."[19]

Starvation became rampant in Cambodia. Nixon detailed the Khmer Rouge brutality: "Married couples were prohibited from engaging in prolonged conversation. This was punishable on the second offense with death. ... Children were forced to watch as their parents were decapitated or stabbed, bludgeoned, or tortured to death."[20]

Similar atrocities were prevalent when the North Vietnamese took over South Vietnam: "Hanoi conducted widespread executions to take its revenge against Saigon's defeated government. A former National Liberation Front (NLF) agent was in a position to know about Hanoi's executions. He said the death toll reached in the tens of thousands."[21] The communists built dozens of prisons or "Re-education Camps." Hard labor camps, torture, and executions were not new to the North Vietnamese. It was more than even some communist leaders could take—a good example of this is Bui Tin.

James Webb, former Secretary of the Navy, wrote in the foreword of Colonel Tin's book, *Enemy to Friend*, "Disillusioned by the repressive and excessively vindictive postwar policies of the government for which he had fought, former North Vietnamese Col. Bui Tin abandoned a life of relative comfort and prestige and left Vietnam in late 1990, … Since that time, he has lived as a political exile in France and has worked assiduously to bring better conditions, including democracy, to his native land."[22]

Disillusionment with the War and its aftermath was not confined to Vietnam. One of the serious results of the anti-war sentiment on college and university campuses during the war is that many of these protesters became the education "elites" in our colleges and universities of today. Others managed to embed themselves in the bureaucracy, constituting what fifty years later is regarded by many Americans as the "deep state."

Their anti-American philosophy has influenced countless students since the Vietnam War.

But not at College of the Ozarks. Love for country and willingness to defend it are at the heart of the Patriotic Goal of the College. Learning this firsthand from Vietnam veterans is indeed an instruction like no other. (Figure 113) The entire country needs to take note.

Figure 113: 2014 "Class Picture" Veterans, Students, and Staff. Photo by John Luck.

PART V
EVALUATION

At the conclusion of a traditional college class, a letter grade is given based on individual accomplishments such as tests, papers, performance, etc.[1] Below, a **Report Card** (Figure 114) reflects how each of the stakeholders' participation is viewed. Grades are subjective and based on personal experience and extensive interviews; they are supported by two visits to Vietnam and years of research, as summarized.

VIETNAM WAR (1965-1975)
REPORT CARD

STAKEHOLDERS	FINAL GRADE
Celebrities	F
Higher Education	F
Politicians	F
Media	F-
Public	I
Military	A

A = Excellent   B = Good   C = Satisfactory
D = Needs Improvement   F = Fail   I = Incomplete

COMMENTS: *Many stakeholders misrepresented the truthful actions of the military.*

Figure 114: Author's evaluation of key stakeholders in the Vietnam War.

KEY STAKEHOLDERS OF THE VIETNAM WAR

CELEBRITIES

Celebrities, and those viewing themselves as such, were quite visible during the Vietnam War—thanks to media attention. Some such as Jane Fonda, Tom Hayden, Daniel Ellsberg, Benjamin Spock, Bob Dylan, and others became well-known. Some of these activists contributed to undermining public confidence and military morale.

Noted author and decorated Vietnam veteran B.G. Burkett later wrote, "We tried not to think about what was going on in the States politically...we looked at their activity [anti-war] as treason, actively encouraging the enemy to kill us."[2]

Perhaps no protester received as much attention as did actress and agitator Jane Fonda. James Rothrock summarized Fonda's contributions. "She made 21 broadcasts from Hanoi, many of which were aimed at U.S. servicemen fighting in Vietnam." Rothrock's analysis of her broadcasts revealed outrageous assertions such as "a description of U.S. bombing of dikes...terrorist tactics...among other things."[3]

❝ ...Jane Fonda, Clark, and many other like-minded American citizens constituted what James Rothrock appropriately called a *Band of Traitors.* **❞**

If nothing else, a picture of Fonda sitting on an anti-aircraft gun emplacement will always remind the public of her anti-American field trip, which resulted in her "Hanoi Jane" moniker. Jane Fonda's activities were in no way restricted to one visit to Hanoi. She was a frequent speaker at coffee houses and universities across America. Speaking at Michigan State to raise funds for Defense of GIs in Trouble, Vietnam Vets Against the War (VVAW), and the Black Panther Party, she stated, according to the Detroit Free Press, "I would think that if you understood what communism was, you would hope, you would pray on your knees, that we would someday become communists." She went on to say, "Viet Cong are *the conscience of the world*."[4] This is a strange accolade for a group known for cutting off limbs of children. Years later her apology fell on deaf ears—too little, too late.

Activist Ramsey Clark, former attorney general under Lyndon B. Johnson, said, "It is known that military men detained in Vietnam (i.e. POWs) are in good health and they are given humane treatment."[5] Many no doubt thought Ramsey Clark to be a fool, or liar, or both. Further, Jane Fonda, Clark, and many other like-minded American citizens constituted what James Rothrock appropriately called a "Band of Traitors."[6]

Jane Fonda and Ramsey Clark are but two examples of those who provided propaganda for North Vietnam. The communists were likely very pleased.

GRADE: F

HIGHER EDUCATION

The Report of the President's Commission on Campus Unrest, in reporting to the American people, laments:

"The crises on American campuses has no parallel in the history of the nation.... Too many Americans have begun to justify violence as a means of affecting change or safeguarding traditions."[7]

"No progress is possible in a society where lawlessness prevails."[8]

"A *new* culture is emerging, primarily among students."[9]

"Faculty members who engage in or lead disruptive conduct have no place in the university community. ... Academic institutions must be free—free from outside interference, and free from external intimidation."[10] Though the Commision Report was written in 1970, it sounds like 2021!

Students and faculty at the University of Michigan developed a new way of discussing the Vietnam War, the *teach-in*. The concept of a *teach-in* evolved from the ranks of some 58 professors who wanted to strike because of their unhappiness with the War. The idea of a strike was replaced by what was called a *teach-in*—meetings to discuss the ramifications of the War. Oddly enough, the first *teach-in* occurred about two weeks after Marines had come ashore near Da Nang on March 8, 1965.

Following the Michigan event, the *teach-ins* spread quickly. Columbia University and many other colleges and universities staged similar occasions—Wisconsin, Washington University, University of Chicago to name a few. Even a national *teach-in* was held, which drew a very large crowd.

Campus unrest began to take on various forms. Writer Tom Wells attempted to put things in perspective: "In many cities, students blockaded streets, bridges, or highways. Some harassed draft boards. Although the May protesters were overwhelming peaceful, violent demonstrations erupted on many campuses. During the month's first week, ROTC buildings were exploding or igniting at the rate of more than four a day. The police and National Guard—toting bayonets and live ammunition—were called out to more than a hundred schools. Students in Buffalo, New York, pelted police with rocks, shouting, *Shoot me; shoot me.* Arrests skyrocketed. The month witnessed the greatest display of campus discontent in American history."[11]

Ironically, it would not be the last!

Clearly, the higher education community failed in its leadership role. It was infiltrated by several radical groups (i.e. Students for a Democratic Society) that had their own agenda—not always the Vietnam War. Vietnam became a catalyst for every conceivable grievance.

GRADE: F

POLITICIANS

Colonel Bui Tin, a retired North Vietnamese officer, reveals in his book, *From Enemy to Friend*, the place and problems of politicians in the Vietnam War: "My impression is that the generals [U.S.] did not have full power to propose and implement their war plans. It is evident that they were controlled and kept on a tight leash by the President of the United States, by the U.S. Congress, and by political circles in America."[12]

One does not have to be a scholar of the War to see the fingerprints of politicians in plans and decision making. After all, it started at the top. President Johnson made the statement, "They can't hit an outhouse without my permission."[13] Such a foolish statement speaks volumes about how the War was to be conducted.

Many believe the timing of the Gulf of Tonkin response was tainted by an upcoming election. But this sort of micromanagement was minor compared to the undermining that occurred by those who had served at high levels and subsequently gave aid and comfort to the enemy. The Communist Politburo of North Vietnam must have been ecstatic seeing an endless stream of anti-war visitors come to Hanoi and berate their own country. Some, like former Attorney General Ramsey Clark must have given the communists hope after they had absorbed one horrendous battlefield loss after another.

 The unpatriotic acts of Ramsey Clark and countless others pale, compared to the near continuous congressional actions during the last few years of the War.

Much of the propaganda espoused by Mr. Clark and others was broadcast to U.S. servicemen in English on Hanoi Radio. According to James Rothrock in his well-documented book, *Divided We Fall*, "Clark said he would publish evidence on U.S. bombings of dikes and other civilian targets in North Vietnam..."[14] Upon Clark's return to the United States, Representative Fletcher Thompson of Georgia accused Clark of lending support to enemy propaganda attacks on the United States.[15]

The unpatriotic acts of Ramsey Clark and countless others pale, compared to the near continuous congressional actions during the last few years of the War. With one amendment after another, the American efforts to save an ally from being overrun by Communist North Vietnam were undermined profoundly.

The Cooper-Church Amendment, the McGovern-Hatfield Amendment, the Case-Church Amendment, the Fulbright-Aiken

Amendment, and the War Powers Act provided plenty of encouragement to Communist North Vietnam to carry out its plan to overrun South Vietnam. This it did on April 25, 1975, as the world stood by and watched. Shortly before the collapse of South Vietnam, then President Gerald Ford appeared before a joint session of Congress to ask for additional aid, claiming that "we cannot...abandon our friends while our adversaries support and encourage theirs."[16]

Unfortunately, we did.

GRADE: F

MEDIA

There are reasons why this is the lowest grade on the "Stakeholders Report Card." After two trips to Vietnam, personal conversations with numerous veterans, and extensive research, it is my belief that the media not only deserves the lowest grade, but also influenced the low grades of other stakeholders. Other authors have aptly stated this to be true.

> "...it was the television coverage which shattered public morale and destroyed the support of the War in the United States."

Phillip B. Davidson in *Vietnam at War* writes, "One correspondent with several years' service in Vietnam, Robert Elegant, has scathingly reproached his colleagues for their misleading reports, not only on the Tet Offensive, but on the entire War."[17] He further states, "Most correspondents reported the War negatively because other newsmen covered it that way...the reporters who refused to accept and report the negative views of his journalistic brethren risked professional and personal ostracism."[18] Davidson believes that "while misrepresentation of the Tet Offensive by the print media as an allied defeat shook the American people, it was the television coverage which shattered public morale and destroyed the support of the War in the United States." The television coverage of the Tet Offensive revealed the awesome power of that medium to influence national events. Quoting author Peter Braestrup, Davidson writes, "Rarely had contemporarty crisis-journalism turned, in retrospect, to have veered so widely from reality."[19]

So misled was the public and Congress that such misrepresentations helped fuel the anti-war movement and likely prolonged the War.

It doesn't take a military genius to understand that North Vietnam was on the ropes. According to NVA Colonel Bui Tin, communist losses during Tet "were staggering and a complete surprise...our [VC] forces in the South were nearly wiped out."[20] Tens of thousands of communist soldiers were killed.

Instead of a well-deserved victory with its ally South Vietnam, not only Tet but the entire War, American forces were portrayed by the media as having lost. President Johnson decided not to seek reelection, fruitless negotiations with the North started, and the communists took advantage of the lull in bombing to recover from the disaster.

GRADE: F-

PUBLIC

Public opinion was strongly supportive of the Vietnam War early on. Despite the media continually referring to the Tet Offensive as a defeat for the U.S. military, public support for Johnson fell more so than did support for the War.

In Peter Braestrup's *Big Story*, he explains how the public reacted differently than did the Congress after the Tet Offensive: "Opinion polls show that approval of Johnson's handling of the War remains low. Support of the War itself, however, seems to have risen since the Communist Tet Offensive."[21] He goes on to cite a Gallop survey that asked people to classify themselves as hawks or doves. He said, "Hawks have increased from 51 to 61 percent, and the doves have decreased from 28 to 23 percent." In addition, Braestrup cites a Harris poll showing "support for the War increased from 61 percent to 74 percent."[22] As media reporting became even more negative and congressional unhappiness increased, public support dropped. Some think it was because in the months building up to Tet (late January), President Johnson had brought General Westmoreland back who gave speeches that painted a rosy picture of how the War was going. The public deduced things were going so well that the impending end of the War was in sight!

The irony was that the War could very well have been near the end, as tens of thousands of NVA/VC troops had been killed. Westmoreland needed more troops for reserves to counterattack but the 200,000 troops request was politicized, and few troops were forthcoming. And, the execution of a VC in downtown Saigon by police didn't help. The public, instead of seeing victory, saw President Johnson announce he would not run for reelection, a bombing pause (worthless as usual), peace talks (a meaningless stall), and more trouble ahead (with Congress, anti-war protests, and riots). Before year-end, Richard M. Nixon was elected, troop withdrawals soon started, and the Communist Politburo in Hanoi must have cheered.

The public was to endure a few more years of up-and-down hope, feeling weary, misled, deceived, and disgusted.

GRADE: I

MILITARY

The military in the Vietnam War was asked to do the impossible under the guise of President John F. Kennedy's exhortation to "pay any price, bear any burden, meet any hardship."[23] Early in the War it became painfully obvious just exactly who would be paying the price, who would bear the burden, and who would suffer the hardship. All in the name of freedom, the American military came to the defense of an ally, South Vietnam, facing an imminent invasion by Communist North Vietnam.

❝ ...the U.S. military was not only asked to fight against the communists via the North Vietnamese and the Viet Cong, but also against the media, celebrities, the politicians, and the anti-war activists. ❞

As it turned out, the U.S. military was not only asked to fight against the communists via the North Vietnamese and the Viet Cong, but also against the media, celebrities, the politicians, and the anti-war activists. Despite such a task, the U.S. military managed to win every major battle, only to have a victory taken away by the 94th Congress in 1975, which betrayed the results of their sacrifice.

It was shameful for Americans to be asked to fight a war under less than optimal conditions. In review, some glaring examples:
- A lack of commitment to winning
- An underestimation of enemy resolve
- An erroneous assumption the War wouldn't last very long
- Shortages of troops and supplies
- A strategy of gradualism (with intermittent bombing halts)
- Mismanagement from Washington, D.C.
- Crippling rules of engagement
- Political decision-making

All of this resulted in the death of large numbers of American personnel. There are many, many examples spread throughout the War.

A statistical profile of those who served in Vietnam is revealing: 91 percent of actual Vietnam War veterans and 90 percent of those who saw heavy combat are proud to have served their country."[24] The great majority of the public now hold Vietnam veterans in high esteem.

And we all should. Many states, like Missouri, have memorials (Figure 115) to honor those who gave their lives in service to our country.

GRADE: A

CALL FOR U.S. CONGRESSIONAL RESOLUTION

America sent its sons and daughters to fight a war that was poorly understood, poorly planned, poorly executed, poorly supported, and worst of all, many Vietnam Veterans were poorly treated upon their return to the United States.

Therefore, the following resolution is proposed to set the record straight and recognize Vietnam Veterans and their families for their sacrifice and service:

On behalf of the American people, the Congress of the United States issues this long-overdue formal apology to Vietnam Veterans and their families for the way they were treated, both during and after the War.

Jerry C. Davis
March 29, 2021
National Vietnam War Veterans Day

Figure 115: Missouri Vietnam Veterans Memorial. Photo by Shann Swift.

POSTSCRIPT

*We can't all be veterans,
but we can all be patriots.*

By the time this manuscript was finished, one thing seemed eerily familiar: America has been down this road before. The culture and events of today reflect striking parallels with the culture and events of the late '60s and early '70s. After five decades, the changes in America have reaped troubling consequences far beyond what anyone would have thought possible. It is easily seen—dissolution of the family, an expanding drug culture, a sexual revolution, rampant abortion, and politicized public education, just to name a few.

 ❝ ...one thing seemed eerily familiar: America has been down this road before. ❞

It is amazing that the same strategies used in the Vietnam era are being used again—and with similar results. Consider: property destruction, bombings, riots and violence in numerous American cities—not unlike 1968. Anti-military sentiment has been replaced by a *defund the police* movement. Add to this, attacks by anti-American zealots on free speech and free enterprise, along with the destruction of historical symbols, the further politicization of the media and big business, and it seems like America is going to destroy itself from within.

Appeasement has resulted in an "anything goes" society with identity politics undermining the rule of law. Young people are growing up in a culture without the traditional American value-shaping institutions such as the home, the church, youth organizations, civic organizations, and disciplined public schools. These have been replaced by a cultural rot, eating away at the very foundation of America.

Much of the problem in education is a result of the growth of an anti-American mindset. This has been made possible by the infusion of '60s-influenced teachers or professors and their successors after the Vietnam War. They moved the Academy to the far left. It's as if the taxpayer has been "sucker punched." The public, in good faith, doled out money for education and got left-wing, anti-American indoctrination, instead.

Patriotic Education (Figure 116) is of critical importance. The Patriotic Goal of College of the Ozarks seeks ***to encourage an understanding of American heritage, civic responsibilities, love of country and willingness to defend it.*** The travel programs of The William S. Knight Center for Patriotic Education play an important part in educating the kind of citizens and leaders needed for today. While other institutions and groups tolerate tearing down monuments, the College believes destroying or rewriting history by left-wing ideologues will destroy what our founders intended.

Those who lived through the Vietnam era see the danger. We all should heed President Reagan's admonition that "freedom is never more than one generation away from extinction." This is now a distinct possibility.

Now is the time for the "silent majority" to speak out before our *FREEDOM* disappears.

One final thought: *We can't all be veterans, but we can all be patriots.*

Figure 116: The Eagle, an oil pastels art project, was drawn in 2015 by Bryson Franks, 6th Grade student at School of the Ozarks, a laboratory school on the College of the Ozarks campus.

TIMELINE
SIGNIFICANT EVENTS OF THE VIETNAM ERA

1954

May
French defeated at Dien Bien Phu by Communists (Viet Minh).

July
Vietnam partitioned into North and South at 17th parallel.
Ngo Dinh Diem became president in South Vietnam and Ho Chi Minh assumed leadership in North Vietnam.

1961

April
Bay of Pigs (Cuba) – failed invasion attempt by CIA-backed Cubans.

1962

October
Cuban Missile Crisis – Soviet missile emplacements crisis.

1963

June
A Buddhist monk burned himself to death protesting the Diem regime.

November
President Diem assassinated.
President John F. Kennedy assassinated.
President Lyndon B. Johnson assumed presidency.

1964

February
U.S. Civil Rights Act passed.

✳ Item specifically explained by a veteran in *VIETNAM 101*.

August
Gulf of Tonkin incidents and resolution.

November
President Johnson defeated Senator Barry Goldwater in presidential election.

December
Bombing of North Vietnam commenced.

1965

March
"Teach-ins" began at University of Michigan, followed by such events on campuses across the U.S.
Marines landed near Da Nang, first American combat forces in ground war.

August
Operation Starlite – first major American (only) combat action by Marines destroyed VC stronghold.
Two Medal of Honor recipients awarded.

November
✳ Battle of the Ia Drang (two major battles).
Landing Zone X-Ray and Landing Zone Albany were major battles and first to use air mobility tactics.

1966

January – February
✳ Bong Song Campaign – second major engagement between 1st Calvary Division and North Vietnamese regiments.

May
Watts section of Los Angeles ignited in race riots.

1967

January
Operation Cedar Falls – largest battle to date in Iron Triangle by American 1st and 25th Divisions.

✳ Item specifically explained by a veteran in *VIETNAM 101*.

February

Operation Junction City – offensive near Cambodian border even larger than Cedar Falls.

September

✳ Siege of Con Thien – near DMZ. Marines pushed Communists back with fierce fighting, often with hand-to-hand combat.

November

Battle of Dak To – one of longest and bloodiest series of battles of the War.

1968

January

Beginning of the Tet Offensive – the War's largest offensive; over 100 cities, towns and villages assaulted; became turning point of War, despite heavy NVA losses.

✳ Battle of Khe Sanh – fought by U.S. Marines, ending with Marines taking Hill 881.

Battle of Saigon – one-week battle, NVA/VC driven from city.

✳ Battle of Hué – Marines retook old city. Communists massacred 3,000 men, women, and children.

March

President Johnson reduced bombing, called for negotiations and announced he would not seek reelection.

Mỹ Lai – Army platoon massacred villagers.

April

Dr. Martin Luther King, Jr. assassinated.

May

Mini-Tet – small-scale Tet Offensive (second of year).

Viet Cong attacked Cholon District in Saigon (third offensive of year).

June

U.S. Senator Robert F. Kennedy assassinated.

✳ Item specifically explained by a veteran in *VIETNAM 101*.

October
Bombing of North Vietnam halted.

November
Richard M. Nixon elected President of the United States.

1969

January
Peace talks began in Paris.

April
U.S. troops peaked at 543,482.

June
"Vietnamization" (American troops to be replaced by ARVN) announced.

July
Walk on moon by American Neil Armstrong.

August
Woodstock – 400,000 gathered in Bethel, New York, for music festival, a countercultural event.

September
Ho Chi Minh, leader of Communist Vietnam, died.

November
Vietnam Moratorium in Washington, D.C.; 500,000 – largest crowd ever.

1970

April – June
✳ Cambodia Campaign – U.S. troops via "Fishhook" and Parrot's Beak" destroyed NVA supplies and delayed NVA plans for two years.

May
Four college students killed at Kent State anti-war demonstrations, Kent, Ohio.

✳ Item specifically explained by a veteran in *VIETNAM 101*.

June

Cooper-Church Amendment (to limit U.S. troops in Laos and Cambodia) passed Senate, but not the House.

Gulf of Tonkin Resolution repealed.

November

Raid on Son Tay to free POWs (had been moved); though unsuccessful, a big boost to POW morale.

December

Hatfield-McGovern Amendment for complete withdrawal of American troops failed.

1971

January – February

"Winter Soldier Investigation" – a media event staged by VVAW (Vietnam Veterans Against the War) and John Kerry about alleged atrocities by U.S. troops.

February

✻ *Operation Lam Son 719* – Laos invaded by ARVN with only U.S. air support. U.S. air support needed to prevail.

June

The Pentagon Papers published by *The New York Times*, revealed a history of U.S. political and military involvement in Vietnam 1945-1967.

1972

February

President Nixon shocked the world with a visit to China.

March – April

Communist North Vietnam launched spring (Easter) offensive and suffered heavy losses.

May

President Nixon visited Moscow.

Operation Linebacker I – U.S. bombing of Hanoi and Haiphong.

✻ Item specifically explained by a veteran in *VIETNAM 101*.

June
Attempted break-in of DNC at Watergate complex, Washington, D.C.

October
Kissinger proclaimed, "Peace is at Hand."

November
President Richard Nixon won presidential election over Senator Eugene McGovern.

December
Nixon ultimatum to North Vietnam to resume talks or "suffer the consequences."
Linebacker II – bombing of Hanoi and Haiphong December 17-30. Bombing stopped, peace talks resumed.

1973

January
President Nguyen Van Thieu's reluctance to go along elicited response from President Nixon, "gravest consequences if you don't."
Paris Peace Accords signed on January 27, 1973, POWs to be returned.

February-March
＊ *Operation Homecoming* – POWs released.

March
Remaining American troops withdrawn.

June
Congress cut funds for Cambodia, Laos, and North Vietnam.

November
War Powers Act passed over Nixon's veto; many regarded this to be an unconstitutional infringement on Presidential authority.

1974

August
President Nixon resigned over Watergate, and Gerald Ford became 38th President.

＊ Item specifically explained by a veteran in *VIETNAM 101*.

December

Congress cut funds to South Vietnam.

North Vietnam began final plan to invade South Vietnam by overrunning Phuoc Long Province.

1975

January

U.S. lack of response to North Vietnam invasion signaled the end for South Vietnam.

March – April

✱ Battles at An Loc, Ban Me Thuot, Quang Tri, Hué, Chu Lai, Da Nang, and finally Saigon fell to Communists.

April

Operation Frequent Wind – evacuated American and South Vietnam troops from Saigon, and Saigon surrendered on April 30.

Death and disaster came to Cambodia, Laos and South Vietnam.

✱ Item specifically explained by a veteran in *VIETNAM 101*.

NOTES

INTRODUCTION

1. Investor's Business Daily Editorial, "Why Are So Many Millennials Ignorant Anti-Americans?" *Investor's Business Daily,* November 28, 2018, accessed September 18, 2020. https://www.investors.com/politics/editorials/millennials-patriotic-survey/.

2. Molly Matney, "Return to Vietnam: How Two Weeks Changed My Life," *Ozark Visitor,* 106, no. 3, (Winter 2015): 6.

ORIENTATION

1. George Esper, "Battle of Dien Bien Phu Shaped Southeast Asia : Vietnam: Peasant Army of Nationalists and Communists Defeated the French 40 Years Ago, Ending Colonial Rule and Setting Stage for U.S. Involvement in Most Divisive War of Its History," *Los Angeles Times,* May 22, 1994, accessed February 26, 2021, https://www.latimes.com/archives/la-xpm-1994-05-22-mn-60690-story.html.

2. History.com Editors, "French Fall at Dien Bien Phu," *History,* May 07, 1954, accessed April 23, 2021, https://www.history.com/this-day-in-history/french-defeated-at-dien-bien-phu.

3. Charles E. Neu, *America's Lost War Vietnam: 1945 – 1975,* The American History Series (Wheeling, IL: Harlan Davidson, 2005), 36.

4. Frank Swygert, interview by Jerry C. Davis about his life and experiences during the Vietnam War, Palm City, FL, June 12, 2017, voice recording and staff-/ student-typed transcript, Point Lookout, MO.

5. Swygert, interview by Jerry C. Davis, June 12, 2017.

6. Swygert, interview by Jerry C. Davis, June 12, 2017.

7. H.R. McMaster, *Dereliction of Duty: Lyndon Johnson, Robert McNamara, The Joint Chiefs of Staff, and the Lies that Led to Vietnam* (New York: Harper Collins Publishers, 1997), 210 – 211.

8. Pat Paterson, "The Truth About Tonkin." *Naval History Magazine* 22, no. 1 (February 2008), U.S. Naval Institute, accessed April 5, 2019, https://www.usni.org/magazines/naval-history-magazine/2008/february/truth-about-tonkin.

9. James B. Stockdale and Sybil Stockdale, *In Love and War: The Story of a Family's Ordeal and Sacrifice during the Vietnam Years* (Annapolis, MD: Naval Institute Press, 1990), 9.

10. McMaster, 125.

11. James B. Stockdale and Sybil Stockdale, 19.

12. James B. Stockdale and Sybil Stockdale, 23.

13. Neu, 86.

PART I – EARLY YEARS (1965-67)

Overview

1. "United States Congress Resolution, Pub.L. 88-408, 78 Stat. 384," (PDF).

2. H.R. McMaster, *Dereliction of Duty: Lyndon Johnson, Robert McNamara, The Joint Chiefs of Staff, and the Lies that Led to Vietnam* (New York: Harper Collins Publishers, 1997), 19-20.

3. Charles G. Cooper and Richard E. Goodspeed, *Cheers and Tears: A Marine's Story of Combat in Peace and War* (Reno: Wesley, 2002), 1-5.

4. McMaster, 328-334.

5. Guenter Lewy, *America in Vietnam* (New York: Oxford University Press, 1978), 95-96.

6. George Haley, "Vietnam Remembered," presentation at College of the Ozarks for a student convocation, Point Lookout, MO, November 9, 2017, slide 16.

7. Haley, slide 19.

8. Michael Beschloss, *Presidents of War: The Epic Story, From 1807 to Modern Times* (New York: Crown Publishing, 2018), 529.

CLASS TOPIC 1: IA DRANG VALLEY, LZ X-RAY (II-CORPS)

1. Class Topic 1 relies upon the important unpublished communications, documents, presentations, and interviews produced by veteran Tony Nadal and student Cody Pentecost in cooperation with the Patriotic Education Travel Program of College of the Ozarks for the Vietnam trip, September 25 – October 9, 2014.

2. Harold G. Moore and Joseph L. Galloway, *We Were Soldiers Once... and Young - Ia Drang: The Battle That Changed the War in Vietnam* (New York & Canada: Random House, 1992), 42.

3. Moore and Galloway, 42.

4. Phillip Jennings, *The Politically Incorrect Guide to the Vietnam War* (D.C.: Regnery Publishing, 2010), 72-76.

5. Jennings, 79.

6. Moore and Galloway, 311.

CLASS TOPIC 2: BONG SON (II-CORPS)

1. Class Topic 2 relies upon the important unpublished communications, documents, presentations, and interviews produced by veteran Steve Hansen and student Blane Bias in cooperation with the Patriotic Education Travel Program of College of the Ozarks for the Vietnam trip, September 25 – October 9, 2014.

2. Steven R. Hansen, interview by Stephane Moutin-Luyat, "Memories of Vietnam," *Armchair General,* July 18, 2006, accessed July 19, 2013, http://armchairgeneral.com/interview-steve-hansen-vietnam-veteran.htm.

3. Hansen, interview in *Armchair General,* July 18, 2006.

4. Hansen, interview in *Armchair General,* July 18, 2006.

5. Blane Bias and Cody Pentecost, "Landing Zone X-Ray: Soldiers and Counselors," *College of the Ozarks Vietnam Tour 2014 Blog,* October 1, 2014.

6. Bias and Pentecost, *Blog,* October 1, 2014.

7. Hansen, interview in *Armchair General,* July 18, 2006.

CLASS TOPIC 3: IRON TRIANGLE (III-CORPS)

1. Class Topic 3 relies upon the important unpublished communications, documents, presentations, and interviews produced by veteran Paul Frampton and student Jonathan Minner in cooperation with the Patriotic Education Travel Program of College of the Ozarks for the Vietnam trip, September 25 – October 9, 2014.

2. William C. Westmoreland, *A Soldier Reports* (New York, NY: Dell Publishing Co., Inc., 1980), 69.

3. *First Infantry Division: In Vietnam July 1965 – April 1967,* Vol. 1, 15.

4. *First Infantry Division,* 225.

5. David Maraniss, *They Marched Into Sunlight: War and Peace Vietnam and America October 1967* (New York: Simon & Schuster Paperbacks, 2003), 284.

CLASS TOPIC 4: CON THIEN (I-CORPS)

1. Class Topic 4 relies upon the important unpublished communications, documents, presentations, and interviews produced by veteran Bill Duncan and student Taylor Johnson in cooperation with the Patriotic Education Travel Program of College of the Ozarks for the Vietnam trip, September 25 – October 9, 2014.

2. Taylor Johnson, "'Proud to Be a 'Replacement'," *College of the Ozarks Vietnam Tour 2014 Blog,* October 5, 2014.

3. History.com Editors, "Thousands Protest the War in Vietnam," *History,* October 21, 1967, accessed January 18, 2018, https://www.history.com/this-day-in-history/thousands-protest-the-war-in-vietnam.

4. Robert Dallek, *Flawed Giant: Lyndon Johnson and His Times 1961-1973,* (New York: Oxford University Press, 1998), 500.

PART II – MIDDLE YEARS (1968-70)

Overview

1. Lewis Sorley, *A Better War: The Unexplained Victories and Final Tragedy of America's Last Years in Vietnam,* (New York, NY: Harcourt Publishing Co., 1999), 15.

2. Walter Cronkite, *A Reporter's Life* (New York: Ballantine Books, 1996), 258.

3. Stanley Karnow, *Vietnam: A History* (New York: Penguin Books, 1984), 336.

4. History.com Editors, "Wise Men Advice President Johnson to Negotiate Peace in Vietnam," *History,* March 25, 1968, accessed April 27, 2021, https://www.history.com/this-day-in-history/johnson-meets-with-the-wise-men-2.

5. Larry Berman, *Lyndon Johnson's War* (New York, NY: W.W. Norton & Company, Inc., 1989), 96.

6. Richard Nixon, *No More Vietnams* (Arbor House, 1985), 106.

7. "The Son Tay Raid," *Psywarrior,* accessed December 12, 2019, http://www.psywarrior.com/sontay.html.

CLASS TOPIC 5: KHE SANH (I-CORPS)

1. Class Topic 5 relies upon the important unpublished communications, documents, presentations, and interviews produced by veteran Don Ballard and student Sara Cochran in cooperation with the Patriotic Education Travel Program of College of the Ozarks for the Vietnam trip, September 25 – October 9, 2014.

2. Congressional Medal of Honor Society, "Stories of Sacrifice: Donald E. Ballard," accessed March 26, 2018, www.cmohs.org/recipient-detail/3222/ballard-donald-e.php.

3. Sara Cochran, "Just Doing My Job," Blog Post, October 4, 2014.

4. Cochran, *Blog Post,* October 4, 2014.

CLASS TOPIC 6: HUÉ 1968 (I-CORPS)

1. Class Topic 6 relies upon the important unpublished communications, documents, presentations, and interviews produced by veteran John Ligato and student Devan Spady in cooperation with the Patriotic Education Travel Program of College of the Ozarks for the Vietnam trip, September 25 – October 9, 2014.

2. Sammy Jackson and Norman Stahl. *Against the Odds the Marines at Hue.* DVD. United States: American Heroes Channel, 2014.

3. Spencer C. Tucker, *Encyclopedia of the Vietnam War: A Political, Social, and Military History* (Santa Barbara, CA: ABC-CLIO, Inc., 1998), 516.

4. William C. Westmoreland, *A Soldier Reports* (New York: Dell Publishing Co., 1980), 415.

5. Westmoreland, 418.

6. Devan Spady, "From the Halls of Montezuma, To the Shores of China Beach," *Blog Post,* October 6, 2014.

7. Charles E. Neu, *America's Lost War Vietnam: 1945 – 1975,* The American History Series (Wheeling, IL: Harlan Davidson, 2005), 126.

8. Neu, 126.

9. Westmoreland, 434.

10. Max Hastings, *Vietnam an Epic Tragedy, 1945-1975* (New York: HarperCollins, 2018), 467.

11. Max Hastings, 483.

12. Ernest W. Lefever, *TV and National Defense: An Analysis of CBS News, 1972-1973* (Boston, VA: Institute for American Strategy Press, 1974), 47.

13. Mark Bowden, *Hué 1968: A Turning Point of the American War in Vietnam* (New York: Atlantic Monthly, 2017), 424.

14. Walter Cronkite, *A Reporter's Life* (Ballantine Books, 1997), 363.

CLASS TOPIC 7: CHU LAI, 91ST EVAC HOSPITAL (I-CORPS)

1. Class Topic 7 relies upon the important unpublished communications, documents, presentations, and interviews produced by veteran Lou Eisenbrandt and student Chase Davis in cooperation with the Patriotic Education Travel Program of College of the Ozarks for the Vietnam trip, September 25 – October 9, 2014.

2. Lou Eisenbrandt, *Vietnam Nurse: Mending and Remembering* (Atlanta: Deeds Publishing, 2015), 1-5.

3. Eisenbrandt, 109-110.

4. Eisenbrandt, 4.

5. Eisenbrandt, 10-14.

6. Eisenbrandt, 17-19, 23-26.

7. Eisenbrandt, 105-111.

8. Eisenbrandt, 109-110.

9. Vietnam Women's Memorial Foundation, "History of the Vietnam Women's Memorial," accessed August 10, 2020, http://vietnamwomensmemorial.org/history.php.

10. Medical Treatment and Facilities, "Medics, the USS Sanctuary, 27th Surg and 91st EVAC," accessed date June 26, 2019, http://www.a-1-6.org/1-6th%20 site/1st%20bn%206th%20inf%20web%20site%20off%20line/cd91stevac.html.

11. Chase Davis, "Just What the Nurse Ordered," Blog Post, October 2, 2014.

12. Davis, Blog Post, October 2, 2014.

13. Davis, Blog Post, October 2, 2014.

14. Kathryn Marshall, *In the Combat Zone: An Oral History of American Women in Vietnam, 1966-1975.* Boston: Little, Brown & Company, 1987, 29.

15. Marshall, 33.

16. Eisenbrandt, *Vietnam Nurse,* 124.

PART III – LATER YEARS (1971-73)

Overview

1. Lewis Sorley, *A Better War: The Unexamined Victories and Final Tragedy of America's Last Years in Vietnam* (New York: A Harvest Book Harcourt, 1999), 29.

2. Neil Sheehan, Hedrick Smith, E. W. Kenworthy, and Fox Butterfield, *The Pentagon Papers* (New York: Bantam Books, 1971), ix—xvii.

3. Richard Nixon, *No More Vietnams* (New York: Arbor House, 1985), 120.

CLASS TOPIC 8: SCOUTS (III-CORPS)

1. Class Topic 8 relies upon the important unpublished communications, documents, presentations, and interviews produced by veteran Jim Greer and student Jessica Turner in cooperation with the Patriotic Education Travel Program of College of the Ozarks for the Vietnam trip, September 25 – October 9, 2014.

2. Donald Porter, "In Vietnam, These Helicopter Scouts Saw Combat Up Close: Cobras and Loaches, Two Vastly Different Aircraft, Relied on Each Other to Fight the Enemy," *Air & Space Magazine,* September 2017, accessed July 31, 2018, https://www.airspacemag.com/military-aviation/snakes-loaches-180964341/.

3. Porter, *Air & Space Magazine*, accessed July 31, 2018.

4. Jessica Turner, "'This Brings Back Memories'," Blog Post, September 29, 2014.

5. Gary Roush, "Helicopter Losses," *Vietnam Helicopter Pilots Association*, https://www.vhpa.org/heliloss.pdf

CLASS TOPIC 9: "DELTA EMERGENCY" (IV-CORPS)

1. Class Topic 9 relies upon the important unpublished communications, documents, presentations, and interviews produced by veteran Tom Egleston and student Jacob Mullet in cooperation with the Patriotic Education Travel Program of College of the Ozarks for the Vietnam trip, September 25 – October 9, 2014.

2. Gary Roush, "Helicopter Losses," *Vietnam Helicopter Pilots Association*, https://www.vhpa.org/heliloss.pdf.

CLASS TOPIC 10: INSTRUCTOR PILOT (IV-CORPS)

1. Class Topic 10 relies upon the important unpublished communications, documents, presentations, and interviews produced by veteran John Sorensen and student Caleb McElvain in cooperation with the Patriotic Education Travel Program of College of the Ozarks for the Vietnam trip, September 25 – October 9, 2014.

2. Caleb McElvain, "Return to a Place that No Longer Exists, But Memories Do," Blog Post, September 28, 2014.

3. McElvain, Blog Post, September 28, 2014.

4. Lawrence H. Johnson, *Winged Sabers the Air Cavalry in Vietnam* (Harrisburg, PA: Stackpole Books, 1990), 116.

CLASS TOPIC 11: POW – NAM DINH (NORTH VIETNAM)

1. Class Topic 11 relies upon the important unpublished communications, documents, presentations, and interviews produced by veteran Bill Bailey and student Haly Johnson in cooperation with the Patriotic Education Travel Program of College of the Ozarks for the Vietnam trip, September 25 – October 9, 2014.

2. Adrian R. Lewis, "Vietnam War POWs and MIAs," *Encyclopedia Britannica*, April 28, 2016, accessed May 12, 2021, https://www.britannica.com/topic/Vietnam-War-POWs-and MIAs-2051428

3. Bui Tin, *From Enemy to Friend: A North Vietnamese Perspective on the War* (Annapolis, MD: Naval Institute Press, 2002), 67-68.

4. Joanne Kimberlin, *Our POWS; Locked Up for 6 Years, He Unlocked a Spirit Inside,* The Virginian-Pilot, November 11, 2008.

CLASS TOPIC 12: POW – HOA BINH (NORTH VIETNAM)

1. Class Topic 12 relies upon the important unpublished communications, documents, presentations, and interviews produced by veteran John Clark and student Molly Matney in cooperation with the Patriotic Education Travel Program of College of the Ozarks for the Vietnam trip, September 25 – October 9, 2014.

2. Benjamin F. Schemmer, *The Raid: The Son Tay Prison Rescue Mission* (New York: Ballantine Books, 2002), 286-287.

3. Lee Ellis, Leading with Honor: *Leadership Lessons from the Hanoi Hilton,* (Cumming, GA: FreedomStar Media, 2016), 104.

4. Ellis, 105.

5. Ellis, 218.

6. Molly Matney, "'Sacrifice, Suffering, and Strength: The Story of an Ex-POW'," Blog Post, October 7, 2014.

7. Stuart I. Rochester and Frederick Kiley, *Honor Bound: American Prisoners of War in Southeast Asia 1961-1973* (Annapolis, MD: Naval Institute Press, 1999), 180-181.

8. Walter E. Orthwein, "Protests Extended War, 2 Returned POWs Say," *St. Louis Globe-Democrat*, article clipping courtesy of veteran John W. Clark.

9. B.G. Burkett and Glenna Whitley, *Stolen Valor: How the Vietnam Generation Was Robbed of its Heroes and its History* (Dallas: Verity, 1998), 23-24.

10. "1973 Economy/Prices," *1970s Flashback*, accessed January 21, 2021, www.1970sflashback.com/1973/Economy.asp.

PART IV - AFTERMATH (1973-75)

1. Fred Pfohl, "Veteran Biography Form" (College of the Ozarks), 2016.

2. Richard Nixon, *No More Vietnams,* (New York: Arbor House, 1985), 38.

3. Charles W. Bray, "The Media and Foreign Policy: Foreign Policy No. 16," *JSTOR*, (New York: Fall 1974), 121, accessed date January 21, 2020, https://www.jstor.org/stable/1147846.

4. Ernest W. Lefever, *TV and National Defense: An Analysis of CBS News, 1972-1973* (Boston, VA: Institute for American Strategy Press, 1974), 157-158.

5. Lefever, 109.

6. Lefever, 150-151.

7. Bruce Herschensohn, *An American Amnesia: How the U.S. Congress Forced the Surrenders of South Vietnam and Cambodia* (New York: Beaufort Books, 2010), 8-9.

8. Paris Peace Accords, "Agreement on Ending the War and Restoring Peace in Viet-Nam of January 27, 1973," ch. IV, arts. 9, 10, no. 13295, United Nations, accessed April 8, 2020, https://treaties.un.org/doc/Publication/UNTS/Volume%20935/volume-935-I-13295-English.pdf.

9. Stewart M. Powell, "Honor Bound," *Air Force Magazine*, accessed January 16, 2020, https://www.airforcemag.com/article/0899honor/.

10. Bui Tin, *From Enemy to Friend: A North Vietnamese Perspective on the War* (Annapolis, MD: Naval Institute Press, 2002), 134-135.

11. Nixon, 137.

12. Bruce Herschensohn interview by Jerry C. Davis about his experiences in the Nixon Administration during the Vietnam War, West Hollywood, CA, February 24, 2020, voice recording and staff-/student-typed transcript, Point Lookout, MO.

13. Nixon, 141.

14. Nixon, 142.

15. Nixon, 146.

16. Nixon, 148.

17. Nixon, 150-154.

18. Nixon, 152-153.

19. Nixon, 155.

20. Nixon, 156.

21. Nixon, 156.

22. James Webb, foreword to *From Enemy to Friend: A North Vietnamese Perspective on the War*, by Bui Tin (Annapolis, MD: Naval Institute Press, 2002), xiii.

PART V – EVALUATION

1. College of the Ozarks, "Grading System," under Academic Policies, *2019-2020 College Catalog*, accessed June 9, 2020, https://catalog.cofo.edu/content.php?catoid=12&navoid=605#Grading_System.

Celebrities

2. B.G. Burkett, and Glenna Whitley. *Stolen Valor: How the Vietnam Generation Was Robbed of its Heros and its History,* (Dallas: Verity, 1998), 23.

3. James Rothrock, *Divided We Fall: How Disunity Leads to Defeat,* (Bloomington, IN: AuthorHouse, 2006), 156.

4. Rothrock, 161-162.

5. Rothrock, 165.

6. Rothrock, 182.

Higher Education

7. *The Report of the President's Commission on Campus Unrest,* (New York: Arno, 1970), 1.

8. *The Report of the President's Commission,* 3.

9. *The Report of the President's Commission,* 4.

10. *The Report of the President's Commission,* 13.

11. Tom Wells and Todd Gitlin, *The War Within: America's Battle Over Vietnam,* (Berkeley CA: University of California Press, 1994), 236, 387.

Politicians

12. Bui Tin, *From Enemy to Friend: A North Vietnamese Perspective on the War,* (Annapolis, MD: Naval Institute Press, 2002), 30.

13. Michael Beschloss, *Presidents of War: The Epic Story, From 1807 to Modern Times,* (New York: Crown Publishing, 2018), 529.

14. James Rothrock, *Divided We Fall: How Disunity Leads to Defeat,* (Bloomington, IN: AuthorHouse, 2006), 164.

15. Rothrock, 165.

16. Charles E. Neu, *America's Lost War Vietnam: 1945 – 1975,* The American History Series, (Wheeling, IL: Harlan Davidson, 2005), 221.

Media

17. Phillip B. Davidson, *Vietnam at War: The History 1946-1975,* (New York, NY: Oxford University Press, 1988), 487.

18. Davidson, 487.

19. Davidson, 485.

20. Davidson, 484.

21. Jim Bancroft, "Vietnam War Interview, Col Bui Tin, Col, NVA and the Antiwar Movement," September 1, 2004, courtesy of *Antiterrorism & Force Protection Fusion, I Corps and Fort Lewis (SAIC), Directorate of Emergency Services,* Ft. Lewis, WA, accessed May 12, 2020, http://www.macvsog.cc/anti-war's_unintended_consequences.htm.

Public

22. Peter Braestrup, *Big Story: How the American Press and Television Reported and Interpreted the Crisis of Tet 1968 in Vietnam and Washington,* (Novato, CA: Presidio, 1994), 500.

23. Braestrup, 500.

Military

24. Henry Kissinger, "White House Years," quoted in Phillip Jennings, *The Politically Incorrect Guide to the Vietnam War* (D.C.: Regnery Publishing, 2010), 161.

25. Don Tortorice, "Time Can Make Us Forget, But Vietnam's Toll Remains," *The Pilot,* September, 23, 2020.

GLOSSARY

A-4 Skyhawk – a single-seat subsonic carrier-capable light attack aircraft

ACAV – armored cavalry assault vehicle

ADC – assistant division commander

ADF – automatic direction finding

Agent Orange – defoliate

AK-47 – Avtomat Kalashnikova, gas-operated automatic rifle used by communists

Ap Bac – Location of first ARVN-Viet Cong battle

ARNG – Army National Guard

ARVN – Army of the Republic of Vietnam (South)

Bay of Pigs – (Invasion April 1961) CIA-backed refugees in Cuba – lost Cuban crisis, pushed Cuba toward USSR. CIA-backed rebels lost Cuban invasion.

Bong Son – a city located within the Central Highlands; second major battle for the U.S. 1st Cavalry Division

Bong Son 1 & 2 – site of major battles in II-Corps

Cayuse – proper name for scout mission helicopter

CEO – chief executive officer

CIA – Central Intelligence Agency

Charm school – orientation for new pilots

Chinook – Boeing CH-47 is an American twin-engine, tandem rotor, heavy-lift helicopter

Chieu Hoi – also spelled "chu hoi" in English, the Chieu Hoi Program was an initiative by the South Vietnamese where leaflets were dropped by aircraft over enemy-controlled areas seeking deserters.

Cobra – attack helicopter made by Bell (AH-1G)

COSVN – Central Office of South Vietnam (North Vietnamese)

CP – command post

CTZ – Corps Tactical Zone (four zones: I-CORPS, II-CORPS, III-CORPS, IV-CORPS)

CW2 – Chief Warrant Officer 2

CW4 – Chief Warrant Officer 4

DEROS – date expected return from overseas

Dien Bien Phu – site in North Vietnam of Communist victory over French

DMZ – so-called Demilitarized Zone, dividing line (around the 17th parallel) between North and South Vietnam

DOA – dead on arrival

F-4 Phantom – McDonnell Douglas tandem two-seat, twin-engine, long-range supersonic fighter-bomber jet

F-8 Crusader – carrier-based, single engine, jet fighter

FACS – forward air controllers

Fake News – deliberately biased reporting to support a narrative

GI – American soldier

GOOK – derogatory term for Vietnamese

Gradualism – gradual escalation of bombing plan

Hanoi Hilton (Hỏa Lò) – central prison in North Vietnam that housed POWs

Ho Chi Minh Trail – infiltration route into the South

Ia Drang Valley – area around the Ia Drang River and location of the first major battle between the U.S. and PAVN

Iron Triangle – Communist stronghold north of Saigon, thick forest, full of tunnels, caves

JCS – Joint Chiefs of Staff

KIA – killed in action

LAW – light anti-tank weapon

LBJ – Lyndon B. Johnson, 36th United States President

Leatherneck Square – section of I Corps, Marine territory

LOH – light observation helicopter

LRRPs – Long Range Reconnaissance Patrols

LZ – landing zone

M113 – APC (armored personnel carrier)

M16 – automatic assault rifle used by American forces

M79 – grenade launcher

MAAG – Military Assistance Advisory Group

MACV – Military Assistance Command, Vietnam

Mad minute – a tactic where an infantry platoon/squad would all fire towards a suspected enemy direction

MC – mobile construction Seabee

Medevac – medical helicopter

MIA – missing in action

Million Dollar Wound – injury sufficient to send home

MOH – Medal of Honor; highest U.S. award for valor

NCO – non-commissioned officer

NVA – North Vietnamese Army

NLF – National Liberation Front; political revolutionary organization of Communist Vietnamese in South Vietnam.

OCS – officer candidate school

OH-6A – scout helicopter; Loach

PETP – Patriotic Education Travel Program

POW – Prisoner of War

Psy-warriors – American counter insurgency operators

PTSD – post-traumatic stress disorder

RFPF – Region Force Popular Force ("ruff-puffs")

RIO – Radar Interception Operator

ROE – Rules of Engagement

Roman plow – tank with wedge blade

ROTC –Reserve Officers Training Corps

RPG – rocket propelled grenade

RTO – Radio Telephone Operator

Rubber ladies – air mattresses

S1 – supply

S3 – operations

SAM – surface-to-air missiles

Scout – officially named "Cayuse", an OH-6A helicopter

SEAL –United States Navy special warfare Sea, Air, and Land teams

Semper fidelis – Always faithful (Marine Corps motto)

Slicks – UH-1 helicopter (workhorse), commonly called a "Huey"

Son Tay – site of raid on NVA-POW facility

SRO – Senior Ranking Officer

TAOR – Tactical Area of Responsibility

TET – Vietnamese Lunar New Year

Tonkin Gulf – Northwest arm of the South China Sea, 300 miles long

USAID – U.S. Aid for International Development, originally the United States Overseas Mission

USO – United Service Organizations, provided shows for military personnel

VC – Viet Cong

Viet Cong – the guerrilla army of the NLF

VHPA – Vietnam Helicopter Pilots Association

Viet Minh – Communist front used to oust French and Japanese.

Vietnamization – gradually turn over to South Vietnam

WP – white phosphorous (willie peter); incendiary munition

XO – Executive Officer

LIST OF FIGURES

Figure 26: Veteran Steve Hansen and student host Blane Bias. Photo by John Luck.

Figure 27: Bong Son plain. Photo by John Luck.

Figure 28: II-Corps map.

Figure 29: Entrance to Battalion HQ. Photo courtesy of Paul Frampton, PETP 2014.

Figure 30: Iron Triangle and surrounding area. Map adapted from public domain.

Figure 31: Veteran Paul Frampton and student host Jonathan Minner. Photo by John Luck.

Figure 32: Booby traps (Viet Cong). Photo by John Luck.

Figure 33: White circle is of a captured VC wearing an American military uniform. Photo courtesy of Paul Frampton, PETP 2014.

Figure 34: Jonathan experiencing a spider hole. Photo by John Luck.

Figure 35: Molly Matney at the entrance of a tunnel. Photo by John Luck.

Figure 36: Cross-sectional diagram of Viet Cong tunnel system used by the communist insurgents during the Vietnam War. Diagram from public domain.

Figure 37: Members of the Blackhorse Regiment (Troop A, First Squadron, 11th Armored Cavalry Regiment) being recognized with the Presidential Unit Citation, 50 years later. Adapted from public domain.

Figure 38: Veteran Bill Duncan and student host Taylor Johnson. Photo by John Luck.

Figure 39: Con Thien location map. Adapted from public domain.

Figure 40: Aerial photo of base at Con Thien. Photo courtesy of Bill Duncan, PETP 2014.

Figure 41: South Vietnam Combat Tactical Zones (I-IV Corps). Adapted from public domain.

Figure 42: Duncan and his RTO on mission. Photo courtesy of Bill Duncan, PETP 2014.

Figure 43: Northwest aerial view of Con Thien, handwritten annotation by Col. Duncan. Photo courtesy of Bill Duncan, PETP 2014.

Figure 44: Sketch of the American military base at Con Thien. Drawing by Col. Bill Duncan, PETP 2014, Jerry C. Davis, and Sara Franks.

Figure 45: Hill Locations. Adapted from public domain.

Figure 46: China Beach. Photo by John Luck.

Figure 47: Rockpile. Photo by John Luck.

Figure 48: Col. Duncan explaining battle at Con Thien (note greenery). Photo by John Luck.

Figure 49: Tet Offensive (major attack sites). Adapted from public domain.

Figure 50: Student host Sara Cochran and veteran Don "Doc" Ballard. Photo by John Luck.

Figure 51: Don Ballard at old runway, Khe Sanh. Photo by John Luck.

Figure 52: Ho Chi Minh Trail. Adapted from public domain.

Figure 53: Example of a trap. Photo by John Luck.

Figure 81: Student host Jacob Mullet and veteran Thomas Egleston. Photo by John Luck.

Figure 82: IV-Corps map. Adapted from public domain.

Figure 83: Flight package for hunter-killer mission. Illustration by Jerry C. Davis, Beth Blevins, Sara Franks, and JaMarie Thompson.

Figure 84: John Sorensen and Tom Egleston. Photo courtesy of Tom Egleston, PETP 2014.

Figure 85: Veteran John Sorensen and student host Caleb McElvain. Photo by John Luck.

Figure 86: IV-Corps map. Adapted from public domain.

Figure 87 (left to right): Student Caleb McElvain, veteran John Sorensen, veteran Thomas Egleston, veteran Jim Greer, student Jessica Turner, and student Jacob Mullet in front of a Huey. Photo by John Luck.

Figure 88: Student host Haly Johnson and veteran Bill Bailey. Photo by John Luck.

Figure 89: Picture from student play, *Four-Star Country Boy*. Photo courtesy of Public Relations, C of O.

Figure 90: POW Camps, North Vietnam. Adapted from public domain.

Figure 91: North Vietnam site (Nam Dinh) where Cdr. Bailey was shot down. Map adapted from public domain.

Figure 92: The Hanoi Hilton in a 1970 aerial surveillance photo. Photo from public domain.

Figure 93: Yankee Station, *U.S.S. Constellation*. Photo from public domain.

Figure 94: An F-4, like what Bailey flew. Photo from public domain.

Figure 95: *A tinker toy* (A-4 Skyhawk). Photo from public domain.

Figure 96: Letter from Bill Bailey's mother. Courtesy of Bill Bailey, PETP 2014.

Figure 97: Veterans (POWs) John Clark and Bill Bailey in front of Hanoi Hilton. Photo by John Luck.

Figure 98: Cdr. Bill Bailey examines Hanoi Hilton propaganda. Photo by John Luck.

Figure 99: Cdr. Bailey shares POW bracelet with student Haly Johnson. Photo by John Luck.

Figure 100: Student host Molly Matney and veteran John Clark. Photo by John Luck.

Figure 101: North Vietnam site (Hoa Binh), where Col. John Clark was shot down. Map adapted from public domain.

Figure 102 (left to right): Student host Molly Matney, veteran John Clark, veteran Bill Bailey, and student host Haly Johnson. Photo by John Luck.

Figure 103: Aerial image of Son Tay. Photo from public domain.

Figure 104: Col. John Clark, assisted by Molly Matney, hold John's rendering of the Tap Code as he shows-and-tells, "down first, across second." Photo by John Luck.

Figure 105: Col. Clark and Molly Matney look at POWs being freed. Photo by John Luck.

BIBLIOGRAPHY

"1973 Economy/Prices." *1970s Flashback*. Accessed January 21, 2021. www.1970sflashback.com/1973/Economy.asp.

Alvarez, Everett, Jr., and Anthony S. Pitch. *Chained Eagle*. New York: Donald I. Fine, 1989.

Ambrose, Stephen E. *Nixon: Ruin and Recovery 1973-1990*. New York: Simon & Schuster, 1991.

—. *Nixon: The Education of a Politician 1913-1962*. New York: Simon & Schuster, 1987.

—. *Nixon: The Triumph of a Politician 1962-1972*. New York: Simon & Schuster, 1989.

Asselin, Pierre. *A Bitter Peace: Washington, Hanoi, and the Making of the Paris Agreement*. Chapel Hill: University of North Carolina Press, 2002.

Ball, George W. *The Past Has Another Pattern: Memoirs*. New York: W. W. Norton & Company, 1982.

Bancroft, Jim. "Vietnam War Interview, Col Bui Tin, Col, NVA and the Antiwar Movement," September 1, 2004. Courtesy of *Antiterrorism & Force Protection Fusion, I Corps and Fort Lewis (SAIC), Directorate of Emergency Services*. Ft. Lewis, WA. Accessed May 12, 2020. http://www.macvsog.cc/anti-war's_unintended_consequences.htm.

Beech, Keyes. *Not Without the Americans: A Personal History, a Clear and Hopeful Look at the U.S.-Asian Scene by the Dean of Far East Correspondents*. Garden City, NY: Doubleday & Company, 1971.

Berman, Larry. *Lyndon Johnson's War*. New York: W. W. Norton & Company, 1989.

Beschloss, Michael. *Presidents of War: The Epic Story, From 1807 to Modern Times*. New York: Crown Publishing, 2018.

Borling, John, and John McCain. *Taps On The Walls: Poems From The Hanoi Hilton*. U.S.: Master Wings Publishing LLC, 2013.

Botkin, Richard. *Ride the Thunder*. Los Angeles: WorldNetDaily, 2009.

Bowden, Mark. *Hué 1968: A Turning Point of the American War in Vietnam*. New York: Atlantic Monthly, 2017.

Bows, Ray A. *Vietnam Military Lore, Legends, Shadows and Heroes*. Hanover, MA: Bows and Sons Publishing, 1997.

Bows, Ray A., and Pia Bows. *In Honor and Memory: Installations and Facilities of the Vietnam War*. New Smyrna Beach, FL: Bows & Company, 2015.

Braestrup, Peter. *Big Story: How the American Press and Television Reported and Interpreted the Crisis of Tet 1968 in Vietnam and Washington.* Novato, CA: Presidio, 1994.

Bray, Charles W. "The Media and Foreign Policy." *Foreign Policy,* no. 16. (Fall 1974): https://www.jstor.org/stable/1147846.

Brelis, Dean. *The Face of South Vietnam, Part 1.* Boston: Houghton Mifflin Company, 1968.

Bullington, James R. *Global Adventures on Less-Traveled Roads: A Foreign Service Memoir.* North Charleston, SC: CreateSpace Independent Publishing Platform, 2017.

Burkett, B.G., and Glenna Whitley. *Stolen Valor: How the Vietnam Generation Was Robbed of Its Heroes and Its History.* Dallas: Verity, 1998.

Clark, Allen. *Wounded Soldier, Healing Warrior: A Personal Story of a Vietnam Veteran Who Lost His Legs but Found His Soul.* St. Paul, MN: Zenith, 2007.

—. *Valor in Vietnam 1963-1977: Chronicles of Honor, Courage, and Sacrifice.* Havertown, PA: Casemate Publishers, 2012.

Colby, William, and James McCargar. *Lost Victory: A Firsthand Account of America's Sixteen-Year Involvement in Vietnam.* Chicago: Contemporary Books, 1989.

Coleman, J.D. *Pleiku: The Dawn of Helicopter Warfare in Vietnam.* New York: St. Martin's, 1988.

Collier, Peter, and David Horowitz. *Destructive Generation: Second Thoughts About the Sixties.* New York: Encounter Books, 1989.

Congressional Medal of Honor Society. "Stories of Sacrifice: Donald E. Ballard." Accessed March 26, 2018. https://www.cmohs.org/recipient-detail/3222/ballard-donald-e.php.

Cooper, Charles G., and Richard E. Goodspeed. *Cheers and Tears: A Marine's Story of Combat in Peace and War.* Reno: Wesley, 2002.

Copeland, Ron. *Sons of the Greatest Generation: Snapshots and Memories of Vietnam, October 1967 to October 1968.* Victoria, BC: FriesenPress, 2016.

Coy, Jimmie Dean. *Prisoners of Hope: A Gathering of Eagles, Book Three.* Mobile, AL: Evergreen, 2005.

—. *Valor: A Gathering of Eagles.* Mobile, AL: Evergreen, 2003.

Crocker, H.W. *Don't Tread on Me: A 400-Year History of America at War, from Indian Fighting to Terrorist Hunting.* New York: Three Rivers, 2006.

Cronkite, Walter. *A Reporter's Life.* NY: Ballantine Books, 1997.

Dallek, Robert. *Flawed Giant: Lyndon Johnson And His Times 1961-1973.* New York: Oxford University Press, 1998.

Daughterty, Leo J., and Gregory Louis Mattson. *Nam: A Photographic History.* New York: MetroBooks, 2001.

Davidson, Phillip B. *Vietnam At War: The History 1946-1975*. New York: Oxford University Press, 1991.

Day, George E. *Return With Honor*. Mesa, AZ: Champlin Museum Press, 1989.

Diem, Bui, and David Chanoff. *In the Jaws of History*. Bloomington: Indiana University Press, 1999.

Donlon, Roger H.C. *Beyond Nam Dong*. Leavenworth, KS: R ∞ N Publishers, 1998.

Dougan, Clark, Stephen Weiss, and the editors of Boston Publishing Company. *The Vietnam Experience: Nineteen Sixty-Eight*. Boston: Random House, 1983.

Dougherty, Kevin, and Jason Stewart. *World History Timeline: The Timeline of the Vietnam War - The Ultimate Guide to This Divisive Conflict in American History*. San Diego: Thunder Bay, 2008.

Downs, Donald Alexander. *Cornell '69: Liberalism and the Crisis of the American University*. Ithaca, NY: Cornell University Press, 1999.

Dramesi, John A. *Code of Honor*. New York: W.W. Norton & Company, 1975.

Duncan, David Douglas. *War Without Heroes*. the Netherlands: Harper and Row Publishers, 1970.

Eisenbrandt, Lou. *Vietnam Nurse: Mending and Remembering*. Atlanta: Deeds Publishing, 2015.

Ellis, Lee. *Engage with Honor: Building a Culture of Courageous Accountability*. Cumming, GA: FreedomStar Media, 2016.

—. *Leading with Honor: Leadership Lessons from the Hanoi Hilton*. Cumming, GA: FreedomStar Media, 2012.

Esper, George. "Battle of Dien Bien Phu Shaped Southeast Asia : Vietnam: Peasant Army of Nationalists and Communists Defeated the French 40 Years Ago, Ending Colonial Rule and Setting Stage for U.S. Involvement in Most Divisive War of Its History." *Los Angeles Times*, May 22, 1994. Accessed February 26, 2021. https://www.latimes.com/archives/la-xpm-1994-05-22-mn-60690-story.html.

Fall, Bernard B. *Street Without Joy: The French Debacle in Indochina*. Mechanicsburg, PA: Stackpole Books, 1994.

Ferguson, Amanda. *American Women of the Vietnam War*. New York: Rosen Publishing Group, 2004.

First Infantry Division: In Vietnam July 1965 – April 1967. Vol. 1.

Flanagan, John F. *Vietnam above the Treetops: A Forward Air Controller Reports*. New York: Praeger, 1992.

Gabriel, Richard A., and Paul L. Savage. *Crisis in Command: Mismanagement in the Army*. New York: Hill and Wang, 1978.

Giap, Vo Nguyen. *Big Victory Great Task: North Viet-Nam's Minister of Defense Assesses the Course of the War*. New York: Frederick A. Praeger, Publishers, 1968.

—. *How We Won the War*. Philadelphia: RECON Publications, 1976.

Gibbons, William Conrad. *Part 1: 1945-1960, The U.S. Government and the Vietnam War: Executive and Legislative Roles and Relationships*. Princeton: Princeton University Press, 1986.

—. *Part IV: July 1965-January 1968, The U.S. Government and the Vietnam War: Executive and Legislative Roles and Relationships*. Princeton: Princeton University Press, 1995.

Goodwin, Doris Kearns. *Lyndon Johnson and the American Dream: The Most Revealing Portrait of a President and Presidential Power Ever Written*. New York: St. Martin's, 1991.

Gottlieb, Sherry Gershon. *Hell No We Won't Go: Resisting The Draft During the Vietnam War*. New York: Viking Penguin, 1991.

Greene, Wallace Martin. *The Greene Papers: General Wallace M. Greene Jr. and the Escalation of the Vietnam War*. Quantico, VA: History Division, United States Marine Corps, 2015.

Halberstam, David. *HO*. Lanham: Rowman & Littlefield Publishers, 2007.

—. *The Best and the Brightest*. New York: Ballantine Books, 1992.

—*The Powers That Be*. Chicago: University of Illinois Press, 2000.

Haley, George. "Vietnam Remembered." Presentation at College of the Ozarks for a student convocation, Point Lookout, MO, November 9, 2017.

Hastings, Max. *Vietnam an Epic Tragedy, 1945-1975*. New York: HarperCollins Publishers, 2018.

Herman, Arthur. *Douglas Macarthur American Warrior*. New York: Random House, 2016.

Herring, George C. *America's Longest War: The United States and Vietnam, 1950–1975, Fifth Edition*. New York: McGraw-Hill Education, 2014.

Herschensohn, Bruce. *An American Amnesia: How the U.S. Congress Forced the Surrenders of South Vietnam and Cambodia*. New York: Beaufort Books, 2010.

Hershberger, Mary. *Jane Fonda's War: A Political Biography of an Antiwar Icon*. New York: The New, 2005.

Higgins, Marguerite. *Our Vietnam Nightmare: The Story of U.S. Involvement in the Vietnamese Tragedy, With Thoughts on a Future Policy*. New York: Harper & Row, Publishers, 1965.

Hirsch, James S. *Two Souls Indivisible: The Friendship That Saved Two POWs In Vietnam*. New York: Houghton Mifflin Company, 2004.

History.com Editors. "French Defeated at Dien Bien Phu." *History,* May 07, 1954. Accessed April 23, 2021. https://www.history.com/this-day-in-history/french-defeated-at-dien-bien-phu.

History.com Editors. "Thousands Protest the War in Vietnam." *History,* October 21, 1967. Accessed January 18, 2018. https://www.history.com/this-day-in-history/thousands-protest-the-war-in-vietnam.

History.com Editors. "'Wise Men' Advise President Johnson to Negotiate Peace in Vietnam." *History,* March 25, 1968. Accessed April 23, 2021. https://www.history.com/this-day-in-history/johnson-meets-with-the-wise-men-2.

Hoplin, Nicole, and Ron Robinson. *Funding Fathers: The Unsung Heroes of the Conservative Movement.* Washington, D.C.: Regnery Publishing, 2008.

Hubbell, John G., Andrew Jones, and Kenneth Y. Tomlinson. *P.O.W.: A Definitive History of the American Prisoner-of-War Experience in Vietnam, 1964-1973.* United States: Reader's Digest Association, 1976.

Hutchens, James M. *Beyond Combat.* Chicago: Moody, 1969.

Investor's Business Daily Editorial. "Why Are So Many Millennials Ignorant Anti-Americans?" *Investor's Business Daily,* November 28, 2018. Accessed September 18, 2020. https://www.investors.com/politics/editorials/millennials-patriotic-survey/.

Isaacs, Arnold R. *Without Honor: Defeat in Vietnam and Cambodia.* New York: Vintage Books, 1984.

Jackson, Sammy, and Norman Stahl. *Against the Odds The Marines at Hue.* DVD. United States: American Heroes Channel, 2014.

Jennings, Phillip. *The Politically Incorrect Guide™ to the Vietnam War.* Washington, D.C.: Regnery Publishing, 2010.

Johnson, Lawrence H., III. *Winged Sabers: The Air Cavalry in Vietnam.* Harrisburg, PA: Stackpole Books, 1990.

Johnson, Lyndon Baines. *The Vantage Point: Perspectives of the Presidency 1963-1969.* New York: Holt, Rinehart, and Winston, 1971.

Jordan, Kenneth N., Sr., *Marines Under Fire - Alpha 1/1 in Vietnam: From Con Thien to Hué to Khe Sanh.* Baltimore: PublishAmerica, 2008.

Karnow, Stanley. *Vietnam: A History.* New York: Penguin Books, 1997.

Keith, Phillip. *Black-Horse Riders.* New York: St. Martin's, 2012.

Kelley, Michael P. *Where We Were In Vietnam.* Central Point, OR: Hellgate, 2002.

Kendrick, Alexander. *The Wound Within: America in the Vietnam Years 1945-1974.* Boston: Little, Brown & Company, 1974.

Kennedy, Robert. *The Road to War: Congress' Historic Abdication of Responsibility.* Santa Barbara: Praeger, 2010.

Kimberlin, Joanne. "Our POWS; Locked Up For 6 Years, He Unlocked a Spirit Inside." *The Virginian-Pilot*, November 11, 2008. Accessed January 20, 2021. https://www.pilotonline.com/military/article_a812005a-5111-59ee-96e6-d63072685f5e.html.

Kissinger, Henry A. *Years of Upheavel*. Boston: Little, Brown & Company, 1982.

—.*White House Years*. Boston: Little, Brown & Company, 1979.

Langer, Howard J. *The Vietnam War: An Encyclopedia of Quotations*. Westport, CT: Greenwood, 2005.

Lanning, Michael Lee. *Inside the LRRPs: Rangers in Vietnam*. New York: Presidio, 2006.

Latigue, Martin. *How to Pray In Combat When Your Mind Is Off*. United States: LitFire Publishing, 2016.

Lefever, Ernest W. *TV and National Defense: An Analysis of CBS News, 1972-1973*. Boston, VA: Institute for American Strategy, 1974.

Lehrack, Otto J. *The First Battle: Operation Starlite and the Beginning of the Blood Debt in Vietnam*. Havertown, PA: Casemate, 2004.

Lewis, Adrian R. "Vietnam War POWs and MIAs." *Encyclopedia Britannica*, April 28, 2016. Accessed May 12, 2021. https://www.britannica.com/topic/Vietnam-War-POWs-and MIAs-2051428.

Lewy, Guenter. *America in Vietnam*. New York: Oxford University Press, 1978.

Linderer, Gary A. *The Eyes of the Eagle: F Company LRPs in Vietnam, 1968*. New York: Ivy Books, 1968.

Logevall, Fredrik. *Choosing War: The Lost Chance for Peace and the Escalation of War in Vietnam*. Los Angeles: University of California Press, 1999.

—. *Embers of War: The Fall of an Empire and the Making of America's Vietnam*. New York: Random House, 2013.

Maclear, Michael. *The Ten Thousand Day War – Vietnam: 1945-1975*. New York: St. Martin's, 1981.

—. *Vietnam: A Complete Photographic History*. Photographs edited by Hal Buell. New York: Tess, 2003.

Macdonald, Peter. *Giap: The Victor in Vietnam*. New York: W.W. Norton & Company, 1993.

Maraniss, David. *They Marched Into Sunlight: War and Peace Vietnam and America October 1967*. New York: Simon & Schuster, 2003.

Marshall, Kathryn. *In the Combat Zone: An Oral History of American Women in Vietnam, 1966-1975*. Boston: Little, Brown & Company, 1987.

Matney, Molly. "Return to Vietnam: How Two Weeks Changed My Life." *Ozark Visitor*, Winter 2015.

McDaniel, Eugene B., and James L. Johnson. *Before Honor.* Philadelphia: A. J. Holman Company, 1975.

McDonough, James. *Platoon Leader.* Novato, CA: Presidio, 1985.

McMaster, H.R. *Dereliction of Duty: Lyndon Johnson, Robert McNamara, The Joint Chiefs of Staff, and the Lies that Led to Vietnam.* New York: Harper Collins Publishers, 1997.

McNamara, Robert S., and Brian VanDeMark. *In Retrospect: The Tragedy and Lessons of Vietnam.* New York: Vintage Books, 1996.

Medical Treatment and Facilities. "Medics, the USS Sanctuary, 27th Surg and 91st EVAC." Accessed date June 26, 2019. http://www.a-1-6.org/16th%20 site/1st%20bn%206th%20inf%20web%20site%20off%20line/cd91stevac. html.

Miller, John Grider. *The Bridge At Dong Ha.* Annapolis, MD: United States Naval Institute Press, 1989.

Moore, Harold G., and Joseph L. Galloway. *We Were Soldiers Once...and Young: Ia Drang - The Battle That Changed the War in Vietnam.* New York: Random House, 1992.

—. *We Are Soldiers Still: A Journey Back to the Battlefields of Vietnam.* New York: Harper Perennial, 2009.

Morrissey, Thomas F. *Between The Lines: Photographs From The National Vietnam Veterans Memorial.* New York: Syracuse University Press, 2000.

Moyar, Mark. *Triumph Forsaken: The Vietnam War, 1954—1965.* New York: Cambridge University Press, 2006.

Nahas, Albert J. *Warriors Remembered: Vietnam Veterans – Welcome Home.* Indianapolis, IN: IBJ Book Publishing, 2010.

Neu, Charles E. *America's Lost War Vietnam: 1945 – 1975.* The American History Series. Wheeling, IL: Harlan Davidson, 2005.

Newby, Claude D. *It Took Heroes: A Cavalry Chaplain's Memoir of Vietnam.* New York: Ballantine Books, 2003.

Nixon, Richard. *The Memoirs of Richard Nixon.* New York: Grosset & Dunlap, 1978.

Nixon, Richard. *No More Vietnams.* New York: Arbor House, 1985.

North, Oliver L. and William Novak. *Under Fire: An American Story.* New York: HarperCollins Publishers, 1991.

O'Brien, Tim. *The Things They Carried.* New York: First Mariner Books, 2009.

Oberdorfer, Don. *Tet!: The Turning Point in the Vietnam War.* Baltimore: Johns Hopkins University Press, 1971.

Palmer, Bruce, Jr. *The 25 Year War: America's Military Role in Vietnam.* Lexington: University Press of Kentucky, 1984.

Paris Peace Accords. "Agreement on Ending the War and Restoring Peace in Viet-Nam of January 27, 1973," ch. IV, arts. 9, 10. No. 13295. United Nations. Accessed April 8, 2020. https://treaties.un.org/doc/Publication/UNTS/Volume%20935/volume-935-I-13295-English.pdf.

Parker, James E., Jr. *Last Man Out: A Personal Account of The Vietnam War*. New York: Ballantine Books, 1996

Paterson, Pat. "The Truth About Tonkin." *Naval History Magazine* 22, no. 1, (February 2008). U.S. Naval Institute. Accessed April 5, 2019. https://www.usni.org/magazines/naval-history-magazine/2008/february/truth-about-tonkin.

Piotrowski, Pete. *Basic Airman to General: The Secret War and Other Conflicts – Lessons in Leadership and Life*. N.p.: Xlibris, 2014.

Pike, Douglas. *PAVN: People's Army of Vietnam*. Novato, CA: Presidio, 1986.

Plaster, John L. *SOG: The Secret Wars of America's Commandos in Vietnam*. New York: Simon & Schuster, 1997.

Podhoretz, Norman. *Why We Were in Vietnam*. New York: Simon & Schuster, 1982.

Porter, Donald. "In Vietnam, These Helicopter Scouts Saw Combat Up Close: Cobras and Loaches, Two Vastly Different Aircraft, Relied on Each Other to Fight the Enemy." *Air & Space Magazine*, September 2017. Accessed July 31, 2018. https://www.airspacemag.com/military-aviation/snakes-loaches-180964341/.

Porter, Gareth. *Vietnam: The Definitive Documentation of Human Decisions*. Stanfordville, NY: Earl M. Coleman Enterprises, 1979.

Powell, Stewart M. "Honor Bound." *Air Force Magazine*, July 11, 2008. Accessed January 16, 2020. https://www.airforcemag.com/article/0899honor/.

Puller, Lewis B., Jr. *Fortunate Son: The Healing of a Vietnam Vet*. New York: Grove, 1991.

Radford, Mike. *The Salute to Service: The Rebirth of Patriotism*. Green Forest, AR: New Leaf, 2004.

Riordan, John P., and Monique Brinson Demery. *They Are All My Family: A Daring Rescue in the Chaos of Saigon's Fall*. New York: Public Affairs, 2015.

Rochester, Stuart I., and Frederick Kiley. *Honor Bound: American Prisoners of War in Southeast Asia 1961-1973*. Annapolis, MD: Naval Institute Press, 1999.

Rothrock, James. *Divided We Fall: How Disunity Leads to Defeat*. Bloomington, IN: AuthorHouse, 2006.

Roush, Gary. "Helicopter Losses." *Vietnam Helicopter Pilots Association*. https://www.vhpa.org/heliloss.pdf.

Schandler, Herbert Y. *Lyndon Johnson and Vietnam: The Unmaking of a President*. Princeton, NJ: Princeton University Press, 1977.

Schemmer, Benjamin F. *The Raid: The Son Tay Prison Rescue Mission*. New York: Ballantine Books, 2002.

Sheehan, Neil. *A Bright Shining Lie*. New York: Vintage Books, 1989.

Sheehan, Neil, Hedrick Smith, E. W. Kenworthy, and Fox Butterfield. *The Pentagon Papers*. New York: Bantam Books, 1971.

Shelton, James E. *The Beast Was Out There: The 28th Infantry Black Lions and the Battle of Ong Thanh Vietnam, October 1967*. Wheaton, IL: Cantigny First Division Foundation, 2002.

Shkurti, William J. *The Ohio State University in the Sixties: The Unraveling of the Old Order*. Columbus: Ohio State University Press, 2016.

Shulimson, Jack, and Charles M. Johnson. *U.S. Marines in Vietnam: The Landing and the Buildup 1965*. Washington, D.C.: U.S. Marine Corps History & Museums Division, 1978.

Sorley, Lewis. *A Better War: The Unexamined Victories and Final Tragedy of America's Last Years in Vietnam*. New York: A Harvest Book Harcourt, 1999.

Stearman, William Lloyd. *An American Adventure: From Early Aviation Through Three Wars to the White House*. Annapolis, MD: Naval Institute Press, 2012.

Taylor, Maxwell D. *Swords and Plowshares*. New York: De Capo, 1972.

—. *The Uncertain Trumpet*. New York: Harper & Brothers, 1960.

The Report of the President's Commission on Campus Unrest: Including Special Reports - the Killings at Jackson State, the Kent State Tragedy. New York: Arno, 1970.

"The Son Tay Raid." *Psyop and Military*. Accessed December 10, 2019. http://www.psywarrior.com/links.html

Thi, Kim Phuc Phan. *Fire Road: The Napalm Girl's Journey Through the Horrors of War to Faith, Forgiveness, and Peace*. Colorado Springs, CO: Alive Literacy Agency, 2017.

Thompson, W. Scott, and Donaldson D. Frizzell. *The Lessons of Vietnam*. New York: Crane, Russak & Company, 1977.

Tin, Bui. *From Enemy to Friend: A North Vietnamese Perspective on the War*. Annapolis, MD: Naval Institute Press, 2002.

Townley, Alvin. *Defiant: The POWs Who Endured Vietnam's Most Infamous Prison, the Women Who Fought for Them and the One Who Never Returned*. New York: St. Martin's, 2014.

Tucker, Walter Carter. *Men Who Fought…Boys Who Prayed: A Combat Chaplain's Story: Vietnam*. Mustang, OK: Tate Publishing, 2013.

Tucker, Spencer C. *Encyclopedia of the Vietnam War: A Political, Social, and Military History*. 1 vol. Santa Barbara: ABC-CLIO, 1998.

—. *Vietnam*. Lexington: University Press of Kentucky, 1999.

"United States Congress resolution, Pub.L. 88-408, 78 Stat. 384." (PDF).

Dung, Van Tien. *Our Great Spring Victory: An Account of the Liberation of South Vietnam.* New York: Monthly Review, 1977.

Vietnam Women's Memorial Foundation. "History of the Vietnam Women's Memorial." Accessed August 10, 2020. http://vietnamwomensmemorial.org/history.php.

Walt, Lewis W. *Strange War, Strange Strategy.* New York: Fund & Wagnalls, 1970.

Ward, Geoffrey C., and Ken Burns. *The Vietnam War: An Intimate History.* New York: Alfred A. Knopf, 2017.

Webb, James. *Fields of Fire.* New York: Bantam Books, 1978.

—. Foreword to *From Enemy to Friend: A North Vietnamese Perspective on the War,* by Bui Tin. Annapolis, MD: Naval Institute Press, 2002.

Wells, Tom, and Todd Gitlin. *The War Within: America's Battle Over Vietnam.* Berkeley: University of California Press, 1994.

Westmoreland, William C. *A Soldier Reports.* New York: Dell Publishing Co., 1980.

Willbanks, James H. *The Tet Offensive: A Concise History.* New York: Columbia University Press, 2007.

Willink, Jocko, and Leif Babin. *Extreme Ownership: How U.S. Navy SEALs Lead and Win.* New York: St. Martin's, 2017.

INDEX

Symbols

✳ Denotes a student or veteran participant with the Patriotic Education Travel Program (PETP), who went to Vietnam in 2014.

✳ Denotes a student or veteran participant with the Patriotic Education
Travel Program (PETP), who went to Vietnam in 2014.

* Denotes a student or veteran participant with the Patriotic Education Travel Program (PETP), who went to Vietnam in 2014.

✳ Denotes a student or veteran participant with the Patriotic Education Travel Program (PETP), who went to Vietnam in 2014.

* Denotes a student or veteran participant with the Patriotic Education Travel Program (PETP), who went to Vietnam in 2014.

✳ Denotes a student or veteran participant with the Patriotic Education Travel Program (PETP), who went to Vietnam in 2014.

* Denotes a student or veteran participant with the Patriotic Education Travel Program (PETP), who went to Vietnam in 2014.